the Essential Blender

Guide to 3D Creation with the Open Source Suite Blender

the Essential Blender

Guide to 3D Creation with the
Open Source Suite Blender

blenderfoundation

produced by Ton Roosendaal and edited by Roland Hess

the Essential Blender

Guide to 3D Creation with the Open Source Suite Blender

Information in this book has been obtained by the Publisher from sources believed to be reliable. However, because of the possibilty of human or mechanical errors, the Publisher does not guarantee the accuracy, adequacy, or completeness of any information and is not responsible for any errors or omissions or the results obtained from use of such information.

The original text of this book is available under the Blender Open Content license, and is included on the CD-ROM and available on www.blender.org.

Editor and Lead Author:
Roland Hess

Contributing Authors:
Kevin Braun, Erwin Coumans, Ryan Dale, Andy Dolphin, Tommy Helgevold, Colin Litster, Modron, Tom Musgrove, Mathias Pedersen

Authors contributing through the Blender Summer of Documentation:
Ryan Dale, Colin Litster, Michael Worcester

Cover Images:
'Starry Nights': Mathias Pedersen, 'Mice': Hans Schwaiger, 'Whole in the Sky': Roland Hess, 'Cerebus': Giuseppe Canino, '21': Mike Pan, 'Hunt': Cristian Mihaescu

Designer:
Sandra Gilbert

Copy Editor:
Kevin Maine

Technical Editors:
Giuseppe Canino, Bob Holcomb, Rich Fenner, Michael Fox, Bassam Kurdali, Kamil Makowski, Kent Mein, Tom Musgrove, Doug Ollivier, Kenneth A. Strom, Juho Vepsäläinen, Timothy Wakeham, Jeremy White

Publisher:
Ton Roosendal
Blender Foundation
Oostelijke Handelskade 1107
1018 AD Amersterdam
the Netherlands

www.blender.org
info@blender.org

Printed and distributed by No Starch Press, Inc., 555 De Haro Street, Suite 250, San Francisco, CA 94107, United States of America
www.nostarch.com

Library of Congress Cataloging-in-Publication Data

The essential Blender : guide to 3D creation with the open source suite Blender / Blender Foundation ; edited by Roland Hess.
    p. cm.
   Includes bibliographical references and index.
 ISBN-13: 978-1-59327-166-4
 ISBN-10: 1-59327-166-2
1. Computer graphics. 2. Blender (Computer file) 3. Computer animation. 4. Three-dimensional display systems. I. Hess, Roland, 1970- II. Blender Foundation.
T385.E76 2008
006.6'930285536--dc22
                2007031160

Blender Foundation Foreword

by Ton Roosendaal

Introduction

by Roland Hess

Chapter 0

Chapter 1

Chapter 2

Chapter 3

Chapter 4

Chapter 5

Chapter 6

Chapter 7

Chapter 8

Chapter 9

Chapter 10

Chapter 11

Chapter 12

Chapter 13

Chapter 14

Chapter 15

Reference

Foreword

Many people have asked me — and maybe you find yourself wondering the same thing having picked up this book — what is this strange "Blender" thing about? The answer I usually give is:

"Blender is about people."

It's as simple as that. Yes, it's a wonderful 3D creation tool and an inspiring free and open source development project. But it's really about the people who are making it: people who work with it, people meeting together on-line or in real life to share experiences and who inspire each other to become better artists or developers or designers.

This book is also a reflection of an investment of time and energy by a dedicated group of people. The documentation for Blender is being written mostly by volunteers and is freely available on-line. Thanks to a couple of dedicated authors, and especially thanks to editor Roland Hess and designer Sandra Gilbert, I can proudly introduce to you the new, official Blender manual.

When we worked on the previous manual, the Blender 2.3 Guide, it kept growing and growing and we were hard pressed to keep it under 800 pages. That was without Python scripting or game creation! Three years have passed, and both Blender and its community of users have expanded in surprising directions. Making a single book that would cover all of it and appeal to everyone has become impossible. Instead, we decided it would be better to work on a series of books, each tailored to more specific topics and audiences.

"The Essential Blender" is the first book to emerge from that process. We needed a book that could serve as an efficient introduction to Blender: for artists motivated to get started in 3d creation or for those already experienced with other 3D packages. Such a book was also high on the wish list of an emerging group of trainers and educators worldwide; a standard guide helping to lead students through the major areas of Blender.

I'm very proud of the achievement that we present here. Hopefully, you will get as much joy from reading this book and learning Blender as we had in making them.

Amsterdam, May 2007

Ton Roosendaal
Chairman Blender Foundation

An Introduction From the Editor

This book is a practical guide for using Blender, whether you are completely new to 3D Art, or are adding Blender to your ever-growing set of 3D skills. This book is organized in such a way that it can be useful for everyone.

If you're completely new to 3D graphics and animation, you'll want to start with Chapter 1: An Introduction to 3D Art, and proceed straight through the book.

If you're already familiar with another 3D package and are looking to expand your skills and add Blender to your portfolio, you can skip the "Introduction to 3D" chapter and start with Chapter 2: "The Blender Interface" and Chapter 3, which covers basic object manipulation and animation. After that, you can pick and choose as you wish. The examples and tutorials in each chapter are atomic, meaning that they don't depend on having completed the tutorials and examples from other chapters. If you're a modeler and your studio just plopped Blender in your lap, feel free to jump right into the sculpt modeling chapter. At the end of the book, you will find an index section for each of the major 3D applications, giving the name of the feature or tool from your native application, what its Blender analogue is, and where in the book you can find it.

If you're an old hand at Blender, this book can still be of great use! There are no doubt areas of Blender you've shied away from, content to get by with the absolute bare minimum. Each of the tutorial sections of this book holds little moments that will have you saying "Ah ha! I didn't know that!"

With a few exceptions, each chapter is divided into two sections: an in-depth tutorial, followed by a practical discussion of the topic, the available options and Blender's approach to it. If you learn best by doing, work the tutorial before reading the discussion. If it's the other way around for you, get yourself a good background by reading the discussion first. There is no right or wrong order, and the book has been designed to accommodate different workflows.

Finally, I consider this a "sharing" book. Hopefully, the knowledge you gain as you work through it will stick with you and become a part of your daily work flow. If that happens, I encourage you to share the book with someone else who might be wondering if Blender is right for them. Of course, you ought to buy another copy of the book to have on your shelf, just in case you need it while your first one is away!

Enjoy the book, and happy Blending,

Roland Hess

Errors in or clarifications for the content of this book can be reported and found at the official wiki page:
http://wiki.blender.org/index.php/Books/Essential_Blender

Roland Hess – harkyman

Roland scrounged his allowance and summer earnings when he was eleven years old to buy the Extended Basic cartridge for his TI-99/4A computer, giving him access to the wonderful joys of character-based sprites, animation control and all sorts of other things that come standard in the free handheld game from your local fast food kids meal these days. Since then, he's spent his time alternately writing, producing conventional and computer-based art, coding, raising a family, performing, and working as a digital prepress expert and IT Manager in the printing industry.

Some people think that a critical lack of focus is the cause of more failure in life than anything else, but he heartily disagrees.

Roland can be found online as "harkyman," with his project pages available at harkyman.com. He also blogs at hessreport.harkyman.com and steelcitycowboy.harkyman.com.

How to Get Blender and Install It

How To Get Blender and Install It

What Is Blender?

Blender is a free, Open Source program for Windows, Mac OS X and Linux computers that lets you create images and animations through 3D modeling and rendering.

As Blender is freely available and you're reading this book, you have probably downloaded, installed and run it at least once already. If not, though, this mini-chapter will help to get you going.

Where To Get Blender

If you have the disk that came with this book, versions of Blender for several operating systems can be found on it in the folder called "blender." If you do not have access to the disk, Blender can be downloaded for free from the Download section of the official Blender website:

http://www.blender.org/

The officially supported systems are: Windows (98/2000/XP/Vista), Macintosh OS X (both PowerPC and Intel), Linux on Intel and PPC, Solaris and FreeBSD.

How to Install Blender

The great news is that Blender is almost entirely self-contained. It will not add files all over your system directories or change your system's settings.

To learn how to install Blender, find your operating system below:

Windows

The installer is called "blender-2.44-windows.exe". Double-clicking will run an installation wizard that copies Blender to your hard drive and registers Blender's .blend file type with Windows. It will also create a Blender program group in your Start menu and add an icon to your desktop, if you choose. Simply accept the wizard's defaults for a trouble-free installation.

To run Blender afterward, either double-click the shortcut that was added to your desktop, or find "Blender" in the "Blender Foundation" folder that has been added to your Start menu.

Macintosh OS X

Depending on whether you have one of the older PowerPC-based Macs (G5, G4), or one of the newer Intel macs (Mac Pro, newer iMacs, MacBook Pro, etc.), find the appropriate folder.

MacPPC: The file is called "blender-2.44-OSX-10.3-py2.3-powerpc.zip". This version of Blender works with OS X version 10.3 or later.

MacIntel: The file is called "blender-2.44-OSX-10.4-py2.3-i386-bz.dmg". This version of Blender works with OS X version 10.4 or later.

When copied to your desktop and decompressed, these files create a folder with everything you need inside. This folder may be moved into your Applications folder. To run Blender, simply double-click on the Blender icon inside the folder. No installation procedure is needed.

Linux

The Linux version of Blender comes in two flavors, one for Intel machines and one for PowerPC. You will find the archive file inside the appropriate folder:

LinuxIntel: The file is called "blender-2.44-linux-glibc232-py24-i386.tar.bz2"

LinuxPPC: The file is called "blender-2.44-linux-glibc2.3.2-powerpc.tar.bz2"

Both versions use Python 2.4, and require glibc 2.3.2. The archive can be decompressed, and the resulting folder moved to the location of your choice in your Home directory.

Solaris

The Solaris version, called "blender-2.44-solaris-2.8-sparc.tar.bz2", in the Solaris folder, requires Solaris 2.8 / Sparc. The unzipped directory can be moved to the path of your choosing.

FreeBSD

The FreeBSD version, called "blender-2.43-freebsd-6.2-i386.tar.bz2", in the FreeBSD folder, requires FreeBSD 6.2. The unzipped directory can be moved to the path of your choosing.

Troubleshooting

Blender will not run at all...

Windows

One of the major reasons that Blender (rarely) fails on a Windows system is a lack of proper support for OpenGL. OpenGL is a cross-platform industry standard library, and the graphics system that Blender uses. Almost all video cards support OpenGL, but some support it better than others. If Blender will not run on your Windows system at all, try to update your video card drivers.

Mac OS X

Most likely, you are using the wrong version of Blender for your computer (Intel vs. PPC). Simply try the other one.

Users running OS X 10.4.3 with Nvidia video cards will need to upgrade their OS to 10.4.4 for some crucial video driver bug fixes.

Linux

Make sure that you have the required libraries (glibc 2.3.2). Also, Blender uses Python 2.4, and runs with your system OpenGL libraries. If your Linux is 64-bit, be aware that Blender is currently a 32-bit application.

Blender runs, but it seems to get slower and slower as you work...

This is most likely the "ATI bug." Certain versions of the ATI Catalyst drivers (around 3.1 and up) have problems with the heavy use that Blender makes of OpenGL. Currently, the only way around this is to revert to an older version of their OpenGL driver.

Blender runs, but the display is blurry/shows strange colors/etc...

Most likely, OpenGL anti-aliasing has been enabled in your video card settings. Disabling video-card based anti-aliasing will solve this problem. Also, if color problems persist, or buttons seem to be blacked out, try setting a different color depth for your monitor (16-bit, 24-bit, etc.).

Where To Get More Help

The best source of help are the user forums which can be found at:

http://blenderartists.org/forum/

Be sure to look at the "Solutions to Common Problems" thread in the "Basics & Interface" forum. It has detailed explanations and solutions for almost every little problem new users commonly encounter.

Introduction to 3D

An Introduction to 3D Art

If you are completely unversed in 3D art, then this introduction is for you. If you already know what you're doing and are just using this book to get yourself up to speed with Blender, then skip right on to Chapter 2, The Blender Interface. (Of course, if you did that you would miss out on a fantastic analogy for 3D art that might give you inspiration some day when your mouse just doesn't want to do its thing and all you can think of are chrome spheres and checkerboard planes.) Please note that the screen shots and references to Blender in this chapter are not tutorials – they are simply general examples of what can be done. You won't find step-by-step instructions on how to recreate them. We'll get to all that later.

Taking Pictures of Tiny Little Houses

3D Art is little more than building a model and taking a picture of it.

A tiny model house.

Did you ever build a little setup with toy houses, put miniature figures in it, maybe snap off twigs and bits of bushes and stick them in clay to look like little shrubs? Did you take a picture of it, close enough to the ground to try to make it look like the town was real? Did you spend countless hours in your room as a kid trying to make the whole thing as realistic as possible, while all the other kids taunted you and called you the "Hermit King?"

Okay, maybe that was just me.

But that, minus the taunting, is the essence of 3D art. Creating and taking pictures of models. Admittedly, 3D Art is a much deeper topic than that, but that is where we'll start.

Raw Materials

If you were going to build a diorama of a downtown street, what would you need? Boxes, for the buildings. A knife or scissors to cut windows and doors, or maybe just a marker to draw them on, depending on how fancy you want to get. Colored paper and odd bits of cardboard to make things like the road, the sidewalks and curbs, the trash bins and benches. Maybe if you were feeling lazy, you'd just buy a couple of miniature benches and street signs from a hobby shop. If you were feeling especially clever, you might make a mixture of glue and colored sand to simulate roofing material. You'd need a couple of clippings from live plants to stick around as trees and bushes.

The raw materials and tools to build a model.

If you had all of that, you could build yourself a nice little street scene.

When it was built, and it looked the way you wanted, you could set a digital camera on the ground, frame up the picture in the viewfinder and snap away. You could move the camera to get shots from different angles. If you really wanted to, and you had built things properly, you could have some action figures taped to sticks running around the place while one of your friends recorded it with her nice digital video camera.

Working in computer generated 3D art is almost exactly like this, except that you don't risk slicing the end off your finger with an artist's knife.

First, you build your model. Then, you paint it. Then you arrange all your models where you want them and start snapping pictures.

Building Models

In 3D art (commonly referred to as CG – Computer Graphics, CGI – CG Imaging, or simply 3D) almost all models are built from triangles. It may not seem so at first, because many modeling tools let you work with quadrangles, curves, bevels, mathematical surfaces and a bunch of other stuff I'm not even going to mention. But in the end, it's all triangles. Why, you might wonder? Remember all the times that you've smacked your computer and said "stupid machine"? Well, you were right.

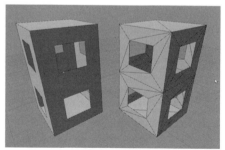

This is a triangle.

Computers are stupid. Way down in their guts, all they understand are triangles, so that's what you're stuck with. Fortunately, computers are really good at calculating and drawing triangles, and there are a lot of very smart people out there (like the people who wrote and maintain Blender) who know how to build tools that make it so easy for you to work with triangles that you often don't even realize that's what you're doing.

And so, from triangles, you will see that you can build a quadrangle.

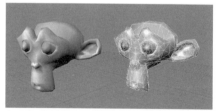

These are quadrangles.

With triangles and quadrangles (quads, for short), you can build anything you like. A box for a diorama street scene. A monkey. Something beautiful.

A simple 3D model, showing its triangle construction on the right.

A monkey head (Suzanne, Blender's mascot), showing triangles.

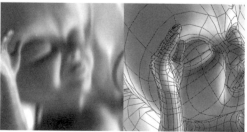

Detail of "Miracle" by Robert J. Tiess

The tools that have been developed to help you work with triangles let you move their corners, their edges or the whole thing at once. They let you duplicate them, smooth the angles between them, split them apart and weld them together. They let you push them around like clay, order them in rows or rotate them in space around an arbitrary axis.

Let's take a look at some of the shortcuts and tools that are available to you when building 3D models. (The following is *not* a tutorial, so we don't recommend trying to do this yet. It's just a sample of the kinds of things you can do.)

Modeling Tools

In Blender, as in all 3D graphics applications, you have access to a number of different very basic models to help get you started.

The primitive shapes accessible through the toolbox.

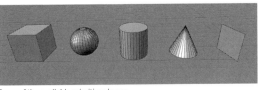

Some of the available primitive shapes.

From this beginning, you can use the other tools to grow, shape and refine your model. If, for example, you wanted to take that cube and build a 3D plus symbol out of it, you could use one of the most popular modeling tools available: the Extrude tool.

A standard cube, with the top face selected.

The top face, extruded upward.

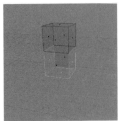

Two of the sides and the bottom face selected.

Those faces extruded, to form a plus (+) symbol.

Now, you might want to change the shape of the plus symbol, making each arm grow in the middle. To do something like this, you would use another popular tool: the Loop Cut tool.

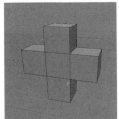

Loop Cut tool in use on the top arm.

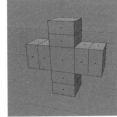

Loop Cut made around the center of each arm.

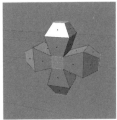

End and center faces scaled down to make a nice new shape.

In the last illustration, you shrunk (scaled down) the quads on the ends of the plus, and the ones that made up the center, giving you a nice new shape. Now, you might think the edges are too sharp, so you use a combination of the bevel tool and the smooth tool until your model looks like this:

Okay, you might be thinking, I only see a few triangles there.

Ah. There they are.

A beveled, smoothed plus symbol.

Blender, like most 3D packages, offers you dozens of modeling tools that you can combine in an almost infinite variety to produce any kind of model you can imagine. Try doing that with a cardboard box.

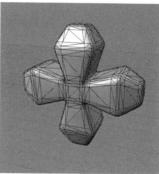

The plus symbol with triangles made visible.

Materials

Let's go back to your little cardboard box model of the street. If you just stick a bunch of plain boxes in a row, it's not going to give a very good illusion of a street. To make it better, you need to make the boxes look more realistic. Let's say that you want the Post Office to look like it's made of brick. You have some options: 1. draw bricks directly on the box with markers or paints; 2. find a picture of a brick wall, cut it out and glue it to the box; 3. make an actual brick-like surface out of glue and red sand, apply it to the box, and painstakingly carve the mortar lines into it.

Of course, to do a good job, you'd have to finish the rest of the box. Paint trim around the door and window holes. Maybe cut and fasten rectangles of clear plastic to make windows. Come up with something neat for the shingles. For a nice little detail, you can draw a little sign on the door that displays the office hours.

So, how does this translate to 3D? In 3D, you define and apply different materials to your models, just like you would for your diorama.

In Computer Graphics, you can get your materials in a variety of ways. First, you must tell the computer what kind of properties you want your material to have: should it be shiny or dull? Rough or smooth? How should it react to light hitting it from different angles?

All of these questions are answered by using different Shaders. In Blender, you can choose from a variety of shading models, each suited to slightly different tasks.

Ball with Lambert shading. Basic shading model.

Ball with Oren-Nayer shading. Good for rough surfaces.

Ball with Minnaert shading. Good for velvets and cloths.

Ball with Toon shading. Simulates cartoon-style

Materials

Once you've chosen the basic properties for your material, you move on to defining things like colors. If you just want the whole thing to be a uniform color, it's pretty simple. If you want to get more complex, though, say, to make your material look like bricks for example, you need to add Textures. And just like texturing a diorama, there a number of ways you can obtain digital textures.

You could use a digital photograph of a brick wall. You could use Blender's texture generation tools to make a simulation of brick. You could use Blender's 3D painting tools to paint bricks directly onto the surface.

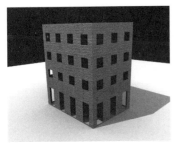
Rendered wall using photo texture map.

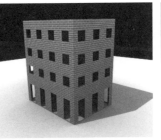
Rendered wall using procedural brick texture.

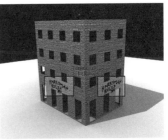
Rendered wall that has been painted on directly.

Of course, there are a few more things to worry about than just that. You have to tell Blender how to orient the texture on the model, so things look right.

There are other properties and things that you can do with materials, such as defining transparency, reflection and bumpiness. You can even use the texturing tools to affect settings other than color: your brick texture could be used to define brick-shaped areas of greater or lesser transparency, different levels of shininess or bumps.

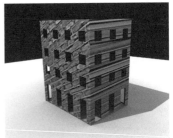
A bad angle and scale for this texture.

Transparency map

Specularity map

Bump map

Thus far, you've made your models and told Blender how you want them to look by defining and applying materials. There's one more thing you need to do before you start taking pictures.

Lighting

You've no doubt seen model railroad displays of varying quality, often at a science center, a museum, or in your weird uncle's basement. One of the things that makes a model set come to life is proper lighting. There is a model railroad display in the Carnegie Science Center in Pittsburgh, Pennsylvania that covers over four hundred square feet. The lighting of the miniatures is impressive as each street lamp, railroad crossing, street intersection and building is lit with painstaking detail. Hidden lamps help to make different sections appear to have different seasons. Other lamps and miniature interior lights cycle to simulate day and night.

Lighting can make or break a scene. Great lighting can make the most simply built and textured model look like a real physical object, despite its other deficiencies. Bad lighting can lay waste to hours of careful modeling and texturing work.

A very simple box model with no textures, lit well and rendered to be fairly realistic.

The same model rendered with a non-shadow point light source.

Blender, like most other CG applications, gives you many options for lighting your models, allowing you to create setups that mimic natural conditions (Sun and Hemi lamps, with something called Ambient Occlusion) and studio settings (Spot and Area lamps), and from there to create lighting schemes that would never be possible in the real world, but that can, as you'll see, help to give drama and depth to your scenes. Lights can be set to different colors and intensities, can be set to cast shadows or not, and can even be set to only affect certain objects, leaving others alone.

Snap Away!

So now, you've created your models and textured them. You've decided how to light everything. It's time to start taking pictures.

In the world of 3D graphics, this is called Rendering. Usually, you create a camera object, aim it and adjust it like you would a real camera, then tell the 3D application to render the image that the camera sees. This is where everything we've talked about up until now comes together.

When you tell Blender to render an image, the first thing it does is to break up your models into triangles. Don't worry – you won't see the triangles. However, recall that triangles are (mostly) the only way the computer understands geometry, so triangles it is! Once Blender has made its own internal model of everything based on triangles, it does some calculations to determine how to cast shadows from different light sources and a few other things.

Then, it starts to generate the image.

Digital images, whether computer-generated, scanned, or captured with a digital camera, are made up of a grid of Pixels

Digital images are made of pixels, which can be seen when zoomed in.

Just to give you an idea of pixel sizes, the computer monitor you're using right now most likely has a dimension of around 1024 x 768 pixels (almost 750,000 pixels!). U.S standard television broadcasts at 648 x 486 pixels, while the European standard is 720 x 486. A 3 Megapixel digital camera will take shots in the range of 2000 x 1500 pixels. A nice glossy magazine cover image will be around 2700 x 3600 pixels.

When you first run Blender, it defaults to rendering images at 800 x 600 pixels.

For each of those pixels, your 3D application decides which triangle from your models is the closest to the camera, which lights affect that particular point on the triangle and how much, and what color it should be, based on the chosen shaders and texturing options from the Materials. Once it has all of that figured out, it stores that result in the image. When it has calculated a result for every single pixel, your image is done. Rendered.

If you're new, you get something like this:

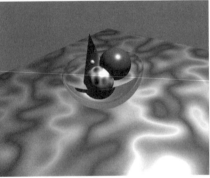

A first attempt at using Blender.

Still from the HD version of Elephants Dream.

If you are a Living Legend of CGI, you get something like the picture on the left:

And now you have a pretty (or not) picture of your model. That's great, but what good is it? Well, for many uses, architectural visualization, making fake product shots for marketing campaigns, doing artwork for personal enjoyment, it is enough. A nice still image is the end.

Snap Away!

But, for many others, this is not the end of the process. You might need things to move. It could be as simple as moving the camera around your model to show off your hard work. If you wanted to really show off, you might make the models of trees appear to sway gently in the wind and have the striped pole on the barbershop spin slowly. Then, a car speeds down the road. Chased by a huge boulder. Chased by a giant, three-headed robot.

That's animation.

Animation

In CG, there are basically three ways to create motion.

The first is to tell certain objects (like a car) where to be, and at what time. Essentially, you say:

"Car, I would like you be at this side of the street when I start rolling the camera, and over at the other end of the street three seconds later. Can you handle that?"

And the car says: "Dude, I'm not real! I'm not even constrained by the laws of physics. I can do anything you want!"

And you say "Awesome!" because it really is.

Animating by telling things where to be and when to be there is called Keyframing.

Each rendered image that makes up part of an animation is called a Frame.

And so, to animate with this method, you go to a Frame (that's the "when") and set a Key (that's the "where") for the location of the object. To make the Car example a little more technical, you would go to Frame 1 in your 3D application (the start of the animation), use the application's tools to put the car at the beginning of the street, and set a Key. Then, you would move the application's time counter three seconds ahead in time, move the car to the end of the street, and set another Key.

Rendering all of the images that represent those three seconds of time, then playing them back in sequence, will show the car moving from the beginning of the street to the end.

The second division of animation, Character Animation, is really just keyframe animation – the same basic procedure of telling "where" and "when" is used – but as it requires a different set of skills, it is usually thought of separately.

What kinds of different skills? Well, the method of animation we just discussed is good for moving objects around that don't change shape. It's pretty straightforward: the object starts here, goes somewhere else, and ends up over there. Maybe it topples over onto its side. That is considered "object level" animation, and more or less, anyone with half of pint of imagination and visualization skills can pull it off.

Character animation is different. Some people might think that character animation is most akin to the clay and model based stop-motion animation popularized in a glut of Christmas specials and sometimes bad/ sometimes brilliant motion picture and television features. Not so.

Character animation is a combination of technical skill, imagination, acting ability and puppetry. Yes. Puppets. There is a reason that a certain high-profile animation studio's in-house character package is called "Marionette". A well set up system of controls for character animation will react more like a complex puppet than anything else.

In Blender, the structure that controls character animation is called an Armature. Armatures can resemble skeletons like the one below:

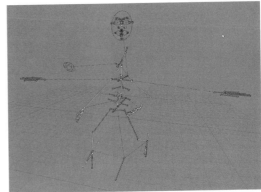

Or something a bit more esoteric like the one on the right:

The odd shapes floating over the head are the face controls, which act

An armature skeleton appropriate for character animation.

The "Ludwig" rig by Jason Pierce.

exactly like the controls on the large-scale multi-operator puppets used for motion picture and television special effects.

But those skeletons and additional controls still function under the same principle as object-level keyframe animation. Place the Arm bones where and when you want them and set a Key. Move the eyebrow controllers to make a goofy face at the right frame and set a Key. Play the whole thing back and each bone and controller will hit their spots at the times you told them to, making a (hopefully) brilliant character animation.

The clever armature and controls move the (equally brilliant) model you've already built of a person, causing it to not only move from place to place, but to change shape as it does so. This change in shape is called Deformation.

None of this is limited to human beings, though. You could make an armature that was just a chain of four bones, attach it to a model of a soda can, and keyframe the armature so that the soda can wriggles around on the ground like worm. Or hops about like a kid jazzing on four bars of high-test chocolate.

A rig in rest position with a character mesh around it.

When the rig is posed, the mesh follows.

The third method of animation is called Simulation or Procedural Animation. Those are just different ways to say "the computer figures it out for you." All natural processes, like a block wall collapsing on itself or the motion of poured water splashing into a glass, are governed by the laws of physics and can, with a greater or lesser degree of success, be simulated by a computer program. Often, as in the case of water splashing into a glass, a computer can do a much better job of animation than a human being can, because it can actually simulate the physics of the situation. The same applies to a falling wall of blocks or a flag flapping in the wind.

Since these are physical simulations, you have to tell your CG application the basics about what you're simulating, which usually include values for gravity, elasticity, mass, wind, etc.

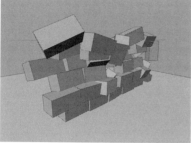  

Rigid Body Physics: A block wall in mid-tumble.　　*Fluid Simulation: Water pouring into a glass.*　　*Soft Body Physics: A flag in the wind.*

In addition to built-in simulations like these, (Blender has rigid body physics – think bowling balls falling down stairs; soft bodies – think an overweight stomach jiggling when slapped; and fluid simulation built right in) many 3D applications, including Blender, allow you to write little programs (usually called Scripts) that can control and generate animation. These can be as simple as a script that makes objects follow the contours of the ground, or as complex as full applications that can produce and animate large-scale battle scenes.

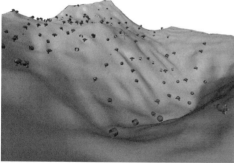 

Objects littered around a terrain by a script.　　*A large-scale combat simulation.*

Conclusion

In this mental exercise, you've made models of buildings, lampposts and a street. You've created and applied appropriate materials to everything. Lights are strategically placed to give a realistic feeling of being outside on a sunny day. Cars, boulders and robots are zooming down the street. Now they're smashing into the wall of the post office, whose bricks tumble realistically to the pavement below, coming to rest beside a little burbling fountain.

We set the frame counter to 1 and place the camera.

Now, all we have to do is press the Render button.

It's that easy.

Really.

Well, okay. It isn't.

But now that you've had your introduction, let's start learning how to actually do this.

Let's Talk About Art.

Don't expect Blender, or any other 3D application for that matter, to substitute for a lack of artistic knowledge and skill. 3D applications are tools, and nothing more. In the hands of a skilled artist, they can produce moving pieces of art. In the hands of a hack, they will produce junk.

Even if you have no artistic background though, all is not lost. There are some basic rules for creating artwork that can be gleaned from a simple web search or a trip to your local library. In my experience, 3D art is an interesting combination of photography and illustration. From photography, you take the techniques of lighting and composition. From illustration (painting, drawing, etc.), you take all of the artistic decisions of working in a non-realistic medium. In other words, at some point you have to decide what portions of reality you will try to reproduce, and what portions you will omit or only suggest.

For a better example of what I am talking about, use as a reference any of the 3D animated feature films produced in the last five years. None of them could be said to be completely photorealistic. In other words, reality does not look like those films. And yet, as we watch them, we are drawn into their shorthand for reality, and our minds fill in the blanks.

It turns out that your toughest job as a 3D artist is exactly that: decide which portions of reality you will omit or imply, and which portions you will recreate. The rest is mechanics.

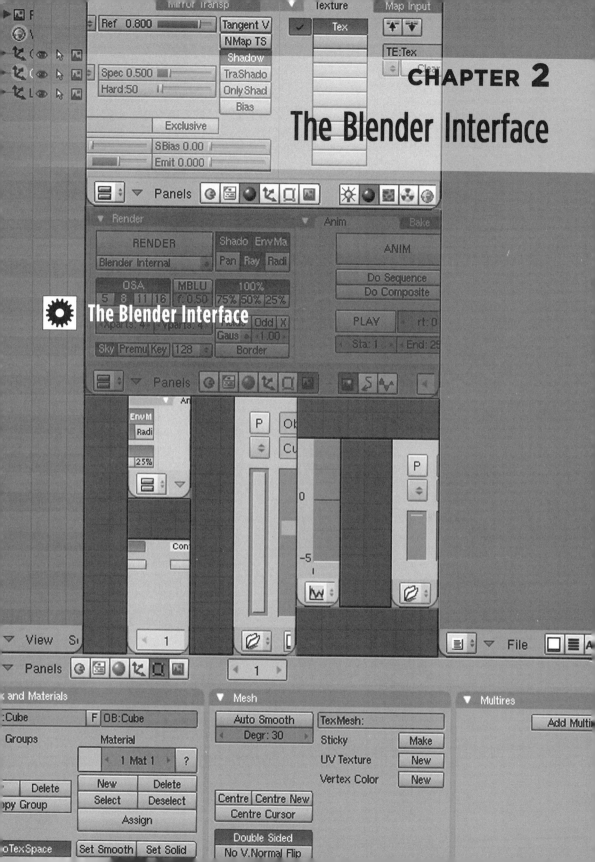

The Blender Interface

It won't be taking a huge gamble to say that the Blender interface is different from anything you have worked with before. Some people seem to get it intuitively; others, not so much. The bad news is that it is not the kind of thing you can enter without instruction — the interface was not designed to allow a new user to sit down and be able to guess their way through a major project.

But really, that's the good news. Blender was designed by professional animators *for* professional animators. Many of the things that can make a program simple for beginners end up constraining even intermediate users. So you should know this: the time spent learning the core principles of Blender's interface will pay you back many times over.

Clear your mind of what you think you know, and let's begin.

The Most Basic Blender Interface Advice Possible

One hand on the mouse. One hand on the keyboard.

Blender was designed with this in mind. The interface is flexible. There are controls built in so that if you want to skip learning most of the keyboard shortcuts and rely on the mouse, you can. But in most situations, you will work more efficiently with a mouse/keyboard combination approach.

Launch Blender. (You already have Blender, right? If not, go to Chapter 0: Installing and Running Blender).

Mac OSX and Linux users will see the application start up and fill the screen. Windows users will too, but they will see an additional window and item in the taskbar. Don't close this extra window (which some people mistakenly call the "DOS" window, because it resembles the black Windows command line utility), as it will cause Blender to close as well. Since you're just getting started, think of it as Blender's annoying kid brother and ignore it.

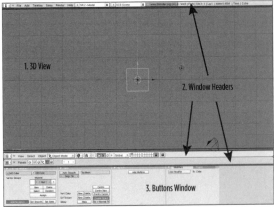

The Main Blender Window:
Key: 1. 3D View   2. Window Headers   3. Buttons Windows

Is Your Mouse Mighty Enough?

Blender works best with a three button wheel mouse. It is useable with a two button mouse, or without a scroll wheel, but it's not recommended. Likewise, you can use the touch pad or control-stick solutions on a laptop in a pinch, but an external mouse will be better. If you need to use a mouse with only two buttons (and forget about using the one-button mouse bundled with older Macs), holding down the Alt key and using a left click will simulate the Middle Mouse Button. Of course, you can quickly find yourself doing a spider crawl around the keyboard if you use this technique. That's why we recommend getting a three button mouse.

Throughout this book, we will use these abbreviations for the different mouse clicks:

LMB = Left Mouse Button click
MMB = Middle Mouse Button click
RMB = Right Mouse Button click

Navigating the 3D Space

How to rotate the view, switch between orthographic and perspective modes, and how to switch between solid and wireframe views.

Let's focus on the 3D view for a moment and how to get around in it.

Place the mouse cursor over the 3D view and roll your scroll wheel back and forth. The view zooms in and out. The scroll wheel, which doubles as the Middle Mouse Button (MMB) on most mice, zooms the 3D view.

Now MMB click and drag. Holding down MMB and dragging freely rotates the 3D view.

Using a combination of view rotation (MMB drag) and zooming (scroll wheel), you can get to any view of the objects in the 3D window that you care to see.

One last mouse view navigation tool for the 3D window, and the first time that *ohomohok* (yes, that's an acronym for One Hand On Mouse, One Hand On Keyboard) comes into play. Hold down the Shift key as you MMB drag. The view simply translates along with your mouse movements. Many users refer to this as "panning" the view.

In addition to mouse-based navigation in 3D space, there are several keyboard shortcuts to help you along. In order to quickly give yourself front, side and top views, you can use the 1, 3 and 7 keys on the number pad (Numpad), located on the right side of almost all full sized keyboards.

Within a few days, using these keys to shift your view will be second nature, but until then it might help you to remember to conceptualize the numpad as viewing through a sphere, with the number keys corresponding to "where" you're viewing things from.

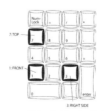

Using the Number Pad to change the view.

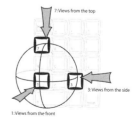

Of course, that mental model might start you wondering if there are shortcuts for the "ignored" positions, namely behind, to the left, and down. Each of those can be accomplished by using the Ctrl key modifier. Ctrl Numpad-1 views from behind. Ctrl Numpad-3 and -7 view from the left and below, respectively.

Changing the Way that Objects Are Drawn: Solid and Wireframe

Moving on from controls that change your point of view, let's learn about some of the different ways to visualize the 3D objects themselves.

You may have noticed when playing around and practicing with the view rotation, translation and zoom controls that the cube in the 3D window is shaded and resembles a solid box. Press the Z-key once. The 3D display changes so that the cube loses its solidity and is shown only by its edges. Press the Z-key again to go back into the solid display mode.

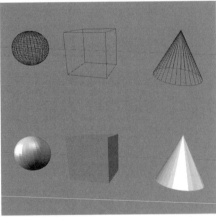

Some simple primitives in both wireframe and solid modes

Of course, you could use the iconic dropdown menu in the header to do this too.

The Shading mode menu on the 3D header.

Yes, you *could* use that menu. But you won't. Why not? Because at first, 95% of the time you'll be working in either Solid mode or Wireframe mode (the one with the edges). Often, it is useful to quickly switch between the two modes to make sure you have the correct edge selected, or to check the overall look of something you've done, and if you rely on the dropdown menu for this most basic thing, it'll be your first step on the road to slooooooow Blending. Use the Z-key. *Ohomohok*.

Changing the Way the View Deals With Distance: Orthographic and Perspective

The other view toggle we'll examine for now is Numpad-5. Numpad-5 toggles the 3D view between orthographic and perspective modes (and if you don't know what that means, you can check out the Orthographic and Perspective sidebar). Press Numpad-5 to toggle Perspective. Now, use the controls you've already learned — zoom, rotate and translate —to move around. The controls feel a bit different in Perspective mode.

As an exercise, you might want to try to get Blender to show you a nice view of the bottom side of the default cube that's there when you run Blender, zoomed to fill most of the screen. Try it in both Orthographic and Perspective modes. If you get lost or disoriented, use Numpad-1 to set you back into a front view and try again.

Orthographic and Perspective Views

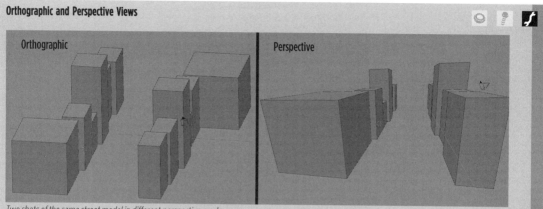

Orthographic

Perspective

Two shots of the same street model in different perspective modes.

"Perspective" refers to the way you see things in real life. Objects close to you look larger than objects which are far away. This is just the way you see things. Blender can display 3D views to look like this as well. In fact, if Blender couldn't display things with perspective, it would be fairly useless as it would never be able to produce images that gave the illusion of reality.

It turns out, though, that many modeling and animation tasks don't work so well in perspective mode. It can be difficult to align items in perspective mode, or to visualize the true shape of a large object when it is constantly distorted by the effects of perspective. For that reason, most modelers and animators work in Orthographic mode.

"Orthographic", or "Ortho" removes the shortening due to distance that is found in perspective, making things appear "flat". If you're not familiar with the effect, a few minutes of toggling between the modes and observing your models from different angles will acquaint you with it.

In Blender, new 3D views default to Ortho mode, making them easier to work in. Camera views (cameras are detailed in Chapter 13) default to Perspective mode, to aid with final visualization.

A Practical Example: Viewing Hidden Items in Solid Mode With Perspective and Zooming

Sometimes when working in one of the solid modes in Orthographic 3D views, you will find that there are objects you cannot see. If you are creating an interior room scene, for example, which is constructed of a cube for the walls, ceiling and floor, entering solid mode will make your furniture and other interior objects impossible to see.

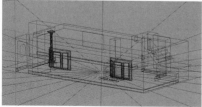

A wireframe view of a room in Ortho mode

A solid view of the same model. No matter how far you zoom in, you won't see the interior

One way to take a good look around in such a situation is to use Numpad-5 to enter Perspective mode. Center the room in the 3D view, then start rolling the scroll wheel to zoom in until your viewpoint has passed through one of the walls of the room.

With careful control, and the use of Perspective mode, you can see objects that would normally be obscured in solid view.

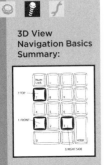

3D View Navigation Basics Summary:

• Numpad-1, 3 and 7 show front, right side and top views.

• Ctrl-Numpad-1, 3 and 7 show back, left side and bottom views.

• The Z-key toggles between wireframe and solid views.

• Numpad-5 toggles between orthogonal and perspective modes.

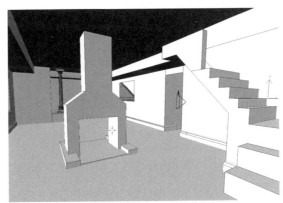

Using Perspective mode, zooming now takes you "inside" the model.

The Toolbox

When working in the 3D view, the toolbox is one of your best friends. Place the mouse over the 3D window and press the Spacebar. The toolbox pops up under the mouse cursor. It functions just like any other hierarchical menu you've ever used.

The toolbox contains almost any command you can use in Blender.

The toolbox contains almost any command or tool you would care to use in Blender. In fact, to get a good idea of the kinds of things you can do with Blender, it is instructive to use the Spacebar, bring up the toolbox, and begin to browse. There are controls there for creating objects of all kinds, moving into different modes, grouping, selecting, rendering, transforming and generally everything else you can do.

One little hint for using the toolbox: if you find yourself going to the toolbox more than twice for the same item, see if the command has a keyboard shortcut listed beside it. If it does, drag your mouse away from the toolbox to close it, then use the keyboard shortcut. Sure, you can be the kind of user who always goes three levels deep into the toolbox to find "Apply Scale/Rotation", but then all of your friends will laugh at you, because *they* realized it was better to simply press Ctrl-A, just like it said in the toolbox. Of course, you don't have to learn *every* keyboard shortcut, nor should you try. But for commands that you find yourself using again and again, the small amount of effort you spend to make yourself use the keyboard will save you time and help your workflow.

The Buttons Window

The default Buttons window and its major components.

A Buttons window shows a series of panels and tabs that are populated by various controls. Depending on which Context you have selected, these controls can affect objects in the 3D view, set options and properties (like Materials), and trigger procedures (like Rendering).

What is a Context? That's just the technical name for the different groupings of controls, selected by either clicking on the appropriate button, as highlighted in the illustration above, or by using the associated hotkey. Hotkeys for the different contexts can be found in the hotkey index and in the chapters relevant to each context throughout this book. For our purposes, we will be focusing on the four rightmost context icons: Shading (hotkey F5), Object (F7), Editing (F9) and Scene (F10).

For now, press F5 to enter the Shading Context. You will see that a new set of icons has appeared to the right of the original context buttons. These are called Subcontexts, but don't let that scare you, as they are just gateways to more groups of controls.

Shading subcontext buttons.

Subcontexts function the same way as contexts: they display a different set of panels and tabs with controls. In the case of the Shading Context we just entered, there are five subcontexts: Lamps, Materials, Textures, Radiosity and World. Keeping hotkeys in mind, try pressing F5 several more times.

Doing this quickly cycles you through the different Shading subcontexts. In fact, this technique holds true for all contexts, allowing you fast keyboard-based access to different sets of controls.

Naming shortcuts
It would become tedious and probably confusing to always be talking about contexts and subcontexts when referring to different sets of controls. For that reason, most Blender users simply refer to different sets of controls by more common names. The Materials subcontext is commonly called the Material buttons. Likewise, the Editing context and Texturing context are called the Edit buttons and Texture buttons, respectively.

These sets of controls are grouped in panels and tabs. Use F5 to get yourself to the Material buttons (or just LMB click on the Material button) and take a look at the layout.

The Material buttons.

The panel/tab interface is quite flexible. You can LMB-click and drag a tab into a different panel if you don't like the current organization. You can drag tabs out of a panel, dropping them into the background to become their own panel. Also, you can drag and drop entire panels, causing their neighbors to shuffle aside and rearrange.

As an exercise, try dragging all of the tabs in the Material buttons into only two panels, then drag some of those tabs off again, creating their own panels. That's not the way you would want to work, but it will give you the idea of how panels and tabs operate.

Panels and tabs can be dragged and joined.

Now, let's look at the actual controls. Press F7 with the mouse over the Buttons Window to bring up the Object buttons.

The Object buttons.

Most of the controls in Blender function like their counterparts in any other piece of software, but since Blender uses its own visual scheme, we'll go over them to alleviate any confusion.

The color references in this section only apply if you are using the basic Blender theme. You can find out how to change the look of Blender in Chapter 14: Customization with Options and Preferences. Almost all tutorials, including the ones in this book, show Blender with the standard interface, so you should probably leave it as it is for now.

1. Toggle button: Aqua buttons that have two settings: On and Off. In certain parts of the interface, they can toggle through three different settings, the third looking like On, but with the button's label appearing in yellow. Toggle buttons are usually used to indicate settings.
2. Button: Pink buttons are used to initiate actions. They will not stay pressed.
3. Text Block: These controls allow you to type text — usually the name of an object or other Blender element. If there is a group of related Text Blocks, you can usually use the Tab key to move between them for faster text entry.
4. Drop Down Menu: Grey controls that have an up/down arrow widget on their side. These function mostly like dropdown menus in any other program, allowing you to select from a predefined list of options. There are times, though, when you will see something like this:

The dropdown menu for managing links.

In these types of dropdown menus, selecting "Add New" will create a completely new item appropriate to the menu (for example, it creates a new Material instead of selecting an existing one). Also, clicking the "X" to the right of the menu will clear any selection from the menu, basically telling it that you want to select "nothing."

5. Spinners: Darker gray controls with left/right arrow heads on either side. Spinner controls are a little more complex than the others. They are used for setting numeric values. Clicking on the label or the actual value in the Spinner will temporarily turn it into a text box, allowing you to enter a value directly from the keyboard. Clicking on either arrow head will raise or lower the value, respectively. And finally, clicking and dragging anywhere within the Spinner will "spin" the value up or down, depending on whether you drag to the right or the left. Try it on one of the Spinners in the Object buttons to see how it feels. Some keyboard modifiers can help with Spinners, too: holding Shift while you drag makes the values advance more slowly, while holding down the Ctrl key makes the value advance by a different increment (usually 10). So using the click-drag method on a Spinner control while holding down Ctrl-Shift would slowly advance the values in increments of 10.

Buttons Window Basic Summary:

• A Buttons Window contains controls for settings values, triggering actions and toggling modes.

• The controls are grouped in Contexts, the more popular of which are accessible by hotkeys.

• Within each context, controls appear on tabs and panels that you can rearrange to suit your workflow.

Over time, the Blender interface has seen a lot of growth, as well as some wear and tear. You may find toggle buttons that are not Aqua. You may find dropdown menus that appear at first to be standard buttons. If you're the picky type, you can make a list of such irregularities and send it to the developers so they can unify the whole thing. If you're not, don't worry about it. Just hit the button and see what it does. You won't blow up your computer or anything (that'll be one of the cool 3.0 features!).

Headers

Each window in the Blender interface can have a header.

The User Preferences header.

Headers always contain menus, and often other controls relevant to the particular type of window to which they're attached. In the figure, we see the User Preferences header.

Clicking on the File menu shows what you are used to seeing from a file menu in a graphics program: commands for opening, closing, saving, importing and exporting files. Note the keyboard shortcuts that appear beside the commands. Most are different from the ones you are accustomed to from other interfaces. Because they *are* different from 99% of the programs you will use, we'll go through the more popular ones here:

The contents of the File menu.

New: shortcut: Ctrl-X. This dumps whatever you are currently working on and sets up a fresh work space. It also pops up the scary, cryptic "OK? Erase all" message that you need to confirm by LMB-clicking. Blender will never ask you if you want to save your current work with a "You haven't saved your work. Do you want to save?" message.

Don't worry, though — this "Erase all" message does not just delete all of the objects and settings in your current project while leaving the project open for you to accidentally save. This is Blender's way of saying "Do you want me to clear my memory and start a new project?"

Open: shortcut: F1. Shows the file browser window, where you can find files to open.

Headers

The Blender File Browser

Because Blender is intended to work on many different platforms (Linux, Windows, OS X, etc.), and because it is intended to be self-contained, it uses its own unique method of browsing for files. Many people find it confusing at first, and it is most likely fairly different from what you are used to. Here is the way it works:

Blender's file browser window.

The hardest thing to wrap your head around here is that the columns in this view flow like columns of text in a newspaper or magazine. Using the scroll wheel here will seem odd until you understand how the columns flow into each other.

Beyond that, using the LMB will put the filename you clicked into the "ready" station. Sometimes a file browser might allow you to select several files at once, in which case you can use RMB to highlight the filenames you need. When you have the files selected that you want, clicking the "Open File" button will load that .blend file. Alternately, you can simply MMB click on the file you want, and it will load the file straight away.

Navigating through folders is a bit less graphical than the file browsers you are used to. Folder names appear at the top of the file listings in white type. A single click on the folder name will take you into that folder. To go back up and out of a folder, you can either click on the "P" button in the upper left, use the P-key hotkey, or LMB on the ".." in the folder listings (I know, I know).

Of course, the Cancel button is still Cancel. Things aren't *that* different.

Also, this same file browser dialogue is used for saving, selecting images for textures and even for browsing through .blend files themselves for linking data. The interface is always the same, though, and playing with it until you have the hang of it will be worth your time.

Open Recent…: shortcut: Ctrl-O. Pops up a list of recently saved files for you to choose from.

Save: shortcut: Ctrl-W. While many applications throughout the world use this shortcut to Close a document, Blender uses it to Save. Under most conditions in Blender, you can also use the traditional Ctrl-S to save, but due to conflicts with hotkeys in certain modes, it's not guaranteed. Ctrl-W will always work.

Quit: shortcut: Ctrl-Q. Pressing Ctrl-Q brings up the "OK? Quit Blender" popup, which must be confirmed by a mouse click. Once again, a reminder is in order that Blender will not prompt you to save your work in progress. The best way to avoid quitting without saving is to drill into your reflexes that the Quit command is really Ctrl-W, Ctrl-Q. That'll be a Save, followed by a Quit.

Other menus in the headers will contain sets of commands relevant to their particular window type. For example, the header menus attached to the 3D Window contain many of the same controls that are available from the spacebar toolbox. Browsing these menus is a great way to go Easter Egg hunting for undiscovered, unpublicized features.

For now, though, don't worry about the individual controls on the different headers. We'll go over the useful items in them in their specific chapters.

Making Changes: How To Adjust the Layout of What You See

If shuffling tabs and panels was the extent of the configurability of Blender's interface, it would be kind of sad. Fortunately, it is not.

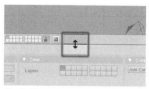

Hover your mouse over the border line between the 3D window and the Buttons window. When you have it just right, it will display as a little double-headed arrow.

LMB click and drag. The border moves up and down, and when you release the mouse button, the windows resize to adjust.

The double arrow, ready to change the interface.

Now, put your mouse over the border again, and this time click with the MMB. A small menu pops up asking you whether to Split or Join the areas, and also gives you the option of "No Header". Choose Split.

Blender makes a vertical border line that follows your mouse as you move it. If you place the cursor in the 3D window, the border appears only there. Likewise for the Buttons window. Move the mouse over the 3D window so the border line follows it. Put it near the center of the screen, and click the LMB.

You've just divided the 3D view into two separate windows. Each window functions independently of the other. You can place your mouse over the left window, press Numpad-7 to put it into top view, then jump over and use Numpad-1 to put the other window into front view.

Here's the cool part. Click on the grid popup menu icon at the far left of either 3D window's header.

The menu that comes up shows you the sixteen different window types available in Blender. From this menu, choose "Buttons Window" since you're already familiar with that. Bingo. The 3D window is now a Buttons window. Use that same menu again and change it back to a 3D window.

The Window type menu. Any window can show any type of information.

This is how deep the Blender interface goes: you can subdivide the interface into almost any configuration of windows you find useful by using the Split/Join tool on window borders. Any of those created windows can be set to any of the window types you just saw in the menu. You can create several windows in a row, each showing a Buttons window set to a different context, so that you can work on, say, materials and textures at the same time without constantly switching window contexts.

That's actually a lot to take in, and your odds of coming up with the Best Blender Configuration Ever on your first trip through are pretty slim. So try this instead:

Click on the dropdown control that reads "SR:2-Model". From the dropdown menu that appears, click "1-Animation". A whole different configuration of windows and controls appears, helpfully optimized for animation.

Selecting a different screen configuration from the Screens menu.

Check out the other choices from that menu: Material, Sequence and Scripting. Lots and lots of buttons, huh? Don't be scared. You can learn all of that stuff later. For now, it's good enough to know that Blender offers you different Screens, accessible through that dropdown menu, that allow you to create and organize any set of window and control configurations that you come up with.

Although you won't need it for any individual tutorial in this book, using different Screens is one of the things that divides Blender pros from ones who reconfigure their workspace by hand each and every time they want to do a different task. Experienced users generally have a set of Screens they have developed, often based off of these default ones, but sometimes entirely of their own creation, that they rapidly jump between during the course of their work. Of course, there is a set of hotkeys for switching between Screens, and although you'll most likely forget it due to lack of use until you are doing more involved Blender projects, we'll tell you anyway, just for the sake of completeness. Ctrl-Left Arrow and Ctrl-Right Arrow move to the previous and next Screen, respectively.

Interface Configuration Basics Summary:

• Change the size of windows by LMB dragging their borders.

• Split or Join windows by MMB clicking on their borders.

• Change the window type by choosing from the Window Type popup menu at the far left of every header.

• Switch between different workspace Screens by using the Ctrl-Left Arrow and Ctrl-Right Arrow hotkeys.

So, remember how we mentioned the hotkeys for switching to different types of buttons windows (F5, F6, F7, etc.)? If you start to use the different screens for different parts of your work, you'll find that you won't have to switch between different kinds of buttons windows as often. So, instead of memorizing a number of function keys, you can begin to work by using Ctrl-Left Arrow and Right Arrow to switch to a screen that is already pre-configured with the tools that you need.

Saving Your Configuration

After your first major Blender project, you will probably have configured the interface to really fit your workflow. You may have gotten rid of the Scripting Screen, and seriously restructured the Animation and Material Screens to better fit the way you work. You would like to use this configuration on all of your future work. What do you do? Ctrl-U. Ctrl-U saves the current Blender workspace, Screens, Objects and all, as the startup default. The next time you run Blender (or do the New/ Ctrl-X command) this exact configuration is what you will see.

Rendering: Isn't This The Entire Point?

Before you move on, there's one last thing to do: render your first Blender scene.

Use Ctrl-X to start a new Blender session. You'll see the default cube, as well as a camera and a lamp. That's everything you need in order to render.

Before you do an official full render, let's get a preview. With the mouse over the 3D view, press Shift-P. Shift-P toggles the Render Preview panel on and off. The panel can be moved around by LMB dragging on its header bar, and removed by either clicking the "X" in its upper left corner or pressing Shift-P again. The panel can be resized by LMB dragging the lower right corner.

The Preview panel will generate a fast render of whatever falls behind it, so it can be used to get an ongoing, quickly updated render of certain small areas

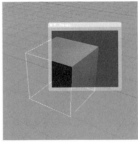

The render Preview panel.

Saving Your Configuration

you may be adjusting. If you like, use the MMB to adjust the rotation of the default view. As soon as you release the MMB, the Preview panel will attempt to display the render preview of the new scene behind it.

On to the Final, Full Render

Press F12. (Mac users beware — F12 is most likely chained to one of OS X's snazzy Exposé or Dashboard features. Go to the Scene buttons, F10, and click the big tan RENDER button. Then go change your Exposé shortcut in the Mac's control panel, because you'll be using F12 all the time in Blender.)

A render of the default scene.

The default cube renders from the perspective of the camera, lit by the single lamp. Woo hoo! Once you're done marveling at this 3D masterpiece, press the Esc-key to put the render window in the background and return to the main Blender interface.

So, now you know the overall basics of the Blender interface. That wasn't so bad, was it?

Admittedly, there is a lot more to learn, but the great thing is that at this point, you can pick it up as you go. If you came to this book wanting to learn just a specific section of Blender, you're now equipped to jump to that part of the book and start in. Of course, you're still invited to stick around for the whole show. You've done the hard part, which is just getting past the look and feel of the interface.

The rest will be easy.

Promise.

CHAPTER 3

Object Manipulation

 Object Manipulation and Basic Animation: Hands On

 Object Manipulation Basics

 Object Animation Basics

Object Manipulation and Basic Animation: Hands on

In this tutorial, you'll learn about object creation, manipulation and organization in Blender, as well as different techniques of object-level animation. In this tutorial, we will be make a model of a molecule that will allow us to experiment with different methods of creating motion through animation.

Use Ctrl-X to begin a clean session of Blender.

At this point, it wouldn't be a bad idea to review the interface elements for changing the 3D view (Numpad-1, 3, and 7 for front, side and top view; Numpad-5 to toggle into and out of perspective mode; Z-key to toggle shaded view, as well as the MMB and scroll wheel to freely zoom and rotate the view. If you haven't already worked through Chapter 2: The Basic Interface, now would be a good time to do so). Once you're done getting your 3D legs, its time to start creating your molecule.

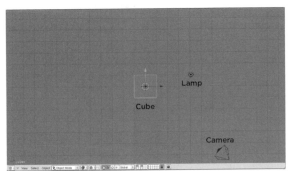

The default 3D view, with a cube, a lamp and a camera.

First, you must get rid of the default cube. If your zooming about in the previous paragraph has resulted in the default objects being off screen, press the Home key and Blender will auto-zoom the view so that all objects are visible again. Now, press Numpad 7 to move into a top view.

Select the default camera by placing the cursor over it and pressing the Right Mouse Button (RMB). Many new users are thrown off by this unconventional selection method (many programs use the Left button for selection). Learn, right now, that RMB selects in the 3D view. When you RMB the camera, you will see that its outline is highlighted in light pink. This pink outline indicates that the object, in this case the camera, is selected.

RMB the cube and you will see that it is now outlined in pink (selected), while the camera has returned to its original state. Selection in Blender is accumulated like most other programs with which you are familiar, with the Shift key. With the cube still selected, hold down the Shift key and RMB the camera. Keep holding the Shift key and RMB select the default lamp. Your selection has been extended to all three objects: the cube, camera and lamp.

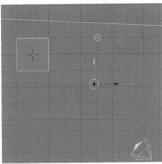

The default scene with everything selected.

But you don't want all of that to be selected. You only want the cube selected.

Press the A-key. A-key toggles selection on and off for everything.

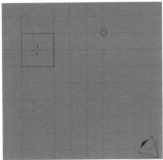

The default scene with nothing selected.

Object Manipulation and Basic Animation

Pressing A-key once selects everything (you can think of it as 'select All'). Pressing it again deselects everything. Do you want to make sure that nothing is selected? Press A-key twice.

Of course, when you just pressed the A-key, everything most likely deselected. Why? Well, remember that by Shift-RMB clicking you had already selected all the objects in the Scene. So, if nothing is selected, you're where you need to be. If instead everything is selected, press the A-key one more time. Get the current scene to a point where nothing is selected. Now, you'll learn one final method of selection.

With your cursor over the 3D window, press the B-key, and watch the cursor become the target of moving crosshairs. These moving guidelines indicate that you are in Border Select mode. Simply LMB click and drag across the 3D window, and any object that falls within the area of the box shape that your dragging creates becomes selected when you release the mouse button. Unlike RMB selection, border select is always cumulative and will add to your previous selection. If you want to use border select to *deselect* objects, then drag with either the MMB or RMB instead of the LMB.

You might want to try using the B-key and border selecting objects for practice, clearing your selection each time with the A-key.

When you're done, use the selection method of your choice to select only the default cube.

Press the X-key to delete the cube. You will be prompted "OK? Erase selected object(s)". Click the LMB to accept this and erase the cube. Over time, you will probably find that the combined motion of X-key/LMB to delete an object will become second nature, and that you'll probably forget there's a click-through confirmation there.

- **Right Mouse Button selects in the 3D view.**
- **Shift-RMB builds selection.**
- **A-key toggles between Select All and Select None.**
- **B-key enters border select mode.**
- **Dragging with LMB selects.**
- **Dragging with RMB/MMB deselects.**
- **X-key deletes selected objects.**

Undo

But wait, you didn't want to remove that cube! Why? Well, let's pretend for a second that the cube was in fact a head model that you've just worked on for eight hours straight without saving once. And you accidentally deleted it.

Ctrl-Z, like in many other programs, is Undo. Press Ctrl-Z to bring the cube you just deleted back from the great digital beyond. Ctrl-Shift-Z is the Blender equivalent of Redo, sending the cube back to the netherworld. Unlike other programs, however, there is no menu entry for Undo or Redo, so learning to use the hotkey combination for this one is essential.

The 3D Cursor

The 'aiming sight' that you've seen hanging around in the 3D view is the 3D cursor. The 3D cursor is where new objects and items will appear when created in the 3D workspace. It can also be used to control how objects rotate and scale.

The 3D cursor.

If you're like most new Blender users, you've mistakenly LMB clicked somewhere in the 3D view, hoping to select something (and select is RMB, remember?). Using LMB in the 3D view sets the location of the 3D Cursor. Before you begin creating your first model, we'd like to make sure that the 3D Cursor is in the center of the 3D world.

• LMB in the 3D view sets the location of the 3D Cursor

• Shift-C centers the 3D Cursor in the global workspace.

Go into front view (Numpad 1) and LMB as close to the center of the intersection of the blue and red (z and x) axes as you can. The 3D Cursor jumps to the position of your click. Now go into side view (Numpad 3) and LMB once again at the intersection of the blue and green (z and y) axes, if the 3D Cursor isn't already there. Use Numpad 1 to return to a front view. Great. Now you're set.

We wanted you to practice using the LMB to set the 3D Cursor in the previous example, but there's an even easier way to return the 3D Cursor to the origin. Shift-C snaps the 3D Cursor to the center of the 3D world.

Adding Objects

With the cursor over the 3D window, bring up the toolbox by pressing the Spacebar.

As you can see in the illustration, there are many different kinds of objects you can add to the 3D view, but for this chapter we're going to focus on the Mesh category. From within the Add->Mesh section of the toolbox, choose Icosphere, then click OK when a pop-up says 'Subdivision: 2'. You've just added a mesh sphere object to the 3D world, and it has been created at the location of the 3D cursor.

The toolbox, about to add an Icosphere.

If you've done this, but don't see anything resembling a sphere on your screen, you may be zoomed in or out too far, or have panned the view too far off to one side. Try pressing the Home key, which will auto-zoom and pan the view to show all available objects.

The icosphere will most likely be a lavender or purple color with yellow edges covering its surface. This is because new objects are created in Edit Mode, which allows you to change the mesh's shape and geometry. You won't be dealing with that yet, but you can learn about it in Chapter 4. For now, get out of Edit Mode by pressing the Tab key. When you do it, the mesh lines disappear, the faces turn gray, and the entire object is given a light pink outline. If you'll recall from earlier in the chapter, that pink outline indicates that the icosphere you just created is currently selected.

So, adding a new object does three things:

1. Creates a new object wherever the 3D Cursor is;
2. Puts the object in Edit Mode (if such a thing is possible for that object. For example, Lamps do not have an Edit Mode);
3. And automatically selects the new object.

Just to give you enough examples to work with, your sample atom will have three protons and three neutrons in its nucleus, so you're going to need to create a few more objects. If you just added several more with the spacebar toolbox right now, they would all be created at the location of the 3D cursor, meaning that they would be created in the same space as your first icosphere. Of course, this is a virtual world, so doing this won't hurt anything. It would only make it difficult to keep track of how many objects you have and where they are. You already know how to set the location of the 3D Cursor, so go ahead and reposition it away from the first sphere.

LMB a short distance away from the original icosphere. Then, use the spacebar toolbox to add another icosphere. Don't forget to hit Tab afterward to get out of the default Edit Mode.

The 3D cursor positioned away from the icosphere.

Getting Oriented

The axis icon in the 3D view.

Before you start moving things around, you need to get oriented in 3D space. Use Numpad-1 to make sure you are looking at the scene from the front. Notice the little icon in the lower left of the view: a vertical blue line labeled Z that meets a horizontal red one labeled X.

This icon is to help you remember that the x axis runs left to right, and the z axis runs bottom to top. Press Numpad-3 to move into side view, and you will see that the icon still shows the z axis, but now also shows the y axis. The y axis runs from back to front.

If you're completely new to 3D, a little explanation is in order. An 'axis' is a convenient way to refer to a direction. 3D objects are located by finding their location along each axis. A more detailed explanation is in the discussion section of this chapter if you should need it.

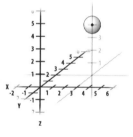

In the illustration, the object is said to be located at (3,2,4), with each of those numbers corresponding to its location along the respective axes (x,y,z).

So, in Blender, the axes are:
- X: left/right
- Y: back/front
- Z: bottom/top

This will have to become second nature to you, and, if you use the keyboard shortcuts for object manipulation and again later for modeling, it will.

Moving, Rotating and Scaling Objects

There are three main things you can do to an object once it has been created. Move it around, rotate it, and change its size (usually called scaling). All together, these kinds of changes are referred to as "transformation".

RMB on one of the icospheres to select it.

To rotate the icosphere, press the R-key. Now start moving the mouse in circles around the icosphere. You will see it rotate to follow your motion. When you're done, RMB will cancel this rotation mode, returning the sphere back to its original orientation. Try it again, by hitting R-key, then rotating, but this time, end the motion with the LMB instead. The sphere leaves rotation mode, but now stays wherever it was when you hit LMB.

This is the main workflow for manipulating objects and using tools in the 3D workspace throughout Blender. A hotkey (R in this case), followed by a mouse motion, ending either with RMB to cancel and return to the previous state, or with LMB, which confirms the change.

Since the R-key triggered a rotation, any guesses as to how to go about scaling an object?

S-key, followed by mouse motion, ending in either LMB (accept) or RMB (cancel). Try scaling one of the spheres. Select it, use S-key, and make it grow to twice the size of the other. LMB to accept the change.

Now, use the same procedure to try to return that icosphere close to its original size. If things get really messed up, remember that you can use Ctrl-Z to Undo.

And finally, movement. In Blender, although R rotates and S scales, it is the G-key that moves objects. G stands for what? Most Blender users think of it as "Grab". If it helps you to remember it, you can too.

The original sphere, scaled to double its size.

Select your icospheres and use the G-key to move them around. Once again, RMB cancels the movement, resetting things to how they were before you pressed G, while LMB accepts the movement.

Now, let's put your knowledge of the axes (x,y,z) to work in conjunction with these basic motion tools.

• G-key lets you move (Grab) an object.
• R-key lets you rotate an object.
• S-key lets you scale (resize) an object.
• With these operations, LMB accepts your changes.
• RMB cancels and returns the object to its original state.
• While in any of these transformation modes (G/R/S), pressing the X, Y or Z-keys constrains you to transforming along that axis.

Using the MMB, click-drag in the 3D window to rotate the view until you have something similar to this (it doesn't really matter as long as you have a nice angled view).

Select one of the icospheres and press G-key to "grab" and start moving. While you're still in Grab mode, moving the sphere around, press the X-key. Suddenly, a line appears through the sphere, running parallel to the X axis, and you find that the object will only move along that line. You have *constrained* the object's motion to the x axis. Now, without RMB canceling the movement, press the Y-key. The guideline shifts to parallel the Y axis, and the motion is constrained to only front/back. You know what the Z-key will do.

Moving, Rotating and Scaling Objects

So you see that if you want to move an object up a bit, you select it, press the G-key, then press the Z-key. When you do that, you can be sure that the object will *only* move up and down. And that's why it's important to learn which axes are which when you are moving things around. You will not always be in one of the straight-on views (front, side, top, etc.), and it can often be essential to be certain of which direction you are moving things.

Manipulators

You've eaten your vegetables and learned the main hotkeys for transforming objects in Blender. Let's look at two alternate workflows for doing the same thing that may suit your way of thinking better.

With the 3D window still at an angled view, re-examine the selected sphere.

Those red, blue and green arrows sprouting from the center of the sphere are its translation manipulators. LMB click and drag on the blue arrow head.

The sphere moves along the z axis (vertically). When you release the LMB, the motion stops and the sphere comes to rest in its new location. Try it with the green and red arrow heads. Each one controls translation along a different axis.

Now, take a look at the manipulator controls on the 3D view header.

The manipulator buttons on the 3D header.

Each button enables a different manipulator, all of which function the same way: LMB and drag. Particularly useful are the visualizations for the rotation manipulators, which actually show the growing angle as you rotate the object.

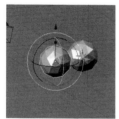

The Combo Manipulator.

Just like holding down the Shift key with RMB builds a selection of 3D objects, holding down Shift while clicking the manipulator buttons in the header builds a selection there as well. In fact, by using Shift-LMB, you can enable all three manipulator types at once, giving you quick access to all transformation features directly in the 3D view.

Give them a try. They might fit the way you work better than the hotkeys. Later on, during character animation and certain kinds of mesh modeling, there are tasks for which the manipulators are very well-suited. Of course, the manipulators are not for everyone, and if you find that you don't care for them and would prefer to have them out of your way, you can. The "pointing finger" icon, shown in the illustration, will turn the manipulators off.

Gestures

Blender also allows users to trigger the basic transformations through mouse gestures. Try this: RMB select one of the spheres. Now, LMB click and drag, slowly carving a circle like this:

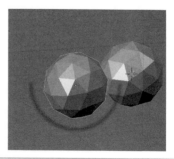

When you release the LMB, you will find that the sphere is now in rotation mode as though you had pressed the R-key. Using the LMB again will confirm the rotation, and RMB will cancel it.

The other mouse gestures are:

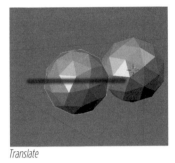

Translate

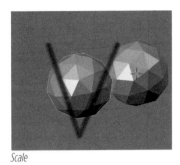

Scale

Some experienced Blender artists swear by the mouse gestures, as they allow them to position and construct their scenes with minimal interaction from the keyboard. They are not for everyone, but definitely worth a try!

Duplication

Back to our atomic example. To make the little atom have the right stuff inside, it will need three protons and three neutrons. You could move the existing icospheres away from the 3D Cursor and add four more from the toolbox. Or, you could make use of what you already have.

RMB select one of the icospheres, then press Shift-D.

Shift-D duplicates the selected objects. The duplicate object is created at the location of the original object, and is put into Grab (move) mode. Move the new object away from the original and press LMB to lock it into position. Note that pushing RMB to cancel Grab mode after duplication does *not* cancel the duplication. A duplicate will still have been made, but will be "hiding" at the exact location of the original. For that reason, if you accidentally duplicate an object, it's better to get into to the habit of moving it away from the original, LMB, then deleting it with the X-key.

You need a total of six icospheres to make up the atom's nucleus. RMB select one of the icospheres you have so far. Next, use the B-key area selection method to select the other two as well. If you accidentally select the camera or lamp object, you can remove them from the selection by holding down the Shift key and RMB (probably twice) on them until they are no longer outlined in pink. Alternatively, you can press the A-key twice (once to select All, and again to deselect everything), then begin from scratch.

When you have the three icospheres (and nothing else) selected, press Shift-D to duplicate all three at once.

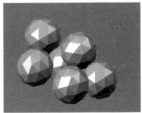

Shift-D duplicates
selected objects.

Using different views (Numpad 1,3,7 and MMB drag), the Grab/move tool and the x, y and z movement constraint hotkeys (or the manipulators!), move the six icospheres together to form a nice, messy, nucleus. It doesn't matter if

The completed nucleus.

it matches the illustration or not. The point is for you to start to become familiar with the tools you will be using all the time.

Moving On

At this point, it's best to spell out what goals we would like you to accomplish to get the big picture. You still need to add three electrons and animate them so they fly around the nucleus. It would also be nice to add some sort of animation to the nucleus as a whole, so it's not just sitting there in quantum laziness the entire time.

Before you begin animating, you should adjust your workspace to one more suitable to the task than the one you've been using up to this point. Do you remember from the Interface chapter that Blender's workspace is highly configurable, and that the default installation comes with several different screens, each suited to a different task? Now's the time to start making use of it.

Use the Ctrl-Left Arrow hotkey to change working screens. If you are using the default Blender installation, this hotkey will have placed you in a screen labeled "1-Animation". Alternately, and a little more slowly, you could have chosen that option from the Screens drop down in the main header.

Choosing the Animation screen from the header.

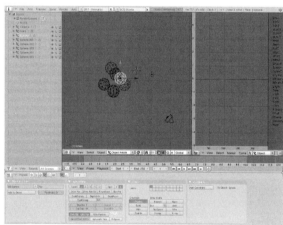

The default Animation screen.

Lots of new stuff here, but no need for panic. In fact, the only really important stuff you'll be dealing with right now is the timeline, the 3d view (which you already know), and something called the Ipo view.

The timeline is pretty self-explanatory. It is the timeline in seconds over which your animation takes place. Controls on the timeline are simple as well. Start and End represent the start and end frames of the animation, and can be changed by clicking on them and entering new values. The "play" button plays your animation in the 3D view. Pressing it again halts animation. The "skip to start/end" buttons do exactly as advertised. LMB dragging within the timeline window plays through any animation you have created in other windows. Moving through an animation by dragging the mouse over a timeline is known as "scrubbing".

The timeline can display either seconds or frames. With the cursor over the Timeline window, the T-key toggles between these display methods. Press the T-key and choose "Frames" for now. (If you're completely new to animation and need an explanation of time in animation and what the term "frame" means, check out the "Frames and Time" sidebar.)

The Timeline window.

Frames and Time

In animation (and television and film), time is divided into Frames. Each frame is a still image that represents a slice of time. When played one after the other quickly enough, these individual frames give the illusion of motion.

Different media have different frame rates. For most film productions, each second in time is divided into 24 frames. The common terminology is to say that film runs at 24 frames per second.

For North American television (NTSC), the rate is 30 frames per second (fps).

For European TV (PAL format), the rate is 25 fps.

It is important that you know your target media before you begin to animate, as changing the frame rate mid-way through an animation can lead to poor results, as objects and effects animated at a different frame rate will appear unnatural.

Empties

Sometimes, it would be nice to create an object that you can animate or use as a reference, but that you won't need to render. A simple mesh could be used, but it would be even more efficient if there was a type of "placeholder" object. What would something like that be useful for? Well, let's say that you would like to make the entire nucleus of your atom pulsate (shrink and grow repeatedly). Since the nucleus consists of a number of objects, you would like to have a way to only animate such an effect once, as opposed to animating each object individually. In Blender, placeholders to help with such things are called Empties. You create an Empty object, then animate it to grow and shrink. Afterward, you get all the parts of your nucleus to follow that animation.

Let's add an Empty to your Scene.

First, to make sure that you can see it clearly when it's created, LMB somewhere away from the icospheres, setting the 3D cursor. Then, use the toolbox to Add->Empty. The Empty appears at the location of the 3D cursor, like any other new object.

The toolbox, about to add an Empty to the scene.

Now, let's do your first bit of animation. In Blender, as in most 3D animation programs, animation is accomplished by changing the location, rotation or scale of an object over time. The markers that keep track of these changes are called Keys.

In the Timeline window, make sure that the green time marker that indicates the current time is as far left as it will go. This should put you on Frame 1 of your animation.

Move the cursor over the 3D window and press the I-key. A menu titled "Insert Key" pops up. Choose "Scale" from the menu, as you are going to only animate the scale of this empty.

The Insert Key menu, prepared to set a Scaling key.

Back in the Timeline window, LMB around frame 80, setting Blender's frame counter to 80. Over the 3D window, press the S-key and scale the Empty up to twice its original size. LMB to confirm the change in scale.

Empties

Now, press the I-key again and choose "Scale."

You will notice that the timeline now contains two small yellow lines, one at the location in time of each key you just set (i.e. one at frame 1, and one around frame 80). Use the LMB to scrub the timeline between these two yellow markers. Watch the 3D view as you do it. You will see the Empty change scale as you scrub back and forth.

As you can see, the Start and End frames for your animation are set to the defaults of 1 and 250, and you need to set a few more keys to fill out the space. Continue positioning the frame counter in the timeline with LMB, then scaling the Empty and inserting Scale keys for it. As you will see, fewer keys in the timeline will result in slower animations, while dense groupings of keys will lead to rapid changes. Remember to press the timeline's play button to have Blender play back your animation for you. Really, it doesn't matter how many keys you insert, or how you decide to scale the empty in this step. If you're the kind of person that needs detailed Instructions though, try setting a new key every twenty frames, alternating between a large scaled empty and a small scaled one.

Another popular method of playing back your animation is to position the cursor over the window you would like to see animated (most likely the 3D view), and pressing Alt-A. Pressing Alt-Shift-A will accomplish the same thing, but will run the animation in all windows on the current screen.

Now you have your Empty shrinking and growing. In the next step, you'll connect the spheres of your nucleus to it.

Parenting

In the real world, children inherit traits from their parents. In the world of 3D graphics, you can give your objects parent-child relationships. A child object will inherit certain character-istics (like scaling) from its parent: if the parent object scales, so will the child. The child can have its own characteristics — it can move, rotate and scale on its own — but anything that its parent does, it will do too. So, if you have an Empty with animated scaling like you just created, making that Empty the parent of your sphere nucleus objects should cause them to scale just like it.

• I-key brings up a menu of available properties on which to set animation keys.
• Alt-A plays animation in a particular window.

Before you do the next bit, let's make sure that nothing is selected. Press the A-key twice to clear any selections that are currently made. Use the method of your choice (RMB, B-key border) to select all the icospheres that make up the nucleus of your atom. Then, holding down the Shift key, RMB select the Empty.

Something we haven't mentioned before is the distinction between "selected" objects and the "Active" object. Notice how the Empty, which was selected last, is a brighter shade of pink than the other selected objects? This brighter selection indicates that the Empty is the "Active" object. The Active object will always be the last one that you select. Having an Active object is important when you will be performing an operation (like Parenting) in which one or more objects will be linked or referenced in some way to a target object. That target will always be the Active object.

So, with all of your icospheres selected, and with the Empty as the Active object, press Ctrl-P and click through the "OK? Make Parent" message that comes up.

The icospheres are now the child objects of the Empty. In some tutorials and references other than this book, they are said to be "parented" to the Empty, even though they are its children. Although that is a common usage, it is technically inaccurate and counterintuitive so we will avoid it here.

RMB select the empty, and use the G-key grab tool to move it around the 3D view (then RMB to cancel the move). The spheres move with it. Use the R-key to rotate the empty and see how the spheres move with it again (then RMB to cancel). RMB select one of the icospheres and move it around by itself (don't forget to RMB to cancel the operation). Child objects can still be moved independently, but follow the motion of their parents.

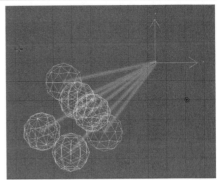

The lines indicating a parent/child relationship are highlighted here.

Press the Play button in the Timeline window (or Alt-A over the 3D view) to see how parenting has caused the icospheres to inherit the scaling animation of the Empty.

Weird, huh? The icospheres grow and shrink with the Empty, but their distance from the Empty changes as well. That's not what you wanted. What is happening is that the children are changing size, but they are changing size as though they and the parent Empty are all one large object, growing and shrinking overall. Let's change this so it works correctly. If you wanted to, you could repeatedly use Undo (Ctrl-Z) to back step until the parenting relationship is removed.

• Ctrl-P creates a parent-child relationship between objects, with the Active object as the parent.
• Alt-P breaks the parent-child link of a selected child object.

Instead, select the icospheres and press Alt-P. An "OK?" menu pops up, with "Clear Parent" already selected. LMB to accept this (or you can press Enter on your keyboard for the same effect). The dashed lines that had been an indicator of the parent-child relationship have disappeared, showing that the spheres are no longer the children of the Empty.

To get the correct effect this time, you would like to put the empty in the middle of your nucleus, so that when it grows and shrinks, the nucleus will follow it properly. You could just use the G-key to position the Empty somewhere near the middle, but there is a more accurate way.

Snapping

Select the icospheres of the nucleus. Press Shift-S. A "Snap" menu pops up, with five options. There are only two that you should really be concerned with: "Selection to Cursor" and "Cursor to Selection". Select "Cursor to Selection". This option places the 3D cursor at the center of the current selection.

The Shift-S snap menu.

So, how do you get the Empty to the exact center of the nucleus? Select the Empty (only the Empty, nothing else!), press Shift-S and this time choose "Selection to Cursor". This option moves any selected objects to the location of the 3D cursor.

You can see then that the workflow for precision movement in Blender is a two step process. First, position the 3D cursor via selection and Snap "Cursor to Selection". Then, Select the object you wish to position and Snap "Selection to Cursor".

In the example above, you've used the Snap menu to position your animated Empty in the center of the nucleus icospheres.

Use B-key to select the icospheres. The Empty, which was selected in the previous step, remains selected and is, in fact, the Active object, as you can see by its brighter color. (If the Empty is not the Active object, hold down the Shift key and RMB click it to make it so.)

With the icospheres selected and the Empty as the Active object, press Ctrl-P to create a parent relationship.

Scrub the mouse back and forth in the timeline. This time, the scaling of the whole nucleus functions as you had hoped. At this point, if you wanted some extra practice, you could create a new Empty and animate it to pulse in a different fashion from the first. Then, you could make half the spheres the children of this new empty, leaving the others as the children of the original. This would create a more complex and hopefully more interesting animation.

The spheres are now the children of the Empty in the middle.

Animation and Keys

Let's get a little more acquainted with Blender's system for creating keys for animation. To do this, you will add an electron to your atom and make it travel around the nucleus.

Shift-S brings up the Snap menu.

Before you do anything else, let's make sure that you are looking at your atom from the front — if you aren't, then some of the following examples will not quite work. Use Numpad-1 to go to a front view.

LMB to the left of the nucleus, setting the 3D cursor there, so that your electron is created at a good location. Use the spacebar toolbox to add an icosphere. Remember to use the Tab key after the object is created, to get out of Edit Mode. Really, you can add any kind of object you choose to experiment with, but our illustrations will use the icosphere. With the S-key, shrink the icosphere so it's a bit smaller than the ones already in the nucleus.

Set the 3D cursor away from the nucleus.

Make sure Blender's frame counter is set to 1 (use the Timeline view for this) and that only the electron is selected. Press the I-key and choose "Loc" (Location) from the Insert Key menu that pops up.

LMB in the timeline to set the frame counter to somewhere around 60. Use G-key to move the electron to a position above the nucleus in the 3D view. Insert another location key.

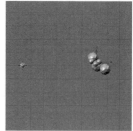

A new icosphere added to be the first electron.

Skip ahead to around frame 120, move the electron to the right of the nucleus and insert a location key. Finally, skip to around frame 180, move the electron below the nucleus and insert a key.

Press the play button in the timeline or use Alt-A over the 3D view to play your animation.

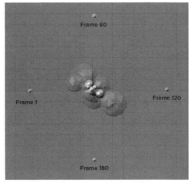

Frame 60

Frame 1   Frame 120

Frame 180

I-key brings up the Insert Key menu, which lets you set animation keys for the Active object.

You'll see that this animation is not satisfactory for two reasons. First, the electron follows more of a diamond shaped path around the nucleus than a circle. Second, the electron stops below the nucleus, instead of continuing back through to its starting point.

The position of the electron at different frame numbers.

First, let's round out the path that the electron follows. With the electron selected, press the K-key. Three olive-colored copies of the icosphere appear, one at each of the locations where we had set a key. The K-key toggles the display of keys in the 3D view.

Scrub with the LMB in the timeline until the electron is halfway between the left and upper keys.

If you try to use the G-key at this point, you will find that the icosphere does not move. This is because in this key view mode your transformations like move, rotate and scale only work on already set keys, not the actual object.

So, let's add a new key here, then move it to create a better circular path. Use I-key, and select "Loc" as before to insert a new key. Then with the G-key, move the key up and to the left. You will see the electron object move too, but this is only a result of moving the key. You are not moving the electron directly.

The electron should be here to make a nice circular path.

Now, as you scrub back and forth in the timeline, you can see the motion for this part of the animation is much closer to circular. Using LMB to move through the timeline, set new keys halfway between the other keys that have already been set, moving them slightly to make the entire animation more circular.

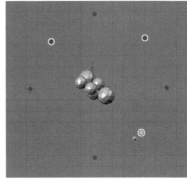

K-key toggles Key mode in the 3D view, which allows you to see and adjust key transformations directly.

You have fixed the first problem with your animation. As you're finished with Key mode for the moment, use the K-key to exit that mode, hiding the keys in the 3D view. Let's move on to the second problem, which is that you would like the electron to end in the exact place it begins.

The new key positions are highlighted.

Working in the Ipo Window

The Ipo window with curves from the orbiting electron.

Let's finally take a look at the Ipo window, shown in the illustration. The first thing to do is to make sure that your orbiting electron is selected in the 3D view. Then, place the mouse over the Ipo window and press the Home key. Recall that in the 3D view, the Home key zooms and translates the view so that every existing object becomes visible. It does the same thing in the Ipo window.

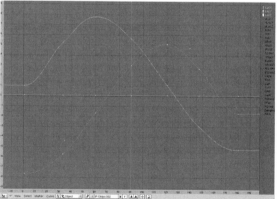

The Home key auto-zooms and pans a window to show everything.

The curves in this window represent the object's motion through space. You can see that there are three curves, each color coded to match one of the labels on the window's legend at the right. (If instead of colored curves you see a bunch of vertical yellow lines and gray curves, press the K-key. We'll explain in a moment.)

If you look along the bottom of the Ipo window, the ascending numbers indicate frames. Along the left side of the window is another scale that indicates values (locations in this case). So, LMB somewhere in the Ipo window to move the frame counter to that frame, just like the Timeline window. Use LMB to place the frame indicator line near frame 50. The legend on the right of the window tells you that LocZ (Location on the Z axis) is represented by yellow. In the Ipo window, then, find where the vertical frame indicator crosses the yellow curve. Look to the left-hand scale to see the approximate value of that orange curve at the intersection. In the illustration, it appears to be around seven.

This means that at frame 50, the Z location value for the selected object is close to seven.

Remember how objects are created in the 3D view in Edit Mode, which allows you to change their shape and geometry? When working with 3D objects, you have always used the Tab key to return to Object mode. As with 3D objects, the Tab key also lets you enter and exit Edit mode on Ipo curves.

RMB on the LocZ (yellow) curve to select it (RMB functions as select in more than just the 3D view). Now, press the Tab key.

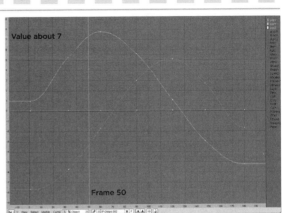

Users who are completely new to 3D probably aren't going to need to directly edit these Ipo curves for a while, but suffice it to say that the same tools that worked in the 3D view (Grab, Scale, RMB select, etc.) all work for editing and moving the points along the curves. Users who do want to edit curves directly like this will be helped by pressing the N-key, which pops up a panel that allows examination of and changes to the actual numeric values of the curve points.

You don't really need to edit anything here. The point is to show you that the curves are editable on a very fine level, if you should ever need to do so. Now that you've noted that, press the Tab key again to leave Edit Mode.

When we left the example, your first electron only went three quarters of the way around the nucleus. You would like it to end up exactly where it started so the circle is complete. Of course, you could just move it with the G-key and set a key frame, hoping to hit the same spot. Or, if you remembered the snapping functions of the 3D cursor, you could set the frame counter to 1, snap the 3D cursor to the electron; then advance to frame 250, snap the electron to the 3D cursor and set another key.

But just to demonstrate the use of the Ipo window, we'll accomplish the task there.

The Ipo view has another visualization mode — one that shows vertical markers on every keyframe. Just like the K-key showed keyframe markers in the 3D view, it does so in the Ipo window as well. Press the K-key, and your Ipo view changes to something like this:

Each of those dull yellow vertical lines indicates that there is a key set on that frame. You're going to do some work in the window now, so use the mouse's scroll wheel to zoom the window out a bit. You'll need some unused space on either side of the first and last keyframes.

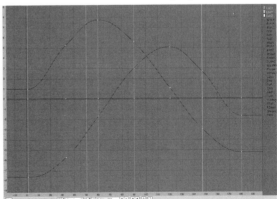

The Ipo view in Key mode.

Select the vertical keyframe marker that sits on frame 1 by RMB clicking on it. Its yellow becomes brighter, indicating that it is selected. Recall that Shift-D duplicated an object in the 3D view. Press Shift-D with the key marker selected and the same thing happens: the set of keys marked by the selected line are duplicated and put into Grab mode. Move that Grabbed line to the right until it is over the indicator for frame 250, the last one in the animation.

You will notice as you move the line that a readout at the bottom of the window tells you how far you have moved. As you move the line, and before you use LMB to confirm the move, try holding down the Ctrl key. You will see that instead of moving smoothly, the line moves in steps, one whole number at a time. Using the Ctrl key during a transformation constrains the transform to operating in nice even steps, and can be very useful, for example, when trying to move something exactly 250 frames.

So now that you've duplicated the location keys from the first frame and moved them to frame 250, your animation starts and begins in the same place, meaning that it will work seamlessly if played in a loop.

Layer Management

Most creative programs, 2D and 3D, have the ability to group objects by layers. Layers can help you to keep your workspace organized. Imagine a large scene based on a tourist attraction that includes a parking lot with cars, grass, a monument and models of people. When working on the monument portion of the scene, having the cars, grass and people cluttering the 3D view can be distracting and make work more difficult than it needs to be. If you put each set of objects into its own layer, it becomes possible to easily hide or show any set of objects as you need to work with them.

Let's create another electron, then start practicing with layers.

Select the already-existing electron and use Shift-D to create a duplicate, moving it about halfway toward the nucleus before using LMB to accept the move. Look at the Ipo window for this newly created and selected object. It contains the exact same animation curves as the original object. In fact, both the original and the duplicate object are linked to the same Ipo curves, meaning that if you were to play the animation right now, the duplicate object would immediately jump to the same position as the original and follow it exactly throughout the timeline. Obviously, you don't want that to happen.

To remove the link between your newly duplicated object and the old animation curve information, click the "X" beside the "IP: ObIpo.001" drop down menu in the Ipo window header. (If the dropdown doesn't appear on your Ipo header like it does in the illustration, try MMB dragging the header to the left to show additional header items.) This drop down menu contains all of the sets of animation curves you have created so far, including the scaling animation you did earlier with the nucleus' Empty parent. The "ObIpo.001" is just the name of this particular set of Ipo curves and can be changed to something relevant like "electronOrbit" if you so choose. In any case, clicking the "X" beside the name removes the link between your new object and the Ipo curves, freeing it up for other purposes.

• Ipo curves are a graphical representation of each animated value of an object.

• Ipo curves can be worked with and transformed like any other Blender object, using the Tab key, RMB for selection, Shift-D for duplication and G-key and S-key for movement and scaling.

• K-key toggles between curve view and key view.

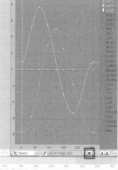

Pressing the "X" will unlink the Ipo from the Object.

Placing the mouse cursor back over the 3D view, press the M-key. A little grid of twenty boxes and a large Okay button appear. Press the number 2 on your main keyboard (NOT the one on the Numpad), and hit Enter. The electron disappears. We'll find it in a moment.

Begin to RMB on the nucleus until you have the nucleus' parent Empty selected. Shift-D to duplicate the Empty and RMB again to cancel any movement of the duplicate. At this point our duplicate Empty is selected, but resting in exactly the same position as the original. Press the M-key, followed by 2 again, and Enter.

The "send to" layers popup palette (numbers are only for illustration).

You may (or may not) suspect that you've just sent these two objects (the electron and the new Empty) to Layer 2 of your scene.

Each Scene in Blender is comprised of twenty layers. An object can exist on several layers at once. You can set Blender to display any combination of layers that you need to see. In your current scene, the nucleus and first electron exist by default on Layer 1. You have placed the new Empty and second electron on Layer 2. Let's find them.

LMB on the button in the 3D window header that corresponds to Layer 2. Immediately, Layer 1 objects disappear and Layer 2 objects are shown. LMB on the Layer 1 button to go back to the original view. Like other selectors in the computer world, you can build a selection or take away from it by holding down the Shift key while selecting. Hold the Shift key and LMB on the Layer 2 block. Now, both Layer 1 and Layer 2 are showing.

Remember when you sent the objects to Layer 2? You simply used the number 2-key on the keyboard. That works here as well, and it would be a good idea to get in the habit of using the number keys to address layers. Just for fun, press the 1-key, then the 2-key. It has exactly the same effect as clicking on the buttons in the 3D view header. Now, hold down Shift while you press the 1 and 2-keys. It adds to and subtracts from the layer selection, just like the mouse clicks.

• Layers control which objects are displayed in the 3D view.

• Layers can be turned on and off either with their number keys or by clicking on the buttons.

• The Shift key adds to and takes away from layer selection.

• M-key in the 3D view pops up a layer button selector that is used to send objects to other layers.

Sending objects to another layer is as simple as selecting the object, pressing the M-key to bring up the Move-to-Layer widget, then selecting the target layer and hitting okay. As with the earlier example, you can also use the number keys to assign a layer and the Enter key to accept the changes, meaning that you can keep your mouse cursor focused on your work. In fact, you will probably get to the point where layer assignment and selection is second nature — your fingers will just hit the right keys when you decide you want to work on a different layer.

Now that we've covered the basics of working with layers, let's look at a different method of making your new electron circle around the nucleus. This way builds on things we've already covered, and adds one more trick.

Using either the mouse, or the 2-key, show only layer 2 of your Scene.

Select the Empty. Before you do anything else, remember that this Empty is a duplicate of the one in the middle of your nucleus, meaning that it is still linked to the same scaling animation

Layer 2 contains the Empty and Icosphere.

you made before. Go over to the Ipo window header, like you did with the duplicate electron, and break the link by LMB clicking on the "X" next to the Ipo name.

Now, make sure that you are on Frame 1. Use I-key and set a "Rot" (Rotation) key for the Empty. Pick a frame further on in the animation, say, 50 or so. Rotate the Empty along several axes, making it a fairly significant rotation from the original. Place another rotation key. If you like, play back the animation (Play in the timeline or Alt-A) to see the Empty do its rotation.

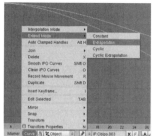

The Extend mode part of the Curve menu.

Now, switch your focus to the Ipo window, and use the Home key to make sure that it shows you everything that's available. You will see three curves, each representing the Empty's rotations along different axes. Use the A-key to make sure all the curves are selected (selected curves have white key points; unselected have black).

From the "Curve" menu in the Ipo window header, choose "Extend Mode", then "Extrapolation". On either side of the outermost keys, the curves turn into straight lines extending off into infinity. What does this mean? Play the animation now. The empty continues to rotate, even after the last frame with a key — Blender is extrapolating a continued animation based on the keys you had previously set.

Part two of this bit of animation is very simple. Return the frame counter to Frame 1. Select the electron, followed by the Empty (both should be selected, with Empty as the Active object). Use Ctrl-P to make the electron the child of the Empty. Play the animation and smile. That was easy.

Constraints

Before we end this basic discussion, we'll look at one more method of animating objects in Blender. This one doesn't even use key frames.

Return the animation to Frame 1. Duplicate both the Empty and the electron. You can select them both and use Shift-D, which creates two new objects with the same parent-child relationship as the originals. When you duplicate the objects, move them away from the others a bit so you have room to work.

RMB on the new electron and move it so its position relative to the new Empty is different than that of the original's, but try to keep it about the same distance.

Now, RMB select the original electron, then hold down Shift and RMB on the new Empty. If you do it correctly, both the original electron and the new Empty will be selected, but the Empty will be the Active object (brighter pink). Use the keyboard combination "Ctrl-Alt-C", and a menu titled "Add Constraint to Active Object" will pop up. From this menu, choose "Track To".

The set of objects on the right are the new duplicates.

Instantly, the empty rotates so that it points toward the original electron, moving its child with it.

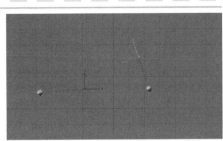

What you've just done is added something called a "constraint" to the Empty. Constraints are mostly used in Blender to limit or change locations, sizes and rotations of objects. In the case of the "Track To" constraint you just added, the constraint changes the rotation of the constrained object (the Empty) so that it always points to the target object (the original electron).

Notice in the buttons window below the 3D view how a Track To constraint has been added to the Constraints panel.

The Constraints panel in the Object buttons.

Ctrl-Alt-C brings up the Constraint menu, which adds a constraint to the Active object, using the other selected object as its target.

You could have used the "Add Constraint" button in this panel to do the same thing you've just done in the 3D view, but you would have had to fill in the proper object name in the panel's "OB:" field to get things to link up properly. Using selections and the Ctrl-Alt-C hotkey builds the constraint for you automatically.

What is the final effect? Move the new empty back to its original position (just using G to move it by hand will surely be close enough, but if you'd like to practice your precision movement, you can always use the Shift-S snap method described earlier). Play the animation.

The new Empty rotates, without any keys, so that it always points to ("tracks") the electron to which it is constrained. Its child electron, in turn, follows the Empty's rotation, most likely generating some neat orbital motion.

Finishing Up

Use Shift-1 (or Shift LMB on the layer 1 button) to add Layer 1 back to the display. Play the animation to see it in all its silly glory. While the animation is playing, you'll learn one more trick.

Let the animation run, and as it plays, try using the MMB-drag in the 3D view that you've used before to rotate your view. It works while the animation plays back! The other view translation controls work as well, although you'll have to use Ctrl-MMB for zoom, as the scroll wheel won't work in this mode.

Now that you've made three protons, three neutrons and three electrons in orbit, you have yourself a finished atom. If you would prefer to have some more practice, add some objects to the nucleus and toss in some more electrons until you have the element of your choice.

Rendering for Animation

In the Interface chapter, you rendered a still of the default cube which was, without a doubt, thrilling. Since you've just animated a nucleus, let's render it and watch it move.

The Render icon on the 3D header.

On the far right of the 3D window's header (you may have to MMB-drag the header to see it) is a small Render icon. LMB click it.

Almost instantly, the render window appears with a preview image of the Scene, drawn in whatever style (solid/wireframe) and from whatever perspective the 3D window is using. This sort of preview render (technically, it's called an "OpenGL" render) can be triggered from any 3D view by LMB on the render icon in its header.

Now, Ctrl-LMB on the same render icon. This time, the preview seems to animate, albeit slowly. What it's really doing is creating 250 OpenGL preview images and saving them somewhere (secret!) on your hard drive. If you don't feel like waiting for this to happen, you can cancel it (or any render, even one with a single frame) by pressing the Esc key.

When it has finished making the preview renders, you can press the Esc key to go back to the main Blender window. From there, find the Scene buttons (F10), and press Play.

![The Play button in the Scene buttons.]

The Play button in the Scene buttons.

A new window opens and your animation will play in a continuous loop.

Okay, that was the fast, crummy OpenGL preview render. It's great for checking your animation to make sure that everything is moving correctly, but not nearly suitable as a final product.

Chapter 12 contains full instructions for rendering animations to disk, so we're just going to take a shortcut here:

Zoom outward in the 3D view until you can see the Camera. RMB select it. Now, with the mouse still over the 3D view, press Numpad-0 to switch to the view from the camera.

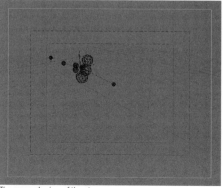

The camera's view of the atom.

The outer solid border in this view represents the camera object itself and should be pink. If it's not, then you may not have the camera selected (just RMB on the solid border to select it). At the moment, your atom is most likely not in the center of the camera's view. Press the R-key twice to put the camera into an "aiming" mode and fiddle around by moving the mouse until your atom seems to be reasonably in the center of things.

If you're up for it, and you have some time to kill, press the Anim button in the Scene buttons (F10). Blender will begin to actually render your scene, frame by frame. Even on a speedy computer, this will take several minutes, so go get yourself a drink.

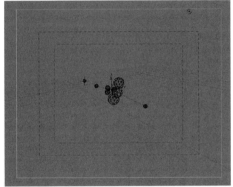

The camera is now aimed a little better.

When it's done, press the play button again to see the finished, rendered animation.

It doesn't look so hot, does it? Even rendered. Don't despair — you haven't learned modeling yet, or materials. Or lighting for that matter. But you know the basics of working with Blender objects and animation now, so the rest will come easily.

Object Manipulation Basics

For almost every hotkey function in this chapter, there is a corresponding entry in the Select and Object menus in the 3D View header. Although Blender's hotkey system was originally designed for maximum efficiency (and still retains much of that quality), it can be a bit daunting to new users. If you find yourself at a loss for the hotkey for a particular function, check out the menus. In fact, periodically browsing the menus is a great way to discover new functionality. This book is really just a primer — there is a lot more depth to be found, and the menus are a nice way to start experimenting once you've mastered the basics.

Coordinates

Understanding the coordinate system is the absolute baseline of 3D manipulation. If you have any experience with this at all, you can skip to the next section without fear.

In the illustration, you'll see a line labeled "X", with value markings along it, and a circle whose center is a dot. The circle's center dot rests on the marker labeled "3". In graphics terminology, you would say that the location of the circle is, "(3)"

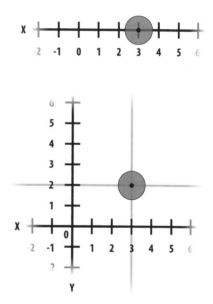

Now, we've added another dimension to the illustration. This time, the center of the circle can be traced down to the "3" on the "X" line and to the "2" on the "Y" line. Each of these lines is called an "axis". When you talk about the location of the circle, you say that its x and y coordinates are 3 and 2. This is commonly written as "(3,2)".

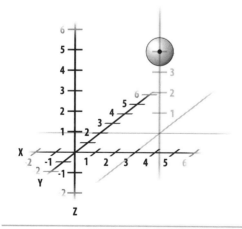

We're in 3D now (3 Dimensions: x, y and z). The center of the circle is still at (3,2) along the x and y axes, but we've added a third axis, z. The circle's center point is four units up on the z axis, so it's final coordinate is (3,2,4).

As you can see on the axes in the illustrations, the coordinate systems go off into both positive and negative directions, so (x,y,z) values will not always be positive.

The 3D Cursor

The 3D Cursor is a focus for activity in Blender's workspace. You set its location by using LMB in a 3D view. When new objects are created and added to a Scene, they are born at the location of the 3D Cursor. When objects are rotated or resized, the 3D Cursor can be used as the center of the transformation. Some beginners find it useful to think of the 3D Cursor like the standard cursor in a word processor: you set its location with the LMB, and when you type, it's where the letters appear.

The 3D cursor.

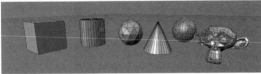

LMB click sets the location of the 3D Cursor.

The 3D Cursor is also useful as a quick reference point when you are animating. For example, if you are animating a character and want to make sure that its elbow remains still, despite the rest of the body moving around, you could set the 3D Cursor to match the starting location of the elbow, giving you a quick visual reference for adjusting the elbow's location later.

Types of Objects that Can Be in a Scene

Scenes are made up of geometry objects, control objects that can affect geometry objects' motion and shape, lamp objects that provide light, and camera objects that provide a viewpoint from which to render. Of the available types of objects, the most commonly used are:

A selection of mesh primitives.

Mesh: Most of your 3D models will be Mesh objects. There are many starting points for Mesh objects, all accessible from the toolbox Add menu, including a cube, cylinder, plane, circle, cone and two kinds of spheres.

Empty: An Empty object functions as a sort of placeholder in 3D space. They have many uses that you will find throughout the rest of this book.

Several different visualizations of Empty objects. The default method is shown in white.

Lamp: Lamp objects are used to define from where light is cast within a scene. The type of lamp object determines what style of light is produced.

An assortment of lamp objects.

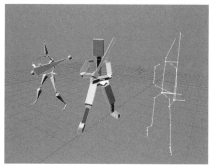

There are several drawing methods for armatures.

Armature: Armature objects are best thought of as skeletons. They do not show up in images you create, but are used as control objects to change the shape of (usually) Mesh objects, in much the same way that your own skeleton defines and controls the overall shape of your body.

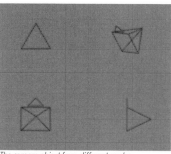

The camera object from different angles.

Camera: Scenes can be viewed and rendered from the perspective of Camera objects. You can have several cameras in the same scene.

Creating and Adding Objects

The Add menu in the toolbox.

Objects are created and added to a Blender scene by using the Toolbox, which is brought up by pressing Spacebar in the 3D view. From the toolbox, the Add menu contains all of the kinds of objects Blender has available.

Objects are created and added to a Scene through the toolbox, which is accessed by pressing the Spacebar.

When you use the toolbox's Add menu to create an object, it is added to the scene at the current location of the 3D Cursor. You will also find that objects are added to a scene with their orientation facing directly toward the current 3D view. This means that if you create an object while in some odd viewing angle you've achieved through MMB view rotation, the object will face directly toward your view, and will begin its life with corresponding rotation values.

Mesh objects, and other editable object types, are created in Edit mode. Edit mode allows you to change the structure of the object (adding several faces to a cube, shrinking the center rings of a sphere, etc.). However, when you want to move objects around, for animation purposes or just to organize your Scene, you need to be in Object mode. Notice in the illustration below how the structure of the object is highlighted in Edit mode, making it easier to modify. To put the object into Object mode, press the Tab key.

The Tab key toggles between Edit mode and Object mode.

The object on the left is in Object mode; the one on the right, Edit mode.

There are too many combinations of display, selection and mesh modes to give you a hard and fast rule for determining whether objects are in Edit or Object mode. The surest way to tell is to look at the Mode menu in the 3D view header.

You can always tell the mode of the Active object by looking at the 3D header.

Creating and Adding Objects

Making Selections

Selection in Blender is accomplished with the RMB. RMB clicking on consecutive objects will make each one the only selected object. A selected object has a pink outline when in solid view mode, and pink edges when displayed as a wireframe. If you want to select multiple objects, hold down Shift while using RMB.

When you first select an object, whether through a plain RMB click or through Shift-RMB, it is called the Active Object. Regardless of how many objects are selected, there can only be one Active Object. It is outlined with a brighter pink than the rest of the selected objects. Many operations, such as copying object attributes, creating parent-child relationships and adding constraints, will use the Active Object as their target.

• RMB selects an object, and makes it the Active Object.
• Shift-RMB builds selection.
• Shift-RMB on the Active Object deselects.

Using Shift-RMB to click on the Active Object will completely deselect it. If you have been holding down the Shift key and using RMB to select several objects in a row, only the last object selected will be designated as the Active Object. In order to deselect one of the other, non-Active, objects, you must Shift-RMB click on it once to make it the Active Object, then Shift-RMB click on it again to deselect.

There are other methods of selection useful when selecting objects that are all within a certain area of the view. Pressing the B-key in the 3D View puts the cursor into Border Select mode. Dragging with the LMB draws a box on the screen, and any object that has a portion of itself within that box will be selected when you release the mouse button. You can also use Border Select to deselect as well — after pressing the B-key, dragging with the MMB will deselect anything that falls within the dragged box.

• B-key with LMB border selects.
• B-key with MMB border deselects.

Many times it is necessary to select everything in a scene, or to make sure that nothing at all is selected. The A-key can be used for that. Pressing the A-key while even a single object is selected will clear all selections. However, when nothing is selected, the A-key selects all objects in the Scene. It is quite common to find experienced Blender users pressing the A-key twice in rapid succession, once to clear all selection, and again to select all.

A-key selects everything in a Scene if nothing is currently selected. Otherwise, it clears all selections.

Once your scenes start to become more complex, it can be difficult to select everything you would like to "by hand". Blender has additional selection tools located in the Select menu in the 3D View header. You can select objects that are grouped together, objects of certain types like Meshes, Lamps and Armatures, objects that have the same materials, and in a variety of other ways. Make sure to explore the Select menu at some point!

Snapping

The key command Shift-S pops up a snapping menu. In Blender, as in many art and drawing packages, "snapping" refers to moving things to a specific, predefined location. From this menu, you can choose to have the 3D Cursor snap to the location of the selected object. If you have more than one object selected, the 3D Cursor will move to the average location of all selected objects. You can also choose to have the selected objects snap to the location of the 3D Cursor.

The snapping menu.

The standard workflow for moving one object to the exact location of another object is to first snap the 3D cursor to the object you are targeting, then select the object you would like to move and snap it to the new location of the 3D Cursor.

Shift-S in the 3D view brings up the Snap menu.

Object Information

There are a number of ways to find out information about the objects you have selected, but the simplest way is through using the Transform Properties panel. Within the 3D view, pressing the N-key brings up a panel that contains information about the Active Object. There are other screens in Blender that use the same hotkey to bring up a properties panel for selected objects, like the Ipo Window and NLA Editor. Pressing the N-key again will hide the panel.

The Transform Properties panel.

The panel shows the current location, rotation, scale and overall dimensions of the object. In addition to simply showing information about the object, the panel can also be used to change those values. Each of the controls is a spinner, allowing you to either LMB click on the value itself to type a new one, LMB click on the right and left arrow to raise and lower the value, or to LMB click and drag inside of it.

In addition, any of the values can be locked by LMB clicking on the grayed-out lock icon beside its spinner. Locking a value on the transform panel will prevent the object from being moved, rotated or scaled along that axis. For example, if you had an object like a sliding door that was supposed to only move left to right, you could lock both its z and y axes so that it could only be transformed along the x (left/right) axis.

N-key toggles the Transform Properties panel in the 3D view.

Transforming Objects

Objects can be transformed ("transformed" is an overall term for moving, rotating and scaling) in a number of ways. As seen above, location, rotation and scale can be changed by entering values in the transform properties panel. Of course, this being an interactive 3D application, these transformations can also be accomplished visually — and much more intuitively — in the 3D view.

Transforming with Hotkeys

Often, the fastest method for transforming objects is to use the hotkeys G (for Grab/Move), R (for Rotate) and S (for Scale, or Size). When you use the transform hotkeys, the selected object (or objects) enters a transformation mode that allows you to move it freely with the mouse. If at any time during a transform you want to cancel the operation, click the RMB. When you have the object transformed as you like, clicking the LMB accepts the operation.

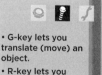

While you are transforming an object, it is often useful to limit the change to a certain axis. For example, if you are trying to make an egg shape from a sphere, you would only want to scale the sphere along, say, the z axis, creating an oblong, egg-like shape.

• G-key lets you translate (move) an object.
• R-key lets you rotate an object.
• S-key lets you scale (resize) an object.

• X, Y, or Z-key constrains transformation to each axis.

• Shift-X, Y or Z constrains transformation within each plane.

This sort of transform limitation is accomplished with the X or Y or Z-keys, used while the object is in transformation mode. So, to move an object only along the Z axis, you would press the G-key, followed by the Z-key. Using Shift with the axis keys does the opposite, allowing an object to transform along the other two axes. For example, pressing the G-key, followed by Shift-Z, would allow the object to move freely in along the X and Y axes, while not allowing vertical (Z axis) movement.

Of course, there is more than one way to do this in Blender. Pressing the G-key (or R or S), then beginning a transformation and clicking the MMB will constrain the object's transformation along whichever axis you have begun the motion. Clicking the MMB again while still in transformation mode removes the constraint, giving you complete freedom of movement again.

There is one further way to limit transformation with these hotkeys, and that is to press the axis key (X, Y or Z) not once, but twice. The second key press causes the object to use what is called the "alternative transformation space". Which

The Alternative Transformation Space menu on the 3D header.

Pressing one of the axis constraints (X, Y, Z-key) twice during transformation constrains the transform to each axis in the alternative transformation space, which is local space by default.

alternative space is used is defined in the header of the 3D Window, and can also be set by the Alt-Spacebar hotkey.

In the case of a rotated cube, transforming the cube with the G-key followed by the Z-key will move it directly upwards in the scene. However, with the alternative transformation space set to "Local", a second press on the Z-key will move the cube vertically in relation to its current orientation.

A cube is shown moving away from the origin, constrained in both Global and Local spaces.

Transformation Center

When rotating or scaling objects, Blender, by default, causes the rotation or resizing to occur relative to the object's center. Pressing the R-key on a cube, then moving the mouse will cause the cube to rotate in place, around its own center. But what if you want to use a different center point for rotation or scaling? Blender can be set to several different methods for determining what to use as an object's transformation center, all accessible in the "Rotation/Scaling Pivot" menu in the 3D view header.

The Pivot Point menu on the 3D header.

Although each option in this menu is useful under certain circumstances, the two most commonly-used are "Bounding Box Center" (the default), and "3D Cursor". In fact, each of these options has a hotkey attached to it: Comma-key (",") for Bounding Box Center, and Period-key (".") for 3D Cursor. It is not unusual to see an experienced modeler or animator rapidly switching between these two modes when making transformations.

Two cubes, the left rotating around its Bounding Box Center, the right rotating around the 3D cursor.

The "Bounding Box" referred to above is just the outer limits of an object.

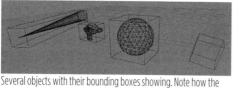

Several objects with their bounding boxes showing. Note how the cube's bounding box is just itself.

Of course, you already know how to set the location of the 3D Cursor (LMB). A word of warning when using the 3D Cursor as the pivot point for a rotation or scale transformation: make sure you set the 3D Cursor from two different views (like front and top). If

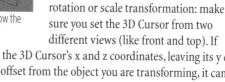

Change the rotation and scaling pivot point through the menu on the 3D header, or with the hotkeys Comma (for Bounding Box Center) and Period (for 3D Cursor).

you set it in front view alone, it will only set the 3D Cursor's x and z coordinates, leaving its y coordinate unaltered. If that y coordinate is drastically offset from the object you are transforming, it can lead to unexpected (read: bad) results.

Transform Manipulators

In many cases, using the G/S/R hotkeys for transformation can be the most efficient method. However, it is not for everyone, and Blender provides tools that can accommodate many different working styles.

The Manipulator controls on the 3D header

The graphical transformation manipulators give users direct, mouse-based access to all of the transformation controls. The manipulator is turned On by default, and can be switched on and off either through its button on the 3D View header, or by choosing "Enable/Disable" from the Ctrl-Spacebar menu in the 3D View.

There are separate manipulators for movement (called translation), rotation and scaling. Each manipulator functions in a similar fashion: simply LMB-drag on the manipulator handle that corresponds to the axis you wish to transform. The rotation manipulator in particular gives excellent visual feedback, showing a "pie chart" representation of the current rotation.

The three different types of manipulators.

Like many things in Blender, the transform manipulator icons on the 3D header can be Shift-clicked to build a selection, allowing you to show and use up to all three manipulator types (move, rotate and scale) at once.

One more interesting aspect of the visual feedback that manipulators give is that locking transformation in the Transformation Properties Panel (N-key, discussed earlier) actually removes that axis from the manipulator, making it impossible for you to use the manipulator to transform along a locked axis.

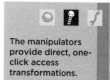

The manipulators provide direct, one-click access transformations.

We encourage you to become comfortable with the hotkeys G, R and S and the axis constraints (x, y, and z) before you start to use the manipulators. The manipulators are generally considered to be more intuitive, and in certain circumstances (like moving vertices relative to their normals during mesh editing and rolling and rotating bones in armatures for character animation) are perhaps the best way to accomplish the task.

If you find that the manipulators are not to your taste, you can get them out of the way (they can cause trouble with selections in cluttered environments) by disabling them with their button on the 3D Header or through

---

the Ctrl-Spacebar menu. Don't forget they are there, though — they may come in handy someday. Whatever the case, make sure that you try out both methods of working so you can find the one that suits you best.

Clearing Transforms

• Alt-G clears all translations.
• Alt-R clears rotations.
• Alt-S clears scaling.

Sometimes, it is helpful to completely remove any movement, rotation or scaling from an object. While this can be accomplished by entering zeros in the Location and Rotation sections of the Transform Properties panel and ones in the Scaling spinners, there is a simpler way. Adding the Alt key modifier to the transformation hotkeys clears that particular transformation. Alt-G returns the object to coordinates (0,0,0). Alt-R clears all rotations, and Alt-S sets any scaling that has been done to an object back to 1.

Applying Transforms

There are cases when you may have transformed an object by changing its scale and orientation in order to get it into a beginning state for animation or other work. Perhaps you imported a model of a car from an Internet repository, and it was of a completely different scale and rotation than the rest of your scene. Using the S and R-keys, you adjusted the model to fit in with everything else. When it was done, your Transform Properties panel looked like this:

The Transform Properties panel.

Ctrl-A applies scaling and rotation to an object, resetting them to their base values without transforming the object.

You could proceed with the construction of the scene and eventually animate just like this. However, it would be nice when animating to start with a "clean slate," especially for rotations.

Pressing Ctrl-A and LMB clicking through the popup that reads "OK? Apply scale and rotation" will reset both Scale and Rotation values to their defaults (ones for Scale and zeros for Rotation), while leaving the object exactly as it appeared before.

Duplicating Objects

Shift-D creates a complete duplicate of the selected object.

There are two ways to duplicate objects in Blender, each suited to a slightly different task. The first is the standard duplication which is accomplished by selecting an object (or objects) and pressing Shift-D. This creates a full, independent copy of the object, including any data, such as mesh data, that might be linked to it. The new object can be edited without affecting the original.

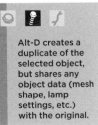

Alt-D creates a duplicate of the selected object, but shares any object data (mesh shape, lamp settings, etc.) with the original.

The other method of duplication uses Alt-D instead, and creates a new object whose data is still linked to that of the original. For example, a duplicate of a Mesh object that was created with Alt-D will actually share the mesh with the original. If the Mesh of either object is modified in Edit mode, the change will show up in both objects, in real time. One excellent use for this method of duplication is for lighting setups: creating a series of Alt-D duplicated lamps would allow you to adjust the lighting intensity on one lamp and have that change used for all of the duplicates.

Copies made with Alt-D are referred to as "linked duplicates".

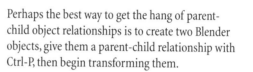

Parenting

Many graphics applications allow you to create parent-child relationships between objects. In a parent-child relationship, any transformations that you perform on the parent also happen to the child. In fact, when transforming a parent, the child is transformed as though the parent and child together were a single larger object, with the parent's center being the overall center of the object. For example, rotating a parent will cause not only the parent to rotate, but the child to move in a curve through space, as though they were connected by a rigid bar. Directly transforming a child object still works as you would expect, but it has no effect on the parent.

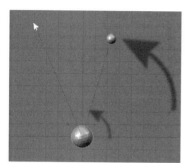

When the central parent object is rotated, the child follows as though it were part of the parent.

To create a parent-child relationship, select more than one object, press Ctrl-P, then LMB to accept the "OK? Create parent" prompt. The active object becomes the parent, and any other selected objects become the children. A dashed line appears between parent-child sets, allowing you to visually keep track of which object is related to which.

To clear a parent-child relationship, select the child object and press Alt-P.

Perhaps the best way to get the hang of parent-child object relationships is to create two Blender objects, give them a parent-child relationship with Ctrl-P, then begin transforming them.

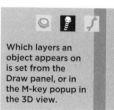

• Ctrl-P causes the active object to become the parent, and any other selected objects to become the children in a parent-child object relationship.
• Alt-P removes the parent-child relationship.

Layers

The layer buttons

Complex scenes can quickly become cluttered with mesh objects, lamps, placeholders and guidelines. When that happens (well, actually before that happens) it becomes useful to sort your scenes into groups of objects that can be selectively hidden when they are not needed. This kind of grouping is best accomplished in Blender through Layers.

The layer buttons on the 3D header indicate which layers are visible and which are hidden.

The same set of buttons is used whenever dealing with layers.

Layer selection follows the same rules as object selection. Using LMB on a layer makes it the current selection, clearing all others, meaning that objects on that layer become visible while all others are hidden. To make several layers visible at once, you build a layer selection by holding down Shift while using the LMB. Shift-LMB more than once on the same layer button will toggle it on and off.

Which layers an object appears on is set from the Draw panel, or in the M-key popup in the 3D view.

An object may be placed on a layer either by clicking the appropriate layer button in the Draw panel of the Object Buttons (F7), or by pressing the M-key in the 3D View to bring up a layer button pop up.

Parenting

Objects can be set to appear on more than one layer. For example, in the case of a farm scene, the farmhouse itself could reside on all layers, while fencing, grass, a barn and animal objects could each reside on their own layers. Having the farmhouse appear in all layers can provide you with a good reference for positioning all the other objects.

In addition to directly clicking on the layer buttons, layers can be activated and set through hotkeys. The keypad numbers 1 through 9 and 0 (which functions as 10 here) are the equivalent of clicking on layer buttons 1

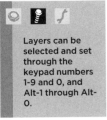

Layers can be selected and set through the keypad numbers 1-9 and 0, and Alt-1 through Alt-0.

through 10, activating the appropriate layer. Holding Shift with 1 through 0 has the same effect as is it does when clicking: it builds and subtracts from the layer setting. Alt-1 through Alt-0 access layers 11 through 20. The "set to layer" M-key popup can also be controlled with the same number keys if you wish. Sometimes, you may be performing an operation with the keyboard in Blender, and suddenly, your entire Scene seems to disappear. Often, it may be that you have accidentally pressed one of the number keys on the main keypad, telling Blender to show only objects on that layer. If your Scene disappears, don't panic — check the layer buttons on the 3D header. It could be that everything is all right, but simply hidden.

Object Animation Basics

Animation information is stored in "keys".

Animation is a change over time in some aspect of your Scene. That change can be something simple, like a change in the color or intensity of a light, or it could be something complicated, like the changes in position and shape of an entire group of characters dancing in time to music, while the camera whirls around the dance floor. Regardless of what happens in your Scene, there must be a way to track and record those changes.

In Blender, as in most animation software, these changes are recorded as "keyframes" or "keys" for short. A key is just a marker in time of some state, value or setting.

Time

Before we review the keying tools, you should learn how to navigate in time.

The most visual method for doing this is to use the Timeline Window, found in the center of the default Animation Screen, but easily accessible in any window from the Window Type pop-up menu. (Remember: to access the default Animation Screen, use the Screens menu from the header at the very top of the Blender window.)

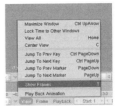

The View menu on the Timeline window header.

The timeline can be viewed in either seconds or in frames. Blender's default is to break each second into 25 frames, the PAL video standard. (Most film/movie work uses 24 frames per second, while the North American video standard, called NTSC, uses roughly 30 frames per second). To change the display method of the timeline, you go through the Timeline Window header's View menu, or simply press the T-key with the mouse over the timeline. Frames per second can be set either with the "Set Frames/sec" entry in the Playback menu, or on the "Frs/sec" spinner in the Render buttons (F10).

The vertical green marker in the Timeline indicates the current frame. Using LMB in the timeline sets the marker and the current frame. The current frame is also displayed in the lower left hand corner of the 3D view, and in the header of the buttons window.

The current frame can be set by LMB clicking within the timeline.

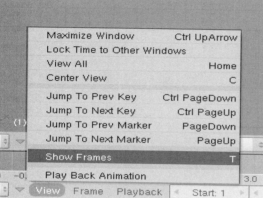

In addition to using the timeline to navigate through time, you can also use (surprise!) keyboard shortcuts.

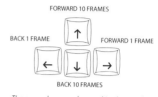

The arrow keys can be used to change the current frame.

The current frame number can be found in many places on the default animation screen.

The Right and Left arrow keys step forward and backward one frame. Up and down arrows step forward and backward by ten frames. Shift-Left arrow moves to the Start frame, while Shift-Right arrow moves to the End frame.

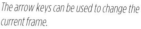

• Right and Left arrow keys change the frame by one.
• Up and Down arrow keys change the frame number by ten.

The Start and End frames, which can be set in either the timeline's header or in the Render buttons, indicate the range of frames that will be shown when you give a "play back" command. You can tell Blender to play the animation between the Start and End frames in a couple of ways: the "play" button on the timeline header or with Alt-A in a 3D Window.

Alt-A with the mouse over a 3D view plays the animation in that view.

Creating Animation Keys

Keys can be set throughout Blender with the I-key. Pressing the I-key will almost always pop up an "Insert Key" menu, with entries appropriate to the mouse's location.

If the mouse is over the 3D window when the I-key is pressed, a key will be set for the active object.

Blender's basic animation workflow is simple:

1. Use the time tools to find the frame where you would like to record a setting for animation;
2. Adjust your object how you want it to be at this point in time (location, colors, shapes, etc.);
3. Use the I-key to bring up the "Insert Key" menu, then select the appropriate key.

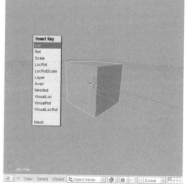

The Insert Key menu for the active object.

Creating Animation Keys

All objects can have Rotation, Location or Scale keys. The Insert Key menu shows several different combinations of those choices. In the menu, Loc stands for Location and Rot for Rotation. Thus, the LocRot entry in the menu creates a key for both Location and Rotation. LocRotScale creates keys for Location, Rotation and Scale. If you are only changing the location of an object in your animation, just use the Loc type key. Likewise, if you are only rotating an object, you would choose Rot.

The Layer entry on the I-key menu sets an animation key for the layer settings of an object. You can make objects appear and disappear from a scene by keying them to move to a hidden layer at a certain frame.

Explanations for the rest of the entries in the object I-key menu wouldn't make much sense to you at this point, so we'll leave them for a more advanced text.

I-key brings up the "Insert Key" menu that lets you save states and settings for animation.

Once you have inserted a key for an object, you continue throughout the timeline to create your animation: pick a frame, adjust your object, set a key. Pick, adjust, set.

Many settings in Blender are keyable beyond simple object transformations. You can consult the documentation to find a comprehensive list of which settings and values can be keyed, but a better way to find out is to hover the mouse over the window of the item you would like to key and press the I-key.

The I-key brings up a keying menu appropriate to the window you are working in.

Ipos and Ipo Curves

The upper right portion of the default Animation screen is used as an Ipo Window. Many new and migrating users are confused by the term Ipo, but it's simple, really. In order to create the animation between different keys, Blender (like any other 3D program) must "interpolate" between the keys. "Ipo" is just an abbreviation of InterPOlation. So the Ipo Window is just a window in which you can view the actual interpolation between animation keys.

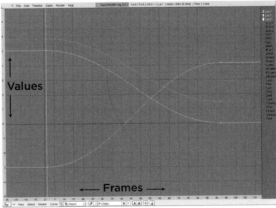

The Ipo window.

Once you have created keys for an object, they will show up, along with some curves, in the Ipo window. Each different setting gets its own curve, and in the illustration you can see that there are curves for LocX, LocY and LocZ — the x, y and z locations of the object. The Ipo window will show the curves for the active object in the 3D window, so if you want to see the Ipo curves of a different object, select that object in the 3D view.

You can drag with the LMB in the Ipo window to scrub through the animation, just like you could in the Timeline window. In fact, the horizontal axis in the Ipo window is the timeline, in frames, with current time marked by the vertical green line. The vertical axis shows the actual values of the keys.

Rotation Key Values

The exception to the rule about the vertical axis in the Ipo window is rotation keys. Rotation keys are represented in the Ipo window as one tenth of their actual value. In other words, a cube with a Y rotation of 125.25 degrees will show in the Ipo window as 12.52. This is done simply to keep the scales of the different curves in the Ipo window relatively similar. Although confusing at first, you'll soon not think twice about it.

Working with Ipo Curves

The Ipo window shares controls with other areas of Blender. The scroll wheel and MMB function as zoom and view changing controls like they do in the 3D view (MMB only pans the view here). Also, the Home key automatically zooms and translates to show all the available objects, which in this case are keys. Curves can be selected with the RMB, and the G-key and S-key will move and scale the entire curve. With a curve selected, the Tab key can be used to enter Edit mode, allowing you direct access to the key points which you may move as you choose.

• The Ipo window shares hotkeys and functions with the 3D window.
• RMB, and G-key and S-key for selecting and transforming curves.
• Tab key for Edit mode on curves.

The Transform Properties panel for the Ipo window.

Like the 3D window, the N-key brings up a Transform Properties panel that shows the exact values of selected curves and key points, and lets you edit them directly by typing in new values.

Although you can use these tools to change the actual key values (like changing an x location key from x=5 to x=10), you will most often use the Ipo window to change curve interpolation styles, to set the extend mode and to adjust key timing, as you'll see next.

N-key brings up Transform Properties panel for curves and keys.

Interpolation Styles

Blender allows three different ways for values to change from key to key.

The default, which you've seen in the illustrations so far, is called "Bezier" mode, and refers to the style of curve in the preceding section. This mode leads to smooth transitions between key values, slower at the beginning and end of the change, and faster in the middle. Using the example of a ball moving between two locations, Bezier interpolation would have the ball start out slowly, reaching its maximum velocity halfway between the keyed locations, then slowing down before coming to a stop on the last key.

Working with Ipo Curves

T-key brings up the Interpolation mode menu, letting you choose from Bezier, Linear and Constant.

Linear mode moves between keys at a constant velocity. This interpolation type is useful when animating mechanical or non-natural motion.

Constant mode is of limited use. It causes values to stay the same (constant!) until the next key is reached, at which point they immediately change to the new value. It would be used, for example, to cause an object to seem to "teleport" from one location to another.

Interpolation styles can be set by selecting the curves whose style you wish to change, then selecting the appropriate style from the Interpolation Mode entry in the Curves menu of the Ipo Window header. Alternately, you can use the T-key shortcut (think "inTerpolation") to pop up a menu directly within the Ipo window.

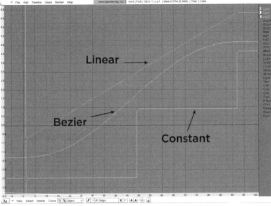

Choosing interpolation types from the Curve menu on the Ipo window header.

The different interpolation types.

Extend Modes

Sometimes, you will want to create a bit of animation that continues forever. A quick way to do this is to create one piece of the animation, and then use Ipo Extend Modes.

Very simply, if the Ipo curves in this illustration represent the motion of an object moving around in a circle:

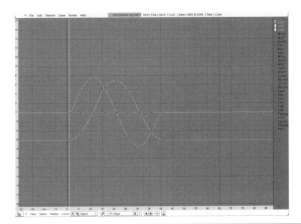

Then this illustration represents that same motion repeating over and over.

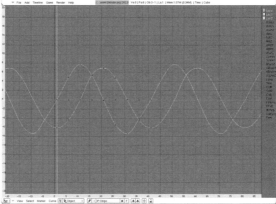

The same Ipo curves in Cyclic mode.

You access Extend Modes by selecting the Ipo curves you wish to extend, then choosing the extend style you would like from the Extend Mode entry in the Curve menu on the header.

Constant: this is the default Extend Mode that all Ipo curves have. This is what you would consider "normal" Ipo curve behavior, and the only one you have seen so far.

Extrapolation: this mode takes the slope of the curve at the first and last keys and simply extends them, forward and backward in time, forever.

Choosing an Extend mode from the Curve menu on the Ipo window header.

Cyclic: cyclic extend causes the animation between the first and last keys to repeat over and over, resetting each time.

Cyclic Extrapolation: this mode repeats the animation like cyclic mode, but instead of resetting, it uses the last repetition's endpoint as its starting point.

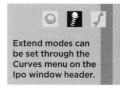

Extend modes can be set through the Curves menu on the Ipo window header.

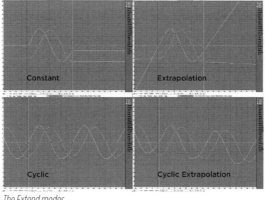

The Extend modes.

Key Timing

When you are setting keys for your animations, you probably will be guessing as to how long certain actions should take. How quickly should the ball fall toward the floor? How long does it take for a character to turn his head in surprise? The odds are that you won't know the answer until you play back your animations to see what looks right. Although the proper location and rotation keys may be in place for such things, their correct timing is just as crucial.

Adjusting key timing in the Ipo window is quick and easy.

Within the Ipo window, press the K-key to enter Key mode. Every frame that has a key now shows a vertical line that is selectable with the RMB. Using the G-Key to move that vertical line will move all keys that fall along it to the left or right (backward or forward) along the timeline.

This illustration shows the circular motion animation curves in Key mode. The keys on Frame 16 have been RMB selected.

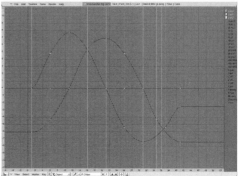

The Ipo window in Key mode.

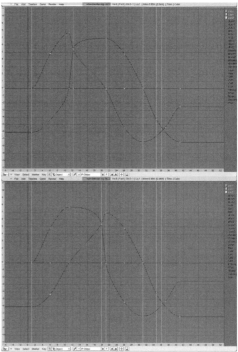

The curves adjust to follow the movement of keys.

The K-key toggles Key mode in the Ipo window, which lets you quickly adjust the timing of your keys.

Using the G-key, you can move the entire set of keys from Frame 16 to the left or the right to adjust their timing. As you do this, the curves update in real time.

While this chapter has shown you the mechanics of moving and animating objects in Blender, it hasn't even touched on the artistic aspects of animation. Indeed, entire books have been written on the subject. Once you are comfortable with the mechanics of animation in Blender, you're encouraged to start practicing and improving your art.

CHAPTER 4

Mesh Modeling

 Mesh Modeling: Hands On

 Mesh Modeling: Discussion
by Kevin Braun

Kevin Braun (HumanForum)

Kevin Braun is a multimedia professional specializing in all forms of interactive development. He received his BFA from the University of Massachusetts at Dartmouth in 1995 and since then has served world-class clients such as Harvard University, MIT and Cisco Systems. When he and his wife Christine take a moment from raising their three boys they conspire on how to save the world using their combined artistic skills.

To learn more or see examples of his work visit:
http://www.brauninteractive.com

Mesh Modeling: Hands On

In the previous chapter, you learned how to manipulate objects in Blender. You've seen how to move, scale and rotate objects, as well as some ways to set Blender to different modes.

But now we want you to actually edit the object itself. Blender has several modes for dealing with objects, but the two most frequently used are Object Mode and Edit Mode. In Object Mode you work with the object as a whole - you can move objects, scale them and rotate and parent them. In Edit Mode you concentrate on one particular object, and make changes to the mesh that gives the object its shape.

So, what's a mesh? I hear you asking. Usually, Blender (and computers in general) represents 3D objects by a set of vertices (or points) connected by edges. Three (or sometimes four) vertices can form the boundaries of a "face". A face is just a part of a mesh that is "filled in", and will look solid when rendered. Vertices and edges do not render, but faces do.

Here are some images to attempt to make this clearer.

In Edit Mode, you manipulate the object at the vertex level.

This model is what we hope to achieve in this tutorial. In theory, you could come close to making this all in object mode, but what you need to learn is when and where to use the different tools Blender has to offer. Knowing that this is the product of experience, doing this tutorial will give you some idea of how to choose your tools.

Where we'll be heading in this tutorial.

Anyway, enough about theory. Let's get down to modeling. Start up Blender (or use Ctrl-X to begin a new session if Blender is already running) and press the Z-key. The Z-key toggles between shaded mode and wireframe mode. You can switch between these two modes whenever you want to see how you're model is coming along. In this tutorial, some screenshots will be in wireframe mode and some will be in solid mode. You don't have to be there too, though. We tried to choose the best mode just to let you see what was going on in the illustration.

RMB select the default cube in the center of the scene, then press the X-key and confirm its deletion.

The first thing you are going to do is to create the basic shape of one of the pillars. You could do this with a simple cube, but as the pattern on each side of the pillar is identical, you are going to create one side, then duplicate it.

The toolbox, about to add a cube.

Use the spacebar to bring up the toolbox, then select the following menu items: Add, then Mesh, then Cube. I know, you just deleted the default cube, but we want to get you familiar with using the toolbox.

You may remember from the previous chapter that when you add a new object, that object begins its life in Edit mode. You should be able to see 4 yellow dots at the corners, which are called vertices. A yellow vertex means that it is currently selected.

The cube in Edit mode.

Press the A-key and watch all the vertices turn pink. (This is also the case for edges and faces.) To recap, just as the A-key toggles select all/deselect all for objects, it does the same in Edit mode, only with vertices.

Selecting Vertices

There are several ways to select vertices in Blender.

- RMB. Just like object mode, clicking on (or near) a vertex with the RMB will select it. Holding down Shift while RMB clicking will build a selection. RMB on an already selected vertex will deselect.

- Border select. Press the B-key, then LMB drag over the area you want to select. Border select is always additive, so using it will add to the selection set you already have.

- Circle select. Press the B-key twice, and the cursor turns into a circle. You are now in circle select mode. You can "paint" a selection with this circle by LMB dragging. MMB dragging deselects. The mouse's scroll wheel increases and decreases the size of the circle. RMB ends circle select mode.

- Lasso select. Holding down Ctrl while LMB dragging lets you "lasso" vertices for selection. As you draw around the vertices you would like to select, a dashed line is drawn to show where you have dragged so far. Releasing the LMB completes the shape you have been drawing, then selects any vertices that fall within it.

Using Numpad 7, view the cube from the top.

Now, select the four verts nearest to the top of the screen. There's only two, you say? Remember that for right now, you're looking straight down on the top of a three dimensional cube, and can only see two vertices because the others are directly behind them. If you like, you can rotate the view a bit by dragging with MMB just to make sure (or toggle in and out of perspective mode with Numpad-5), then return to the top view with Numpad 7.

So, using any of the above selection modes, except for standard RMB, select the four vertices (which will look like only two) nearest to the top of the screen. Press the X-key, then select "Vertices" from the Erase menu that pops up.

The cube with the top vertices selected.

Just so you can see what you did, here's an off-axis view of the cube with those four vertices removed. It's now just a square.

Use Numpad-1 to change to a front view. A-key to select all the vertices (or you can Shift-RMB all four for practice), then press G-key to enter Grab mode. We would like you to move the quad to be in the exact position as the next illustration:

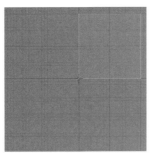

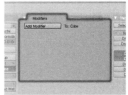

The plane that's left when you delete the vertices.

Notice that the lower right vertex is exactly at the intersection of the red and blue axes (x and z). In order to move the quad exactly onto that, hold down the Ctrl key while moving in Grab mode. With the Ctrl key down, the movement snaps to a grid, allowing you to easily put the lower left vert exactly on the origin.

The remaining quad with its lower left vertex at the origin.

Here's an alternate trick for doing precision movement. Undo (Ctrl-Z) the translation you just performed. Now, press the G-key to enter Grab mode, followed by (and type exactly what is inside the quotes) "x1". Then hit Enter. Now, type "gz1" and hit Enter. The quad should have moved one full unit to the right, then one full unit up. Blender accepts numeric keyboard input in transformation modes. Obviously, you won't use that trick all the time, but it's excellent, for example, if you want to move something along a single axis for a specific distance, or to scale something to exactly twice its original size.

You might have noticed in the original image that the faces of the pillars below the bridge are symmetrical. This will allow you to take advantage of one of Blender's most powerful mesh tools: modifiers.

Using Modifiers

In the Buttons window below the 3D view, use F9 to get to the Editing buttons, and find the Modifiers panel.

Modifiers make on-the-fly changes and additions to meshes.

Click the "Add Modifier" button, then choose "Mirror" from the popup menu. Some new controls will appear. You will also notice that in the 3D view, the quad has been mirrored along the X axis. This mirrored copy is a "live" effect, and can be reconfigured at will in the modifiers panel.

The modifiers panel before adding modifiers.

Using a mirror modifier means that any changes you make on the original portion of the mesh will be reflected in the mirrored portion. And, since the pillar you are trying to make is symmetrical both left to right and top to bottom, you'll add a second mirror modifier.

Click "Add Modifier" again, and choose "Mirror". Another mirror modifier appears in the Modifiers tab, below the first one. Nothing happens in the 3D view. This is because the second modifier is set up exactly like the first, creating a second copy mirrored along the X axis, overlapping the first. You want this copy to be top-to-bottom, so change the axis of the second modifier by clicking its "Z" button. When you do that, you see the quad now mirrored along two axes, like the next illustration.

Notice the ghosted items to the left of and below the main mesh.

Another way to create this modifier would be to press the "Copy" button on the original mirror modifier, making a duplicate below the original that can be changed to suit your needs.

Finally, turn on the "Do Clipping" option in both modifiers. This will prevent any vertices you move from crossing the X or Z axes, which would cause overlapping meshes at the mirror point. The option "clips" any transformation that crosses its axis. When you have the modifiers set up properly, the panel should look like this:

The Modifiers panel with both mirror modifiers in place.

Now, with all four vertices still selected, use the G-key again, and see how things function with the modifiers in place. Moving the quad away from the mirrored axes does the same for all four copies. Moving it toward the axes actually changes its dimensions as the "Do Clipping" option keeps the vertices from crossing the axes. Move it around until it looks something like the next illustration, then LMB to accept the transform.

Subdivision

One way to begin adding detail to a mesh model is through subdivision. Subdivision is simply dividing faces like your quad into smaller faces that take up the same space. Blender has several tools for dividing faces and edges, and you'll use one of them now.

Try to move the quad around until it looks like this.

This quad has been subdivided.

With all four vertices of the quad selected, press the W-key to bring up the Specials menu. This menu contains a lot of common mesh modeling operations. In the menu, LMB on "Subdivide Multi", and accept the default "Number of Cuts: 2" that appears. The quad is divided twice in each direction, leaving you with something like this:

As was mentioned before, some screenshots, like the previous one, are in wireframe mode, and may not match your screen. You can toggle between wireframe and solid modes by using the Z-key.

We would like some of those faces to form the basis of a nice border for your pillar, but you need to adjust them a bit first.

Working with Edges

Up until now, you've been working with vertices. It is also possible to work directly with edges (the lines that connect vertices) or faces (the filled spaces defined by edges). On the 3D header, click the Edge button, as shown in the illustration:

These three buttons choose different select modes.

In the 3D view, the vertices disappear. You were working in Vertex mode before, but now you are working in Edge mode. All the same selection tools (RMB, Border, Lasso, etc.) apply to edges that applied to vertices and objects, but you get a few new and very useful tools as well.

Subdivision

While holding down the Alt key, RMB on any edge in the quad. The entire line of edges associated with the one you clicked is selected. This is called Edge Loop selection. Now, Edge Loop select (Alt-RMB) one of the interior vertical edges.

Press Ctrl-E, and a menu titled "Edge Specials" appears. From that menu, LMB select "Edge Slide". The edge loop you have selected enters a special kind of grab mode that allows you to slide it between the edge loops on either side. As with any other transform mode, LMB accepts the change and RMB cancels.

Using a combination of Alt-RMB select and the Edge Slide tool, try to select and move the interior edges up and to the right so that your model looks like this:

Try to get the subdivided edges to line up like this.

Now, you're going to subdivide the big face that's on the lower left of the quad. In fact, the first thing you'll do is change it from a quad into two triangles. With the mouse over the 3D view, press Ctrl-Tab, then select "Face" from the menu that pops up. The Ctrl-Tab menu is an alternate way of changing the select mode between vertices, edges and faces. Notice that once you are in Face select mode, all faces have a little point in their centers. This helps to differentiate them from areas that might be bound by vertices and edges, but are not true "filled in spaces" like a face.

RMB select the large face in the lower left, then press Ctrl-T to split the face into two triangle faces. If the triangles in your model appear differently than the ones in the illustration (the diagonal runs the other direction), use the Flip triangles command, Ctrl-F, to change it.

The Knife Tool

The lower left face has been split into two triangle faces.

With the two triangle faces still selected, press the K-key to bring up the cutting tools. Select "Knife (Exact)" from the menu. The Knife tool lets you draw directly on the screen by either dragging with the LMB or by repeatedly LMB clicking for straight, point-to-point lines. The lines that you draw will be used to cut any selected edges and divide any faces that they make up. At any point during the process, you can click with the RMB to cancel.

After you've pressed the K-key and selected "Knife (Exact)", LMB drag to create a line that looks something like this:

When you have that, press the Enter key to accept the cut. Now that the cut is made, switch to Edge select mode (with either Ctrl-Tab or on the 3D header), and using the Knife (Exact) tool, make another similar cut, just inside the first.

The line your knife cut should follow.

The mesh after accepting the knife cuts.

Pulling Vertices Into Line

This new set of cuts will form a second, interior border on your column. Right now, though, the cuts you've made are kind of crooked. To fix that, you'll learn a technique that is so frequently used it will become almost automatic to you eventually.

Go into Vertex select mode (Ctrl-Tab or 3D header), and select only the two rightmost of the cuts you just made.

Move the mouse cursor to the right of the model, but still within the 3D window. Now, press the S-key for Scaling, and begin to move the mouse toward the model. The vertices will move toward each other. As you move the mouse to the left, click the MMB one time. A horizontal line appears. Clicking the MMB while moving the mouse during a transform constrains that transformation along the axis nearest to the motion of the mouse. In this case, because you were moving the mouse from side to side when the MMB was clicked, it constrained the scaling transform along the X axis.

While still in the Scaling transform mode, hold down the Ctrl key. As you learned before, holding down Ctrl during a transformation snaps the values to even intervals. Continue to move the mouse toward the line between the vertices. When the mouse is very near to the edge, it will become perfectly vertical and the readout on the 3D header will display "Scale: 0.0000 along the global X axis". When you see that, press the LMB to confirm the move.

That was just a very detailed explanation of what turns out to be a simple effect. The reason we went into such detail is that this technique is an important tool that you will use again and again in your modeling.

If you would rather use the keyboard to do the same thing, you could select the vertices, then press "sx0" and Enter.

Using this technique, straighten the three other edges that were created with the knife tool. Remember that you will want to scale along the Z axis for the vertices whose connecting edges are horizontal.

> To align selected vertices along a single axis, use the S-key, MMB click to constrain the scale along a single axis, then hold down Ctrl to snap to exact values. Reduce the scale to 0 and LMB.

Using the aligning technique, you should be able to arrive at this.

Depth Through Extrusion

Select these five faces.

Go into Face select mode and select the five faces that will form your borders. Using the MMB, rotate the 3D view off-axis a bit, like the illustration, so you can get a better view of the next step.

"The extrude tool is applied to a face or a group of faces. It creates a new face of the same size and shape which is connected to each of the existing edges by a face. Thus, performing the extrude operation on a square face would create a cube connected to the surface at the location of the face." - Wikipedia entry for "Construction of Polygon Meshes"

If that went straight over your head, fear not! You shall learn by trying. Press the E-key and select Region from the popup that appears. This will duplicate the selected part of the mesh and connect the newly created section to the currently selected part. Blender automatically puts you in translation mode, constrained to the direction perpendicular to the previously selected face (in this case, that's along the Y axis). Translate (remember, you don't need to press anything, you're already in the correct mode) until your model looks something like the illustration.

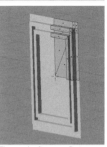

The mesh after your first extrustion (shown in Solid mode).

If you cancel the transformation with the RMB after doing an extrude, it's important to know that the extrude itself is not undone. The new geometry that extrude creates remains in the model, exactly on top of the original geometry that was selected. If you cancel out of the transform portion of an extrude, make sure that you delete (X-key) the new geometry, which should be the current selection.

From the illustration, and in your own model, you can now start to see the power of the mirror modifiers. Whatever you do to the original instance of the mesh is mirrored in real time on the duplicates, in this case creating two raised borders the whole way around the face of the pillar.

We'd like to make a nice ornament in the center of the pillar, so go to front view (Numpad-1). Select the edges and use the K-key Knife (Exact) tool to make a cut as shown in the illustration to the right.

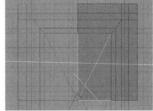

In face select mode, select the two innermost faces that were just created. With those faces selected, you'll use the "Subdivide Multi" option from the W-key Specials menu. This time, you'll increase the number of cuts to 3.

The path of the Knife cut.

Back in vertex selection mode, RMB select every other vertex on the long diagonal edge of the ornament. Using the G-key, followed by the Y-key to constrain the motion to the Y axis, move those vertices outward from the face of the pillar.

The two center triangle faces subdivided at multi level 3.

The vertices select.

The selected vertices moved along the Y axis. (Shown in Solid mode.)

Using the Proportional Editing Tool

RMB select the vertex at the very lower left of the model, which you can now easily see is really the center of the mirrored model.

On the 3D header, click the icon menu designated by the little donut. This menu changes the standard mesh transformations like translate, rotate and scale into what is called "Proportional Editing" (PET). In Proportional Editing, more vertices are transformed than just the selected ones. Depending on how it is set, selecting and moving a single vertex will also move the vertices around it as well, with the influence of the move falling off the further you get from the selected vertex.

Let's See How it Works.

Use the MMB to give yourself an off-axis view like you did when extruding a little bit ago. If you are not already in wireframe mode (Z-key), get there now.

With the lower left vertex selected, either choose "On" from the PET menu on the header, or use the O-key (the "O" looks like the donut on the menu). The PE tool is now on. Press the G-key and start to move the mouse. Things kind of go crazy. First of all, press the Y-key to constrain translation to that axis. That should settle things down and let you get your bearings.

As you move the mouse and see the translation on the screen, you will see that indeed, many vertices other than the one you have selected will be moving. There will also be a large gray circle superimposed on the model. This circle shows how far the "influence" of the selected vertex extends, and can be changed by using the scroll wheel. For a moment, try not moving the mouse, but scrolling the wheel back and forth. As you do, you can see the influence of your transformation grow and shrink.

When you're done playing around with it, press the RMB to cancel. Use the Z-key to get into solid mode. Then, G-key again, followed by Y to constrain. By moving the center vertex and adjusting the PET influence with the scroll wheel, try to get the center portion of your mesh to look like this illustration:

Let's add some more detail to this little dome. First, use the O-key or the 3D header menu to turn off the PET. You can tell it's off when the donut icon on the header is gray. Then, using the RMB, select several of the vertices on the dome it doesn't really matter which ones. Four or five will be fine.

The center ornament moved with the Proportional Editing Tool

Here's a new method of moving vertices: Alt-S. While you may recall from object mode that Alt-S clears any scaling on an object, in edit mode it triggers a Shrink/Fatten transformation. This method of moving vertices (it works for edges and faces too) translates vertices along their normal. A vertex's normal is the direction it is "facing" on a surface. For example, the normal of a vertex that makes up part of the outside of a sphere points directly away from the surface of the sphere.

So, with your fairly random selection of vertices, use the Alt-S Shrink/Fatten transform to push those vertices inward or outward. It doesn't really matter which way you take it - you're just trying to make the ornament look interesting. If you find that more than just your selection is moving, though, it probably means that you forgot to turn off the PET.

With that done, let's make a test render and see how it looks.

Get out of Edit Mode (Tab-key) and press Numpad-0 to see things from the default camera's point of view. Most likely, things are a bit off center

RMB select the outermost solid line in the camera view. That outer line is actually the camera, which is now selected. Press the R-key twice. This lets you aim the camera in a very intuitive way by moving the mouse. If you like, you can also use the G-key to move the camera around, then re-aim it with the double R-key technique. Get things so that the panel you've created appears nicely in the center of the camera space, then press LMB to confirm the camera's transformation.

The scene out of center from the camera's view.

Now, a little rendering trick to show off the detail of your model. Press F8 to change the buttons window into the World buttons, then select the "Amb Occ" tab. Click the "Ambient Occlusion" button to turn it on, and turn the "Samples" up to around 7. You can see the lighting and rendering chapters for a more in-depth look at this, and other, rendering topics.

The same scene, now in center.

The Ambient Occlusion panel in the World buttons.

Press F12 to render and get a good look at your work so far.

From that render, I'm thinking that the two borders stick out a little too much. It's easy enough to fix. If you're happy with yours, just leave it alone, but if you'd like to make an adjustment, just enter Face select mode, select the front faces of the borders, and G-key then Y-key to move them back a bit along the Y axis.

The Loop Cut Tool

I'd like to make that inner border a little more detailed. From an off-axis view, hover the mouse over the diagonal corner edge of that inner border and press Ctrl-R. Ctrl-R is the hotkey for the Loop Cut tool, which will add an edge along an edge ring and subdivide the faces that it crosses. Ctrl-R places you into a mode where purple lines will pop up with every edge you move your mouse over, showing you where the loop would be cut if you clicked the LMB. In fact, try moving the mouse around over the model right now and see how the loops appear and disappear.

A render of the panel you've created.

When you're done with that, bring the mouse back to the corner edge, so the purple loop looks like this:

Press the LMB to start the cut. The loop cut begins its life in Edge Slide mode, which you're already familiar with. Move the loop about a third of the way toward the outer edge of the border and press the LMB to confirm. Now, make another loop cut, just inside the first, so that when you're done, the border is divided into three parallel sections.

In face select mode, select the central row of faces.

Use the E-key to extrude that selection back into the main face of the pillar, which,

The loop cut tool preparing to cut.

when viewed in solid mode, should look something like this:

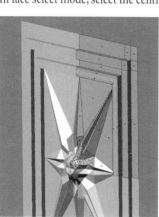

You've now finished the main modeling on a single face of your pillar. In the next part, you'll learn how to use the Array modifier to make offset and rotated copies of a mesh.

Faces selected for another extrude.

The Array Modifier

Just like the mirror modifier created a mirrored virtual copy of your mesh, the Array modifier makes non-mirrored duplicates, with versatile options for arranging them.

The result of extruding the faces back into the panel.

Go back to the Edit buttons and find the Modifiers panel. Add a new modifier, this time choosing Array. The array modifier will appear below the two mirror modifiers, and will most likely fall off the bottom of the screen. You can MMB drag the buttons window to show the whole thing. Or, to make some more space in the buttons window, you could click the triangle in the upper left side of the mirror modifiers to collapse them. When the array modifier is created, you will see a copy of your mesh appear to the right of the original.

An array modifier.

Because we want you to have your array form a nice rectangular pillar, you need some way to have it rotate the copies. Although there don't seem to be any settings in the modifier for causing a rotation, it can be done with the "Object Offset" controls. Object Offset uses the coordinates of an external object, like an Empty, as a guide for creating offsets - this includes any scaling or rotations the Empty might have.

Before you use Object Offset, turn off Relative Offset by un-clicking its button.

Let's create an Empty object to use. First, use the Tab key to get out of edit mode on the pillar. We'd like to create the Empty at the center of the Blender world, and as it will be born where the 3D cursor currently is, you need to move the 3D cursor to the origin. You could place the 3D cursor close to the origin by using the LMB, then selecting "Cursor-> Grid" from the Shift-S snap menu, or you can just use the Shift-C hotkey. Shift-C returns the 3D cursor to the origin.

In a top view, use the toolbox to add an Empty. RMB select the pillar, and type the new Empty's name "Empty" in the Object Offset box in the array modifier (names in Blender are case-sensitive, so make sure to type a capital "E"). Click the "Object Offset" button to turn it on. Nothing happens. RMB select the Empty, and do some kind of transform on it: Grab, Rotate, Scale... it doesn't matter. You'll see a copy of the mesh begin to move around. RMB to cancel that translation.

Try transforming the Empty again, this time using the R-key for rotation, and holding down the Ctrl key so that you snap exactly onto 90 degrees.

Nice, but if you look at the corner where they meet, the instances overlap. You don't want that. Of course, fixing it is as simple as selecting the Empty and G-key moving it until the edges seem to meet.

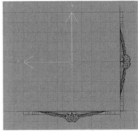

The mesh is duplicated, offset and rotated 90 degrees.

There are two more things to adjust. Set the "Count" spinner up to 4, so you have four sides on your pillar. Make sure that the "Merge" and "FirstLast" buttons at the bottom of the modifier are turned on. These two buttons determine whether Blender treats joints like the corner you just fixed as separate items, or if it joins matching edges and vertices, creating a single larger piece. You want the corners to be joined, so we've turned these options on.

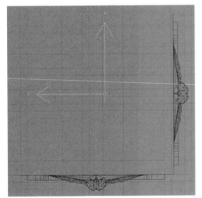

The vertices in the lower right now meet.

The array modifier, with Merge and FirstLast enabled and Count set to 4.

Array Power

The array modifier is powerful. Using several array modifiers with different objects can quickly create hundreds or even thousands of mesh instances. While it is very fast, always be sure not to crank things too high too quickly, or you might find yourself with a sluggish Blender session. As a demonstration of how using the array modifier beats simply duplicating parts of a mesh by hand, take a look at this illustration:

Here, the exact same model is used, but the array count has been set to ten, and the Empty has been rotated and moved slightly so that everything lines up correctly. This sort of change and rearrangement would be very difficult with more traditional modeling techniques.

The same pillar panel with the array count set to 10.

Turning Modifier Instances Into Real Geometry

At some point, you might need to do something to the mesh that won't necessarily work with modifiers in place. For example, you may have been using the mirror modifier to create a symmetrical human face, but now would like to start making it more realistic by adding asymmetric details. To convert a modifier's virtual copies of a mesh into real geometry, press the Apply button on the right side of the modifier.

Modifiers can only be applied in object mode, and if you try to do it in edit mode, Blender will warn you that it's not possible. So, go into object mode and press the Apply button on all three modifiers (two mirror and one array), starting with the top-most, and working your way down.

When you've finished and the Modifiers panel is empty, go into edit mode and take a look at the full, selectable geometry of the pillar.

A render at this point should give you something like this:

Closing the Top

One last trick to learn: with Alt-RMB, select the upper edge of the pillar. Ensure you are in Edge selection mode when you do this, as using Alt-RMB in Face or Vertex selection mode can lead to different results.

A render with all four sides on the pillar.

Click the E-key to extrude, and then, before you use LMB to accept the extrusion, press the S-key. The transform mode after extrude doesn't limit you to just translation - all the transform modes are accessible. Once the S-key is pressed, scale the new edge inward a bit, then confirm with the LMB.

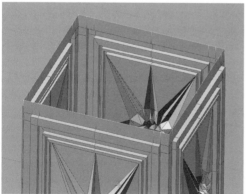

The upper edge selected.

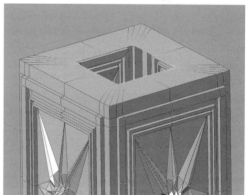

The upper edge has been extruded and scaled inward.

With that new extruded edge still selected, press the W-key for the specials menu and choose "Merge". A popup will ask you if you want "At Center", "At Cursor" or "Collapse". Choose "At Center". All of the vertices along that edge are averaged, then joined into a single vertex - effectively joining all of the associated edges and making a solid top. The Merge menu can be accessed directly by pressing Alt-M.

The Merge menu.

A new render shows the finished pillar.

At this point, you're going to finish the bridge, but only using tools that you've already learned in this tutorial, with one exception. That being the case, we're not going to give you every shortcut or explain every single detail of each step. See if you can follow along.

Create a new Empty (probably called "Empty.001") at the location of pillar.

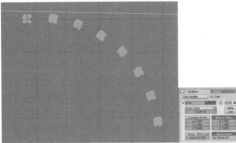

The array modifier with settings, and the result in the 3D view.

Add an array modifier to the pillar. Give a decently high count (I used 8, but you don't have to), change the Relative Offset X value to 3.0, and enable Object Offset. Put the name of the new Empty in the Object Offset text field. Select the Empty and rotate until your array of pillars looks something like this illustration:

Go back into Edit mode on the pillar and select all of the edges that make up the top. Using the K-key knife tool, choose Knife (Midpoint) and draw the cut line in a full circle around the center. Pressing Enter to accept the cut should show this:

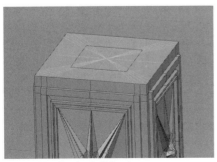

The top of the pillar after the Knife cut.

Select this new cut (Alt-RMB Edge Loop select will work), then extrude it upward.

With the top extruded edge still selected, use the Shift-S snap menu to bring up the "Cursor->Selection". In top view, use the toolbox to add a mesh plane to the existing

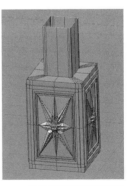

Closing the Top

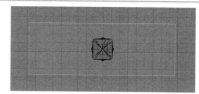

mesh (Add->Mesh->Plane). Using either the scaling or grab tools, change the plane to look like this:

Notice how the other arrayed instances started scooting out of the way as you made the plane larger? That's because you were using "Relative Offset", and as the spacing was relative to the size of the mesh, it changed as the mesh's size changed. That's not going to work, so turn off Relative Offset in the array modifier, and turn on Constant Offset.

Top view of the pillar, with a plane added to begin the bridge deck.

The next part will take some fine tuning, but I'm sure you can handle it by now. Start by setting the X value of the Constant Offset controls to somewhere around 18.0. The edges of the planes on each array instance should be fairly close to one another. Work with that offset setting until the lower corners are as close as you can get them. There's no need to be exact, just get it as close as you can with the offset value.

Then, with the plane still selected, use the rotation and scaling tools to try to get the lower corners to meet exactly.

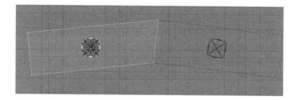

Now, adjust each of those two corner vertices individually so that they match the left edge of the arrayed instance.

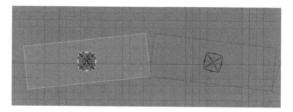

Get to an off-axis view through MMB view rotation. Extrude the entire plane upward a short distance. Make two loop cuts (Ctrl-R) along the length of the bridge deck, and edge slide them toward the outsides.

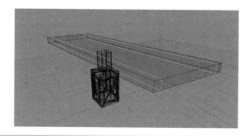

Select the two outermost faces of the top of the bridge deck, Shift-D duplicate them and move them upward (Z axis) a bit.

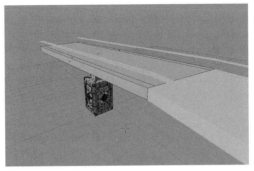

Extrude those new faces upward to form the guide rails of the bridge.

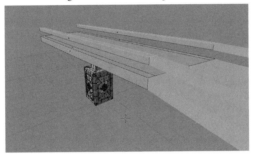

Back in a top view, LMB to position the 3D cursor inside one of the guide rails. From the toolbox, add a mesh tube to the model.

Here's the one new thing: you would like this tube to render smoothly, not showing each of its faces.

Adding a tube to the mesh with the toolbox.

Set Solid

Set Smooth

Blender can render edges in two ways: smooth and sharp. The default method, the one used for all toolbox primitives, is sharp. To change this, you use the "Set Smooth" button on the Links and Materials panel of the Edit buttons. Select the portions of the mesh that you would like to render smoothly, in this case the tube support, and press the button. You can change it back by pressing the "Set Solid" button. If you have a model (like a human head) that should be rendered entirely smoothly with no sharp edges, you can also use the "Set Smooth" in Object mode, in which case it applies smooth rendering to the entire model.

This tube will be the support for the guide rail, so make sure to scale it so it fits inside of the guide rail's area. In a side view, move the tube vertically (Z axis), if it needs to be moved, in order to go between the guide rail and bridge deck. Also, you will probably need to scale it along the Z axis to have it reach the distance from the rail to the deck.

Back in a top view, Shift-D duplicate the tube support several times, placing it along the length of both guide rails.

And with that, you've achieved the model from the introductory render. You can, of course, move the camera around

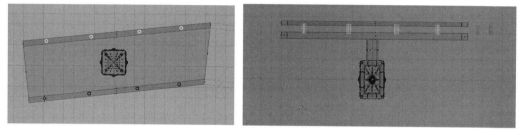

to get more dramatic rendering angles of the entire construction. Some people like to move the camera directly in the camera view as you did earlier, but some find this unintuitive. If you didn't like doing it that way, you can try this instead.

Using a MMB-click at the bottom of the 3D window, split the view into two parts (see Chapter 2 if you forget how). Use Numpad-0 to set the right hand window to a camera view. Then, select the camera in the left hand view and start to transform it. The transforms you make to the camera also show in the camera view, letting you move the camera in a more familiar object-like way, while seeing the results in real time.

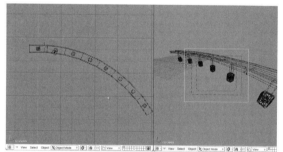

The 3d window split for camera positioning.

When you have the camera somewhere that provides a nice view... render!

Of course, it's still easy to add details to the bridge. And, as the array modifier is still live, any changes you make to one portion will be repeated on the others, allowing you to quickly make something much nicer. The final illustration was made in under five minutes from the same basic model that you've just created, using only the tools you've learned.

Set Smooth

The modeling tools and techniques that you've used in this tutorial are applicable to a wide range of modeling tasks. Hopefully, it will have given you a good basis to continue learning and improving.

A more detailed bridge model.

A finished scene built from this tutorial.

Modeling Tools

Introduction

What is Polygon Modeling?

Polygon, or "Poly," Modeling is the process of creating a 3D model using basic 3D elements called vertices, edges and faces. A vertex (more than one vertex are called vertices) is a point in 3D space. An edge is a line connecting two vertices. Three edges together form a triangle face, while four edges together form a quad face. Those triangle and quad faces of filled space are the polygons.

A vertex, an edge, and a face.

One of the main advantages of polygon modeling over other modeling methods is the ability to easily add detail to specific areas without having to add more complexity to the rest of the model. Other advantages include speed of rendering in real-time environments and relative ease of texturing.

Modeling Tools

Working with Vertices

Selecting / Deselecting

The first thing you'll need to know in order to begin modeling is how to select and deselect vertices. Run Blender, or if it's already running, clear the current scene with Ctrl-X. There should now be a square in the center of your screen, highlighted in purple to indicate that it is selected. In the introductory chapters, you worked with objects in Object mode, and always used the Tab key to leave Edit Mode when an object was created. Now, we want you to actually work in Edit Mode. So, use the Tab key to enter Edit Mode with the default cube still selected, and you'll see that the four edges (straight lines) and four vertices (points at each corner) that make up this polygon are highlighted in yellow.

The Tab key toggles between Edit and Object modes

If you press the A-key with your cursor in the 3D viewport, you can toggle between selecting and deselecting all of the vertices in this object, just like you could when working with multiple objects in Object Mode. Putting an

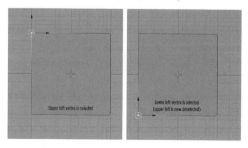

object into Edit Mode makes it function in many ways like a mini-version of the whole scene - a lot of what you have already learned will apply within this new, smaller scope.

Make sure all vertices are deselected and then right click on the vertex in the upper left corner to select just that one. If you now right click on the vertex in the lower left corner, the one you previously selected will become deselected and the lower one will now be selected. You can select (or deselect) multiple vertices at the same time by holding the Shift key down while right clicking (RMB) on each vertex you would like to select.

Deleting

- In Edit Mode, selection works for vertices just like it does in Object Mode:

- RMB selects, while Shift-RMB builds and takes away from the selection.

The next thing you'll need to know is how to delete a vertex. First you'll want to get a good look at all the vertices that are in this object. By pressing Numpad-5 you can toggle your view between Perspective and Orthographic view (see Chapter 2 for more on the difference). Switch over to perspective view and use the techniques you just learned to select all of the vertices except the one in the upper-most left corner and then press the Delete key (or the X-key). A menu will appear with a number of different options - this is where things start to differ from object mode. Choose "Vertices" from the menu to delete the vertices that you have selected. You may notice that a side effect of deleting the vertices is that the edges and faces are also deleted. This is because the faces are made up of edges and the edges are made up of the vertices you just deleted. Removing the vertices necessarily removed the other things they had built. If you had chosen "Edges" or "Faces" from the Delete menu you could have removed only the edges or faces respectively, leaving the vertices in place, but unconnected.

X-key or Delete key brings up the delete menu, allowing you remove vertices, edges or faces.

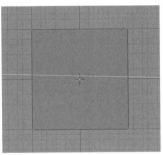

Ortho: Orthographic view.

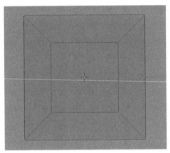

Perspective: Perspective view.

Moving

Transform keys in Edit Mode carry over from Object Mode: G-key (Grab), S-key (Scale), and R-key (Rotate), as well as axis constraint shortcuts, transformation manipulators and mouse gestures.

At this point you'll want to move the remaining vertex closer to the middle of the screen so you can begin working with it. To do this you'll need to select it, then press the G-key to "Grab" it. Once you press the G-key the vertex will move to follow the movements of your mouse, just like an entire object would in Object Mode. Move the vertex near the center of the screen and press the LMB to place the vertex and confirm the translation. Of course, the keyboard constraints that you learned in the Object chapter also apply here: hitting the X, Y or Z-keys will constrain vertex movement to that axis. Pressing them twice uses the alternative transformation space as defined on the 3D header.

Exact Positioning

Using the G-key is a great way to move things as long as you don't need to be precise. In fact, most of your modeling will be done using this method. However, there are times when you'll need exact positioning. To

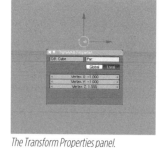

The Transform Properties panel.

achieve that kind of precision in Blender you'll use the "Transform Properties" panel. To access the transform properties dialog make sure you have something selected (the remaining vertex in this case) and press the N-key.

In the Transform Properties panel you'll see that you have a number of different options. Here you can rename your object by modifying the text in the "OB:" text field (the object in the example is named "Cube"), or place the object exactly where you want it by modifying the numbers in the various X, Y and Z text fields. To place the vertex in the exact center of the 3D workspace hold the Shift-key and click the LMB in the "Vertex X:" spinner control. This makes the field instantly editable. Type the number "0" and press Enter. To complete the process, repeat these steps for the "Vertex Y:" and "Vertex Z:" fields. For faster access to the Y and Z controls, you can simply hit the Tab key when you've entered your value in the X control. When entering values into fields in Blender, the Tab key functions much like it does in other programs you might be familiar with, taking you to the next text field.

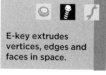

N-key brings up the transform properties panel for numeric positioning.

The Extrude Tool

A vertex by itself will not show up in a render. So what can we do with vertices? Combine them into edges (which still don't show up in a render) and then into faces. Faces render. There are several ways to create edges from a vertex.

The easiest way is to extrude the vertex. Extrusion is simply taking one thing, like a circle, and extending it into space. Extruding a circle into space creates a cylinder. Extruding a square creates a box. Extruding a vertex in Blender will create another vertex and an edge that links them. To do this, make sure the vertex is selected and press the E-key. Now move the mouse around and you'll notice that you are moving another vertex, and that an edge attaches the two vertices like a string. To place the new vertex where you want, press the LMB. To add some precision to your placement you can hold the Ctrl-key while moving the vertex and it will "Snap to" the nearest increment in Blender units. Of course, you could also use the Transform properties dialog.

E-key extrudes vertices, edges and faces in space.

If you need to create a whole chain of vertices, there is a simpler workflow than using the E-key for extrude. With a vertex selected, clicking with Ctrl-LMB in the 3D view creates a new vertex at the location of the click, selects it and links it with an edge to the original vertex. By holding down the Ctrl key and LMB clicking repeatedly, you can quickly build a chain of vertices linked by edges. This fast extrusion feature will actually work with any mesh selection: vertices, edges or faces.

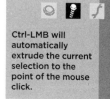

Ctrl-LMB will automatically extrude the current selection to the point of the mouse click.

Another easy way to create an edge is to duplicate a vertex by selecting a vertex and pressing Shift-D. After using the LMB to place the duplicated vertex, Shift-RMB selecting the original and pressing the F-key will create an edge between them.

Removing Extra Vertices

There are many cases where you may end up with vertices that occupy nearly the same space. You may have imported a mesh model from a CAD program that has portions of the mesh duplicated in the same spot as the original. You may be trying to join two parts of a mesh into one, scaling vertices toward each other until they occupy the same point. In any of those cases, you need to remove the extra vertices and join the edges and faces that they help to define.

To remove extra vertices and join the edges and faces that they build, select the vertices in question and press the W-key, choosing "Remove Doubles" from the popup menu that appears. Remove Doubles works with a distance threshold value, adjustable in the Mesh Tools panel of the Edit buttons (F9) with the Limit spinner, so you can, for example, select all vertices in the entire mesh and use the function without fear that it will remove all but one of your vertices.

In the illustrations, you see two halves of a cube, separated, then with the vertices scaled together.

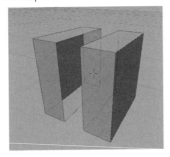
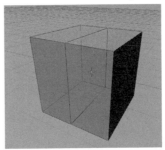

Although the vertices occupy the same space, the edges and faces they build are not connected, and will render with ugly lines at the gaps. As you can see in the next illustration, the vertices are still independent, and can be selected and moved apart from each other.

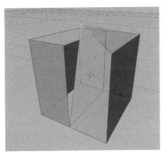
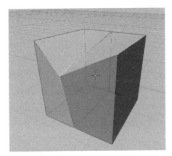

With the vertices joined into one, the two halves are now one continuous mesh

Remove Doubles, from the W-key specials menu and Mesh Tools buttons, merges vertices that are very close together.

Once the vertices of the cube have been selected and the Remove Doubles function has been used, the vertices are merged into one, and the edges and faces they build are now truly connected.

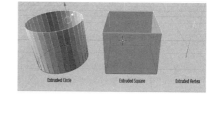

A common technique is also highlighted in the next example. When trying to get vertices close together for a merge, it is often easier to use the Scale command (S-key), scaling them down to 0 with the help of the Ctrl key, than it is to move one (G-key) and trying to line it up with the other on screen.

Working with an Edge

With edges, the same rules and methods that you have learned with vertices apply, plus more. You might be wondering why working with an edge (or face) is important since you already know how to work with vertices. By being able to work with all three, you will be able to take full advantage of Blender's tool set and learn to work as efficiently as possible.

Selecting

Blender has tools made just for selecting edges. To activate Edge select mode, click the icon on the 3D header that looks like a diagonal line. It's between the Vertex select (four dots) and Face select (triangle) icons. Once Edge select is activated, you'll be able to RMB click anywhere along the edge to select it. To select multiple edges, you can hold the Shift key while RMB clicking on other edges.

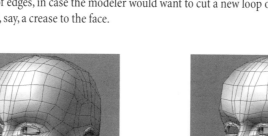

Blender also has tools for selecting multiple edges. Under the Select menu on the 3D header, you'll see the Edge ring and Edge loop options. These can be used to easily select complex groups of interrelated edges, and are especially useful when working with character models.

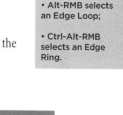

- Alt-RMB selects an Edge Loop;

- Ctrl-Alt-RMB selects an Edge Ring.

In the case of this head model, Alt-RMB selects the loop of edges that runs around the mouth, giving the modeler easy access to this crucial area. Also, Ctrl-Alt-RMB will select the corresponding ring of edges, in case the modeler would want to cut a new loop of edges through them to add, say, a crease to the face.

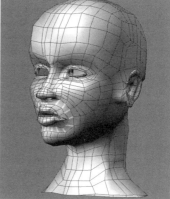

Edge loop selected around the mouth.   *Edge ring selected around the mouth.*

Working with an Edge   103

Working with Faces

Creating a Face

Faces are created with a selection and the F-key. To create a face, you need to have either three or four vertices selected (three will build a triangle face, four will build a quad face), or two edges.

F-key creates a face from three or four selected vertices or two selected edges

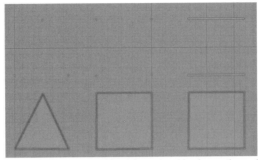

Pressing the F-key to create a triangle face and quad face from vertices, and a quad face from two edges.

Selecting

As with anything else in Blender, the quickest way to select faces is to switch over to Face Select mode and use the RMB. The Face Select mode button is to the right of the Edge Select mode button on the 3D header and has a triangle as its icon. Another way to change select modes is by pressing the Ctrl-Tab keys. You'll get a menu that allows you to choose your select mode without having to use the icons.

Adding Detail to a Mesh

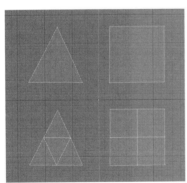

A triangle and quad face, before and after subdivision.

If you are constructing a model and you find that you need more detail in a certain area, one way to achieve this is to "subdivide" the face (or faces) that you are working with. Subdivision cuts a face into four new faces that take up the same space as the previous single one did. To subdivide a face, make sure you have one selected, then click the Subdivide button on the Mesh Tools panel in the Edit buttons. Subdivide can also be found in the Specials menu by pressing the W-key.

You'll see that there are some other subdivision options in the Specials menu. The "Subdivide Multi" option allows you to perform more than a single slice at once on the selected faces, and is quicker than selecting "Subdivide" many times in a row. "Subdivide Multi Fractal" does basically the same thing, but moves the resulting extra vertices around randomly. It's great for creating terrain, or any surface that needs to have a rough, random mesh. Immediately below that on the menu is "Subdivide Smooth", which will not only subdivide the selected portions of a mesh, but will simultaneously attempt to smooth out all edges created by the process.

The W-key Specials menu with Subdivide Multi selected.

Another way to add detail is to use the Knife tool. This tool allows you to cut Edges by drawing with the mouse. The best way to see how this works is to select all the vertices in a subdivided square and press Shift-K to bring up the Knife subdivide menu. From the menu, choose "Midpoints" and the cursor will change to a knife icon. Press and hold the LMB, drawing a line that intersects several of the edges that make up the square. When you are finished, press the Enter key, and Blender will cut each edge that your line crossed, placing vertices at their centers and creating some new faces in the process. The "Exact" function of the Knife tool cuts the edges exactly where the mouse crosses them, as opposed to their centers.

Shift-K brings up the Knife tool for cutting faces and edges into parts.

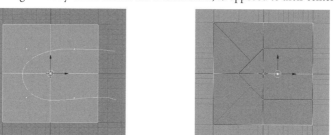

Knife cut tool before pressing Enter to activate the cut, and showing the result.

Filling

Up until now you've been looking at fairly regular shapes. Let's examine a random shape and see how Blender helps to organize it into a group of faces that you can work with by using the Fill and Beauty Fill tools.

Take a look at the graphic below:

A shape made of edges, but not filled with faces. *The shape filled with faces by using the Shift-F fill command.* *The faces rearranged more pleasingly with Beauty Fill.* *Any triangles that can be converted to quads have been.*

You could start to select sets of vertices or edges and use the F-key to build faces for this outline one at a time. A faster (though messier) way is to simply select all of the vertices with the A-key and press Shift-F to use Blenders Fill tool. Blender will fill the shape with the appropriate number of faces. This method doesn't always create the cleanest models, though, so once the shape is filled, Blender's Beauty Fill tool can help to clean things up.

With all of the vertices in the shape selected, press Alt-F to activate the Beauty Fill function, and Blender will attempt to clean up the model.

If you need to clean things up even further, you can even have Blender attempt to join triangles into quads with either the "Convert Triangles to Quads" command from the Mesh menu's Edges section, or use the Alt-J hotkey.

• **Shift-F attempts to fill an area of selected vertices or edges with faces.**

• **Alt-F attempts to make a nicer arrangement of faces.**

• **Alt-J will convert available triangles into quads.**

Subsurf

Up to this point you've only worked on models and objects with sharp edges. When rendered, the models look just like they did in Edit Mode. That would be fine if you only modeled machines or other artificial objects. However, if you tried to model an organic shape or something like a perfectly smooth circle using the methods we've gone over so far, it would take a lot of vertices, exacting placement and a lot of time. That wouldn't be an efficient use of your time and would make your computer work very hard when it came time to render. Fortunately, Blender has a tool made just for this type of modeling called the Subsurf modifier. Subsurf is short for a process called Subdivision Surfacing. In Subdivision Surfacing, a simple low-polygon model (like the default cube) can be used as a "control cage" for a more complex organic model like a ball.

To add a Subsurf modifier to a mesh object, first make sure the object is selected in the 3D view. From the Modifiers panel in the Edit buttons, click the "Add Modifier" button, then choose "Subsurf" from the resulting menu.

The Subsurf modifier panel.

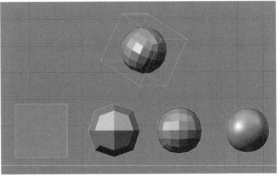

A cube, with progressive levels of subsurfing.

The default setting is 1 level of subsurfing for both editing and rendering. These values can be changed in the modifier panel, but be careful: subsurfing actually has Blender create extra geometry behind the scenes. Turning levels up too high, especially on models that are complex to begin with, can quickly have your computer trying to perform calculations for millions of polygons, and can bring your system to a crawl.

To keep things working better while you model, you can set the subsurfing level for the interface and the renderer separately. Setting the subsurf Levels control to 2 will probably give you a good balance for most work. Try rendering your subsurfed model with Render Levels set to 2 as well. If the results are not smooth enough,

increase the value in Render Levels one at a time until they are.

The real value of Blenders Subsurf tools becomes evident when working on a more complex organic model like a human head. The only difference between these two illustrations is that the second has a Subsurf modifier applied to it.

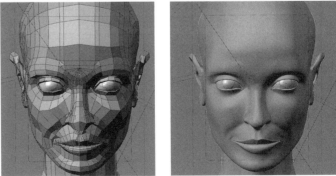

A head model before and after the Subsurf modifier.

Adding a Subsurf modifier is such a common practice in Blender that there is a direct hotkey for it: Shift-O. Shift-O will add Subsurf modifiers to any selected objects that are currently in Object mode. Furthermore, using Ctrl-1 through Ctrl-4 will set the Subsurf levels for those objects, making it possible to manage your Subsurfing for an entire Scene without ever touching the Edit buttons' modifier panel.

The Add Modifier button in the Modifiers panel of the Edit buttons lets you make a standard mesh into a Subsurfaced subdivision mesh.

Working with Normals

Understanding the Normal

There is one last element of a polygon model in Blender that you'll need to understand before you finish. That element is called a Surface Normal, or Normal for short. Its function is to tell Blender (and the user) which direction a Face is pointing, and to help calculate how light behaves when reflected off of your model.

Sometimes when working on a complex model it is possible to end up with adjacent faces whose normals are pointing in opposite directions. This can cause undesirable results so it's best to make sure they are all pointing where you want them.

The illustration below shows the default cube with "Draw Normals" activated. The "Draw Normals" button is found in the "Mesh Tools 1" panel of the edit buttons. (In the default configuration of Blender, this panel is actually scrolled off the right side of the screen on most monitors. MMB drag to the left in the Edit buttons area to bring it into view.) You can also change the length of the line that indicates the direction of the normal by changing the value in the "NSize" field just above the Draw Normals button.

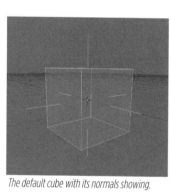

The default cube with its normals showing.

With Draw Normals activated, small teal lines stick out of each face in your model. These lines represent the direction the Normal is facing. Pressing the W-key and selecting "Flip Normals" from the Specials menu changes the direction of the normals of any selected faces. If you have a model with "normal problems", i.e. strange black seams in solid mode and render, you can force Blender to recalculate all normals to face the outside of the model by selecting everything in Edit Mode, and pressing Ctrl-N. Pressing Ctrl-Shift-N will set all of the normals to point toward the inside of the model.

Ctrl-N recalculates the normals of a model.

Tips and Additional Tools

Now you know the basics of how Blender handles the various tasks related to polygon modeling. Let's conclude this introduction with some tips that will give you a little more power.

Vertex Groups

Vertex Groups allow you to save selections of vertices, so that later you can reselect them easily. This is useful when creating complex models that may need adjustment later. For example: when working on a face, if you find that you are constantly selecting the same group of vertices around the nose, it would make sense to save that selection for easy access. It's important to understand that the selected vertices haven't actually been "put" into a group, though. Vertex groups just contain lists of vertices. So, there is no reason that a vertex cannot be listed in several different vertex groups.

Vertex Groups are created in the "Links and Materials" panel of the Edit buttons, in the Vertex Groups section of buttons. With your selection of vertices made as you like, press the "New" button in the Vertex Groups panel. Some new controls will appear, including a naming field and popup menu button for choosing other, already created vertex groups.

The Vertex Group controls.

The default name for the first vertex group created is simply "Group", but can be replaced with something that will help you to remember its contents better. Once you have entered a name, click the "Assign" button to assign the selected vertices to the named group. Remember that simply clicking the "New" button only creates an empty vertex group - your selection will not be saved into it until you click the "Assign" button.

The other controls in that part of the panel do the following:

Delete: Deletes the named vertex group. Note that this does not delete the vertices, it just removes the saved selection.

Remove: Removes the selected vertices from the currently active vertex group.

Select: Examines the named vertex group and selects its vertices in the 3D view. This is an additive selection, so anything that was already selected in the 3D view remains selected.

Desel.: The opposite of Select. Any vertices that are selected in the 3D view, but are in the named vertex group, are deselected.

Mirroring

Another time-saving feature in Blender is the Mirror modifier. It allows you to only model half of a model and see it duplicated in mirrored form, creating the other half. It is useful for modeling symmetrical things, like this head as seen in the illustration below.

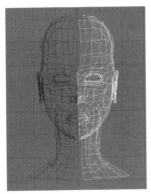

Adding a mirror modifier in Blender is just like adding a Subsurf modifier: click the "Add Modifier" button on the Modifiers panel of the Edit buttons and choose "Mirror". The mirrored half will appear as ghosted lines in Wireframe mode, but will be fully solid in Solid mode.

Enabling the "Do Clipping" button in the Modifiers panel will prevent any vertices you transform from crossing the center line of the mirror effect. When you have finished symmetrical modeling, pressing the "Apply" button in the Modifiers panel will make the mirrored half of the model into actual geometry that can be selected and modified independently.

Loop Cut

In addition to the other subdivision controls that you have learned, the loop subdivide tool allows you to quickly and uniformly subdivide all the edges that are within the same "loop". In the illustration below, you can see the cut line looping around the eye, which will allow the modeler to add crease lines. To initiate a Loop Cut, press Ctrl-R and move the cursor over the model. While moving the cursor, you'll notice that when Blender detects groups of edges that it can cut, a magenta line will appear to indicate the location of a possible loop cut. When the magenta line indicates the loop that you would like to cut, press the LMB once to begin the cut. Then, Blender will allow you to slide the cut back and forth between the outer edges by moving the mouse. You can even increase or decrease the number of cuts made along the loop by using the scroll wheel. When you have the cutting line positioned exactly as you like, pressing the LMB will have Blender make the cuts. Pressing the RMB at any point in the procedure cancels the cut.

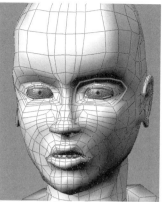

A new loop is being cut around the eye on the right side of the image.

Edge Slide

Once you begin using the Loop Cut tool to add detail to your models, you may find that edge loops become even more useful. For example: what if the cut that was made around the eye in the previous illustration fell along the center of the edges, but you had really wanted it nearer to the exterior loop? Instead of moving each edge individually, you can simply Alt-RMB select the edge loop, then choose "Edge Slide" from the Ctrl-E Edge Specials menu in the 3D view. This allows you to slide the edge back and forth between the two bounding loops. LMB accepts the slide, while RMB cancels. This tool will actually allow you to slide any selectable edge loop, regardless of what tools were used to create it.

Edge Loop Delete

One of the elements in the X-key delete menu we have not mentioned is the "Edge Loop" option. With an edge loop selected, using this option from the X-key delete menu will remove the edges, but join the faces on either side. The effect is as though an edge loop had never been cut there. This is a great tool for cleanly reducing the polygon count of your meshes once you have them looking the way you want.

Conclusion

In this introduction, you have seen the basic tools for polygon modeling in Blender and learned a little about how you can begin to work with them. If you haven't already worked through the tutorial section of this chapter, it's a good way to see this theory put into practice, and to learn a few more tricks as well.

Best of luck,
Kevin Braun

CHAPTER 5

Sculpting and Multiresolution Modeling

 Sculpting: Hands On
by Tom Musgrove

 Sculpting: Discussion
by Tom Musgrove

Tom Musgrove

Tom is a writer, a student, a researcher, and commercial fisherman in Alaska. His volunteer work with Blender includes release management, assisting new coders in finding the relevant experts for their projects, documentation work, and occasional coding and python script review.

Multiresolution Sculpting: Hands On

Multiresolution sculpting is an approach to mesh modeling that allows you to intuitively shape and add detail to a mesh by pushing and pulling polygons, similar to how you might model with clay. Multiresolution sculpting can create the rough forms of a model from a simple mesh primitive, or add greater detail to and improve the form of existing models.

Sculpting a Monster Head

For this tutorial you will be sculpting a monster's head. A monster's head is ideal for a first attempt at sculpting because:

1) It allows exaggerated detail, which frees you to play around with the tools without worrying about unrealistic results;

2) It can have horns and other protrusions that make perfect sculpting examples;

3) You can play with a wider variety of interesting textures for your monster's skin; and

4) When you show your work to your critics (i.e. friends and family) they'll be much more likely to call your first sculpting attempts "genius" than if you had tried a realistic human head.

A Primitive Base

Before you begin sculpting, you need a base. For this tutorial, you'll start with the default cube. If you're not already working with a new Blender session, start one now (Ctrl-X).

The View Properties panel.

If you like, you can turn off the view's grid and axis lines, which will de-clutter the view, by choosing View Properties from the "View" header menu and adjusting the panel to match the illustration. Also, you can turn off the transform manipulator (Ctrl-Spacebar, then choose Disable) as it can get in the way of sculpting.

Multiresolution

Normally, when working with a mesh, the addition of detail is more or less irreversible. If you want to make a large-scale change after adding detail, say, drastically increasing the size of the upper portion of a model, you must select and transform all of the small faces and hope for a smooth transition. With multiresolution modeling, this restriction is removed. Even if you add the equivalent of four rounds of subdivision to a mesh, you can still return to the very basic, undivided shape and change it, with those changes propagating through to the other levels of detail.

Choosing View Properties from the View menu.

Let's make the cube "multiresolution." RMB to select the cube and press "Add Multires" in the Multires Panel of the Editing buttons (F9).

The Multires panel of the Editing buttons.

You should see a new button, "Add Level," appear in the Multires Panel. Press the Add Level button four times. You will see additional buttons and some sliders appear in the panel. The slider immediately below the Add Level button should read "Level: 5." If you look in the upper right hand corner of your Blender application header you should see "Fa: 1536," meaning that your object now has 1,536 faces.

Clicking on Add Level.

The Multires panel after adding five multires levels.

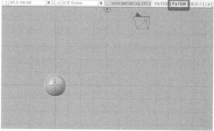

The face count on the main header.

Sculpting panel

Now you will enable sculpt mode. From the mode menu (which currently reads "Object Mode"), select "Sculpt Mode." On the Multires panel, two additional tabs appear: "Sculpt" and "Brush."

Choose Sculpt Mode from the header dropdown menu.

Pressing the N-key in the 3D view brings up a floating panel that contains many of the same options as the Sculpt and Brush panels. If you like the convenience of a floating panel, feel free to use it. Be aware, though, that instructions pointing you to the panels on the Edit buttons should be redirected to the floating panel.

At the bottom of the Sculpt panel are three Symmetry buttons. Enable the "X" Symmetry button. Much like the mirror modifier in standard mesh editing, symmetry will allow you to sculpt on one side of the model and have your work duplicated on the other side automatically.

The Sculpt panel in the Edit buttons.

The Sculpt floating panel.

X Symmetry enabled.

Zoom in so that the head fills the 3D view. Before using the scroll wheel for a standard zoom, try this: press Shift-B and LMB drag a box tightly around the default cube. When you release the mouse button, the view will zoom to the space you just outlined.

Draw Brush

Finally, you're ready to sculpt.

Take the brush — represented by the circle in the 3D view — and place it at about two thirds of the way up the model. Do a LMB drag along the surface of the model forming the brow ridge of your monster. While the LMB is held down, you can scrub back and forth over an area to transform it even further. If you don't like how your stroke went, Ctrl-Z to undo and try again.

The brow ridge.

Notice how the sculpting is duplicated on the other side of the model as you work with the brush. MMB rotate the view to ensure that the stroke looks okay from different angles. You can also split the 3D view into separate parts and set them to different viewing angles.

You will probably want to have only a single 3D view when working with very high resolution models, as multiple views during sculpting can slow things down considerably.

Brush Size and Strength

Although you can use the sliders on the control panels to change the size and strength of the sculpting brushes, there is a faster, more intuitive way to do so. With the mouse in the 3D view, pressing the F-key lets you resize the brush by moving the mouse. Similarly, Shift-F will adjust the brush strength. As with other transformations in Blender, clicking with the LMB accepts the change, while RMB clicking or pressing the Esc-key will cancel it.

After you've created the brow ridge, rough in a ridge for the nose as well. Right now you are just trying to lay things out and give a general form to the head. A very rough shape is fine.

You'll now use the Subtract mode of the Draw brush to hollow out the eyes a bit. This can be done in one of two ways — either by clicking the "Sub" button on the sculpt panel, which will switch the brush to subtract mode; or by holding down the Shift key while sculpting. Holding the Shift key reverses the brush mode temporarily. If you will be continually sculpting in Subtract mode, it's best to use the Sub button, but since you are only doing a brief subtract, simply use the Shift key method.

The nose roughed in.

Back in regular Add mode (let go of the Shift key), you can add a line to represent the lips.

You now have a goofy looking blob person.

The eye areas hollowed out by drawing in Subtract mode, and a very rough lip form added.

Draw Brush

Grab Brush

Let's give your head some more realistic and interesting proportions.

Switch to the Grab brush: either with G-key in the 3D view, or by pressing the Grab button in the Sculpt panel. Notice that it doesn't have any add, subtract, or airbrush buttons. Nor does it have a strength slider.

> *The Size slider value is not the same as it was for the Draw brush. Each brush has its own control set, and keeps its own settings for size and strength. However, Symmetry settings are shared by all brushes.*

Set the size of the Grab brush to 200, its maximum setting. Now "grab" the mesh by clicking and holding the LMB. Drag the mesh to where you want it and release the LMB.

If you are zoomed out you can grab more of the mesh in a single click. Grab and pull some of the mesh to form the jaw. Also, you can grab and pull the side of the head to make it wider or narrower. You will find that in some view angles it is easier to grab and position the mesh to your liking than in others. Be sure to rotate the 3D view to ensure that your shaping of the model looks okay from different angles. You won't be able to achieve something like the illustration with a single grab and pull.

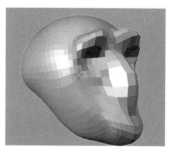

Try to think of using these brushes like actual paint brushes — several small, light strokes in an area will give more control and better results than hammering away with a house-painting brush.

Let's add two more levels of resolution. Press the Add Level button in the Multires panel twice. You should now be at level 7 multires and the main header should show 24,576 faces.

What you are trying to achieve with the Grab brush.

Layer Brush

It's time to add the basic shape of the ears. First, change to the Layer brush, either with the panel controls or the L-key. Set the Strength of the Layer brush to its maximum. The Layer brush raises the mesh a preset amount, and never more. So, if you need to build up a volume greater than the preset, you will need to repeat the stroke a number of times. Rotate to a view that shows the side of the head and draw an ear shape. You should repeat the stroke until you have a decent amount of ear built up.

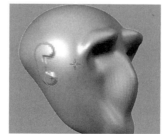

One pass of the Layer brush.

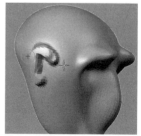

The ear after five or six Layer brush passes.

Inflate Brush

The Inflate brush can be used around the edge of the ear to give it a bit more thickness. Press the I-key (or the Inflate button on the panel) and draw with the Inflate brush along the edge of the ear. Once again, several small overlapping strokes at a lower strength will give a more organic effect than a single, high-strength attack.

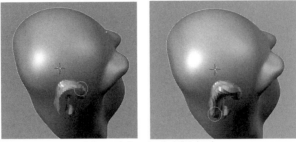

Before and after using the Inflate brush.

Use the Layer brush (L-key) in subtract mode to push the interior of the ear in a bit.

Now, go back to the Inflate brush (I-key). This time, put it in subtract mode and bring the size down to about 15. Use it to hollow out an area behind the top of the ear, giving it some separation from the rest of the head.

Switch to the Grab brush (G-key) and adjust the shape of the ear a bit more. In the illustration, we've stretched the tips up to give the ears a more wolfish look and rotated them out from the head a little more.

Hollowing out the area behind the ear.

Change to the Smooth brush using the S-key and get rid of any lumpy, spiky or flat areas on the ears or skull that were created when making the ears. Start with the Smooth brush's size at about 100, and adjust it as you see the need.

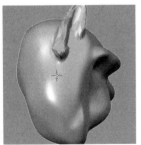

The adjusted ears.

Using the Inflate brush in add mode, draw on the tip of the nose to make it more bulbous. Switch to subtract mode with the Inflate brush (Shift-key) to hollow out the nostrils. Once again, use the Smooth brush (S-key) to smooth out any geometry that has become sharp or too strange looking.

At this point, you can fool around with the tools to create some horns, spines and bumps on the top of the head. Try making several protrusions, each using a different tool (Draw, Grab, Inflate, Layer) to see how the results differ. In the sample model we'll forgo horns and a spine, opting for some nice teeth instead.

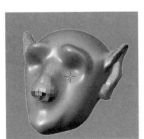

The tip of the nose has been inflated, and the nostrils deflated.

You'll be adding some finer details now, so add another level of resolution with the Add Level button.

　　　　　　　　　　　　　　　　　　　　　　　　　Inflate Brush

Improving Performance

Depending on the power of your computer, you may have begun to experience a bit of slowdown in the responsiveness of the tools. Here are a couple of ways to speed things up.

Partial Redraw

When you entered Sculpt mode in the 3D view, a new menu appeared on the header. In the new Sculpt menu is a "Partial Redraw" option. Enabling this can give a substantial boost in sculpting speed, but may also introduce some display artifacts. When in Partial Redraw mode, you will no longer see the individual faces — the model will be smooth. It may look a bit different, but can be worth it when working with high Multires levels.

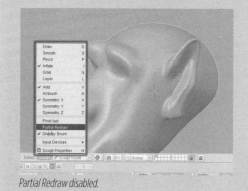

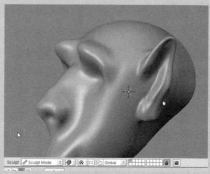

Partial Redraw disabled.　　　　　　　　　　　　　　*Partial Redraw enabled.*

Another useful speed trick is to hide a part of your mesh. There are three ways to do this, each with a slightly different effect.

Mesh Hiding

Press Alt-B then LMB drag across a portion of the model. At first, it seems as if the view has simply been cropped to only show a part of the mesh. Not so. Use the MMB to rotate the view, and you will see that the view itself is still intact. The model only displays the faces that were within the dragged rectangle, as though it had been used to core the mesh like an apple. When working with the Alt-B hiding method, be aware that sculpting strokes that travel into invisible areas will still sculpt, so be careful! Press Alt-B again to view the entire mesh.

Ctrl-Shift-LMB is another method of mesh cropping. This version actually removes the hidden parts of the mesh from the sculpting tools' influence, meaning that sculpting into hidden parts of the mesh will have no effect on it. This includes any parts of the mesh that would normally be affected because of the Symmetry buttons — sculpt strokes made on a mesh will not be reflected onto the other side if that portion is hidden. While using this method of hiding, be aware that adding or changing a multires level will cancel it, showing the entire mesh. To view the whole mesh, either Ctrl-Shift-LMB drag in an empty area of the 3D view or press Alt-H. This method gives the best performance boost of any of the hiding techniques.

Shift-B and LMB drag. This is the "zoom to border" trick you learned at the beginning of the chapter. While it's not exactly a method of hiding geometry that would otherwise be on screen, zooming tightly into an area for detail work results in large portions of the mesh being off screen, and can increase performance.

Wrinkles Using Inflate and Pinch

Monsters are usually worried or concerned about something, so let's add forehead and brow wrinkles with the Inflate and Pinch brushes.

Wrinkles Using Inflate and Pinch　　　　　　　　　　　　　　　　　　　　117

Ctrl-Shift-LMB drag a rectangle across the forehead region to hide the rest of the model. With the Inflate brush's strength set fairly low, make two parallel strokes on the forehead, about a brush-width apart.

Drawing a rectangle with Ctrl-Shift-LMB to show only the forehead.

The wrinkles inflated.

Press the P-key to select the Pinch brush. Pinch pulls any parts of the mesh within its area of influence toward the center of the brush. Drag the Pinch brush along the crease. The gap between the two inflated ridges will begin to close. Make several passes with the Pinch brush until the valley begins to look more like a crease.

With the Smooth brush, blend the transition from forehead to wrinkle. You can use the Grab brush to pull parts of the wrinkled area back into the forehead if they seem too lumpy.

The wrinkles pinched.

Wrinkles between the eyebrows, before smoothing.

Repeat the procedure to add vertical wrinkles between the eyebrows.

Once you're happy with the wrinkles, you can reveal the whole mesh by pressing Alt-H.

Saving Your Work

Multires meshes, especially when used at higher levels, can make for fairly large files. Hard drive space is cheap these days, but there's no reason to be wasteful. So, before saving, enable the "Compress File" option on the File menu. If you haven't saved your sculpt model up until this point, you should do so now.

Eyes

There are two ways to create eyes for a model. The first, and the one necessary if you are planning to animate later, is to carve out eye sockets, create entirely separate sphere objects, and place them "inside" the head. Then, it is a matter of shaping the eye openings to properly fit the eye objects, and sculpting details such as eyelids and creases. However, if you are creating a static image and want to have a "complete" sculpture, you can simply sculpt the eyes as part of the model.

In this example, you will be adding the eyes directly to the sculpture. In a front view, use Ctrl-Shift-LMB drag to hide everything but the area around the eyes.

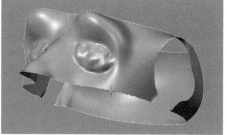

Using the Draw brush (try Size: 27; Strength: 25), start to build up the eyes. You are just drawing strokes for volume, and it won't look very eye-like for now. After you have the basic volume created for the eyes, change over to the Smooth brush. Drop down a multires level or two by clicking on the left side of the Level spinner to make smoothing go faster.

Roughing out the eyes.

Once the eyes look fairly smooth, use the Level spinner to return to multires Level 8. Then, add a level of multires, taking you to Level 9. Inflate and draw the general form of your eyelids. Remember to draw them closed a little, and not to put the eyelid lines at the seam between the eyeball you've created and the rest of the head.

Continue alternating between smooth and inflate until you're happy with the shape of your eyelid and eye.

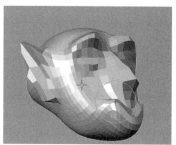

The eyes with protuberant eyelids.

Working in Lower Multires Levels

We'd like you to step back from details for a moment and change some of the larger structure of the head. In particular, you need to actually create a mouth and redefine the lower half of the face. While this could be done at the current high level of detail, there is an easier, faster way.

Using the "Level:" spinner on the Multires panel, turn the level down to 5. The model is now significantly less detailed, showing more general forms. One of the great things about multires modeling is that any changes you make to the mesh on a lower level carry through to the higher levels, and vice versa. Even though you didn't shape the level 5 mesh like this, it has been pushed and pulled into this state by the actions you've taken at other levels.

The rougher forms of level 5.

If Partial Redraw is enabled, disable it now, so that the individual faces show.

With the Grab brush set to a fairly large size (75 or so), drag upward on the lower, outer rim of the jaw to form the basis of a more pronounced jaw and two upward-facing tusks.

The lower jaw pulled out and up.

At this point, your monster head may look significantly different than the one in these examples, and that's fine. Sculpting is a very organic process, and the odds are that even if we recreated all of the illustrations for this chapter, following the exact same process, they would be different each time. Depending on the exact topology of your monster head, the next set of instructions may work more or less well. If you just can't seem to get your tusks and mouth to follow the example exactly, don't worry. The example is just that: a sample to learn from, not something that needs to be duplicated.

With the rough form created for the base of the tusks, move up to multires level 7 to continue adding more detail.

Using the Draw brush, create a fat line around the base of the tusks that will form the lower lip. It'll look fairly ugly at this multires level, but you'll smooth it in a bit.

Up in multires level 8, put a separation line between the base of the tusks and lips.

Switch to the Smooth brush, and give it medium values (50-60) for both size and strength. Smooth the lower portion of the lip into the rest of the face until it blends nicely and seems to be a continuous piece with the rest of the model.

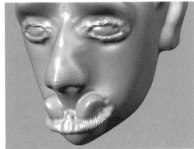

The lower lip drawn in.

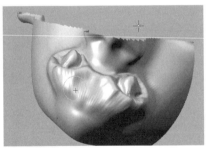

The lip blended into the lower jaw.

You will notice many details in the above illustration. They were created using the same method as you used earlier when making creases in the brow: parallel inflation strokes, then pinch in the middle and smooth. The model itself is done at this point. You can continue to add details, extra tusks, horns, etc., as you like.

Using Textures as Brushes

A monster should have strange skin to go with its horns, long ears and tusks. The sculpting tools allow you to sculpt with a textured brush.

In the buttons window, go to the Texture buttons (F6), and click on the Brush button of the Preview tab. To add a new brush texture, LMB click on the top texture channel to activate it and click the Add New button.

The brush texture panels.

Using Textures as Brushes

Any of Blender's textures, including Image textures, can be used as brushes. From the Texture Type menu that appears, choose "Musgrave." Many of the texturing options are described in greater detail in Chapter 9.

The Musgrave options panel.

From the Musgrave panel that appears, change the "Multifractal" setting to "Rigid Multifractal." All you've done here is chosen a texture that will look sufficiently nasty when applied to a skin. Finding a good noise texture for your projects is mostly a matter of trial and error, although the Materials and Texturing chapter of this book can give you a good starting point.

With the Musgrave noise texture set, move back to the Edit buttons (F9). In order to use the new texture brush, either go to the Brush tab in the Edit buttons or focus on the "Texture" section of the Sculpt Properties floating panel.

The Brush panel.

If it's not already active, click on the texture channel labeled "Tex," then click on the little automobile icon to have Blender assign the name "Musgrave" to the texture. Make the rest of the panel match this illustration:

Enabling the 3D button will apply the texture to the model throughout 3D space, as opposed to "painting" it onto its surface. When 3D is enabled, a Size control will appear. Like the SizeX/Y/Z controls in the Map Input panel of the Material buttons, this size spinner works the opposite of the way you would expect. Raising the value decreases the size that the texture is applied at. Set the Size control to around 400.

Now, use the Draw brush on the cheeks of your monster and watch the ugly ridges form within its surface.

For some variety, create a different texture brush for the rest of the head. Return to the Texture buttons, and select the next empty texture channel. Add a new texture with the Add New button, and select "Voronoi" from the Texture Type menu. You'll just use the default Voronoi settings, so go back to the Edit buttons and the Brush panel.

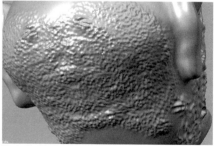

A nasty texture for a nasty creature.

This time, set the brush to "Drag" style instead of "3D." Rotate to the back of the monster head and begin to use the new texture brush in Draw mode. Immediately, you can see the difference between "Drag" and "3D." When working with the 3D option, it was almost like the brush was causing a texture that was already within the model to grow and become clear. With the Drag option, you are using a single instance of the texture, stamping and smearing it as you work the brush.

The back of the head, brushed with a different texture.

Using Textures as Brushes

The finished monster head.

When working in Drag mode, you can change both the size and rotation of the stamped texture interactively. When changing the brush size with the F-key, you actually see a representation, right within the brush, of the texture that will be used. Likewise, you can use Ctrl-F to rotate the texture for even greater variation, and see it rotate right on your display.

All Done

At this point, you can call the model finished. If you were going to go a few steps more, you could disable Symmetry and put in details that differed from side to side like scars and warts. You could also drop down to detail level 5 and pull some of the general shapes out of symmetry as well. Whether you decide to do that or not, you will have learned a great new way to create organic models: Blender's sculpting tools.

One last tip:

The sculpting tools are "experiential," meaning that the more you experience them, the better you will become. We encourage you to start this same tutorial from scratch, and, knowing what you know now, see if you don't come out with a significantly better result the second time.

A second time through the tutorial will give even better results.

All Done

Multiresolution Sculpting: Discussion

Much like Blender's UV unwrapping tools, the multiresolution sculpting work flow is best understood by doing. The tools themselves are fairly simple, but it is in their implementation that they find their power. This discussion section will serve better as a reference for someone who has already acquainted themselves with the general procedures of multires sculpting in the tutorial section. It would also be helpful to have worked through Chapter 4 if you don't already understand the basic concepts and terminology of mesh modeling.

Multiresolution Meshes

Sometimes after you've seriously subdivided a mesh object to add fine details, you wish that you could go back to the un-subdivided version to make large scale structural changes without disturbing the fine work you've already done. Your best bet in that case is to start trying to push and pull the mesh with the Proportional Editing Tool and hope that things don't distort too badly.

With multiresolution modeling, though, you can do exactly that. What begins as a simple mesh can be given increasing levels of detail, yet each level of subdivision is maintained and adjusted as you work on the model, and remains accessible. One could sculpt a head with incredibly fine details, then later decide that the overall proportions of the face were off and fix them simply at a level of detail that could better accommodate such changes.

A mesh is changed into a multiresolution mesh by clicking the Add Multires button on the Multires panel in the Edit buttons (F9).

Once a mesh has been made multiresolution, it cannot have geometry added to or subtracted from it in Edit mode. Existing geometry can still be transformed there, however. Also at this point, Shape Keys (Chapter 8) and multiresolution are not compatible, and Blender will prevent you from using them together should you try.

The Multires panel after clicking "Add Multires."

Multires levels are added by clicking the Add Level button. The current level that is displayed in the 3D view and available to work on is set with the "Level" spinner. The working level may also be set by using the Page Up and Page Down keys. Changes made at any level will propagate to other levels, so if you move the entire right half of a mesh upward at a high level of detail, the low level version will follow, and vice versa. It is best to work in whatever is the lowest level of detail to which the current task lends itself.

The Multires panel after clicking "Add Level."

If you create too many multires levels and realize you don't need them, they can be removed by setting the current Level to the highest one you wish to keep and pressing the "Del Higher" button. In the same way, lower levels of multires that you find no longer useful can be deleted by pressing the "Del Lower" button, which will get rid of all multires levels below the current one.

If you have completely finished using the multiresolution properties of a mesh and want to use it in conjunction with Shape Keys, or to change the actual geometry, use the "Apply Multires" button. This function removes all multires properties, turning the object back into a regular mesh as it appeared at the current multires Level

Multiresolution Meshes

setting. If you have nine levels of detail and press "Apply Multires" when on level six, the resulting mesh will be the one from level six: all finer detail is lost.

Although they are dealt with in the same chapter and often used in conjunction, multiresolution modeling and the sculpt tools can be used independently. Any mesh may be changed using the full range of sculpting tools, just like any mesh can be made multires and worked on with strictly traditional polygon transformation tools.

The Sculpting Tools

Sculpting is begun by selecting a mesh object and setting it to Sculpt Mode on the 3D header. When an object is in Sculpt Mode, the Sculpt and Brush tabs appear within the Multires panel. Also, the floating N-key Transform Properties panel in the 3D view turns into the Sculpt Properties panel, which combines the functionality of the Sculpt and Brush Edit Buttons panels. As in other modes, the Properties panel is shown and hidden with the N-key.

The sculpting tools are utilized by LMB clicking and dragging on the model in the 3D view, as though painting.

There are several sculpting brushes available. Each brush uses its first letter as a hotkey, which makes them easy to remember. If you don't want to learn the hotkeys, Ctrl-Tab will bring up a menu of the different brushes in the 3D view.

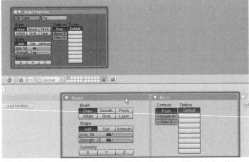

The Sculpt Properties panel, along with the Sculpt and Brush tabs. Note that the Sculpt and Brush tabs have been torn off into separate panels in this illustration.

Draw: Pulls the mesh in the direction of the average of the Normals of all influenced faces. D-key.

Inflate: Pulls each face in the direction of its individual Normal. I-key.

Smooth: Averages the faces of the mesh that fall within its area. Sculpting with the Smooth brush reduces lumps, bumps, wrinkles and any other details it comes across. It is also good for fixing areas of a mesh that have become spiky or crumpled due to over-inflating or pinching, or where a mesh has overlapped itself. S-key.

The bulge on the left was created with the Draw brush. The one on the right with Inflate. Notice how the faces near the center of the inflated area have grown, while the ones on the drawn section have remained the same size.

Pinch: Pulls everything within its brush area toward the center of the brush. P-key.

Layer: Raises the mesh, but only to a certain height that is dependent on its Strength value. Unlike the

Inflate and Draw brushes, Layer will not create a rounded dome if repeatedly applied, but will instead create a plateau. L-key.

Grab: Acts very much like the G-key grab command in Edit mode while using the Proportional Editing Tool. Advantages of using it in Sculpt mode are that it is single LMB-click and drag, without worrying about selecting vertices or faces. G-key.

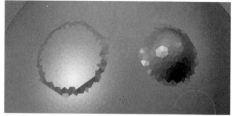

The effects of the Draw brush on the right, with the Layer brush on the left.

Add/Subtract: Draw, Pinch, Inflate and Layer may be used in either Add or Sub (Subtract) mode. Subtract mode simply inverts the effect of the selected brush type. Subtracting in Draw or Layer pushes the mesh instead of pulling; Inflate balloons the mesh away from the brush; Pinch pushes faces away from the center of the brush. The tools default to Add mode, and can be changed to Subtract by clicking the Sub button on the Sculpt panels. Brushes can also be temporarily toggled to Subtract mode by holding down the Shift key while sculpting, or switched permanently by pressing the V-key.

Airbrush: Enabling the Airbrush option causes the selected brush to be applied for as long as the LMB is held down, regardless of whether the mouse is moving or not. A-key.

Adjusting Brush Size and Strength: The size and strength of the brushes can be set by moving the sliders on the Sculpt panels, or with hotkeys. Adjustments to these values are made on a brush-by-brush basis. In other words, each brush (Draw, Pinch, etc.) holds its own settings, which will be retained if you switch brush types and come back.

The hotkey for adjusting brush size is the F-key. When pressed, the brush is resized interactively in the 3D view by moving the mouse until the brush circle is the desired size. Pressing the LMB accepts the new size, while RMB cancels. Shift-F adjusts brush strength in the same fashion. When changing brush strength in the 3D view, please note that a tighter, more concentrated (though smaller) circle indicates higher brush strength, whereas the large but more diffuse circle signals lower strength.

As it is with other transformations, you can also enter a value directly when adjusting size and strength. Pressing the F-key in the 3D view, then typing "25" and Enter will set the brush strength to 25.

Symmetry

Pressing the X, Y, or Z-keys (or the buttons on the panels) enables sculpting symmetry along that local axis. This tool simply mirrors any brush strokes you make along the indicated axes, so if your object is not symmetrical to begin with, it may not produce the desired effect. You can work with any combination of symmetry buttons enabled at once. The normal workflow is to use symmetry during the creation of an organic sculpture, but to turn it off before adding finishing details to make the object more believable.

Textured Brushes

Any of the brushes can sculpt with textures, although its usefulness is limited with the Smooth and Pinch brushes. Textures are created in the Texture buttons (F6, Chapter 9), and can be added to the texture brush

Symmetry

stack directly in the Sculpting Brush panels by selecting an empty texture channel and choosing a texture from the popup menu to the right. Unlike the Material buttons texture stack, the ones here are not layers of a single texture. Each is its own separate brush and will only work when selected.

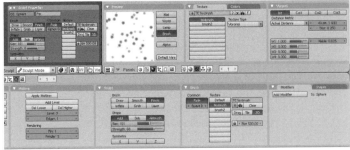

Texture brushes added on the Brush panels, with a Brush texture created in the Texture buttons.

Any texture, including Image textures, will work with sculpting, but the generic noise textures Musgrave, Voronoi, and Distorted Noise are the most frequently used for sculpting textures into organic surfaces.

Textured brushes may be used in three modes: Drag, Tile and 3D, selectable to the right of the texture stack.

3D mode applies texturing based on the 3D coordinates of the faces being sculpted. This texturing mode treats the sculpture as though the texture already exists within and throughout it, and is only revealing it. The Size control that appears when 3D is selected works opposite to the way you would expect. Increasing the Size value decreases the sculpted size of the texture. When working in 3D mode, try a Size value of around 500 to get your bearings.

Drag mode works with a single area of the texture, "stamping" that same texture image over and over as you drag. When adjusting brush size (F-key) and strength (Shift-F) in this mode, a black and white representation of the actual texture is shown within the brush's circle in the 3D view. For variety, the texture may also be rotated interactively with Ctrl-F.

Tile mode works on the same principle as the Drag brush, in that it uses a single portion of the texture, but creates offset instances of the texture, based on the Size control that appears when Tile is selected. This Size control sets the distance over which the brush will repeat the portion of the texture it is using. A Size that is half the value of the current brush size is a good starting point.

Where to Begin?

Multiresolution sculpting can be used on any mesh object. Some sculptors prefer to begin with the mesh primitive that most closely resembles their target sculpture (i.e. a sphere for a head, a four-sided cone for an ancient pyramid, etc.). This will always work, but can lead to tens of thousands of unneeded faces in areas like the back of the head, as all sections of the mesh will receive the same levels of detail. For maximum efficiency, it is often better to work from a mesh that has been carefully subdivided by hand before entering multires mode, creating significantly more faces in areas that will require greater detail during sculpting (like the eyes and mouth), while leaving the back of the head with only a few faces.

Limitations

Currently, the maximum polygon count of a Blender mesh is limited by the amount of RAM that your system can give to a single process. It is also limited in workability by the speed of your processor and the capabilities of your graphics card. Standard Windows XP is limited to 2 GB per process with data limited to roughly 1.5 GB; Mac OS X is limited to 2.4 GB per process. Linux processes can generally access 3GB of RAM.

Through experimentation, we've found that multiresolution meshes are limited to around 3.2 million quad faces on standard Windows XP with 2GB of physical ram. A non-multiresolution mesh can have over 4 million faces. On OS X, a multiresolution mesh has similar but possibly slightly higher limits. On Linux, you may be able to greatly exceed these polygon counts, even for 32 bit systems.

The number of faces that a mesh contains can be seen in the upper right of the main header, beside the version number of Blender ("243 Ve: 57922 | Fa: 57920") The "Fa" refers to the number of faces in the active object.

Some Windows XP systems encounter problems achieving even 1.6 million quads with the above hardware. You'll have to try it with your particular configuration to see.

To achieve very high polygon counts, you will need to disable Global Undo (see Chapter 14) when changing multires levels or changing modes: those actions push the entire current, gigantic mesh onto the undo stack, requiring a significant amount of memory. Once you reach the desired multires level or mode, you can re-enable Undo.

Improving Performance

At high poly counts you may find that the brush begins to lag. Here are some things you can do to speed it back up.

Hiding part of the mesh

You can hide parts of your mesh with Ctrl-Shift-LMB click and drag. Parts of the mesh falling outside of the box you describe will be hidden. You should experience an increase in both your graphics card and sculpting performance. Ctrl-Shift-LMB click and release without dragging, or Alt-H, will reveal the full mesh again.

Partial Redraw

You can turn on 'partial redraw' via the Sculpt menu. This option uses a simplified OpenGL drawing method, causing a possible increase in drawing artifacts, but often giving a substantial increase in drawing speed on most systems. On some graphics cards, however, this option can result in a slow down instead of a speed up.

Disable Brush Drawing

This might provide some speed improvement on ATI cards. Brush drawing, the circle that indicates the current brush size, can be disabled by un-checking "Display Brush" in the Sculpt menu.

Averaging

You can adjust the 'Averaging' setting in the Sculpt menu. This setting interpolates between mouse positions. If sculpt is drawing too slowly, it will assume that you sculpted between your current position and the last position it recalls and fills in between them. This can improve the smoothness of the sculpt, but will decrease the precision of your strokes. In some cases, it may actually decrease sculpting speed.

Only using a single 3D view

At lower multiresolution levels, your graphics card should be able to handle drawing the sculpture in several 3D views at once. At high poly counts, though, you will probably want only a single 3D view open in order to achieve maximum sculpting performance.

Beyond these steps you can take from within Blender, there are more expensive routes to enhancing sculpting speed. Purchasing additional RAM, up to your system's limit, or an entirely new and up-to-date computer system will give the best sculpting experience available. Unfortunately, sculpting is taxing on a system's RAM, processor and video card, so there is nowhere to cut a corner that will not significantly affect its performance. Fortunately, Blender is efficient, and sculpting and multires will function quite well on older, weaker systems, as long as you avoid the enormous face counts of high multires levels.

Odds and Ends

Modifiers and Multires

You can use modifiers with multires, but there are some caveats and limitations. It's not always useful to have modifiers working at the highest multires levels. To set the level of multires on which you would like modifiers to function, use the Pin control on the Multires panel. Modifiers that change geometry in some way, like Subsurf, ignore all multires levels above the Pin setting when rendered. Modifiers that affect the shape of the mesh, like Armature and Curve, will have significantly different results depending on the Pin level at which the modifier is applied. Generally, shape modifiers will give the best results at the lowest multires level.

Creating Normal and Displacement Maps

At this point, Blender does not have the capability of generating tangent space normal or displacement maps. Currently, the preferred method is to export your high resolution mesh object and a low resolution version that have been UV unwrapped and use external tools such as Xnormal on Windows (other options on Windows are ORB, NVIDIA Melody and ATI NormalMapper); ATI NormalMapper for OS X; and DeNormGen for Linux. In order to export the high resolution version of the object, you may need to use the "Apply Multires" button first (remember to do that on a copy of the file so you retain a good, working version of the sculpture). The best exporters for such objects in Blender tend to be OBJ, 3DS, Collada and LWO.

Character Animation: Hands On
by Ryan Dale

Character Animation: Discussion

Ryan Dale

Grad student by day, Blenderhead by night (well, sometimes grad student by night, too), Ryan uses Blender partly for figures in scientific presentations but mostly for playing around with character animation. Ryan participated in the first Blender Summer of Documentation by writing the Introduction to Character Animation tutorial. The full version of the tutorial (only part of which is in this book) can be found on the Blender wiki and covers the workflow of bringing a character to life from modeling and rigging all the way through animating and adding sound.

Character Animation: Hands On

Introduction

In this tutorial, you'll use some of Blender's animation tools to create an action: a wave of the arm. This very simple action will be blended later with a more complex animation.

The Action Editor is where you create individual actions: blinking the eyes, nodding the head, a walkcycle, and so on. Later, you can mix the actions in another window called the NLA Editor. While complex "acting" for the main characters in an animation should probably be done in a single Action, the NLA is excellent for building variety in characters that do not hold the main focus of scene.

In the "examples" folder on the included disk, find the file called "characteranimation.blend" and open it with Blender.

The file contains a fully rigged and skinned character. He's a little goofy looking and rather dynamic. Let's call him Hank.

Setting Up Your Workspace

When you first open the file with Hank, you are in the "1-Animation" screen. This is the default animation screen that comes with Blender, and as it works fairly well, you can use it with some minor adjustments.

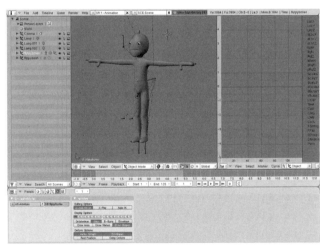

Default screen layout when opening characteranimation.blend

The Ipo window on the right, which you've seen before in Chapter 3, won't be needed right now. Replace it with an Action Editor window. An Ipo window can only show the keys for one object or bone at a time. When working with character animation, you need to see keys for many bones at once so you can easily adjust and align their timing

Introduction

relative to one another. This is the Action Editor's job. As you animate your character, each bone that receives even a single keyframe appears in the Action Editor.

Creating a Wave

RMB click on the armature to select it. The first thing you will notice is that you can't see the armature when it is inside Hank's mesh. How can you work with it if you can't see it? One solution would be to just work in wireframe mode. That could be handicapping, though, as character animation relies on visual feedback from the character itself. The better the visualizations of a character's poses are, the better the final animation will be.

Changing the Ipo view to an Action Editor.

With the armature selected, check out the Armature panel in the Edit buttons (F9). Enable the X-Ray option. Now, the armature is visible regardless of whether it is inside or outside the mesh.

To pose and animate an armature, you need to enter Pose Mode. This can be selected from the main modes pop-up menu on the 3D view header, or with Ctrl-Tab. As the frequently-used Edit mode is the Tab-key, this is a pretty easy one to remember.

Enable X-Ray on the Armature panel.

When you enter pose mode, many of the bones of the armature turn gray, while some are yellow. The yellow bones have constraints on them, which you can learn about in Chapter 7.

Bone transformations work much like object transformations, using the same methods and hotkeys: manipulators, mouse gestures, and G/S/R. One difference you will notice is that sometimes asking for a translation (grab move, G-key), results in a bone rotating instead. Some bones, like the ones in the middle of Hank's arms and spine, are parts of longer chains of bones. They are not free to translate in space. Instead of simply having translation controls for these bones do nothing, they trigger a rotation instead.

Before you begin animating, let's make the job a little easier. In the Timeline window in the middle of the screen are the animation playback controls that were covered in Chapter 3. You'll make use of another one of those controls now. Enable the button with the red dot, commonly seen in audio/video devices as the Record button.

The Record button to enable automatic keyframing.

You have just enabled automatic keyframing, meaning that any bone that moves or rotates will automatically have a keyframe set on the current frame. This will prevent the unfortunately common occurrence of setting a complex pose, then accidentally advancing the frame number and losing it.

If you have been changing your user preferences and have enabled the "Avail" option for keying, you will have to set initial keyframes manually with the I-key. If you haven't changed the keyframing preferences, then you don't need to worry about it for now.

How to Pose

For the wave, you want to raise the hand and arm into the air, tilting the hand outward a bit. By selecting each arm bone and applying rotations, you could achieve such a pose, but it would be difficult and rather unintuitive. If you like, try to use RMB selection and R-key rotation on the arm and hand bones to get something like this pose:

Very difficult, no? One thing you may have noticed when rotating the bones was that as soon as you moved them, they turned a bright blue. The blue color is an indication that a bone has at least one keyframe set. Because of the automatic keyframing you enabled a moment ago, each rotation resulted in a keyframe.

RMB select all of the now-blue bones and use Alt-R to clear any rotations you may have set.

The arm raised to wave.

Now RMB on the bone called "hand.l" to select it. It is the first bone of the left hand immediately following the two longer arm bones. On the Armature panel in the Edit buttons, enable the Auto IK option.

Auto IK enabled.

Use Grab mode (G-key) to move the hand. This time, translating the hand bone pulls the rest of the arm around with it, letting you create the pose much more intuitively. When you have the hand close to what looks like a decent pose for the beginning of a wave motion, disable Auto IK.

Inverse and forward kinematics are covered in Chapter 7: Rigging and Skinning. If you've not worked through that chapter and do not plan to, it's enough to say that IK, Inverse Kinematics, lets you pull an entire chain of bones by moving a target bone, instead of posing each bone individually.

You need to adjust the hand a little so it tilts away from the body. Many Blender animators prefer to use the manipulators for bone rotations like this, as they give excellent visual feedback. If the Transformation Manipulator isn't showing, enable it on the 3D header, or with Ctrl-Space. When the manipulator is visible, set it to Rotation mode.

With the manipulator set to the default Global mode on the header, it's not very useful. Change it to Normal, which will cause the manipulator to align itself with the active bone. Now, LMB clicking on any of the manipulator's orbits and moving the mouse will rotate the bone along that axis.

The hand with the rotation manipulator.

Although you don't have to use the manipulators for bone rotations, they certainly can help. If you prefer, continue to use the R-key. When working with hotkeys and bones, you will probably find it most useful to rotate with the R-key R-key combination to enter trackball mode, or the R-key followed by XX, YY, or ZZ to enter local

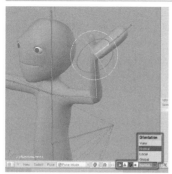

rotation mode with the Alternate Transformation Space set to "Normal" on the 3D header. However, the illustrations in the rest of this chapter will show the manipulator.

Work with the hand in Auto IK mode and by directly rotating it until it looks something like the earlier illustration.

Now, take a look at the Action Editor. It has several rows, or channels, and each has a name that corresponds to a bone in the active armature. When you select a bone in

The manipulator set to Rotate Normal mode.

the 3D view, the corresponding channel in the Action Editor is selected. Just the same, RMB clicking a channel name in the Action Editor selects that bone in the 3D view. In the illustration, the lower_arm.l channel is selected.

The Action Editor.

Notice that some yellow diamonds have appeared within the Action Editor's timeline. These represent the bones' keyframes. They are aligned with the vertical green frame indicator that functions like the ones in the timeline and Ipo windows. Currently you're on Frame 1, and the animation keys were all added there.

Finishing the Wave

Advance to Frame 5, either by LMB clicking in the Action Editor or Timeline, or by pressing the Right Arrow key four times.

The pose from Frame 1.

The new pose on Frame 5.

The pose on Frame 5 was created by RMB selecting the middle arm bone and rotating it slightly on its X axis (the red manipulator orbit).

After rotating the bone, look at the Action Editor and note the following:

- Keys were automatically inserted for the arm bones that were moved. In this case, only the "lower_arm.l" bone was moved.

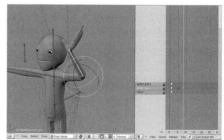

The Action Editor after moving the arm bone on Frame 5.

- No key was inserted for the other arm bones, since they weren't altered in this frame. It is true that they changed position, but they were not directly manipulated, and maintain their position and rotation relative to their parent bone further up the chain.
- The Frame 1 key for "lower_arm.l" is deselected (white) and the new Frame 5 key is now selected (yellow). The keys from Frame 1 for the other bones are still selected, as they didn't receive new keys. .

Bones remain where they are until you tell them otherwise. Since you did not set another key for the "hand.l" bone in frame 5, it will stay in the same position as it was in frame 1.

LMB scrub the timeline back and forth between Frames 1 and 5 to see the animation. It's rather basic, and if that bothers you, feel free to wave with your own hand and arm a couple of times. Watch it in a mirror. Observe how much of the motion comes from the shoulder, the elbow and the wrist. Try to see what the extreme positions of the actual motion are. Then, try to use those positions and your other observations to set new keys on Hank to make a more believable motion.

Completing the Wave Action

Advance to Frame 9.

You'll perform the next bit of animation in the Action Editor itself. Like most Blender window types, the Action Editor uses a common set of selection, transformation, duplication and deletion tools.

- A-key to select/deselect all keys;
- RMB and Shift-RMB to build selections; and
- B-key followed by LMB drag to select an area.

You're going to duplicate the keys from Frame 1 and move the duplicates to Frame 9, copying Frame 1's pose to Frame 10. Doing so will cause the Wave action to start and end in the same position. To get a better view of what you're doing, use the mouse's scroll wheel and MMB-drag to zoom into and position the view of the keys.

Perform the following actions:
- Deselect all keyframes by pressing the A-key;
- Use the B-key to bounding-box select all the keys on Frame 1;
- Duplicate the selected keys with Shift-D; and
- This should seem familiar — the duplicate keys begin their life in Grab mode.
Move the duplicated keys to Frame 9. Don't worry if you hit Frame 9 exactly or not.

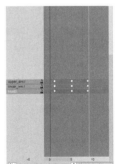

The pose keys from Frame 1 duplicated and positioned near Frame 9.

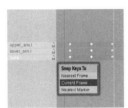

The key Snap menu.

With the new keys still selected, press Shift-S, which, as you may remember from Chapter 3, brings up the Snap menu. Choose "Current Frame" from the pop-up menu, and the keys are snapped to Frame 9. Of course, if you are in the habit of holding down the Ctrl-key while moving key markers, your keyframes will never fall between frames, and you won't need to adjust them afterward like this.

Scrub back and forth between Frames 1 and 9 to make sure you are happy with your animation.

On the Action Editor's header, change the name of this set of keyframes to something useful, like "Wave."

You have now created your first character animation Action.

Creating a Walkcycle

A walkcycle is an Action that includes one full stride of a character walking, both with the left and right feet, that, when played over and over (cycled), gives the appearance that the character is walking.

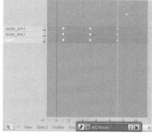

Naming the Action.

Click the "X" next to the name of the Wave action on the header to unlink it. LMB click on the selector and choose "ADD NEW" to create a new, blank Action. If you wanted to work with the Wave action again, it could be accessed by selecting "Wave" from this same menu.

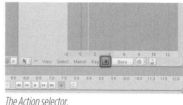

The Action selector.

An armature can have many different Actions, but only one active Action, which is displayed in the Action Editor. This active Action is the one that will receive any new keys you insert, and whose keys you can directly edit.

Set the frame counter to Frame 1.

In the 3D view, use the A-key to select all the bones in the armature, and use Alt-R and Alt-G to remove all rotations and translations, returning the armature to its rest position. Notice that even though the "Record" button is still pressed, keys were not added when you cleared rotation and location. Automatic key insertion does not recognize clearing location or rotation as actual movement.

The Contact Pose

Where we're headed.

In a walkcycle, the contact pose is the point when the leading foot just touches the ground in front of the character. It's generally the first pose to animate in a walkcycle.

In the 3D view, switch to a side view (Numpad-3). Make sure Auto IK is off. The legs are set to already use IK, and Auto IK will cause them to malfunction.

Move the lowest bone in the spine, "spine1," down a little along the Z axis so the legs bend a bit.

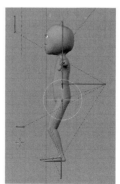

Move the spine down.

Creating a Walkcycle

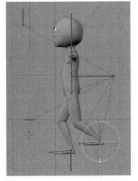

Move the left leg controller back and up.

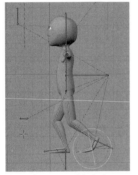

The toe bone rotated clockwise.

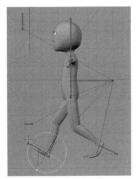

Make the mesh hit an imaginary floor.

RMB select "leg.l." You may have to MMB rotate the view to see and select it accurately, and return to side view after making the selection. Notice that you are not selecting one of the actual leg bones, but the bone that extends below the left foot. This bone is the IK target of the left leg. Move this bone back and up to match the illustration.

With "leg.l" still selected, rotate it counter-clockwise so the toe of the foot passes through the "floor." In this case, it might be simpler to use the R-key, as the rotation you want corresponds exactly to the side view.

The foot rotated.

RMB select the toe bone, called "toe.l," and rotate it clockwise so that it appears to be bent up to meet the floor. Be aware that you may have to alternate between tweaking the foot and toe positions to get this just right.

RMB select the controller bone for the right leg: "leg.r." Move it forward and rotate it clockwise to try to match the illustration.

The goal here is to get the heel of the mesh's right foot to appear to contact the ground at the same level as the toe of the left foot. The right foot should not be so far out in front of the body that the knee becomes completely straight which can cause the foot bones to detach from the leg.

Now pose the arms (illustrations on the next page). Once again, an easy way to do this is to turn on Auto IK and drag the hands into position, bringing the arms along for the ride. Afterward, disable Auto IK and finely adjust the rotations of the arm and hand bones with the rotation manipulator set to Normal mode.

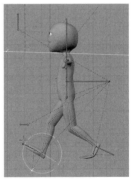

The right leg moved forward and the leg controller rotated.

You may have to rotate or change the view several times to get the arms to go where you want them to. Keep in mind that when people walk, the legs and arms have opposing motion: right leg forward means right arm back. It might take a while to get things just right, but be patient — learning to create poses does not happen in an instant. If you can do so without feeling silly, you should try walking naturally around your work area, observing how your arms and hands swing and twist to give yourself a reference. Of course, if you have a video camera available and record reference motion to play back frame by frame, it can be an even bigger help.

Here are front, side, and top views of the posed arms:

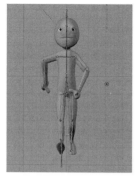

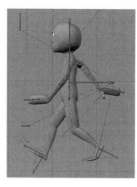

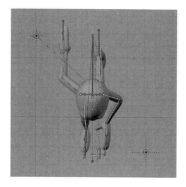

An off-angle perspective view of the pose.

Making a good walkcycle requires more than just arm and foot positioning.

Spend some time on the spine. When walking, the leading hand twists the top of the spine toward it, and the trailing arm twists the lower spine toward it. Be aware, though, that by rotating the lower spine bones, the upper spine, arms, neck, and head will rotate as well. You may have to compensate by rotating the upper spine bones back the opposite way. Rotations of the spine during a walkcycle should be subtle: they add hints to the overall motion. Over-rotating will produce animation that looks wild and unnatural.

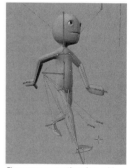

The same perspective view, with the noted spine adjustments added. The differences in a still frame are almost unnoticeable, but will have a good effect when animated.

Flipping the Pose

Select all bones in the armature with the A-key. Click the "Copy Pose" button at the bottom of the 3D Window. This copies any existing keys (location, rotation, and scale) from all selected bones.

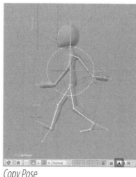

Copy Pose

You may have to use MMB Drag to pan the header of the 3D Window back and forth in order to find these buttons.

Press the Up Arrow key to advance ten frames to Frame 11. Click the "Paste Flipped Pose" button.

This pastes the pose as a mirror-image of the pose you just copied.

Paste Flipped Pose

This is one reason to strictly follow the naming instructions when creating a rig in Chapter 7. Because they end in ".l" and ".r," Blender recognizes that the bones are on the opposite side of the body and does the calculations to automatically insert the mirrored pose for you.

Advance to Frame 21, and this time press the normal Paste Pose button (not Paste Flipped Pose). The effect is similar to when you used Shift-D to duplicate and reposition the keys in the Action Editor in the "Wave" action.

In the Action Editor or the Timeline, scrub the frame slider back and forth between Frames 1 and 21 to see the character walk. From the first contact pose to the opposite contact pose and back to the first again takes 21 frames in this case. Everything else in the walkcycle is just filling in keys between those frames.

Recoil Pose

You made a rough cut of a walkcycle with just one pose and a couple of mouse clicks! When played back as animation, though, it's clearly inadequate. You can improve the walk by adding poses in between the ones you just created.

The recoil pose is where the front foot takes the weight of the body. The forward foot flattens, and the body sinks down a little. Here's how to create it:

Move to Frame 2. RMB select the right leg controller "leg.r." Clear its rotation with Alt-R. You need to set a key with this bone un-rotated, but if you recall from before, clearing a rotation does not set a new key. To do that, press the I-key and select "LocRot" from the keying menu that pops up.

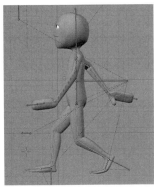

The recoil pose.

Grab the bone at the base of the spine ("spine1") and move it down a little. A new way to approach a small move like this is to press the G-key, and then press the Down Arrow key a couple of times. Pressing Enter confirms the move.

Now, select only the "spine1" and "leg.r" bones. This may be easier to do by RMB and Shift-RMB clicking on their names in the Action Editor. Use the Copy Pose button, and paste the flipped pose 10 frames later into Frame 12.

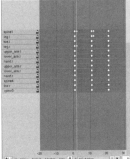

The Action Editor after pasting the flipped recoil pose. The order of channels in the Action Editor depends on the order in which keys were added, so your screen might show a different order than this.

The Passing Pose

Move to Frame 6 and adjust "leg.r" (the leg controller) and "toe.r" so that the foot is flat on the ground. If you are having trouble telling exactly where the ground should be, move to Frame 1 and LMB in the 3D view to set the 3D cursor at the very bottom of the forward foot. When you move back to Frame 6, use the 3D cursor as a guide. Adjusting the right foot and toe rotations will most likely only involve clearing the rotation with Alt-R, then setting a rotation key by pressing the I-key and choosing "LocRot."

Move "spine1" up until the right leg is mostly straight.

Select only the bones moved in this step and copy and paste the flipped pose 10 frames later into Frame 16.

The Passing Pose.

The High Point Pose

Move to Frame 8. Move "spine1" upward a little, so that the right leg straightens completely and just begins to stretch. Fix that stretch by moving "leg.r" until it re-attaches to the bottom of the leg bones. Rotate "leg.r" so the toe goes through the floor just a bit. Rotate "toe.r" so it is level with the floor again.

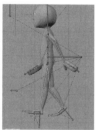

Grab the controller for the left leg, "leg.l," and move it forward and up.

After selecting the four bones that were changed in this step — leg.r, toe.r, leg.l and spine1 — copy the pose and paste the flipped version on Frame 18.

The right foot and leg adjusted.

The left leg moved forward and up.

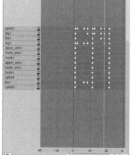

Looping the Animation for Playback

In the Timeline window, set the Start: frame to 1 and the End: frame to 21. This will restrict animation playback to only that frame range, letting you watch your work in a continuous loop. In the 3D view, press Alt-A to start the playback. Pressing the Esc-key stops playback.

The Action Editor after completing the walkcycle.

When looping an animation like this, there will be a slight "catch" as the frame counter returns to 1. This is normal behavior. Don't be fooled into thinking that there is a glitch in your animation. In the next section on the NLA Editor, you will be able to get a better view of how well your Action cycles.

On the Action Editor's header, name this new Action something useful like "Walkcycle." Also, in the timeline view or the Scene buttons, change the overall animation end frame value back to something higher, like 250, so we no longer loop from frame 1 to 21 on playback.

The NLA Editor

You now have two separate actions: "Wave" and "Walkcycle". There's another window in Blender called the NLA Editor (Non-Linear Animation) where you can combine the two actions.

Choosing NLA Editor from the window type menu

Change the Action Editor window to an NLA Editor. This will be your primary workspace.

You can also change the far left window to a new Action Editor, just to make some things clearer in a bit.

This is the NLA Editor. It may not look like much, but it's quite powerful. Right now there are only two rows: "hankbones" and "Walkcycle." "hankbones" refers to the armature you have been working with,

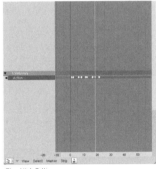

The NLA Editor

although any objects that have Actions associated with them would show up here as well. "Walkcycle" refers to the current action selected in the Action Editor. Just like the Action Editor, the diamonds in the right-hand portion of the window indicate the location of keyframes along the timeline. As opposed to the Action Editor, though, keyframe markers in the NLA view are present if a key exists at that frame for any channel of the associated Action.

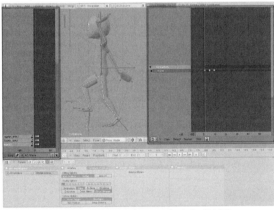

The Wave Action in the Action Editor, also appearing in the NLA Editor.

If you still have an Action Editor window available, use the header Action block selector to switch to the "Wave" Action. If you can't see the Action block selector on the header, you may have to MMB drag on the header to show it. In the NLA Editor, note how the row under Armature has changed, with three diamonds representing the three keyed frames from the "Wave" action.

Converting an Action into an NLA Strip

Switch back to the "Walkcycle" action by selecting it in the Action Editor. With the mouse over the NLA Editor, press the C-key to convert this Action into an NLA strip.

"Walkcycle" converted into an NLA strip.

By converting the Walkcycle Action into an NLA strip, you've created a "window" to the walkcycle, letting you see the Action through the NLA Editor. This "window," the Action strip, can be manipulated without affecting the original action. Strips like this can be scaled and moved along the timeline, blended, stacked and set to repeat. You can create any number of strips that show you the same Action. A single strip represents the entire "Walkcycle" Action. You haven't changed the original "Walkcycle" Action in any way, and none of the transformations you can do in the NLA Editor will affect the original.

The NLA Editor can be bypassed by clicking on the icon to the left of an object's name. Clicking toggles between NLA mode (a series of stacked strips) and Action mode (affectionately called the "shark-attack victim" icon). It doesn't look like a button, but it is. NLA mode, with the strips, tells the object to use the strips in the NLA Editor for its animation. Action mode, with the shark attack guy, tells the object to ignore the NLA Editor and use the Action linked in the Action Editor instead. Before proceeding with this tutorial, make sure that Hank is set to NLA mode.

The "Strips" icon, set to use NLA animation.
The "Shark Attack" icon, set to bypass NLA and use the Action Editor.

With the mouse over the 3D view, press Alt-A to play the current animation. Note that the character takes two steps and then stops at frame 21, because, well… that's the end of the walkcycle. This is about to change.

In the NLA Editor, press the N-key. As in other window types, the N-key brings up a transform properties panel. In the NLA Editor, this panel is used to work with strip settings.

Change the value of the Repeat control to 2. Notice that the NLA strip representing the walkcycle now has a faint line down its center, dividing it into two sections. Play the animation again with Alt-A in the 3D view. The character takes four steps now, because the walkcycle action plays twice. However, the walkcycle is almost too fast to see,

The NLA Transform Properties panel.

because those four steps are being taken in only 21 frames. Twice the number of steps in the same amount of frames equals twice the speed.

In the properties panel, change the Strip End control to 41. Play the animation again. There are still four steps, but they are now taking place over the course of forty-two frames, which gives a better result.

Repeat set to 2 and Strip End set to 41.

By changing the values in the strip properties panel, you can adjust the speed and number of steps of a walkcycle. Strips can also be scaled directly within the NLA Editor with the S-key.

Set the walkcycle to a Repeat value of 5. Make sure the frame counter is on Frame 1. Now, instead of typing numbers into the panel controls, press the S-key to begin scaling.

This is easier if you have the mouse cursor to the right of the end point of the current strip before scaling, otherwise the scaling gets reversed.

The NLA Editor

Scale the strip until its end point is near Frame 120. Now you have 120 frames of walking!

You may have to zoom the NLA Editor out with the mouse's scroll wheel and pan it with MMB dragging in order to show the range of frames from 1 to 120.

Mixing Actions in the NLA Editor

With the mouse over the main workspace of the NLA Editor, press Shift-A. Shift-A brings up a selector of all the actions that are available to add to the selected object. Choose "Wave." Adding an Action Strip can also be done through the Strip menu on the NLA Editor's header.

Repeat set to 5 and the strip scaled to around Frame 120.

Adding an Action to the NLA Editor with the Shift-A popup.

When it is added to the NLA like this, the new "Wave" strip is automatically selected, and its properties are shown in the Transform Properties panel. Using the panel, change the "Wave" Action's Repeat value to 4. Change the "Strip End" value on the panel to 50.

Press the G-key and slide the strip along the timeline until its beginning (its left most edge) is around Frame 23. This is one of the reasons that the NLA Editor is so powerful: once actions are defined in the Action Editor, you can add, scale, move and even duplicate them along the timeline as a single entity.

Press Alt-A in the 3D Window to view the animation. Not bad, eh? The wave and the walkcycle happen simultaneously. Use the LMB to scrub the timeline over the end of the Wave strip, though. When the strip ends and the hand comes back down, it's a pretty abrupt motion.

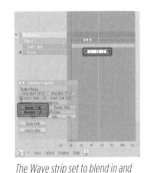

With the Wave action still selected, change the "Blendin:" and "Blendout:" values on the panel to 7. The NLA strip reflects this change by putting "blending" ramps at the beginning and end of the strip. Now, LMB over the beginning and ending of the wave strip again. This time, the animation blends much more smoothly. Press Alt-A in the 3D window to see it play in time.

The Wave strip set to blend in and out over seven frames.

Changing the Stacking Order of NLA Strips

The stacking order of the strips in the NLA Editor is significant. In the example, the top-most strip is the "Walkcycle" action, and under it is the "Wave" action. Strips on the bottom override strips above them.

In other words, the "Walkcycle" action has keys for all the arm bones. The "Wave" action *also* has keys for the left arm bones. As the "Wave" strip is below the "Walkcycle" strip, it overrides any conflicting keys.

To change the stacking order of a selected strip, press Ctrl-PgUp and Ctrl-PgDn. Try this: RMB select the "Wave" strip and move it up one row with Ctrl-PgUp.

Play the Animation

The wave no longer happens. This is because the "Walkcycle" keys for the left arm bones override the "Wave" keys for the same bones.

Change the stacking order of the "Wave" strip so it is under the "Walkcycle" strip again (select "Wave" and use Ctrl-PgDn) and everything is back in working order.

You may be wondering why the walkcycle has Hank essentially treading water. This is the traditional method of producing walking animation. A walk is keyframed "in place," like you have just done, then matched with a whole-body forward motion later. While you can still use this technique in Blender, there is a better way. Before you finish the tutorial, we'll show you how to do it.

Offset Bone

Toggle the NLA Strip/Shark Attack icon so that the NLA is disabled, and the Action in the Action Editor will be used. In your Action Editor window, make sure that "Walkcycle" is selected. The last bit of setup is to LMB click in the upper channel that reads "Walkcycle" in the NLA. This tells Blender to use the timing of the original Action, as opposed to the timing dictated by the strip's length and repeat settings.

Set the frame counter to Frame 1, and make sure that the Record button is selected in the Timeline window so that any transforms you make are automatically keyed. With that done, you're ready to revisit the Walkcycle Action.

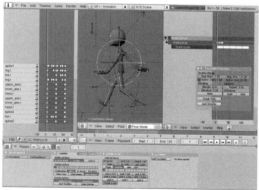

Blender is ready to use Offset bone. The "Wave" Action has been removed from the NLA in our illustrations for clarity

RMB select the bone sticking out of Hank's back called "master." This bone can be used to move the entire armature at once, which is exactly what you're going to do. This bone will make Hank move forward during his walkcycle, and then provide the NLA with a reference when putting together repetitions of the Walkcycle Action.

In the 3D view, go into a side view, make sure that Hank's armature is in Pose Mode, and RMB select the "master" bone. Press the I-key to insert a keyframe, and choose "Loc" from the menu that pops up.

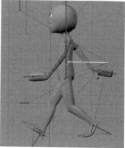

Hank, with the master bone selected, and the 3D cursor set to mark the position of the heel.

LMB click in the 3D view to place the 3D cursor at the base of the heel of the forward foot. The 3D cursor will be your reference point. Use the Left Arrow key to advance one frame. See how the foot moves to the right of the cursor a bit? With the master bone selected, press the G-key to Grab and move it. Moving the master bone moves the entire character, and your goal is to get the base of the heel back into the same relationship it had with the 3D cursor on the previous frame.

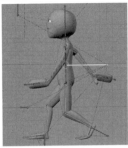

Advance forward one frame at a time, watching as the forward foot moves to the back. Stop advancing frames as soon as the heel comes away from the floor. At this point, you've gone one frame too far. Use the Left Arrow key to go back one frame, the last frame on which the foot is completely flat on the floor. Using the Grab tool again, move the master bone so that the heel of that same foot moves forward until it is once again on the 3D cursor.

At this point, Hank's weight will shift to the toes of this foot. So, LMB click to

By moving the master bone, the heel is kept exactly on the 3D cursor.

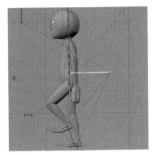

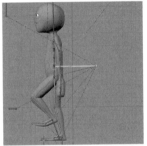

The same frame and pose as the previous illustration, but the 3D cursor has been moved.

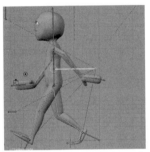

Now that the armature has been moved to match the 3D cursor location on Frame 11, Hank has moved one half of a stride forward.

reposition the 3D cursor at the place where his toes meet the ground. As it is the point of Hank's body that bears his weight against the ground, the toe is the new reference point.

Advance to Frame 11, which is where you have the other foot finally meeting the ground. Move Hank forward using the master bone until the toe of the rear foot hits the center of the 3D cursor.

You can scrub through the first half of the Walkcycle action to see Hank move forward. When you're done with that, return to Frame 11.

The procedure for the second half of the walkcycle is exactly the same as the first:

- Set the 3D cursor to the location of the heel of the forward, weight-bearing, foot.
- Advance one frame, and adjust the master bone location so the heel stays in place with the 3D cursor.
- Advance to the frame just before that heel leaves the ground, and adjust the master bone and armature location again.
- Change the 3D cursor location to the toe of the weight-bearing foot.
- Advance to the last frame of the Action, Frame 21, and move Hank forward one last time so the trailing toe matches the 3D cursor's location.

When you play the Action back now, Hank should walk forward for an entire stride, and his feet should stay planted on the ground reasonably well as he moves.

Offset Bone

This is not the ideal way to use the Offset Bone feature. If you were starting a walkcycle from scratch, knowing you wanted to use the Offset Bone, you would keyframe your character to move forward from the very beginning, with a "master" bone that did not control the feet. This would allow them to be truly anchored in their location when touching the ground.

If Hank is moving forward for you reasonably well, then it's time to return to the NLA Editor. Change Hank's NLA setting back to using NLA strips with the toggle icon. Make sure that the Walkcycle strip is selected, and that it still has a repeat value set (it was 5.0 in the previous example). In the "OffsBone" control immediately below the Repeat value, enter "master" — the name of the master bone you were just keyframing.

Now, if everything happened correctly, playing the animation in the 3D view should show Hank walking forward continuously! You can change how far he goes by adjusting the Repeat value.

The NLA Editor with "master" set in the "OffsBone" control.

If you like, you can add the Wave again as an NLA strip.

Hi Hank!

Character Animation: Discussion

Character Animation is an enormous topic that can take years to master. This chapter will not teach you how to be a successful character animator. What it will do, though, is give you the basic knowledge of Blender's character animation tools so you can begin to learn how to animate. Once you are comfortable working with Blender's tools, we encourage you to check out some of the great work in the Blender Summer of Documentation "Introduction to the Principles of Animation" by Willian Padovani Germano. Much like painting, character animation is a skill that requires going "outside" of Blender to supplement the learning process.

When producing character animation, you will most often work with a skeleton called an "armature." The bones of the armature can be linked to each other in different ways, and, if done properly, can build a fully control-lable, intuitively movable character rig (rigging is covered in Chapter 7). Each bone in an armature can be transformed individually, as though an armature was a collection of smaller, connected objects.

Although certain armature modes can look almost like blocky character meshes, armatures themselves will never show up in a render. Armatures need to be attached to meshes, so the animation of the armature moves the mesh in turn, producing an animated character. Keyframed armature animation is organized into Actions in the Action Editor. For more complex animation tasks, those Actions can be combined and manipulated in the NLA Editor.

Creating Poses and Setting Key Frames

The bones of an armature are transformed and keyframed in much the same way as normal objects. In order to pose an armature and record the poses as keyframes, an armature must be in Pose Mode, which is accessible from the 3D header, and by pressing Ctrl-Tab.

Selecting Pose Mode on the 3D Header.

Once in pose mode, bones may be selected with the RMB, B-key border select, or the Ctrl-LMB lasso.

Armatures are animated in Pose Mode, which is accessed with Ctrl-Tab.

If a selected bone is attached to other bones as part of a chain, it will only be able to rotate. Bones that form the base of a chain, or that are unattached, are free to move, as well as rotate.

The G, S and R-keys perform their standard functions when working with bones. For your convenience, using the G-key on a bone that is part of a chain and unable to translate acts as though it was a Rotation command.

When posing part of an armature that has great freedom of movement, like a head on top of a neck, try pressing the R-key twice to put the bone into Trackball rotation mode. You may find it more intuitive than the standard rotation modes.

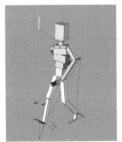

The bones in the middle of the arm can only rotate. The selected bone, which forms the "look-at" target for the character's eyes, is not part of a chain and can be both translated and rotated.

Manipulators

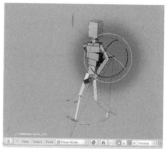

The manipulator enabled in Rotate mode, with the ATS set to Normal. The manipulator is currently applied to the lower left arm bone.

Even if you don't use the Transformation Manipulators when working in other portions of Blender, it's worth it to try them out when doing character animation. Use either Ctrl-Spacebar or the buttons on the 3D header to enable the manipulator and set it to Rotate mode. Once the manipulator is enabled, set the Alternative Transformation Space to "Normal." This will align the manipulator to whichever bone is selected. One thing to watch out for when working with bones is to make sure that the transformation pivot point is set to Median Point (comma-key) and not Cursor, as the latter will give you puzzling results if you are not expecting it.

The advantage of using the rotation manipulator for posing is that it provides one-click access to rolling bones, and excellent visual feedback in what can sometimes be a crowded environment.

G, S and R-keys, as well as mouse gestures, the manipulators and the standard selection methods all function with bones.

Setting Keys

When you translate and rotate bones to create the poses and motion of your armature, you need to set key frames. Pressing the I-key in the 3D view functions exactly like it does everywhere else in Blender. A list of key types appears, allowing you to choose exactly which transformations to key. It is highly recommended, though, that you turn on Automatic Keyframing when working with armatures. Sometimes, you will put several minutes into perfecting a single pose, and it would be a shame to lose your hard work by absentmindedly changing the frame.

Enable Automatic Keyframing by pressing the Record button in a Timeline view.

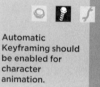

Automatic Keyframing should be enabled for character animation.

The Timeline view and the Record button.

Posing with IK

IK stands for a way of calculating poses called Inverse Kinematics. With IK, you grab and move the end of a chain, say, the foot of a character, and the rest of the leg follows along. Although the foot bone is a part of a chain which would normally limit its movement to only rotation, with IK applied to it, it regains its freedom of movement. You can learn more about setting up IK chains in Chapter 7.

When using a rig with IK enabled, only the target bone of the IK chain needs to be keyframed. The rest of the bones calculate and interpolate their positions on the fly.

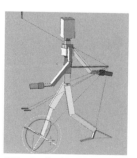

With only a foot bone selected, the entire leg moves to follow.

Manipulators

AutoIK

AutoIK is another posing tool. By enabling "AutoIK" in the Armature panel of the Edit buttons, any bone that is selected and moved becomes the target of a temporary IK chain. In this way, you can start to create poses for non-IK portions of an armature, like the arms and hands, using the convenience of IK, then turn it off and finely adjust each bone's rotation individually.

The AutoIK button on the Armature panel.

As AutoIK is only a posing tool, the bones that it moves will not retain those positions unless each and every one of them receives a keyframe. This is directly opposed to a standard IK chain in which only the target bone receives a keyframe. Of course, if you have Automatic Keyframing enabled as we suggested earlier, keys are set for all necessary bones without you having to worry about it.

The Action Editor

When keyframing object-level motion in Chapter 3, you worked with an Ipo window, which helped you to visualize what was going on with the animation. When working with armatures, though, you may be setting keys for several different bones, in different combinations, at different frames. The Ipo view can only show the curves and keys for one object at a time, so how should you proceed?

The Action Editor shows a high level view of an object's animation.

In the illustration to the right, both the Action Editor and Ipo view are focused on the same piece of object animation. Notice how there is a single diamond along the Action Editor's timeline for each key position in the Ipo window.

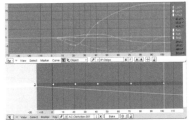

An Action Editor and Ipo window view of the same animation.

This sort of information compression allows you to view animation data from many bones at once.

Each diamond represents some sort of keyframe for the bone that is named at the left of the row. Which kind of keyframe? It could be location, rotation or scale. There is no way to tell short of opening an Ipo window, but in practice it usually does not matter.

The Action Editor showing many bone channels.

The Action Editor is where you keep track of which bones have keys on which frames.

The Action Editor shows keys for many bones at once.

Commands and Functions

Working with the diamond key frames shares a lot of functionality with the objects in the 3D view. Keys can be selected with the RMB, or with the B-key border technique. Keys are moved by pressing the G-key. Holding down the Ctrl-key while moving keys in Grab mode will cause the keys to move in even increments of one frame. When more than one key is selected, using the S-key will scale the selected key positions relative to the current frame marker.

The key in the middle was created by duplicating the key on the left. The yellow bar between them shows you that the position is "held" for those frames.

Keys can be duplicated by selecting them and pressing Shift-D. Duplicated keys, like other Blender objects, begin their life in grab mode, and their positions are finalized by LMB clicking. If you want a bone to hold its position for several frames in the middle of an animation, duplicate the key for the held position and move it several frames to the side.

Sometimes, moving and scaling keys in the Action Editor will result in keys not sitting on exact frame numbers. If you are attempting to line your keys up exactly, this can be a problem. Pressing Shift-S brings up a snapping menu, and allows you to snap any selected keys to the nearest whole frame.

- **Action Editor keys are handled with the same commands as other Blender objects.**

- **Shift-S brings up the key Snap menu.**

Selecting Action Editor Channels and Bones

If you are working with an armature that has dozens of bones, and you are finding it difficult to select the correct bone in the 3D view, try clicking on the bone's channel name in the Action Editor. Doing so selects both the channel in the Action Editor, and the associated bone in the 3D view.

Adjusting the Timing of a Motion

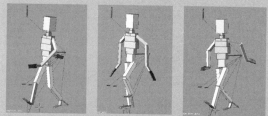

Three frames of a character walking. Note the left arm as it swings back.

Here's an example of how the Action Editor can help you to refine your animation.

The Action Editor looks like this, with the two key markers for each of the left arm bones selected:

Let's say that you wanted the first part of that motion to proceed very slowly, and drastically speed up near the end. You could go into an Ipo window and start messing directly with curves and bezier handles, once for each curve on each bone. But there is a simpler way.

Place the timeline marker halfway between the two keyframes whose timing you would like to adjust. Make sure that the keyed bones are selected. In the 3D view, use the I-key to insert new keys on this frame, using the "Avail" option from the pop-up menu. This will set keys only for Ipos that already have keyframes.

In the Action Editor, two new keyframes spring to life.

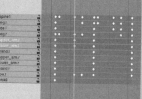

The new keyframes become the active selection in the Action Editor. Using the G-key, move them very near to the set of keys to their right. What this does is to set the midpoint of that motion very near to the end of the motion. The net effect is that the first "half" of the motion takes a long time, while the second "half" happens very quickly.

The new keyframes, which represent the pose at the middle of the motion.

The same technique can give a little life to held positions, too. In this case, though, a set of keys is created very close to one of the endpoints of the motion, then moved to the middle.

Managing Actions

An armature can have many Actions. Actions are created, selected, and destroyed on the Action Editor's header, using the standard Blender data block controls.

Working with the Action Editor View

The Action Editor window is manipulated exactly like an Ipo or other 2D window. All available content can be shown by pressing the Home-key. The view can be zoomed with the scroll wheel and panned by MMB dragging within it. Also, pressing the C-key will center the view on the current frame.

The Action block controls on the Action Editor header.

The NLA Editor

What is NLA, and when should you use it?

NLA stands for Non-Linear Animation. The NLA Editor allows you to take different Actions that were created in the Action Editor, and stretch, combine and order them into a single piece of animation. Where the Action Editor lets you work in detail on a single Action, the NLA Editor lets you see and work with many Actions at once.

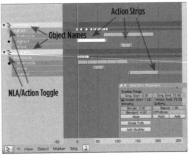

The NLA Editor

The names of the objects that are eligible for NLA appear in the left column of the view. As in the Action Editor, clicking on any of these object names selects that object in the 3D view. NLA information will only display for objects that are on visible layers, so if you know you've used NLA on an object but it doesn't appear in the Editor, the object may be on a hidden layer. Sometimes, objects that should be able to have NLA, like an armature, may not show in the NLA at all. While this can be confusing, it is easily fixed by selecting the object in the 3D view, then using Shift-A to add an Action in the NLA Editor, even though the object doesn't appear there yet. Adding the Action will make the object show up in NLA.

To the right of the object's name and below it are the different strips that represent the Actions. These are called Action strips. Action strips for a particular object can be shown or hidden by clicking on the triangular "collapse" icon to the left of the object's name.

When using NLA, Blender generates animation based on where along the NLA timeline the Action strips fall. If you have an Action for waving with keys on Frames 1 through 25, but wanted your character to actually wave on Frames 65 through 89, you could select all of the keyframe markers in the Action Editor and move them 64 frames forward. Then, any character that used that Action would have to use that same frame range.

However, if you were using NLA, you could simply move the wave Action's strip 64 frames forward on the timeline, and the NLA would produce the animation you wanted, leaving the Action itself in its original condition for easy re-use.

In addition to simply changing locations along the timeline, NLA can be used to cause Actions to occur more quickly or slowly. Making an Action Strip larger causes it to cover more of the timeline, making the original Action play back more slowly. Shrinking a strip will cause the Action to execute more quickly.

Adding and Removing NLA Strips

Action Strips are added to the NLA Editor by selecting the object in the 3D view or the left column of the Editor and pressing Shift-A. A menu pops up with all of the Actions that are available to add to the selected object. Action Strips are added with their first frame wherever the current frame counter is located in the Editor.

Selected Action Strips can be removed with the X-key.

Transforming Action Strips

We mentioned earlier that Action Strips can be moved and resized. The standard Blender methods work in the NLA Editor as you would expect. Pressing the G-key enters Grab mode so you can move selected Strips along their timelines. Strips can be scaled with the S-key. Like collections of key markers in the Action Editor, scaling occurs relative to the current frame bar in the Editor's timeline.

Toggling NLA Mode and Action Editor Mode

The icon to the left of an object's name in the NLA Editor is actually a toggle button, changeable by LMB clicking on it. The two states are:

NLA mode   *Action mode*

When in NLA mode, an armature's animation will be generated by the Strips and settings as configured in the NLA Editor. In Action mode, NLA is ignored, and animation will be generated by whatever Action is set in the Action Editor. If your character seems to be ignoring your NLA setup, this is the most likely culprit.

Layering and Blending Action Strips

As you add more Action Strips to an object, new ones appear below existing Strips. Strips that appear lower in the NLA stack take precedence over Strips that are higher in the stack. If a Strip for walking contains animation keys for legs, feet, arms and hands, and a lower strip contains animation keys for arms and hands, the arm and hand keys from the lower strip will be used in place of the keys from the upper strip.

This is the way that NLA blends animation.

If the stacking of the Strips in the NLA Editor is not working the way you would like, it can be rearranged by selecting a Strip and pressing Ctrl-PageUp and Ctrl-PageDown to move the Strip up and down, respectively.

Strip Properties

Action Strips can do more for your animation than simply changing an Action's location along the timeline and altering its speed. The N-key Transform Properties panel for the NLA Editor lets you set additional options.

The NLA Editor Transform Properties panel.

Strip Start/Strip End: A Strip's location on the timeline and size can be adjusted from the Properties panel with the "Strip Start" and "Strip End" controls. Using the panel, you can enter values directly for the selected Strip's starting and ending points along the timeline, allowing you to perfectly synchronize actions with other events.

Repeat: An Action can be set to repeat by increasing the Repeat value past 1.0. Action Strips that have a Repeat value higher than 1.0 will show small vertical lines wherever the repeats will occur along the timeline. Be aware that using Repeat will not automatically result in a smooth repetition of the Action. If your Action was not created with its beginning and ending pose in the same position, you will see your armature "skip" as it begins each repetition.

Blendin/Blendout: If you layer several Action Strips and scrub over the timeline, you will see that animation for one Strip begins and ends immediately and completely at the start and end of the Strip. This can cause the keyed bones to jump at transition points.

No Blendin/Blendout values on the bottom Strip.   *Blendin/Blendout values have been set.*

To fix this, you can set the Blendin/Blendout values to tell the NLA over how many frames to blend the animation. In the second illustration, the animation for the lower Strip will begin and end its effect more gradually, following the ramp shown on the ends of the Strip. Lower values create a quicker transition, while higher values will take longer.

With the posing and keyframing tools, the Action Editor and the NLA Editor to play with, you'll be busy for a long time learning to make your characters come to life.

CHAPTER **7**
Rigging and Skinning

 Rigging and Skinning: Hands On

 **Rigging and Skinning: Discussion**
by Ryan Dale

Rigging and Skinning: Hands On

The best way to animate a complex mesh object like a character is through the use of Armatures. An armature acts like a skeleton: you actually move the bones of the armature and those bones drive the animation of the character mesh. The process of building an armature is called "rigging," and the process of attaching the armature to a mesh is called "skinning."

Many artists are intimidated by the complicated controls and advanced functionality of the freely available Blender rigs and are put off from rigging altogether due to its perceived complexity. The armatures are excellent, and their creators have put great amounts of time and effort into making them flexible and efficient.

It is possible, however, to create a fairly useful rig without creating dozens of hidden control bones. That is what you're about to do.

Getting Started

Open the file "hank_for_rigging.blend" from the "examples" folder on the included disk.

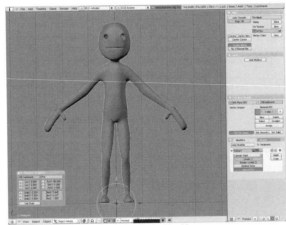

The screen when you open "hank_for_rigging.blend."

This is the Hank mesh that you will be familiar with if you have already worked through Chapter 6. The first thing to notice before you even begin building an armature is that Hank has a rotation and a scale.

It's always a good idea to begin working with character animation and armatures in a completely clean transformational state. With Hank selected, press Ctrl-A to apply the transformations, leaving Hank looking exactly as he does but removing the transformations.

Before working with armatures, use Ctrl-A to Apply all transformations to your mesh.

Now that Hank is ready, create the armature.

The Properties panel for Hank after applying transformations.

Use the spacebar toolbox to Add->Armature. That new object sticking up from the ground at Hank's feet is a bone. Just like adding mesh objects to the 3D view, the armature and bone begin their existence in Edit mode, which will allow you to add and destroy bones, create parent/child relationships between them, and adjust their positioning to fit inside Hank's body. During this stage of armature creation, the Transform Manipulator isn't very useful, so turn it off by using Ctrl-Space->Disable or by clicking the pointing finger disable button on the 3D header.

With the manipulator gone, it's easy to see that the top ball of the bone (called the "tip") is yellow, while the bottom ball (called the "root") is purple. Yellow, as elsewhere in Blender, indicates that the tip is selected. You can see this by pressing the G-key to enter Grab mode and watching the tip move around as you move the mouse. Notice that as you move the tip away from the root, the entire bone grows along with it. When you're done moving it, press the RMB or Esc-key to cancel the transformation, putting you back to where you were when the bone was first created. If you accidentally accepted the transformation with the LMB, remember that you can always Ctrl-Z to undo.

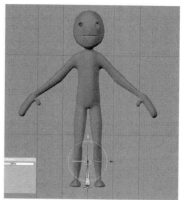

One other thing to notice is that neither R-key rotation nor S-key scaling seem to have any effect on this single bone node.

The new armature, with a single bone.

This bone will be the master bone for the entire armature, meaning that all other bones you add will be connected to it either directly or indirectly, so that when the master bone is transformed, the entire armature will follow it. You could leave it pointing up like this, but most people find that this sort of master bone is better visualized horizontally.

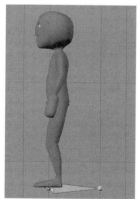

Switch to a side view, and, using the G-key, move the tip of the bone back and downward until it lines up horizontally with the root of the bone. Holding down the Ctrl-key while doing the transformation will help you to get it right on. The length doesn't really matter, but you should make it stick far enough out behind Hank that it will be easy to select even during a cluttered animation session.

RMB click in the center of the bone (anywhere on the bone except the tip and root balls) to select the entire thing. When you do this, more information appears in the Transform Properties panel, as well as in the edit buttons. One of those properties is the bone name. LMB

The tip of the master bone moved back and down.

click on the bone name, in either the Armature Bones or Transform Properties panel, and rename it "master."

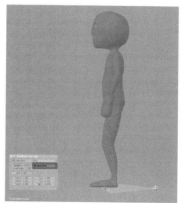

The bone renamed to "master."

• When beginning an armature, add a master bone at the same location as the mesh object's center.

• X-Ray will show bones that would ordinarily be hidden by a mesh.

Notice how a part of the bone is hidden by Hank's feet? When you go to work on the rest of the armature, this could certainly be a problem. If the mesh hides the bones, how can you work on it? You could use the Z-key to toggle into wireframe mode, but there is a better way.

Enable the "X-Ray" button on the Armature panel of the Edit buttons. Now, the armature will always draw in front of the mesh.

The X-Ray button.

The Spine, Neck and Head

You could add a bone for each and every vertebra in the spinal column, but fortunately you don't need that level of articulation. As Hank is a very simple mesh, just two spine bones, with one each for the neck and head, will suffice.

Use the toolbox to add a new bone, with Add->Bone. When the new bone appears, RMB click on the main body of the bone to select the whole thing, then use the G-key to move it so that the root of the new bone rests near the pivot point of Hank's hip.

RMB select only the tip of the spine bone and move it to the small of Hank's back. Although the spine on a character like Hank would be flexible along its entire length in real life, if bent, it would mostly deform the body in two different zones: the upper and lower back. So, it makes sense to put the pivot point of one of your bones at that same point in the body.

From here, the rest of the spine is easy to construct. Hold down the Ctrl key and LMB click on the indicated areas in the illustration:

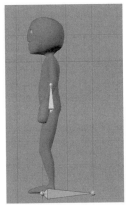

The base bone of the spine, moved into place.

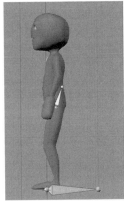

The tip of the spine base, adjusted to the small of the back.

Ctrl-LMB click here to Extrude the base of the spine several times.

The Spine, Neck and Head

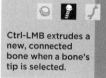

Ctrl-LMB clicking with a bone's tip selected extrudes new bones in a chain. If you've done it correctly, you will have something that looks like this:

Your armature doesn't have to match exactly, but the crucial elements are that the neck bone's root should be at the rear base of the neck and that the head bone be very close to vertical.

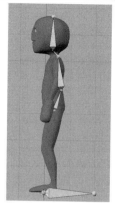

Before you go any further, press the A-key twice to select all of the bones. On the Armature panel in the Edit buttons, enable the "Draw Names" button. You will see that, with the exception of the "master" bone, the rest have fairly useless names like "Bone.001" and "Bone.003". By RMB selecting each of the bones in turn, and using the Properties or Armature Bones panel, change the names to "spine.base," "spine.top," "neck" and "head."

The spine, neck and head bones.

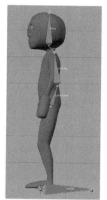

The bones given useful names.

Ctrl-LMB extrudes a new, connected bone when a bone's tip is selected.

Adding Arms

Use Numpad-1 to change back to a front view.

You could now create each side of the body individually, but that would be wasted effort. By enabling the "X-Axis Mirror" button on the Armature panel, you can have Blender help to create a symmetrical armature.

"X-Axis Mirror" enabled.

While X-Axis Mirror will mirror any transformations you make across the center of the armature as long as the bones are named correctly, it will not create the mirrored bones for you. You could create a single bone, then use the duplication and the M-key mirror tools to reflect it on the other side of the armature. This is such a common action, though, that the process has been shortened dramatically for work with armatures.

RMB select the root of the master bone. You might have to MMB rotate the view to get a good shot at it. If so, be sure to use Numpad-1 to go back to the front view before continuing.

Press Shift-E. Shift-E in armature Edit mode triggers a mirrored Extrude. Pull the extruding bone up and to the right until it looks like this:

A mirrored extrusion.

Adding Arms

You may be noticing some differences in the way that your bones have "rolled" around their longest axis, compared to our illustrations. This should not cause any trouble, but if it bothers you, try selecting all of the bones and pressing Ctrl-N to fix their rolls.

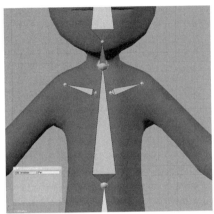

The collar bone in place.

RMB select the right hand bone and move it to the top of Hank's chest. Then, select the tip of the same bone and place it where Hank's shoulder joint would be. The bone on the left side of the screen will follow everything that you do to the right. These will be the collar bones.

RMB select the tip of the collar bone on the right half of the screen. It's now easy to Ctrl-LMB click at the elbow, where the hand joins the arm, at the start of the fingers, and at their tips. Doing so extrudes the bones to form the arm, and, with X-Axis Mirror enabled, the bone creation is duplicated on the other side for you.

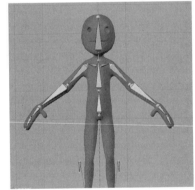

The arms extruded.

Shift-E creates symmetrically extruded bones.

Before things get out of hand with more bones, you should name the ones you just created. The next section shows you how

Naming Symmetrical Bones

RMB select the collar bone on the right side of the screen. In the panels, you can see that the bone is called "master_L." This is because it was extruded from the bone called "master," using the symmetrical extrusion command (Shift-E). Symmetrical extrusion uses the "_L" and "_R" suffixes on bone names to differentiate between the left and right sides of the axis. If you're wondering why the bone on the right side of the screen is tagged with the "_L" suffix, rotate the view a bit and remember that it is the left side of Hank's body.

In order for several rigging and animation features to work properly, these "_L/_R" tags need to remain in place.

Change the selected bone's name to "shoulder_L." Next, select the same bone on the opposite side of the armature and rename it "shoulder_R."

Proceeding down the chain, rename the bones on both sides of the arms to "arm.upper_L/R," "arm.lower_L/R," "hand_L/R," and "fingers_L/R."

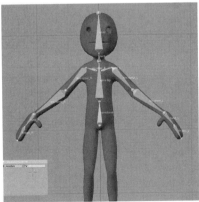

The arm bones on both sides named.

Naming Symmetrical Bones

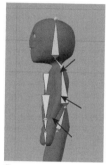

If you are working with an armature and the X-Axis Mirror effect seems to be broken, check your bone names. Not only must bones be in identical locations across the axis, they must also have identical names and the proper suffixes. Working pairs of suffixes for mirrored bones are "_L/_R," "_l/_r," and ".l/.r."

Adjusting the Arms and Hands

If you rotate the view or go into a side view, it becomes obvious that the bones do not follow Hank's mesh very well.

Of course, this is easy to fix. In a side view, RMB click on one of the joints and G-key move it into place. You should only need to move the joints left-right on the screen to get them to fall along the center of the arm's mesh. To restrict motion to left and right only (the global Y axis), you could press the Y-key after the G-key, or click with the MMB once you have started to move the bone toward its position.

The root of the collar bone should be pulled back until it is just inside the mesh.

The arm bones are not even close.

Go into a front view with Numpad-1 and check to make sure that everything still fits, as sometimes the bone positioning can change a little depending on how exactly you performed this last step.

Adding the Legs

The legs will consist of two bones each. RMB select the root of the spine base and Shift-E extrude a new mirrored set of bones down to the knee. RMB back where the roots of the spine base and the two new leg bones all begin. One of the root balls there will be selected, and the only way to really find out which it was is to use the G-key and start to move it. If you grabbed the root of the spine by accident, RMB click to the cancel the move, and use RMB on the same spot to select again.

> You will have to adjust bones in different views to make them fit your mesh.

When you have grabbed and begin to move the root of one of the leg bones, pull it away from the spine until it rests in the middle of the leg/body joint.

Select the tip of the upper leg bone at the knee and Ctrl-LMB extrude to the ankle, which is a little bit above the top of the foot.

The arm and hand bones pulled into place.

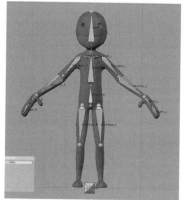

The upper leg bones created and adjusted.

Name the bones "leg.upper_L/R" and "leg.lower_L/R."

Once again, go into a side view and adjust the knee and ankle positions to fall along the centerline of the leg mesh. You will only need to select and adjust the bones for one leg, though, and X-Axis Mirror will continue to take care of the other side for you.

Bone Layers

In addition to the main Layer system for objects, each armature has sixteen layers available for bone organization. For the next part of this exercise, creating the feet, that big master bone will be in the way when making selections and lining things up with the mesh.

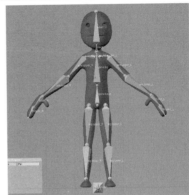

The leg bones named.

RMB select the master bone. On the Armature Bones panel (not the Armature panel), click the layer button on the far right. This set of buttons represents what layers the bone appears on. As soon as you click the far right layer button, both the bone and the contents of the Armature Bones panel disappear. This is because bone Layer 16 is not being shown, removing the bone from the 3D view and deselecting it. Since the Armature Bones panel shows information about selected bones, that information goes away.

The button for bone Layer 16.

Creating the Foot Bones

With the master bone out of the way, you can start to create the foot bones. We're going to tell you how and where to make them now, but we'll explain why later.

In an angled view, RMB select the tip of the lower left leg bone (leg.lower_L). Press Shift-S to bring up the Snap menu, and choose "Cursor to Selection" to move the 3D cursor onto the tip of the bone.

Back in a side view, Ctrl-LMB click behind Hank, at the level of the floor, to extrude a new bone. RMB select the entire new bone and take a look at the Armature Bones panel.

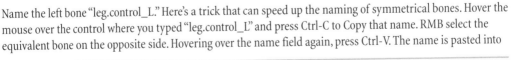

The Armature Bones panel for the new bone.

The "child of" pop-up menu shows which bone the selected bone is a child of. You want this bone, which will be your main foot and leg controller, to not be a child of any other bone. In the 3D view, press Alt-P and select "Clear Parent" from the menu that pops up. You could also have used the menu on the Armature Bones panel to select a blank space for the "child of" control. With the parent relationship removed, the bone is disconnected and can be moved by itself.

Select the leg controller bone on the other side of the armature and clear its parent relationship as well. Unfortunately, X-Axis Mirror will not help you when it comes to these sorts of things.

Name the left bone "leg.control_L." Here's a trick that can speed up the naming of symmetrical bones. Hover the mouse over the control where you typed "leg.control_L" and press Ctrl-C to Copy that name. RMB select the equivalent bone on the opposite side. Hovering over the name field again, press Ctrl-V. The name is pasted into the control, but with an extension: "leg.control_L.001." With the mouse back over the armature, press the W-key and select "Flip Left-Right Names" from the brief menu that pops up. The bone's name changes to "leg.control_R." This not only saves time, but prevents typos.

Select the root of one of the new control bones (you might have to rotate the view a bit to grab one) and move it down until it is aligned along the ground with the bone's tip. If you've un-parented both bones and selected properly, the controller bones should be broken away from the legs, apparently lying on the floor.

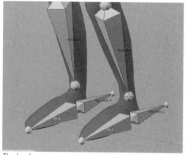
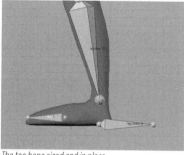

The leg controllers.

From an angled view, RMB select the root of the left leg controller ("leg.control_L"). Back in a side view, Ctrl-LMB click on the toe, extruding a new bone along the length of the foot. Back in an angled view, you will see the mirrored bones, too. Names these bones "toe_L" and "toe_R."

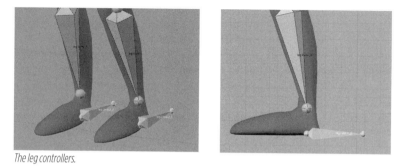

The toe bones.   *The toe bone sized and in place.*

With one of the toe bones completely selected (not just the root or tip), press the S-key to scale. Hold down the Ctrl key to snap the scale to increments of 0.1, and scale the bone down to 0.5. Alternately, you could press the S-key, followed by "0.5 Enter." Next, move the bone forward and up a bit so it touches the front of the toe mesh.

Go back to an angled view and select the root of the "toe_L" bone. In a side view, Ctrl-LMB click once behind the tip of the lower leg bone, then once again a little further back.

Select the joint between the last bone created and the one just before it. Press Shift-S again to bring up the Snap menu and choose "Selection to Cursor." The 3D cursor should still be at the tip of the

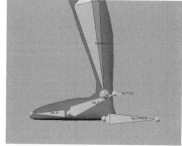

More foot bones.

Creating the Foot Bones

lower leg bone, snapping the new bones' joint to the same place. If you've accidentally moved the 3D cursor by LMB clicking in the 3D view at some point, you will have to reset it by selecting the tip of the lower leg bone and using "Cursor to Selection."

The bones on the other side of the armature should follow along, giving you this:

Name the new bones "foot_L/R" and "ankle_L/R" to match the illustration.

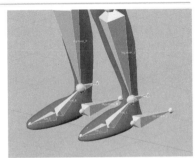

The rest of the foot bones in place, and named appropriately.

Creating Parent/Child Relationships in the Feet

You want the feet and legs to move at the request of the controller bone. You'll get to the legs in a moment, but you can get by with only parent/child relationships for the feet.

Select the "foot_L" bone and Shift-RMB select the "leg.control_L" bone. Press Ctrl-P to make the leg controller the parent of the foot bone. When you make a parent/child relationship with bones, there is one more step than when doing it with regular objects. Upon pressing Ctrl-P, a menu pops up asking "Connected" or "Keep Offset." You've gone to some small trouble to offset the bones in just this way, so choose "Keep Offset."

Now, RMB select "toe_L" and Shift-RMB select the left leg's controller again. Ctrl-P to make it the toe's parent, choosing "Keep Offset." Repeat this procedure on the other side of the armature.

At this point, you have almost all the bones you need to control Hank. The next step will involve adding some constraints, which must be done in Pose mode. Before you temporarily leave Edit mode, though, there is one more thing to do.

Fixing Bone Roll

Remember how you removed the rotation and scaling from the Hank mesh before you began this whole procedure? The same thing needs to be done to the bones before you start constraining and animating.

With the armature still in Edit mode, use the A-key (once or twice, depending on what you currently have selected) to select all the bones in the armature. Press Ctrl-N and accept the pop-up that appears.

Several of the bones, particularly the ones in the arms and legs, roll in place.

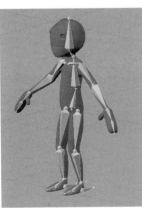
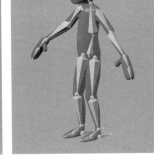

Before and after recalculating bone roll.

What you've just done is recalculated optimized roll values for all the bones. This will make animating significantly more predictable.

With that accomplished, leave Edit mode for a while and see how the armature moves.

Making the Legs Into IK Chains

Armatures can work in three different modes: Edit, Object and Pose. The Tab-key toggles into and out of Edit mode. Ctrl-Tab toggles between Object and Pose modes. Edit mode overrides both Object and Pose modes, so pressing the Tab-key in either mode will take you to Edit mode.

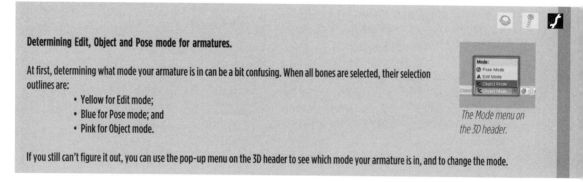

Determining Edit, Object and Pose mode for armatures.

At first, determining what mode your armature is in can be a bit confusing. When all bones are selected, their selection outlines are:

- Yellow for Edit mode;
- Blue for Pose mode; and
- Pink for Object mode.

The Mode menu on the 3D header.

If you still can't figure it out, you can use the pop-up menu on the 3D header to see which mode your armature is in, and to change the mode.

Press the Tab-key to go from Edit mode to Object mode. Then, press Ctrl-Tab to put the armature into Pose mode.

Hank's legs, like the legs of most armatures, will be rigged with Inverse Kinematics, meaning that the leg bones are not posed individually, but by moving a target bone and forcing the legs to follow.

In an angled view, RMB select the bone "ankle_L" and Shift-RMB select "leg.lower_L," in that order. Notice that in Pose mode, selected bones are outlined in bright blue.

Press Ctrl-I, the hotkey for adding an IK constraint. Accept the "To Active Bone" popup that appears. The leg bone should turn a dull yellow. In the buttons window at the right, you will see an IK Solver constraint in the Constraints panel.

Now, to see how this works, RMB select the controller for the left leg and foot, "leg.control_L," and move it around with the G-key. The leg follows the foot, mostly. Now, try some rotations to see how the foot and leg react.

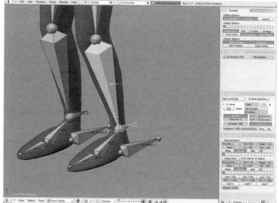

The left leg made into an IK chain.

To work with rotations when posing bones, it is quite efficient to turn on the rotation Transformation Manipulator. By no means do you have to use it, but many animators find that it significantly speeds up their work flow.

Use Ctrl-Spacebar in the 3D view to select "Rotate" from the Manipulator pop-up menu. On the 3D header, make sure that the Alternate Transformation Space is set to "Normal," which will cause the manipulator to operate locally on each selected bone.

With the LMB, click and drag on the different orbits of the rotation manipulator to see how the leg and foot react to rotations of the controller. When you are done playing around, make sure to use Alt-R and Alt-G to clear any transformations you've put onto the bones.

The rotation manipulator, set to Normal space.

One thing you may have noticed is that when rotating the controller around the Z Axis (the blue orbit), the foot turned, but the leg did not follow. This is because IK solving involves the position, not the rotation of the target object. When the controller rotates, the target barely moves; likewise, the leg. Unfortunately, using the "Rot" button on the IK constraint controls does not do the trick.

In order to get the leg to rotate along the Z axis with the controller, you need to add a new bone.

Of course, bones can only be added and removed in Edit mode, so back you must go!

Before switching to Edit mode, RMB select the lower leg bone. Then, use the Tab-key to enter Edit mode. You'll notice that the same bone is automatically selected in Edit mode. Edit mode and Pose mode selections carry over into one another, making it convenient when you are troubleshooting a rig like this.

Adding a LockTrack Constraint for the Knee

You don't necessarily want to have the entire leg chain rotate with the foot. In general, it will be the knee that rotates to keep pace with the foot's direction. If you get up and walk in a circle for a while, you will probably observe that, while the foot can rotate independently of the knee a little, the knee usually follows, a little behind. You can mimic that same behavior by creating a new bone and adding a constraint.

With the lower leg bone selected, go into a side view. Press Shift-D to duplicate the bone and move it forward, away from Hank. Rename this bone "knee_L." Then, scale the bone down until it looks something like this (be sure to scale the bone here, not just grab the root or tip and make it smaller that way. It's fairly important that the bone maintain the same angle and direction as the lower leg bone):

A new bone called "knee_L."

Adding a LockTrack Constraint for the Knee

As you can see from the dashed line, the knee bone is the child of the upper leg bone. You want it to actually be the child of the leg's controller. So, as the knee bone is already selected, Shift-RMB select the controller ("leg.control_L"), and use Ctrl-P to create a parent/child relationship using "Keep Offset."

Press the Tab-key to leave Edit mode. It should have returned you to Pose mode, as that's where you were before. If not, though, use Ctrl-Tab to re-enter Pose mode.

Now, let's add the Locked Track constraint. The easiest way to do this is to first RMB select the knee bone, then Shift-RMB select the lower leg bone. With the mouse still over the 3D view, press Ctrl-Alt-C, which will bring up a list of different available constraints. Choose "Locked Track" and watch your leg bones go kerblooey.

You can always add and configure constraints by using the Constraints panel in the Edit buttons. However, doing it from the GUI saves you from having to enter the names of the target armature and bones.

Locked Track is one of the less-understood constraints. It is like a version of the Track To constraint, whose behavior is obvious, that allows you to prevent the tracking along one axis. So, if you were to prevent the bone from following its tracked target along the Y axis, its length, the bone would rotate only around its length as it followed the target. That is what you would like the leg bones to do.

So, in the Locked Track constraint on the Constraints panel, set the "Lock" control to "Y," so the bone will only roll around its length. But which value to click for the "To" control? If you were to show the Axes for each bone ("Draw Axes" on the Armature panel), you would see that the lower leg bone's Z-axis is the one most closely pointing toward the knee bone. So, in the Locked Track controls, set "To" to "Z." If the Z axis had been pointing away from the knee, the best choice would have been "-Z." When you adjust Lock to Y and To to Z, the leg regains its normal behavior, but with an addition.

Now, selecting the controller bone and rotating with the blue orbit (Z axis) rotates the lower leg bone as well.

To get the upper leg to follow, repeat the Locked Track procedure:
- Select the knee bone first, then the upper leg bone;
- Ctrl-Alt-C and choose "Locked Track"; and
- Adjust the constraint so that "Lock" is Y and "To" is Z.

The next step is for you to repeat this entire portion of the exercise for the right leg. Here's a brief rundown, so you can keep track of what you're doing:
- Create an IK solver on the lower leg, targeting the ankle bone;
- Duplicate, scale and move the lower leg bone in Edit mode to create the knee bone;
- Change the knee bone's parent to the right leg's controller; and
- Add Locked Track constraints to the upper and lower legs, targeting the knee bone.

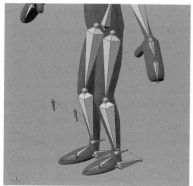

The legs and feet with knee targets and IK in place.

Adding a LockTrack Constraint for the Knee

Restricting Transformations

So you have a leg and foot rig that works reasonably well. But what happens if you (or someone else) grabs one of the foot or knee bones and translates them? Then the rig is ruined. There is a simple way to prevent this.

In Pose mode, make sure that the Transform Properties panel is active. If it isn't, press the N-key to bring it up.

Select the toe bone of the left foot. On the panel, LMB click on the gray lock icons to the left of LocX, LocY and LocZ. This prevents the bone from being moved by a user within the 3D view. The bone can still move as part of a parent/child chain, but direct manipulations are prevented. The front part of the foot should also have some rotation restrictions. LMB click on the lock icon for RotY and RotZ, leaving only RotX unlocked. You will see that on the manipulator, only the red orbit remains.

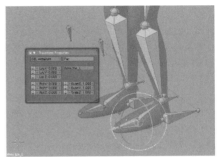

The Transform Properties panel, showing the values for the selected "toe_L" bone. Note that the toe bone's manipulator shows both rotation and translation widgets.

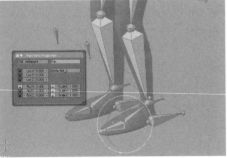

The toe bone locked for translations and most rotations.

Not only does this method prevent a user (or yourself) from breaking your rig during animation, but by removing locked transformations from the manipulator, it gives you instant visual feedback when selecting a bone as to which transformations are available.

Make the same locks on the next bone in the foot, called "foot_L." Lock the bones of the right foot as well. You can duplicate transformation locks by selecting both the bone you would like set up, followed by the bone on which you already have indicated your locks. Then, press Ctrl-C and choose "Transform Locks" from the menu that pops up. This copies the locks from the last-selected bone to the other bones in the selection.

The knee bones that act as the targets for the Locked Track constraints should have their rotations and translations locked, too. Actually, you should leave the LocX control unlocked: translating the knee bones along their X axis can help to control which way the rig's knees point in certain poses.

Finishing the Lower Body Rig

When thinking about other bones to lock the transformations on, the upper leg bones come to mind. In a real person, the upper legs are joined quite tightly to the body — they will never translate. So, locking out translation for those bones is a good idea.

However, there is another feature of a real character that we haven't taken into account. If you grab the base of the spine in Pose mode and move it, the upper legs do not follow, even though in real life, they would be locked together through the pelvis. You want to mimic that behavior in the rig. Having done the work with parenting in the feet, this should be easy.

Use the Tab-key to enter Edit mode.

The natural thing to do would be to make the spine base the parent of the upper leg bones. If you try it, which you can, you'll find that the parent/child indicator line runs to the upper tip of the spine bone. This can lead to some exaggerated motions in the legs when moving the spine. It would be much better to have them linked to the root of the spine, but that's not possible with a normal parent/child relationship.

Here's how to do it:

RMB select the root of "spine.base" and use the Snap menu to place the 3D cursor there. RMB select the tip of "spine.base" and Ctrl-LMB away from it to extrude a connected child bone. Select the tip of the new child bone, and use the Shift-S Snap menu to move "Selection -> Cursor." If you've done it correctly, you'll have a new bone in the same location as the spine base, but upside down.

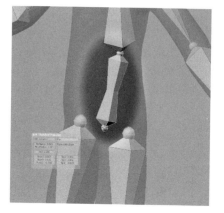

Select one of the upper leg bones, then Shift-RMB select the upside down spine and use Ctrl-P to create an offset parent relationship. Do the same with the other leg.

Adjusting IK Chain Length

Go back into Pose mode and grab one of the leg controllers. Move it around, and see how both legs and spine now move along with the controller. Not the behavior you were looking for. This is happening because an IK Solver constraint, like the ones on the lower leg bones, works the whole way up the parent/child chain. Since you added the spine into the chain of the legs, it is now affected by the IK.

Although it creates some interesting control possibilities, change it back so that the IK stops with the legs.

In Pose mode, RMB select one of the lower leg bones. On the IK Solver constraint in the Constraints panel, set the "ChainLen: 0" control to 2. This value tells the solver how many bones to include in the chain, the first being the constrained bone itself. In this case, setting the control to 2 includes the first two bones in the chain: the lower and upper leg. The default value, 0, causes the solver to affect all bones in the chain.

Set "ChainLen:" to 2 for both of the lower legs' IK Solvers.

With that done, moving the leg controllers affects only the legs and feet. Also, with the upper legs set as the children of the spine, grabbing and moving "spine.base" properly affects the legs.

Adjust chain length to 2.

Linking the Arm to the Spine

If you were just playing with the spine to see how its motion affected the legs, you may have noticed that the arms were not following along.

You should already know what to do to fix this by now.

In Edit mode, make the upper spine bone ("spine.top") the parent of the two shoulder bones ("shoulder_L/R"). You can also lock the translation controls for the shoulder bones, as you don't want to them to change location independently of the rest of the body.

Hybrid Arm IK

Many people prefer to animate arms without IK. In Blender there is a (fairly) simple way of rigging a hybrid method that allows you to create poses with IK tools, but adjust the results with manual rotations.

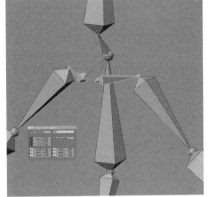

The shoulder bones as the children of the upper spine, with translation locked.

In Pose Mode, RMB select a lower arm bone ("arm.lower_L"). Press Ctrl-I to create an IK constraint. From the popup that appears, choose "Without Target." In the IK Solver constraint on the Constraints panel, set "Chain Len" to 2.

Press the G-key in the 3D view and you'll find that the bone functions as an IK solver for the arm. However, if you press the R-key to rotate, it functions as though it was a regular, unconstrained bone.

Do the same set of actions for the first hand bone ("hand_L"), creating an IK constraint "Without Target," but setting "ChainLen" to 3. Grabbing and moving the hand bone lets you create a pose with an IK feel if you choose, but it remains fully adjustable with rotations.

Duplicate your work on the other side of the armature so that there are "targetless" IK constraints on both lower arms and hands.

Full Body IK

You'll do one last trick before you clean up the armature. The feature you restricted by setting a chain length in the leg IK can actually be useful.

RMB select the bone "fingers_L" at the very end of the left hand, and use the Tab-key to go into Edit mode.

Using Shift-D, duplicate the bone and move it backward to the edge of the hand mesh. Rename this new bone "full.body_L".

Back in Pose mode, use Ctrl-I to add an IK solver to the bone, and choose "Without Target."

Repeat the procedure to create a "full.body_R" bone.

Hybrid Arm IK

In Pose mode, try selecting one of these bones and pulling it around. The entire skeleton moves, with just this one bone! So, if you need to create some radical poses that involve Hank really reaching for something, using these extra full body controllers would be a good place to start. Using them to create the poses of a walk cycle, though, would almost certainly be overkill.

The armature pulled around drastically with the full body IK controls.

Linking to the Master Bone

Remember the very first bone you created, the master bone? It's time to show it by Shift-LMB clicking on the sixteenth (far right) layer button in the Armature panel. With the master bone showing, go into Edit mode and select the base of the spine followed by the master bone itself. Press Ctrl-P and choose "Keep Offset" to make the spine the child of the master bone. Do the same thing for the two leg/foot control bones.

Now, you have a convenient method, via the master bone, of moving the entire armature at once in Pose mode.

Cleaning the Armature

The rigging is finished. You now have a decently functional armature whose feet and legs are each controlled both in translation and rotation by a single controller bone. The toes can be rotated independently. The upper foot can be rotated up and down, leaving the toe in place. Knees can be translated along a single axis to twist the legs, if necessary.

In the spine, each bone can rotate by itself, and translating the base of the spine moves the upper legs fairly well. Arms can be posed with either hybrid IK controls or standard rotations.

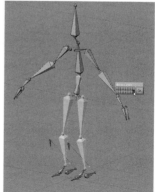

You won't need to see all of the bones in the armature in order to animate effectively. In the interest of simplicity, you can send the unneeded bones to a hidden bone layer, just like you did with the master bone nearer the beginning of the chapter.

Build a selection consisting of the upper and lower leg bones, the "upside down" spine bone and the ankle bones ("ankle_L/R"). Make sure that you are in Pose mode, and press the M-key. This brings up the same style of layer popup as seen when dealing with standard objects. Click on the lower rightmost box, and then on OK to send the selected bones to Layer 16.

And finally, on the Armature panel, change the Display Options from "Octahedron" to "Stick."

Stick mode is a bare bones (ha!) way of showing an armature, allowing the animator to see as much of the mesh as possible. If you get confused or simply don't like it, you can always change back to Octoahedron.

Skinning

Skinning is the process of defining how an armature affects a mesh. Right now, the Hank mesh does not move along with the armature. There are several ways to attach a mesh to an armature, but you're only going to look at one of them here.

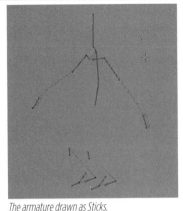

The armature drawn as Sticks.

Use Ctrl-Tab to get the armature into Object mode. You're going to make the armature the parent of the character mesh. Select the character mesh, then Shift-RMB select the armature and press Ctrl-P.

Two new options pop up when doing this. Be sure to choose "Object." Choosing "Armature" from this menu would use one of the alternative, more complicated, skinning methods.

Once that's done, you'll find that transforming the armature in object mode brings the mesh along with it, but that setting a pose in Pose mode still leaves the mesh unchanged.

The Armature Modifier

Armature deformations are best done through the Armature modifier. Select the actual Hank mesh and examine the Modifiers panel in the buttons window.

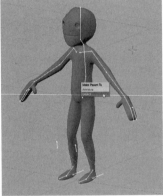

Making a mesh the child of an armature.

Hank's modifier stack, showing only a Subsurf modifier.

Click the "Add Modifier" button on the panel and choose "Armature" from the list that pops up. On the stacking controls at the right side of the new modifier, click the little "up" arrow to move the modifier up in the stack. Disable the button labeled "Vert. Groups."

In the "Ob:" field, enter the name of the armature you've created, which is most likely just "Armature." If you type the name incorrectly, it will disappear, as the text box will not allow an invalid input. You may need to select the armature and look at the properties panel to get the name exactly right.

The mesh Modifiers panel, with an Armature modifier created and tweaked.

Select the armature now, and go into Pose mode. Grab one of the lower arm bones and move it up. Depending on how well you positioned your bones within the arm, you may or may not get something that looks like this:

What's going on?

Each bone has a preset envelope of influence that it uses to deform the mesh around it. In this example, the arm bone envelopes obviously did okay, but the ones on the hand bones didn't work very well.

Hank's poor poor hand.

To see these envelopes, choose "Envelope" from the Display Options on the Armature panel in the Edit buttons.

In the illustration, the ghostly cylinder around the selected arm bone shows the bone's envelope. Envelopes only display for selected bones. We'll show you how to adjust the envelope size and strength on the hands in your model, but depending on how well your bones deformed the Hank mesh, you may need to make some additional adjustments, too.

With the hand bone selected, press Alt-S to scale the envelope while leaving the bone itself untransformed. In Pose mode, Alt-S is your only friend for adjusting envelopes. Here, you can see pictures of the hand bone's envelopes and the deformation of the mesh, before and after adjusting the envelope size with Alt-S.

Envelope view enabled for the armature.

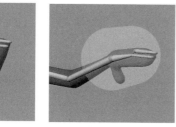

The finger bone's envelope in the example needs to be enlarged, too. A good work flow for adjusting the default envelope skinning is to pose a joint, see how the surrounding bones deform the mesh, and then adjust the envelope sizes while the mesh follows along in real-time. In the next two images, the finger bone has been bent, then the envelope adjusted to give a proper deformation.

You'll notice that the full body controller is still sticking straight out beside the finger bone. That is only a control bone. You do not want it to directly deform the mesh. Its job is to pull around other bones which in turn do the deformation.

The Armature Modifier

The way to prevent a bone from being considered for deformations is to disable the "Deform" button on the Armature Bones panel. Regardless of the quality of deformations on your particular model and rig, select the full body controllers and disable "Deform." Bones that have had their deformation disabled show no envelope when they are selected.

The "Deform" button on the Armature Bones panel.

While disabling deformations for the full body controllers, you should do so for other control and behind-the-scenes bones, namely: the master bone, knee targets, leg controllers, ankle bones and the upside-down spine bone. As several of those are on the hidden layer, now would be a good time to show them again. On the Armature panel, Shift-LMB on the last layer button on the right.

Yikes. Those are some gigantic hip joints, Hank!

Before you tackle that, though, let's see how things deform in the lower body.

Displaying armature Layer 16.

After grabbing the left leg controller and transforming it a bit, it's clear that things are a mess.

Your armature and deformation will almost certainly be different from what you see here. It will depend on exactly where the joints of your armature fell when doing the rigging exercise. For that reason it's important to understand the process of what's going on here so you can adapt it to your own situation.

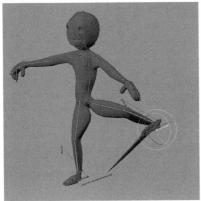

Bad deformations on the feet and legs. The illustration was switched to Stick mode to better see the mesh.

The worst problem is that the foot is clearly not covered by the envelopes. Selecting the bone "foot_L" and using Alt-S to increase the size of its envelope quickly takes care of this.

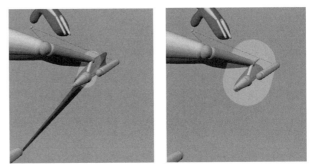

The foot bone's envelope adjusted to fix foot deformation.

Another less obvious problem is how the inner thigh of the right leg seems to be moving along with the motion of the left leg. This is because the envelope of the upper left leg bone extends into the area of the right leg, and up into Hank's stomach. In this case, simply scaling with Alt-S will not work, because the bone itself is so large in this view that you cannot make the envelope small enough.

You can change envelopes on a more detailed basis in Edit mode.

The Armature Modifier

Changing Envelopes in Edit Mode

In Edit mode, the first thing you will see is that any poses you have set in Pose mode are temporarily abandoned. Don't worry — they'll come back when you leave Edit mode.

Edit mode allows you to select the roots and tips of bones, just like you are used to doing, and using the S-key scale method to change their deformation profile. Remember way back at the beginning of the chapter when we said that scaling a single root or tip had no effect on a bone? Well, we lied, but just a little.

By selecting the root of the upper leg bone and scaling, you can change its envelope like this:

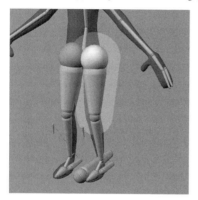 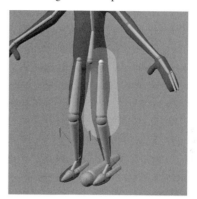

It's important when working with envelopes to look at the mesh and armature from several angles, as an envelope that appears to cover the mesh properly from one perspective may be missing something along another axis.

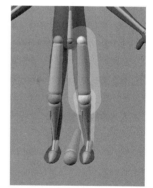

While in Edit mode, selecting an entire bone and using Alt-S will work just like it does in Pose mode: scaling the envelope for the bone.

And so you proceed throughout your entire armature, using each controller and moving each joint to see how the mesh deforms and to spot trouble.

We'll look at one more case of envelope deformation before moving on.

A more reasonable size for bone tips, roots and envelopes.

Adding Bones to Assist Deformation

With this armature, there is no way to have the head bone's envelope be broad enough to deform the entire head without dipping into areas like the shoulder and chest that have no business being affected by the head bone. What to do?

There are several ways to approach it, but the easiest is to add a new bone as a child of the head bone to assist with the deformation.

The head bone in Edit mode, showing envelopes.

To get this configuration, we Shift-D duplicated the head bone, then positioned the new bone's root and tip so it fell perpendicular to the original. After that, the overall envelope size was altered with Alt-S until it appeared to fill in the gaps the original bone had left. Of course, this new bone must be made the offset child of the original head bone or things will go very badly once you begin to animate.

Then, we returned to pose mode and tested it by moving the neck and head. In fact, our first attempt when creating this exercise didn't quite cover the area correctly, and an additional adjustment had to be made to the envelope size.

A new bone to help with head deformation. Notice how the envelopes of the original and new head bones completely cover the head now.

Weight Painting and Vertex Groups

The last way of adjusting mesh deformation that we'll talk about is called Weight Painting. Behind the scenes, it involves the creation and use of vertex groups, but the 3D view interface elements let you work rather intuitively.

In this illustration, Hank's back has been bent backward, showing off a poor deformation in the chest. You could add another bone that was linked to the spine to fix it, but there is another way.

To weight paint your way out of a mess like this, select the mesh object, and on the 3D header choose "Weight Paint" mode. On the mesh's Modifiers panel, enable the "Vert. Groups" button in the Armature modifier.

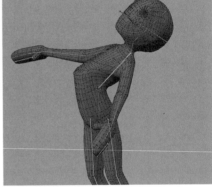

A bad deformation in the chest.

Although the mesh object is selected, you'll find that you can RMB select the bones of the armature, if it was in Pose mode. In this example, the "spine.top" bone has been selected.

At this point, the LMB in the 3D view becomes a paint brush. What the brush is "painting" is really bone influence. As you click and drag on the mesh, it is telling the mesh that it should be influenced by the currently selected bone. In terms of color, dark blue means that the mesh is not influenced by the bone at all, through teal, green, yellow, orange and red, at which point the mesh is influenced by the bone's transformations at 100% strength.

You can choose to what maximum weight you would like to paint in this panel with the "Weight" control, and how much of that maximum value will be painted with each stroke with the "Opacity" control. An opacity of 1.0 will paint the full value of the Weight control with every pass of the mouse.

The weight paint panel on the Edit buttons.

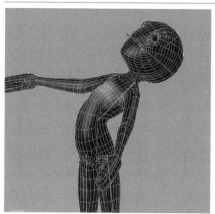

A few mouse clicks on the chest and sternum later.

By painting a few strokes on the poorly deforming area with Weight 1.0 and Opacity .25, this deformation was achieved. A definite improvement. Serious animators will use this technique to finely tune their deformations for nearly each and every bone in their characters.

Wrapping Up

When you have envelopes and weight painting set so that each controller can move, deforming the portions of the mesh you desire while leaving other parts alone, then you are done. Move any deformation helper bones you created to a hidden bone layer so they are out of the way. If you need to revisit your envelope settings or weight painting, though, don't forget they're there!

If you have already worked with Chapter 6, we encourage you to try it again with the rig you just created. It's different than the rig provided with Hank in the previous chapter, and you can learn from the differences in how your rig responds to the same set of instructions.

Rigging and Skinning: Discussion

Imagine how tedious it would be to animate a mesh as complicated as a character by moving each vertex in the mesh where you want it, frame by frame. You'd never get any animation done! In Blender, using an armature makes the task of posing a mesh much easier. If you've worked through Chapter 6, you've already seen this in action on the Hank character.

The process of constructing an armature is called "rigging," while the process of marrying the armature and mesh is called "skinning."

The general workflow for rigging an armature and skinning a mesh is something like this:
- Build an armature inside your mesh by extruding and adding bones;
- Name the bones appropriately;
- Optionally, add constraints to give the rig more functionality, making it easier to use;
- Apply an Armature modifier to the mesh; and
- Using either Envelopes or Vertex Groups (or both), designate which bones should influence which parts of the mesh.

Armatures are used to deform meshes for complex tasks like character animation.

Then you're done! At various points along the way, though, you may have to go back and modify the mesh to make it work better with the armature, or even alter your armature's structure for better functionality. It's an iterative process, and may take a couple of tries, especially during skinning.

More Than Armatures

Blender offers ways to deform a mesh beyond the basic armature. Although not covered in this book, there are a host of other methods at your disposal: hooks, modifiers, curves, lattices and driven keys. Any of these can be used to enhance or even completely drive mesh deformation, meaning that they too fall under the heading of "rigging." In the end, armatures are just one (very important) tool in your rigging toolbox.

The included disk has several examples of alternative approaches to rigging in the folder "rigs," with explanations embedded right within the files. You are encouraged to expand your mind a bit and check them out.

Rigging: Building an Armature

Adding an Armature

To add an armature, use the spacebar toolbox and choose Add->Armature. An armature with a single bone will be added at the location of the 3D cursor, in Edit Mode. As always, it's a good idea to switch to Object mode with the Tab-key and use Alt-R to clear any rotation. Armatures and character animation are even more sensitive to object level rotations than other kinds of objects, and making sure to always build your armatures with no object level rotations will prevent unexpected behavior and problems later on.

If you have solid view turned on, you may not see the bone if it's inside your mesh. You can either use the Z-key to switch to wireframe so you can see the armature better, or you can turn on the X-Ray option in the Armature panel of the edit buttons. X-Ray makes the armature visible through any objects that might otherwise be blocking it.

Anatomy of a Bone

The default bone draw type is Octahedron (more on draw types later), where the bone has a thick end and a thin end. At each end there's a circle. The circle at the thick end is the root of the bone, and the circle at the thin end is the tip of the bone. The root and tip can be selected separately. You can select the entire bone either by RMB-clicking the center of it, or by selecting both the root and the tip of the bone.

A single bone, in wireframe and solid views. The tip is selected, and the root is unselected.

Armature Modes

An Armature has an Object mode and an Edit mode, just like a mesh. Unlike a mesh, however, you will rarely use the Object mode of an armature. Instead, you'll use Edit mode and Pose mode, one that's unique to armatures.

Object mode can be used to place an armature in a starting XYZ position within a scene, but after that it is generally unused. Object mode is denoted by a solid light pink outline.

Edit mode is used for constructing the armature, assigning hierarchical relationships between bones (i.e., parent/child), and adjusting the armature to better fit a mesh. Edit mode is denoted by magenta (for unselected) and yellow (for selected) outlines.

Pose mode is used for assigning constraints to bones and for posing the armature during animation. Pose mode is denoted by a blue outline around bones.

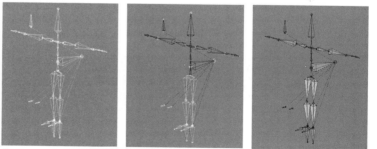

The same armature in Object, Edit and Pose modes.

Switching modes: When you first add an armature, you are in Edit mode, as shown by the yellow and pink bone outlines. You can use Ctrl-Tab to enter Pose mode, indicated by blue bone outlines. Notice, though, that once Pose mode is activated, the Tab-key switches between Edit and Pose modes — Object mode is skipped. To get back to Object mode, Ctrl-Tab deactivates Pose mode.

Armatures are constructed in Edit mode, but animated in Pose mode.

Adding and Moving Bones

Adding a bone: To add a bone to an armature, use the spacebar toolbox and choose Add->Bone while in Edit mode. The new bone will be added at the 3D cursor, and will not have a parent.

Bones can also be added to an armature by selecting an existing bone and using the Extrude command. The part of the bone from which you extrude determines the behavior and relationship of the newly extruded bone.

Extruding from the tip: RMB select the tip of the bone and use the E-key to extrude. The new bone will automatically be a child of the bone it was extruded from, and will automatically be connected to that same bone.

Extruding from the root: select the root of the bone and use the E-key to extrude. A bone extruded from a root will not be a child and will not be connected to the bone it was extruded from. It is equivalent to adding a new bone.

In addition to using the E-key to extrude, a new bone can be extruded by making a selection and Ctrl-LMB clicking in the 3D view. The tip of the new bone will be set wherever you clicked, while the root will be at the tip of the previously selected bone.

Symmetrical extrude: An extremely useful function! Turn on X-Axis Mirror in the Armature panel of the Edit buttons. Activating this feature allows you to use the command Shift-E to symmetrically extrude. If you symmetrically extrude from the tip of a bone, both new bones will be children of the bone they were extruded from. When you move just one side of a symmetrical pair, the other will move as well, saving lots of time when building symmetrical armatures.

In addition, the bones are automatically given "_L" and "_R" suffixes. These suffixes are important. If you remove either one, the symmetrical relationship is broken.

Adding a bone symmetrically: To add a bone symmetrically, extrude (Shift-E) from the root of any bone. This will create a bone without a parent.

If you prefer to work with a single side of an armature at a time, you can always create only, say, the left side, then Shift-D duplicate your work, scale it along the X-axis (use -1 for a scale factor) and use the W-key "Flip Left-Right Names" function to mirror your armature.

Moving bones: To arrange the armature inside the mesh, you can move entire bones or individual roots and tips. When two bones are connected, you can move just the joint between them. Don't forget the snap menu (Shift-S), which lets you use the 3D cursor as a reference point for bones as it does for objects.

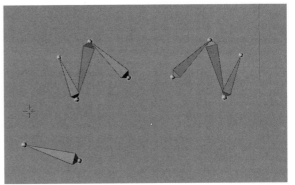

The single bone was added normally, with the toolbox Add->Bone command. The two sets of bone chains were added with Symmetrical extrusion.

       Adding and Moving Bones

Bone Parent/Child and Connected Relationships

Like other Blender objects, bones can have parent/child relationships. Building these relationships correctly is essential to a properly functioning rig. If you recall from the introductory animation chapter, a child object can move independently of its parent, but will be transformed as a single object with the parent if the parent moves. This functionality is much the same with armatures and bones.

For example, the bones of a human arm are arranged in just such a parent/child relationship. The hand can move on its own, as can the lower arm. However, if the upper arm moves, both the lower arm and hand must move with it. So, in this example, the hand is the child of the lower arm, which is in turn the child of the upper arm.

As we mentioned before, bones that are extruded from the tips of other bones are created as children by default. This makes the creation of chains of bones like arms very simple.

If you have already existing bones that you wish to create a parent/child relationship for, when one was not created by default, it is easy to create one. Just as you create the same relationships with regular objects, first select the child object. Then, Shift-RMB select the parent and press Ctrl-P.

There is one major difference, though, between object parenting and bone parenting. With bones, parent/child objects can be either connected or disconnected. A disconnected child bone works exactly like the parent/child relationship you are used to from Object mode. A connected child object, however, cannot translate independently of its parent - its root is the parent's tip. It can still rotate freely, but cannot move away from the parent bone.

So really, in our earlier example of a human arm, it would be more precise to say that the hand is the connected child of the lower arm, which is the connected child of the upper arm. In fact, there are no actual joint relationships in the human body that can be properly termed disconnected, as the human body does not, hopefully, come apart.

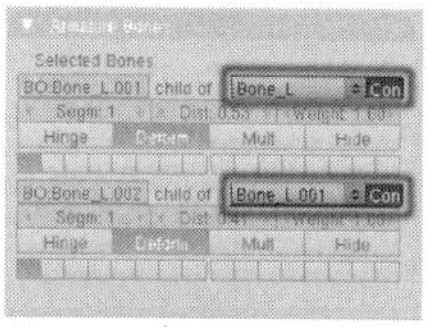

The parent/child controls on the Armature Bones panel.

When you use Ctrl-P to create a parent/child bone relationship, you are given the option to connect the bones, resulting in a connected relationship, or to keep them offset, resulting in a disconnected relationship.

These relationships can also be managed from the Armature Bones panel in the Edit buttons. Parent bones are set from the "child of" dropdown menu, and the "Con" button toggles between connected and disconnected.

Bone Naming

The naming of bones is important for more than just letting Blender know which bones should be considered symmetrical. A versatile armature can have dozens of bones, and when you are animating, the last thing you need is to have to guess whether "bone.001," "bone.015" or "bone.007" is the one you need to select. Although tedious, taking the time to name your bones will save you headaches later.

Sidebar (right column):

• Bones can be added from the toolbox, or by extruding existing bones with the E-key or Ctrl-LMB clicking.

• When "X-Axis Mirror" is enabled in the armatures Edit buttons, changes to one side of the armature also happen to the other. Shift-E extrudes symmetrically.

• Bones in a parent/child relationship can be either connected or disconnected.

• Connected child bones cannot be translated independently.

Selected bones are named in the Armature Bones panel in the Edit buttons, or on the N-key Transform Properties panel.

Fixing Bone Roll

Never begin working in Pose mode before selecting all bones in Edit mode and fixing roll rotation with the Ctrl-N hotkey.

Bones can roll around their length. Although this can be useful when animating, it can ruin an otherwise good armature if improper roll values are included in the original structure in Edit mode. Once you have built an armature, it is essential that you select all the bones and use the Ctrl-N hotkey to trigger a full recalculation of bone roll, making sure that you begin animating from a "clean slate."

For certain effects, you may edit a bone's roll manually. If you have done so, make sure that you do not destroy your hard work by using Ctrl-N on that bone.

A Tour of the Armature Panels

The Armature panel of the Edit buttons.

Armature Panel

This panel has settings that are applied at the object level. The settings here apply to all the bones in the armature.

Editing Options

X-Axis Mirror: Enables mirrored editing for all mirrored bones. This is a great tool that makes armature construction much easier. When this is activated, you can use Shift-E to make symmetrical extrusions as discussed earlier.

X-Ray: Causes the armature to be visible through all other objects, except for other armatures that are X-Ray active. This is useful for when you want to manipulate the armature but also want to see how its linked mesh is deforming, and would rather not keep switching to wireframe view. This is often used while constructing and posing an armature.

Display Options

Bone Layers: These work in the same manner as the main layer buttons. Each button represents a layer. When the button is enabled, that layer is visible. Assign a bone to a layer by clicking a layer button in the adjacent Armature Bones panel (see below). The layer buttons on this panel control which layers are displayed. Sometimes, when using a rig someone else has made, you may suspect that there are bones or controls you cannot see. Most likely they have been set to a layer which is not displayed here. Enable more layers by Shift-LMB clicking on the different layer buttons to find any hidden bones.

Display Modes: These buttons set the armature display mode. Only one bone display type can be activated at a time. Each draw type is useful for showing something different, as there are just too many armature features to be able to visualize them all within a single mode.

Fixing Bone Roll

Octahedron: the default drawing type, which allows you to easily differentiate between the root and tip of the bones. Useful for working on an armature in Edit mode.

Stick: a minimalist drawing type good for reducing visual clutter. Once a rig is complete, the draw type is usually set to Stick to keep the display simple.

B-Bone: "B-Bone" is analogous to "B-spline," a mathematical way of describing curves. In Blender, a B-bone is a bone that can curve along its length. You can add segments to a bone (something you'll only be able to visualize in B-Bone mode) to allow it to curve. B-bones also allow you to scale the display size of a bone without affecting any other parameters. This can be useful if you want to make the pelvis bone look like a large block, or the fingers like small thin bones. Some animators work with armatures without using an attached mesh, and adjust the B-bones to mimic the volumes of a character. Remember that this is a display modification only and does not affect the armature's functionality.

Envelope: this draw type allows you to visualize the "envelope of influence" of a bone and should be enabled if you will use Envelopes to deform a mesh. Envelopes are described more fully in the skinning section of this chapter.

Draw Axes: Draws the axis of each bone in the armature. Useful when working with constraints when you need to designate on which axes they should operate.

Draw Names: Displays the bone names in the 3D view next to each bone.

Deform Options:

Vertex Groups/Envelopes: These buttons are used for certain methods of skinning.

Rest Position: Enabling Rest Position shows the armature without any pose information. You can't pose any bones while the armature is in its rest position. Useful for "freezing" the armature in place, for example, while working on shape keys.

The Armature Bones Panel

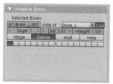

The Armature Bones panel.

When a bone is selected in the 3D view, the following controls are shown for it.

BO: The name of the bone. You can change it by LMB clicking on the name and typing a new one.

Hinge: This option allows bones to defy the rules of the parent/child relationship. When enabled, this feature causes bones to inherit their location from their parent, but to ignore size and rotation. In other words, the child stays connected to the parent, but does not scale or rotate along with the parent.

Deform: Enables bones to affect the vertices of a connected mesh object. Some bones will be used as controls for other bones, or even for complex bone structures, and you won't necessarily want these control bones to affect the mesh directly. To prevent them from deforming the mesh, disable the Deform button.

Deform Options:

Bone Layers: Indicates which layers the selected bone belongs to. Shift-LMB adds to or subtracts from the layer assignment, just like the object-level layer buttons. In complex armatures, there may be dozens of bones that do "behind-the-scenes" work and would only clutter the display. To make life easier when it comes time to animate, bones like this can be moved to a layer that is not displayed. Likewise, controls for different animation functions can be organized together on different layers.

Constraints

Once an armature has been built in Edit mode, it is most likely not ready for serious animation work. While it is certainly possible to move and key each bone independently while animating, it would still be an extremely time-consuming, unintuitive process. A rig really becomes useful after adding constraints, which can add a great deal of functionality and ease of use.

Constraints can only be added in Pose Mode. When in Pose mode, a Constraints panel will appear in the Edit buttons. To add a constraint, select it from the Add Constraint dropdown box. All constraints have similar controls:

Constraints alter the normal function and transformation of a bone, linking it in some way to another bone or object in the scene, called the "target."

The Constraints panel, showing that a Copy Rotation constraint has been added to the selected bone.

All constraints have an OB: name field. When a constraint is added, this name field appears in red, as there is no object assigned yet. Type the name of the intended target object into this field. All constraints require a target object: either a regular object, or a bone. To add a bone as the target, first type the name of its armature object into the OB: field. The constraint control recognizes that it is an armature, and another field, the BO: field, appears. Type in the name of the bone you want to have as the target in this new field.

If the name you typed disappears after you press Enter, it is probably because you spelled the object's name incorrectly. Remember that object names in Blender are case sensitive.

Stacking Constraints

Constraints are evaluated in a specific order, and the order can be viewed and changed inside the Constraints panel. Each Constraint has a pair of arrow buttons in its top right corner, which are used to move the constraint up or down the constraint stack. Constraints at the top are evaluated first, but their effects can be over-ridden by constraints further down in the stack.

Constraint Details

The more commonly used constraints are detailed below.

Copy Location

The Copy Location constraint

Copy Location forces the object to have the same location as its target. Move the target and the constrained bone moves as well, but the constrained bone cannot be moved by itself. The target can be either an object or another bone. The X, Y, and Z buttons indicate which axis is copied from the target. All three are enabled by default, but un-checking any of them will free the constrained bone to move independently along that axis.

Two bones, before and after a Copy Location constraint has been added to the one on the left.

Adding two Copy Location constraints to an object or bone that point to different targets will cause the constrained object to always position itself midway between the target objects, if the Influence slider on the lowest constraint in the stack is set to 0.5.

Bones that are connected children of other bones will ignore Copy Location constraints, as they are not free to translate.

Copy Rotation

The Copy Rotation constraint

Copy rotation causes the constrained object to match the rotation of the target object. Similar to the Copy Location constraint, a Local option appears if the target of the constraint is another bone. As in the Copy Location constraint, having X, Y, or Z enabled means that you cannot change this bone's rotation in that axis. You can only change it by rotating the target bone.

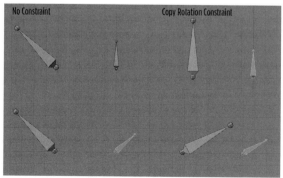

Two bones. The one on the left rotates in both sequences, but in the second, the left bone has been Copy Rotation constrained to follow it.

Copy Location

Track To

The Track To constraint

Track To forces the constrained object to point at the target object. Wherever you move the target, the constrained bone will point to it. Also, wherever you move the constrained bone, it will point to the target. The To: buttons let you choose which axis of the constrained bone should point toward the target (the dashes indicate negative X, Y, and Z respectively). The Up: buttons let you choose which axis of the constrained object should point up. It's a good idea to turn on Draw Axes in the Armature panel in order to see exactly where the axes are.

The bone on the left has a Track To constraint, targeting the bone on the right.

The same axis can't both point to the object AND point up. If you try to do that, the Const box turns red and the constraint won't function correctly.

Locked Track

The Locked Track constraint

The Locked Track constraint is a bit like the Track To constraint, but involves less motion for the constrained object. It allows one axis of the object to be locked, or ignored when tracking. When working with bones, it is often used by locking the Y axis so that a bone will only roll to face the target.

The bone on the left has had it's Y axis locked. The extra bone sprouting from its tip is to show how it rotates to face the target bone.

Floor

Floor constraint

The Floor Constraint allows you to use a target object to specify the location of a plane which the affected object cannot pass through. In other words, it creates a floor! (Or a ceiling, or a wall.) In normal mode, it uses the simple global location of the target object to define the barrier. With the "Rot" option enabled, the target object's rotation will be taken into effect, letting you create tilted floors.

The Max/Min buttons let you choose which location of the target object the bone cannot pass. For a floor, use Z. For a ceiling, use -Z. For walls, use +/-X or Y. The number in the Offset slider lets you move the "floor" or ceiling that many units away from the center of the target object, to take the depth of the mesh's feet into account.

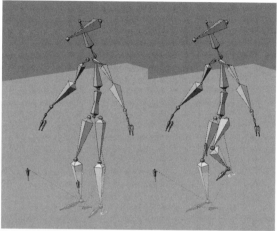

The armature's leg controllers are both below the level of the plane. On the right,
a Floor constraint has been added to one of the controllers.

Sticky: Makes the affected object immoveable when touching the plane (cannot slide around on the surface of the plane), which is fantastic for making walk and run animations. However, it should only be used to generate pose keyframes, as it will not function as you expect in a live animation situation.

Keyframing Tip:
When you animate foot placement with a Floor constraint, **always** be sure to use the option VisualLoc from the Insert Key menu.

Stretch To

The Stretch To constraint

Stretch To causes the constrained object to scale along its Y axis (its length in the case of a bone) toward the target object. It also has volumetric features, so the constrained object can squash down as the target moves closer, or thin out as the target moves farther away. This volumetric effect can be disabled by clicking the "NONE" button.

Floor

The Rest Length control is the bone's length in the armature's rest position. The small "R" button next to Rest Length recalculates the bone's stretch, setting the stretched bone back to its initial un-stretched state.

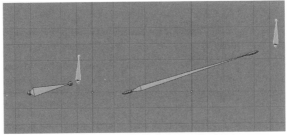

The bone on the left is Stretch constrained to the bone on the right. As you can see, bones can deform significantly when stretching, so use this with care.

Among other things, the Stretch To constraint is used for cartoon-type rigs for squash and stretch.

IK Solver

The IK Solver constraint

The IK Solver constraint is Blender's implementation of inverse kinematics, which is explained in the sidebar. The IK Solver is probably the most frequently used constraint. In fact, it's so often used that it has its own shortcut key, and certain restrictions of constraints, like requiring a separate target, have been removed. Although an IK Solver can have a normal target, which is useful in many rigging situations, it can be conveniently invoked without one.

The ChainLen control allows you to prevent the effects of IK from propagating throughout an entire chain of bones without un-parenting or disconnecting those bones. This would be useful, for example, if your chain of bones included everything from the collar bone through the hand, with the hand having an IK Solver con-straint. If you did not want the collar bone to be affected by the IK solver, you would set the Chain Length control to 2, indicating that the IK effect should only work for two bones up the chain.

When ChainLen is zero, the default, the IK Solver will use all available bones in the chain.

The lower leg bone has an IK Solver pointing to the selected foot controller bone. As the controller moves, it pulls the IK chain with it.

Forward and Inverse Kinematics

A chain of bones is a series of bones where each bone is the child of another bone, whether connected or offset. Imagine that you're animating an arm and hand reaching for an apple. First you would pose the upper arm. The rest of the arm would follow along, since everything else in the chain is a child (or grandchild, etc) of the upper arm. Once you were happy with the upper arm, you would pose the lower arm and the hand would move with it. Finally you would pose the hand. This method of animation, where you start at the base of a chain and pose each bone individually is called Forward Kinematics.

There's another way to set up a bone chain called Inverse Kinematics, activated in Blender through the IK Solver constraint. Using the IK Solver constraint, you can animate the arm that is reaching for the apple in a different, more intuitive way. You can make the hand the target of the chain, and tell the chain of bones in the arm to try to point to that target. It is called "Inverse" instead of forward because all you do is animate the target, and the chain of bones follows in an attempt to reach it. You would move the hand toward the apple, and the rest of the arm would follow.

When should you use FK, and when should you use IK? It's an issue of personal preference, although practical considerations come into play. Generally, any chain whose endpoint will be exerting physical pressure on surrounding objects will use IK. So, legs and feet almost always use IK, as they contact the ground, bear the weight of the character and push against the ground. The rest of the body, including the arms, usually use the forward method. The exception is when a hand needs to contact the outside world, like picking up an apple or grabbing onto a railing. Some people prefer to rig arms with IK, but set its influence to 0 and only use it when necessary. Others prefer to pose such chains with AutoIK, but leave them as Forward Kinematic rigs.

Skinning: Connecting the Armature to the Mesh

Creating and rigging your armature only gets you half-way to actually being able to animate a character. In order to have your armature animations do anything useful, the armature needs to be attached to a mesh object.

Armature Modifier

If you've worked through Chapter 4, you are already familiar with Mesh Modifiers. If not, here's the short version: modifiers are functions that change the way that a mesh appears and acts. Attaching an Armature modifier to a mesh is sort of like using a constraint on an armature: you point it toward your target armature, and it changes the behavior of its host object. An Armature modifier is added to a mesh by first selecting the mesh object, then bringing up an Edit buttons window. From the Modifiers tab, click "Add Modifier" and choose "Armature."

Select the mesh, and in the Modifier panel add a new Armature modifier. Type in the name of the armature that you want to link to your mesh. Do not hit the Apply button. In the modifiers panel, the Apply button removes the modifier and causes any modifications it had made to the mesh to be permanent.

An Armature Modifier

Once the Armature modifier is added to the mesh and properly targeted at the armature itself, there are two options for how it will deform the mesh: Envelopes and Vertex Groups. You can use either one or both. Envelopes use visual areas of effect to determine which portions of the mesh are moved by which bones. Vertex groups allow you fine control, down to the mesh vertex level, over what affects what.

Envelopes

The Armature and Armature Bones panel.

Many people find envelopes an intuitive way to work. To see the envelope of a bone, enable the Envelopes draw type in the Armature panel under the edit buttons. The envelope of a bone is shown by the white ellipse surrounding it. Any area of the mesh that falls within that envelope will be deformed when the bone is moved. The goal when using envelopes is to tweak the size of the envelopes so that they enclose just the area of the mesh that you want to deform with a particular bone, but no more.

Adjustments to envelopes can be made in both Pose mode and Edit mode. Use either Alt-S or the "Dist:" field in the Armature Bones panel to adjust the spread of the envelope away from the bone. RMB selecting a bone in Pose Mode and pressing Alt-S lets you interactively scale the envelope size without changing the size of the bone itself. Likewise, using the S-key in Edit mode while envelopes are displayed scales only the envelopes, not the bones. When in Edit mode, you can scale the envelope for the entire bone, or scale the roots and tips individually, depending on what you have selected.

Since the effect of a bone envelope is determined by these adjustments, you don't have vertex-by-vertex control. If you can get away with using envelopes for your armature, great! However, as envelopes are both less precise and somewhat slower than the other skinning method, for anything of middling complexity, it's necessary to assist envelope deformation with vertex groups.

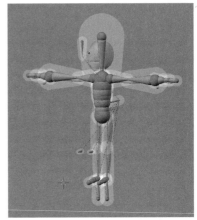

Hank's armature with the envelopes adjusted to cover the mesh.

Vertex Groups

A vertex group is a list of some of the vertices of a mesh. A mesh vertex can appear in as many different vertex groups' lists as you care to place it in, or it could belong to none at all.

When using an Armature modifier that has the Vertex Groups button enabled, you can tell a bone to move part of the mesh by selecting vertices in the mesh and assigning them to a vertex group with the exact same name as the bone.

For even more control, the vertices that are assigned to a group are given a weight. The weight, a value from 0.0 to 1.0, determines how strongly any actions performed on the vertex group will affect that particular vertex. For example, if one vertex appears in two different vertex groups (which happens a lot!) those vertex groups may be pulling their vertices in two different directions. Which group does the vertex follow? Well, if the vertex's weight in each group is 0.5, the groups have equal influence over the vertex, and it ends up splitting the difference. If, however, the vertex has a weight of 0.1 for the first group and 0.9 for the second group, the second group will have more influence, and the vertex will follow the second group's deformation much more closely. Vertex weights are always relative to the weights from competing groups.

One vertex can belong to many vertex groups, and one vertex group can have many vertices, each with a different weight. Assigning these weights is often necessary for organic models, where joints are supposed to deform smoothly. Around a shoulder joint, for example, the weights might have to be adjusted so that the upper arm doesn't pinch too much when the arm is lowered.

Manual Vertex Group Assignment

There are several ways to add vertices to a vertex group. The "manual" way gives you by far the most control. In Edit mode on your mesh, select several vertices. Under the Link and Materials panel in the Edit buttons, there is a Vertex Groups section. Click the "New" button to create a new, empty vertex group.

The Vertex Groups controls in the Link and Materials panel of the Edit buttons.

Then click the Assign button to assign the selected vertices to the just-created vertex group. When you click assign, the selected vertices are added to the vertex group's list, using the weight that is indicated in the Weight field.

If you have changed the Weight control for any reason, either manually or through weight painting, and you click Assign, your vertices will use whatever weight is there, even if it is 0.0. It's a good idea to make sure that it is set to 1.0 before you create and assign a new vertex group. If a vertex group is not acting as you think it should, assigning vertices with the Weight control set to something other than 1.0 could be the culprit.

Different vertex groups can be selected by choosing them from the dropdown box in the Link and Materials panel. Here are some of the controls for working with vertex groups:
- Delete: destroys the vertex group. This will not delete the vertices from the mesh itself — remember, vertex groups are just a list of vertices. This button destroys the list.
- Assign: adds the vertices that are currently selected in the 3D view to the active vertex group
- Remove: removes the vertices that are currently selected in the 3D view from the active vertex group. If the vertices were not in the group already, this has no effect.
- Select: selects any vertices in the 3D view that are assigned to the active vertex group. This adds to the current selection in the 3D view; it does not replace it.
- Desel.: deselects any vertices that are selected in the 3D view and that are assigned to the active vertex group.

Assigning Vertex Groups with Weight Painting

Manually adding vertices to vertex groups quickly becomes tedious. Sometimes you need that kind of vertex-level control, but for more common use, you can graphically assign vertex groups and weights to vertices. This is done in Weight Paint Mode, which can be chosen on the 3D view header.

You should make sure that the armature is in Pose mode and that it is set to X-Ray so it will be visible through the mesh while you work. Upon entering Weight Paint mode on the mesh, it will change color (all dark blue if you haven't added any vertex groups yet) and the cursor will turn into a paint-brush.

Choosing Weight Paint mode.

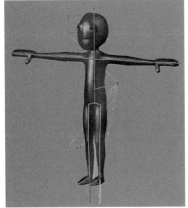

Hank ready for weight painting.

How to Approach Weight Painting

Select the mesh and enter Weight Paint mode. Select a bone — even though the mesh is active, if the armature is in Pose mode you will be able to RMB select individual bones — and press the W-key. This brings up a confirmation for "Apply Bone Envelopes to VertexGroups." LMB click to confirm this and you will see the mesh change color. In terms of vertex group weights, blue means 0.0, red means 1.0, and the rest of the spectrum falls in between. This W-key option auto-paints the mesh with the influence of the selected bone's envelope, which is a good place to begin tweaking.

In fact, if you plan to use vertex groups for your deformation, here's how to proceed: Turn off Envelopes in the mesh's modifiers panel and turn on Vertex Groups. Select the armature, enter Pose mode, and use the A-key to select all of the bones. RMB click the character mesh and enter Weight Paint mode. Before directly selecting any bones, press the W-key and confirm that you want to "Apply Bone Envelopes to VertexGroups." Even though you can't see it, you've just had Blender create beginning weight paintings for every bone in the armature. Now, selecting individual bones will show you their weights on the mesh.

The Paint panel for weight painting.

The actual weight painting works by simply LMB dragging on the mesh model in the 3D view. The Weight control on the paint panel sets the maximum weight that the brush will paint. Opacity indicates how much of that Weight will be painted with each pass of the brush. Of course, the Size control indicates the size of the paint brush itself. Some people find it useful to enable the "Wire" option at the bottom of the panel, which superimposes the mesh's wireframe structure over the painted colors. If you find that you've made a mess of a particular vertex group's paint job, just press the "Clear" button to remove any weight painting for the selected bone.

If you are working with a symmetrical mesh and armature, and the bones are named properly as described before, you can enable the X-Mirror option. X-Mirror allows you to weight paint only one side of a character, and have your painting mirrored to the other, saving you the trouble of duplicating your work on symmetrical characters. Clearing weights with the Clear button does not work symmetrically, regardless of the set up.

With a bone selected, you can use the normal posing tools (rotation, translation) to transform it, letting you see how well your weight painting is working. In fact, you can set a pose on any or all bones, then continue to tweak your weight painting from there. The deformation will update in real time, giving you immediate feedback as to the quality of your work. If you have rotated an arm downward and see that the rib area is deforming too, you can set Weight to 0.0 in the Paint panel, Opacity to around 0.25 and start painting in the areas that deform too much.

In this way, you can continue to weight paint, select and move bones to test, and tweak some more until the mesh deforms smoothly over the range of motion your armature will experience.

Conclusion

Armature creation, rigging and skinning are complex topics, and this is the merest overview of the relevant tools available to the Blender artist. Techniques for creating advanced rigs are constantly evolving, and can only be understood once you have a strong grasp of the basics. Included on the disk with this book are several rigs of varying complexity that have been released for general use. Some of them might function beautifully but be almost incomprehensible from a beginner's standpoint. Fortunately, the artists who created them have explanations and instructions for their rigs which have also been included on the disk. Perhaps the best way to learn some of these advanced techniques, besides sitting down with the artists themselves, is to study these rigs: pick them apart and see how they function.

Of course, you shouldn't feel that you have to create a rig from scratch every time you approach a new piece of animation. Many artists are quite content to use already-created rigs, and there is no shame in it. If you try the tools, though, and find that rigging interests you, you might be the person who creates the next great rig that everyone else is using!

CHAPTER **8**
Shape Keys

 ## Shape Keys: Hands On
by Andy Dolphin

 ## Shape Keys: Tools
by Andy Dolphin

Andy Dolphin (AndyD)

Andy's interest in animation goes back to his childhood. His mother bought Preston Blair's *Animation* book for him and his brothers in the very early 1970's, and he still has that same book today. His fascination with animation led him to experiment with animating building blocks and modeling clay using a super-8 cine-camera in the late 1970's. Since then, Andy's interest in the medium has remained, but opportunities to indulge have been scarce. All that changed when he discovered Blender. Already an accomplished illustrator and fine artist, Andy spends much of his spare time investigating and experimenting with the character animation capabilities of Blender. A regular contributor to Blender discussion forums, he's also written a few Blender tutorials including a very well received tutorial on using Blender shape keys to create lip-synced animations.

Shape Keys: Hands On

Shape Keys are a way of storing changes in the shape of a mesh. Blender shape keys can seem a little daunting at first, but once you come to grips with the basic workflow a whole new world of animation possibilities opens up. Shape keys can range from very simple to extremely complex, but either way the approach to creating, saving and animating them is the same.

One thing to remember when animating with shape keys is that the word "key" is used for two different purposes. A "shape key" stores the locations of vertices in a mesh, ready to be used for animation. On the other hand, a "key frame" records information on the animation timeline and tells Blender what should be happening with an object at a specific point in time as an animation plays or renders. Both terms will be used throughout this tutorial so it's important you understand the distinction.

Note: Before you begin, it needs to be emphasized that you should only add shape keys to a finished mesh. Don't use them on a mirrored mesh or a partially finished model. Adding or deleting vertices, edges or faces can cause unpredictable results or even the loss of the shape keys. This is because a shape key records the changes in the vertices' locations which define the shape of the mesh. Using shape keys is only appropriate for a mesh that is considered "complete".

Fun with Suzanne

Suzanne the monkey is Blender's official mascot, and to celebrate this fact there is a Suzanne mesh included in every Blender release. Poor old Suzanne has been abused in countless ways. She's been turned into stone, glass and all sorts of slimy materials. She's been duplicated, animated and had her head stuck on all sorts of different bodies. Most Blender users have fun with Suzanne at some point, and as a ready-made character mesh she is great for learning new tools and concepts in Blender. So, in order to help familiarize you with the Shape Key user interface, we will have a bit of fun with Suzanne!

The original Suzanne and Suzanne with simple shape keys applied.

Start Blender with a new scene showing the default cube mesh. RMB select the cube in Object mode and delete it by pressing the X-key. Be careful not to click anywhere on the 3D Window or you will move the 3D cursor from the center point (The Global Origin).

Switch to front view (Numpad-1) and use the Spacebar toolbox to Add->Mesh->Monkey. If you haven't met her before, then please say "hello" to Suzanne. You may want to zoom in closer (Numpad + or mouse scroll wheel) to get a better look. If Blender is in a wireframe view, press the Z-key to see Suzanne in all her solid glory. Exit Edit Mode (Tab).

The basic Monkey mesh in front view.

Fun with Suzanne

If you are familiar with mesh modifiers, you may want to add a subsurf modifier and do a SetSmooth to your mesh before making shape keys. For the purposes of this exercise, though, it's not important.

With the monkey mesh still selected, bring up the Editing Buttons (F9). Then go to the Shapes tab and press the "Add Shape key" button. This adds a shape key called "Basis" that stores the basic mesh in its unmodified state. The "Relative" button should be activated by default. This tells Blender to store future shape keys relative to this Basis key, which is exactly what you want. If the "Relative" button is not enabled, the shape keys are stored as absolute shape keys.

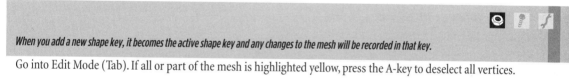

The Basis Shape key added in the Shapes panel.

Since the Basis key stores the unchanged mesh, you don't need to do anything more with it.

Suzanne Grows a Nose

For your first deformed shape key you are going to give Suzanne a long nose like Pinocchio. Press the "Add Shape key" button again. It now says "Key 1", and some key value sliders become visible.

When you add a new shape key, it becomes the active shape key and any changes to the mesh will be recorded in that key.

Go into Edit Mode (Tab). If all or part of the mesh is highlighted yellow, press the A-key to deselect all vertices.

The Shapes panel with Key 1 added.

You want to select the parts of the mesh that form the nose. The easiest way to do this is to work in face-select mode. Choose that option by clicking the triangle on the select-mode menu, or by using Ctrl-Tab in the 3D view. Now Shift-RMB the four faces that make up the front of Suzanne's heart-shaped nose. Switch to side view (Numpad-3) then drag the green arrow on the manipulator or press the G-key to "grab" then Y-key to lock the movement to the Y axis. Now drag the mouse away from Suzanne's head. You should see her nose stretch outwards. Stretch the nose so it is quite long.

Press the Tab-key to return to Object Mode. It will appear that the nose immediately returns to normal, but you've actually just stored a shape key for future use. If you wish to see the key in its modified form or edit it more, press the Tab-key to return to Edit mode with the desired shape key selected in the Shapes panel. You will notice that as you change

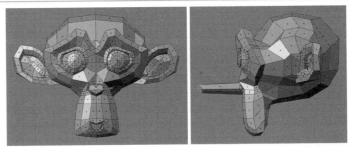

Monkey mesh in Edit mode: A front view with the nose faces selected, and a side view with the nose stretched out.

between the keys using the left and right arrow buttons on the Shapes panel that the mesh will show the selected key for quick reference.

To add another shape key that is derived from the base mesh, first select the Basis key from the shapes menu, then press "Add Shape Key" again.

The menu will now read "Key 2" showing that Blender is ready for you to make and store another shape for this mesh. Tab into Edit mode again. Switch to front view and press the A-key to deselect the nose faces. Shift-RMB select the eight faces that make up the pupil of one eye. Scale the faces up using the S-key and drag until the pupil touches the edges of the eyeball. After making one eye big, deselect its faces. Then, select the corresponding faces on the other eye. Scale this pupil down.

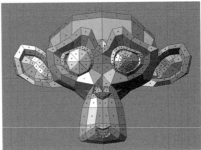

Suzanne's pupils have been resized.

Leave Edit mode to save these changes as Key 2. Again, the mesh will return to normal, but the changes have been stored.

Naming Shape Keys

Each new shape key will be consecutively numbered (Key, 1, Key 2, Key 3, etc.) by default as they are created. This may work well for small projects with few shape keys, but it is good practice to give them useful names so you can easily refer to them later when animating or editing. So far you have two shape keys. Key 1 affects the nose while Key 2 affects the eyes, yet the names don't tell you anything useful. Let's rename your two shape keys now.

Choose Key 1 from the shape key menu. You may notice that when you do this, the shape you saved earlier is immediately displayed in the 3D view. This gives you a quick reference and makes it the active key.

LMB on the text field to select the Key 1 text and type in "Nose Long" to remind you what this shape key represents. Press Return to save the name change. Then select Key 2 from the menu and rename it "Eyes Odd".

Key 1 has been renamed to "Nose Long".

Naming Shape Keys

Add More Shape Keys

Now select the Basis Key from the shapes menu so you can add another shape key. Press Add Shape Key again and LMB on the Key 3 text and rename it "Chin Big". Go to Edit mode and deselect all faces. Go into wireframe view (Z-key) and press the B-key to use the Box Select tool. Drag the selector crosshairs across the region around the mouth and chin (see illustration below). Use the blue manipulator arrow or press the G-key then Z-key to drag this region down and make Suzanne's jaw longer and lower. Use S-key to scale the selection up, making the jaw fatter. Switch back to solid view (Z-key) to see the changes. Press the Tab-key to exit Edit mode and save this shape.

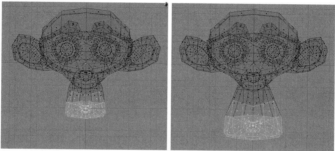

Faces in the chin are selected and re-sized.

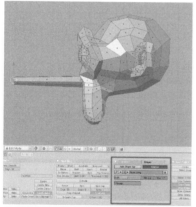

The "Nose Long" shape key.

You can check each shape key by selecting it from the shape key menu in object mode.

You might decide to make Suzanne's nose even longer when it grows. To do this you can edit your "Nose Long" shape key. Select the "Nose Long" shape key from the menu, and Tab into Edit mode. The mesh will display the long nose. Deselect any selected faces. Then, select the four faces on the end of the nose as you did earlier. Go to side view (Numpad-3) and drag the nose out a little longer. Leave Edit mode to save the change.

Let's say that you wanted to make a new shape key, but one that uses the "Nose Long" shape key as a starting point. If you select an existing key from the menu and press "Add Shape Key", the new shape key that is added begins as a copy of the one that was in the menu. This is useful for making variations for a shape key. Let's add a shape key where Suzanne has a long nose that's wide at the tip. Since you already have a shape key where you've stretched the nose, you can use that as the starting point for this new shape key.

In object mode, select "Nose Long" from the shape key menu. Press "Add Shape Key" and rename the new key "Long Wide Nose". Enter Edit mode. You'll see that the mesh is

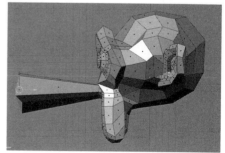

A new shape key with a wide nose, made from the existing "Nose Long" shape key.

Add More Shape Keys

already deformed with the long nose you made earlier. Select the four faces on the tip of the nose, after deselecting any other faces, and scale them to make the nose tip bigger. Leave Edit mode to save the new shape key.

Your shape key menu should now list four shape keys, plus a Basis key.

"Absolute" shape keys do not have this option because they store the absolute position of the vertices.

Min/Max Settings

One of the benefits of using "Relative" shape keys is that you can fine tune how much of the shape key to use. In the Shapes panel you will see Min and Max settings next to each shape key, with the exception of the Basis key. By default, Min is set to 0.00 and Max is set to 1.00. These settings control the range of change that can occur for each shape key, with 1.00 indicating that the shape key is used at "full strength" and 0.00 meaning that the shape key is not applied at all.

Perhaps the easiest way to understand them is to play with them and test the results.

Select the "Chin Big" shape key from the shapes menu. Drag the slider from 1.00 down to 0.50. The chin shape shrinks about halfway toward the Basis key. Move it the whole way down to 0.00, and the "Chin Big" shape key will not affect the shape of the mesh at all.

LMB on the small arrow on the left side of the Min value. The value immediately changes to -1.00. What this means is that the shape key can be applied in reverse, which will move vertices opposite to how they were moved when the shape key was made. Move the key value slider to -1.00 and you'll see Suzanne's chin shrink to smaller than original size. Reset both the slider and Min values to 0.00 for now.

With "Chin Big" still selected in the menu, LMB on the arrow to the right of the Max value. The value changes to 2.00. Drag the slider to 2.00 and see Suzanne's chin grow much larger than you originally intended. Reset the key value slider to 0.00 and the Max value to 1.00 for now.

The "Chin Big" shape key applied at -1.00.

Min and Max values can be useful to exaggerate or reverse shape keys for special effects. You need to use them with care, however, as the results may not always be what you expect.

Animating Shape Keys

Before you begin animating, you should set the animation length by telling Blender how many frames your animation will contain. Go to the Scene Buttons (F10). In the Anim panel, change the "End" value to 100. The "Sta" (start) value should be 1. Your animation will begin on frame 1 and end on frame 100.

Min/Max Settings

Start on frame 1 (Shift-Left Arrow). Select each of the four shape keys one by one from the pop-up shapes menu (Nose Long, Nose Wide Long, Eyes Odd, Chin Big). LMB on the slider and slide it to the right, away from zero. When you release the mouse button, the result will be displayed in the 3D view. You may want to rotate the view a little with the MMB so you can see what's happening. When you move the slider, the selected shape is used in proportion to the value you set. If you slide the "Nose Long" slider to a value of 0.50, the nose will only extend half the distance saved in the shape key.

If you move the slider for each shape key to a non-zero value, you will see that the mesh displays the combination of all these shapes together. The ability to combine multiple shapes is one of the strengths of Blender shape keys and means that it can sometimes be possible to create complex animation with just a few shape keys.

It's important to note that each time you move a shape key slider, it sets a key frame on the animation timeline. For this animation, you want Suzanne to start out looking normal, and then to change shape before returning to normal at the end. So, you want

All the shape keys set to 1.0.

all the sliders set to zero on the first frame (frame 1). Select each shape key from the menu again and set each slider to zero. Suzanne looks normal again.

First, we'll just mess with Suzanne's nose. Move forward thirty frames to frame 31 (Up Arrow three times). Select "Nose Long" from the list and move the slider to 1.00. You'll see Suzanne's nose stretch to full length. A key frame for this shape key has now been set at frame 31. Go back to frame 1 (Shift + Left Arrow), move the mouse pointer over the 3D view and press Alt-A to watch the animation. You'll see Suzanne's nose grow, then stay stretched until the frame counter reaches frame 100. Then, the nose snaps back and re-grows as the animation replays from frame 1 again. Press the Esc-key to cancel the looping animation playback.

Now, move forward to frame 61 and LMB on the slider for the "Nose Long" key again. You don't need to move it — just clicking on the slider sets a key frame and leaves the value at 1.00. Move forward to frame 101 and move the slider back to 0.00. This will cause the nose to return to its normal position by frame 101.

Move the mouse pointer over the 3D view again and press Alt-A to see the animation. Suzanne's nose will grow, stay stretched for a while then shrink before replaying. Press the Esc-key to cancel the playback.

What's Happened?

By setting key frames, you've told Blender how the mesh should be deformed at those points in the timeline. Blender automatically works out, or interpolates, the amount of deformation in between those key frames. You can see the results by looking at the values displayed in the sliders as you change frames. For example, if you move to frame 11, you will see that the slider for "Nose Long" has a value of 0.24 on that frame. The value increases fairly steadily as it approaches the first key frame at frame 31.

To get an even better look at what's happening, select a shape key from the shapes menu, position the mouse cursor over the Buttons Window, then press Shift-Alt-A. Now the animation plays while the sliders indicate the changing values of the selected shape key.

Note that shapes will constantly transform between key frames of different values so if you want the mesh to hold a particular shape for a while before changing, you'll need to set a key at the beginning and end of the block of time when you would like it to remain constant. That's why we set a key frame value of 1.00 at frames 31 and 61: so the nose would stay stretched for a while before shrinking again. In most cases you will find that you will set a key frame where you want the shape to start deforming, another key frame where it will be fully deformed, a third key frame where the shape begins to change back again, then a final key frame to indicate where the change has finished.

Animating Multiple Shape Keys

If you have more than one shape key to animate, or if you want a visual reference for keeping track of key frames, then the above approach becomes too awkward. To continue the tutorial, open an Action Editor Window. You can change the existing Buttons Window into an Action Editor Window via the Window Menu button (Refer to Chapter 2: The Blender Interface if you need to look up how to do this).

In the Action Editor window (usually just called the Action Editor) you will see all of Suzanne's shape keys listed. LMB on the small triangle next to the word "Sliders" to expose a key value slider for each key. These sliders work in exactly the same way as those you used in the Shapes panel, but now you can access them all at the same time without scrolling through a menu. A marker is placed on the timeline for each key frame that is created. These markers can be selected, moved, scaled and deleted in the Action Window (see the Character Animation chapter for more on working within the Action Window).

At this stage, you should already see a marker for each shape key on frame 1, and markers on frames 31, 61 and 101 for the "Nose Long" shape key (press the Home-key to auto-zoom the window to show all of the keyframes). The markers on frame 1 were set when you first clicked each shape key slider and set the values to 0.00. The other markers show the key frames that were set for Suzanne's stretching and shrinking nose.

Action Editor window and Suzanne model before adding additional keyframes

The Action Window also indicates the current frame number with a vertical green line. LMB in the Action Window and the indicator will move to the mouse cursor and set the current frame accordingly.

Morphing Suzanne

LMB on frame 31 in the Action Window to set the current frame to 31. You should see the green vertical line that represents the current frame jump to that frame. Move the sliders for "Eyes Odd" and "Chin Big" to 1.00. Blender sets markers on the timeline. Move forward to frame 61 either by LMB on the timeline or by hitting Up Arrow three times. Move both sliders to 0.50. You can LMB on the number on the slider to quickly type in an exact value if moving the slider isn't accurate enough.

Move forward to frame 81 and set the slider values to 1.00 again. Then move to frame 101 and set the sliders to 0.00. When the animation cycles you should see the nose grow and shrink as before, but now the eyes and chin will grow, shrink a little, grow again then return to normal before the animation replays. Press Alt-A over the 3D view to try it out. If you press Shift-Alt-A with the mouse cursor over the Action Editor, you'll see the slider values change as the animation runs.

Combined Shape Keys

When two different shape keys affect the same part of a mesh, Blender mixes the shapes together. As with many things in Blender, the best way to understand this is to just mess with it, so let's do that next.
Return to frame 31. LMB on the slider for "Nose Wide Long" to set it to a value of 0.00 on this frame. This ensures the shape remains unchanged for the first 31 frames.

Now move to frame 61. Here you see Suzanne's nose fully stretched to the shape you made in "Nose Long". If you remember, you also made "Nose Wide Long" from the "Nose Long" shape but made the tip of the nose wider.

If you set the slider for "Nose Wide Long" to 1.00 on frame 61, you will see in the 3D window that the nose grows even longer. In fact, it stretches twice as far as it was stretched when you made that shape key. The reason is that the vertices of the nose have already moved once due to the "Nose Long" shape key, and Blender moves them again for the "Nose Wide Long" shape key. You can test this by setting the "Nose Long" slider back to 0.00 on frame 61 to see that the nose returns to the shape you made for "Nose Wide Long". Leave it set to 0.00.

Now move to frame 101 and set the slider for "Nose Wide Long" to 0.00. Check the animation with Alt-A.

Editing the Key Frames

The key frame markers in the Action Window can be edited in various ways. We won't go into detail here, but you can play with them to get a feel for what they do. Pressing the A-key in the Action Window selects or deselects all key frame markers. RMB clicking on a marker selects it, and the B-key box select can be used to select multiple markers. You can also Shift-RMB to select multiple markers. Pressing the G-key moves selected markers. Holding Ctrl limits movement to single frame increments. You can delete a selected key frame with X-key. Basically, the key frame markers in the Action Editor can be dealt with just like normal objects in the 3D view. If you find that your animation happens too quickly, or too slowly, you also have the ability to scale the key frame markers. By selecting two markers (from the same shape key) and pressing the S-key you can move them together or further apart.

Deselect all markers. Then, select the two markers on frame 61 for "Eyes Odd" and "Chin Big". Press the X-key to delete these key frames. Now the eyes and chin will no longer shrink in the middle of the animation. Play the animation to see the result.

There is much more you can do with shape keys: pinning shapes to view multiple shape keys at the same time on different instances of the mesh, applying shape keys only to selected vertex groups, and causing shape keys to animate based on the motion of other objects. These are advanced subjects that you can investigate as you progress. Here is a quick overview of their functionality.

With what you learned in this tutorial you know all you need to know to be able to make Suzanne appear to talk. To do this you would need to make shape keys with the mouth in a few different shapes, including wide open, fully closed and pursed into a tight "ooo" shape. You could even import an audio track directly into Blender and, with practice, synchronize your key frames to it.

Now that you are familiar with the Shape Keys work flow, see if you can make it happen!

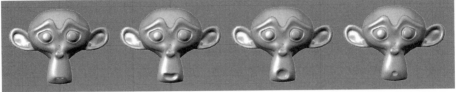

Some simple shape key suggestions for practicing basic lip-syncing with Suzanne.

Shape Keys: Tools

You already know that in Blender you can animate the way that objects move around the 3D world. Blender also gives you the ability to have your mesh objects change their shape over time. These changes, called deformations, are saved in "shape keys". Examples of where you might use shape keys include morphing from one character or shape to another, or adding subtle variations to a shape to add interest to an animation, like having a creature's chest rise and fall to show breathing. One very popular use of shape keys (sometimes called "morph targets") is for character facial expressions and lip-syncing. Shape keys are not restricted to animation however. If you have a model you wish to use in a series of still images, shape keys can be a convenient way of saving shape variations that will be used more than once.

Various facial expressions created only with shape keys.

Shape keys store vertex positions relative to their original positions in the mesh. After the shape key is stored, the deformation can be controlled by influence sliders. Moving the sliders causes the vertices to change from their positions in the original mesh shape and move toward the positions saved in the selected shape key.

Multiple shape keys can also be combined to vary the final shape of the mesh. The original shape of the mesh is saved as a basis shape key. It is always available and can be returned to at any stage, no matter how many shape keys have been made from it. As shape keys are non-destructive, you can try out various ideas on changing or improving a model, and if you find you don't like them, you can delete or ignore them, returning to the basis shape. Keep in mind that shape keys do not allow you to change the structure of the mesh, only the positions of the vertices which make up the mesh. You cannot add or delete vertices when using shape keys.

Making Shape Keys

Before you begin.

Before working on your shape keys, be sure that you are happy that your basic model is finished.

One important point to remember when working with shape keys is that since they store relative vertex positions, the mesh should be in a finished state before applying them. While some editing is possible after shape keys have been saved, it can lead to unpredictable results and may make some of the shape keys useless, in which case you'll need to recreate those shape keys from scratch.

It is common practice to build organic models, like humans and animals, using a mirror modifier so only one half has to be modeled while Blender automatically creates the other half. If you've used a mirror modifier while modeling, make sure to "Apply" it (join the two halves) before proceeding with shape keys, as applying mirror modifiers later will result in the loss of all shape keys.

Shape key controls are found in the Shapes tab of the Editing Buttons (F9). Shape keys are added to a mesh in Object mode. Then, the shapes are made and edited in Edit mode.

The Shapes tab before any shape keys are saved.

If no shape keys have previously been stored for a selected mesh object, the Shapes panel will show a single button with the label "Add Shape Key." When this button is pressed, the panel changes to show a button labeled "Relative," which is active by default, and a drop-down menu with the word "Basis" showing in the text field. This shows you that Blender has stored the current state of the mesh as the Basis shape key. The Basis shape key is essentially the original un-deformed mesh, and all future shape keys for this mesh will be stored relative to this shape key.

The Shapes tab with basis shape key saved.

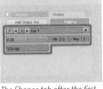

The Shapes tab after the first shape key is saved

Pressing the "Add Shape Key" Button again results in a new shape key labeled "Key 1" being added to the drop-down menu. The key name can, and usually should, be changed to something that will indicate what this shape key represents. For example, when making mouth shapes for lip-sync, the shape keys should be given names that indicate the sound or letter each key represents. If you fail to do this, a lot of time will be wasted when you go to actually use the shapes in an animation. You can edit the name of each shape key by selecting it from the shapes panel menu, then typing a new name into the text field.

When the first new shape key is added, you will see a key value slider, a "Min" and "Max" adjuster and a text box labeled "VGroup:" in the Shapes panel. These give you additional control over the shape key, which will be explained in a bit.

A list of shape keys with sliders also appears in the Action Editor window (Action window), if one is open. When animating with shape keys, it is usually better to do so in the Action Editor as multiple shape keys can be easily accessed without scrolling through a menu, and markers are placed to indicate key frames for each shape key.

The Action Editor window showing a list of shape keys

Once a shape key has been created, a unique target shape can be made by tabbing into Edit mode. Selected vertices, edges or faces can be moved, scaled or rotated to create a new shape. Remember that vertices, edges and faces should not be added or deleted when making shape keys. After the mesh has been modified into the desired shape, it can be stored by exiting Edit mode. Each time the "Add Shape Key" button is pressed, a new shape key is created, ready to store a new shape.

Shape keys can be selected from the drop down menu next to the shape key names or by scrolling through all keys using the "Previous Shape Key" and "Next Shape Key" buttons.

Making Shape Keys

Using One Shape Key as the Basis For a New One

New shape keys are based on the currently selected shape key at the time the "Add Shape Key" button is pressed. So, if the Basis key is selected, the new shape key will be a copy of the Basis key, ready for editing. Sometimes it is useful to have two or more keys that are similar to each other. In this case, an existing shape key should be selected before pressing "Add Shape Key". Then, when entering Edit mode, the mesh will already be deformed to the same state as the previous shape key. From here, minor or major adjustments can be made to the mesh to create the new shape key. This can save quite a lot of time when creating similar shape keys in complex models, as the majority of the adjustments would only need to be done once. Subsequent shapes could be based on the first adjustment.

Editing Shape Keys

As shape keys store positions of vertices relative to the base mesh, it is quite simple to change them, even after they have been used in an animation. In fact, it can sometimes be useful to begin animating and using the shape keys to determine if they need to be tweaked for best results. To edit a shape key, select it from the shape key drop down menu, then tab into Edit mode. Adjust the mesh as desired and save it by tabbing back into Object mode.

One problem that may arise after saving shape keys is coming to the realization that your original shape isn't quite the way you'd like it to be. You may, for example, decide that your character's ears are too small. Simply making them bigger won't deliver the desired result as the smaller ears have already been saved in all existing shape keys and the changes you make will only affect the currently selected shape key.

A very useful feature of Blender shape keys is the ability to change the mesh in one shape key and have that change affect all existing shape keys. Such changes would usually best be done with the base mesh (the Basis key), as this is the un-deformed mesh and any changes will probably be more predictable. So, if you decide the basic shape needs some adjustment, select Basis from the shape key menu and fix the mesh in Edit mode. Then, with all edited vertices still selected, press W-key and choose "Propagate To All Shapes". Return to object mode and examine the remaining shapes to make sure that everything happened as you expected. Remember that you cannot add or delete vertices, edges or faces when you do this. You can only move, rotate or scale existing ones.

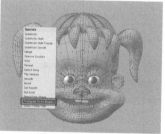

A mesh in Edit mode, showing "Propagate to all shapes."

It is also possible to adjust selected vertices of one shape key by applying vertex offsets from another shape key. Select a shape key from the menu and enter Edit mode. Select some or all vertices and press W-key. Choose "Blend From Shape". A menu pops up with a list of other shape keys to copy from. Select one, then move the mouse slowly in order to see and control the adjustment. Pressing MMB will apply the adjustment at 100%. This feature would prove useful if you wanted your character to have larger ears in some of your existing shape keys, but not

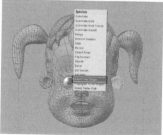

A mesh in Edit mode, showing "Blend to Shape" selected.

all of them. It is certainly quicker and easier than editing the ears in each shape key individually.

If you've already commenced animating, it is important to note that the effect of editing the shape keys or the base mesh will apply immediately to any animation you have already keyed. Be sure to tweak carefully and check the animated results regularly. You may find you'll need to adjust some sliders or edit some key frames to achieve a better result after you've made changes to your shape keys.

Deleting Shape Keys

You can select a shape key from the drop down menu and press the "X" button to delete it. When a shape key is deleted, its influence in an animation is completely removed.

Using Shape Keys

When a shape key is created, the key value slider associated with it will show a default value of 0.0. This means that new shape keys have no influence on a mesh, leaving the mesh un-deformed. If the key value slider is moved forward and released, the mesh will deform. The amount of deformation is relative to the slider value (0.0=0%; 1.0=100%). Note that the slider is not interactive, and the mesh is not updated in the 3D view until the slider is released. Also note that the vertices move in a linear fashion. That is, they move in a straight line from the basis position toward the position stored in the shape key. This linear displacement is important to recognize and understand, as it is one of the main differences between shape key animation and animation using armatures. If you need your mesh to move in a curved motion, such as an eyelid sliding over the surface of a rounded eyeball, shape keys may not be the best option.

The "Min" and "Max" settings next to the key value slider allow you to push vertices past the values saved in the shape key or to move them in the opposite direction, relative to the basis mesh. Pushing a shape to extremes by setting the Max value greater than 1.0 and pushing the influence slider up can sometimes be useful, but it can also deliver unexpected results.

The "Min" setting can be made negative, giving the reverse of the shape key. If a group of vertices was moved to the left in the stored shape key, setting "Min" to a negative value and pushing the influence slider below 0.0 would cause those vertices to move to the right. While this can be an apparently easy way of turning a smile into a frown, for example, it must be approached with caution and is usually best for subtle effects. Values can be negative or positive but the Max value must always be greater than the Min value.

A single Shape key applied to a sphere with its slider set to 1.0 and -1.0

The Pin icon in the Shapes panel can be used to view the effects of a single shape key on a mesh, or an entire set of shape keys at the same time on multiple instances of a mesh. Linked duplicates of the mesh, created by pressing Alt-D on selected objects in Object mode, can be placed side-by-side with each one displaying a different shape key at full key value. A gallery of shape keys can be created using this method. This can be a useful way of comparing different experimental shapes and to choose a preferred shape.

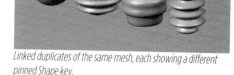

To use shape Pinning, simply find the shape you want to display from the shapes drop down and click the pin icon. Until the pin icon is turned off, the object will display with that shape, regardless of other keys that might have been set.

A More Advanced Trick

The influence of a shape key can also be limited to a

Linked duplicates of the same mesh, each showing a different pinned Shape key.

selected vertex group using the VGroup option, and the result can be further controlled through vertex weight painting. Using this feature, it is possible to create one shape key which contains complex deformations all over a mesh, and then use the shape key in conjunction with different vertex groups to create a whole series of new shape keys, each affecting only a small portion of the mesh. For example, it may be simpler to create an angry face shape key all at once, but you may want access to different components of that shape individually: knotted brow, squinting eyes and snarling lips. It often gives better results to model adjustments all at once, and then to create separate shape keys using vertex groups than it is to create several separate shape keys from scratch.

For more information about vertex groups, refer to Chapter 4.

To do this, create an overall shape key, then create and assign several vertex groups to the mesh, one for each section that would benefit from having a separate shape key. In the VGroup text box of the shape key, enter the name of one of the vertex groups. The shape key is now restricted to only affecting those vertices contained in the group. Press the Add Shape Key button. Normally, this would create a whole new copy of the entire current shape key. In this case, though, it just creates a copy of the shape keys from the vertex group. You can now go back to the original shape key, change the name to that of another vertex groups, and create additional keys.

Animating Shape Keys

Animation occurs when different shape key values are stored at various points along the animation timeline. These values are stored in key frames. Blender displays the current frame number in the header bar of the Buttons window and with a green vertical line in the Action Editor. Frames can be changed using the arrow keys. More information about the animation timeline and changing frames can be found in Chapter 3.

When the key value slider is moved, a key frame is automatically inserted in the animation timeline on the current frame, so the mesh shape at that frame is recorded. Changing frames and moving the slider to various values will result in an animated shape when the frames are played back. If a shape key slider's value is set to 1.0, then the stored values for each vertex affected by that shape key will be applied at 100% on the current frame. This influence will remain unless the slider is moved to a different value on a later frame. Blender creates smooth transitions from one key frame to the next by interpolating values for all shapes between key frames. These values can be seen by setting the frame counter to the desired frame number and reading the value shown in the key value slider in the Shapes panel with the desired shape key selected.

It is often useful to have a mesh change shape over a period of time and remain unchanged for a while, sometimes for just a few frames, before changing shape again. To force a shape to stay at one value for a number of frames before changing shape, it is necessary to set the value slider at the start and end of the fixed-shape period.

Shape Keys in the Action Editor

If your mesh has more than one shape key saved, it is more efficient to animate with the sliders in the Action Editor than to keep switching from shape to shape in the Shapes panel of the Edit buttons. The Action Editor window displays a list of all shape keys associated with the selected mesh. Each shape key has a key value slider that follows the same rules as the influence slider in the Shapes panel. Again, simply moving a slider forward or backward inserts a key frame for that shape on the current frame. You can also see in the Action Window that Blender places a key frame marker in the selected shape's channel. These markers not only serve as a reference for existing key frames but also give the animator access to even greater control over the animation as they can be moved, duplicated or deleted with the standard Blender controls (G-key, Shift-D, X-key).

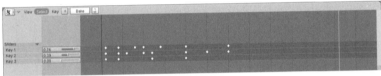

The Action Editor window showing key frame markers.

You can also use the Action Window to edit the name of shape keys or change the Min and Max values. Simply LMB on the shape key name in the list, and a dialog panel will open up, giving access to the shape key values.

The Action Editor window showing the Shape key pop-up panel.

When animating, you may notice some unexpected results when several shape keys are applied at once. If two shape keys affect the same vertex, the final position of that vertex will be determined by the influence of both shape keys added together. For example, if you apply two shape keys to one frame and both keys push the same vertex one unit to the right, the end result will be to push the vertex two units to the right. Conversely, if the second shape key moves the vertex one unit in the opposite direction, the combined result will be for the vertex not to move at all. A practical example of the combined effect of shape keys is given in the tutorial for this chapter.

When Blender saves key frames for shape keys, it can display the values as a set of curves along the animation timeline. These are called Ipo curves and can be viewed by opening an Ipo Curve

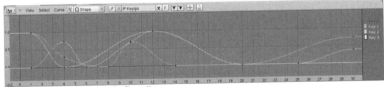

An Ipo window, showing curves for Shape Keys.

Editor window and choosing "Shape" from the Ipo type menu in the window's header. Each shape key has its own curve, identified by the color key in the upper right of the window. Ipo curves can be edited in a variety of ways for advanced animation control. This is often the final step in tweaking an animation. You can refer to the Ipo window section in Chapter 3 for more information on handling Ipo curves.

Crazy Space

When a model is deformed by an armature, it can be difficult to edit the mesh, as the vertices, edges and faces are no longer in their original locations and don't respond to editing as you might expect. Under some circumstances, they might even move away from their intended direction. For this reason, working on a mesh while it is being deformed by an armature is called working in "crazy space". To avoid this problem, select the armature and put it in its un-deformed position using the "Rest Position" button in the Armature tab of the (F9) Editing buttons. This returns the mesh to its default position, and things will behave as expected when editing.

Advanced Uses for Shape Keys

Once you've mastered shape key basics and are comfortable with animating and editing them, you may wish to use automated shape keys in combination with an armature for subtle effects during animation. This automated process is referred to as "driven shape keys".

Shape keys can be "driven" such that when a bone is moved or rotated, the shape key will respond automatically. This feature can be put to great use to prevent meshes from pinching at joints like elbows and knees, or to simulate muscle contraction and expansion as limbs move. Some animators use a combination of bones and driven shape keys for facial animation. Although driven keys are outside the scope of this book, it is good to know that such things can be accomplished.

Conclusion

Shape keys give Blender artists a powerful way to animate and deform their mesh models. They are the primary tool for facial expressions and lip syncing as well as for creating morphing effects. Combined with armatures, they give artists nearly complete control over the shape of their meshes.

Materials and Textures

 Materials and Textures: Hands On
by Colin Litster

Blender Materials: Discussion

Colin Litster – (cog)

Colin Litster started his interest in 3D design after working as a SFX cameraman back in the 1980's. His career progressed into higher education, eventually heading the ICT operations in a large UK university. Colin has maintained his interest in the application of IT to movie production and in 2000 discovered Blender as a viable tool to help produce a 3D feature called *Cog*. Embracing the open spirit of Blender, Colin has contributed many tutorials that have been well received by the community. His contributions in this book will hopefully encourage more 3D artists achieve the impossible.

Materials and Textures in Blender: Hands On

Blender, like any 3D design suite, is essentially a simulation program. Points (vertices) are placed in a virtual 3D space and these points are joined to form faces. Faces are then lit with simulated lights, and a simulated camera is placed to look at your virtual object. All this has to be done before your simulated object and world can be rendered in all its glory.

Blender's Material and Texturing system provides the tools that help you simulate a surface color or property that will turn a boring, gray plastic-looking object into something much more interesting.

This could be based on a photorealistic interpretation of a real material or on some artistic style, like a cartoon, or an impressionistic painting.

A photorealistic render from Blender.

In other words, Materials and Textures offer an enormous palette of color, style, and effect that can be applied to untextured 3D objects, turning them into a truly inspiring picture or animation.

Of course, this means that there is no magic button to press in Blender, or any 3D package, that will automatically produce realistic, or even good-looking, materials. You have to make decisions about many settings, as well as to apply observational and artistic skills. All of these choices can appear daunting to the beginning 3D artist. Indeed, many artists find it difficult to move from more traditional forms of art because of the apparent need to know every aspect of a 3D tool before attempting a still image or animation. Really, though, you only need to know the basics in order to get started. From there, you can build on that knowledge.

Line illustration render from Blender that simulates a hand drawn look.

In this section of the book, we will show you how to quickly simulate a realistic looking material, as well as provide a more general strategy to apply to any material situation. You will also see that you can start to achieve some very good results with only a few tools.

The Material Interface

For purposes of this tutorial, you are going to use the default Material Screen provided by Blender. Start the Blender application, then use either the keyboard shortcut Ctrl-Left/Right Arrow or the Screens dropdown menu to choose the provided Materials editing screen, which looks like this:

Blender comes pre-configured with a Materials editing screen.

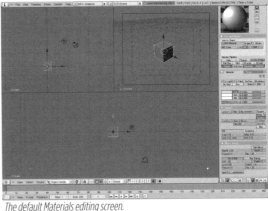

The default Materials editing screen.

Approaches to Simulating a Real Material

Time to get down to creating materials in Blender. For this exercise you will look at how a relatively complex surface material can be created with just a few commands and settings. Also, you'll see an approach to simulating a real material that you can use time and time again to speed up your production pipeline. Don't worry that some commands will be glossed over and given without explanation... we're doing a run-through to get you familiar with the basics. In most cases, we will come back to those areas in more detail later, and in the discussion section after the chapter.

A photograph of an office desk.

The best tools you can employ in creating any material are your eyes. Direct visual interpretation of what you are trying to simulate really is the best way to start material and texture creation. For that reason we will start with a surface to which all of us have fairly easy access.

You will start with the simple desk surface, ignoring for now the power adapter and cables.

Creating the Object and Setting the Lights

Any surface, such as your desktop, either scatters the light toward your eye (this kind of light is called Diffuse), or reflects it directly (called Specular). This means you require some simulated lights to represent the light sources that exist in the real scene. If you need to learn Blender's approach to lighting, you can refer to Chapter 11.

Diffuse Light

Any surface, such as your desktop, has small crevices, nicks and irregularities that prevent light from reflecting perfectly, as though it were a mirror. In fact, most natural surfaces have so much irregularity that they scatter any light that hits them, so the light that reaches your eye from any point on the surface may have come from almost any direction.

Specular Light

Some surfaces will also have specular highlights where the light reflects in a more concentrated manner, giving shininess to the surface.

The position of lighting certainly affects the way your eye perceives a scene, and for that reason it's important to set up the lights in your Blender scene to approximate the ones from the photograph. Without doing that, you can't get a good read on how to set up your Materials.

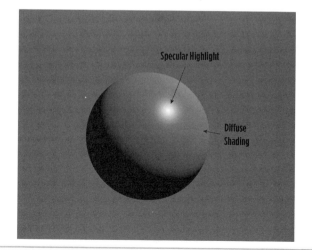

Approaches to Simulating a Real Material

In the example there are 3 lights.

Light 1 represents the outside sunlight that is coming through the window.

Lights 2 & 3 are there to represent light bouncing off of the walls and the artificial light source in the room.

It is possible to set up very realistic lighting that will accurately mimic the properties of real lights, but it is often better to use quite simple setups that copy the general location and brightness of real world lights. Simple setups mean that you can easily arrange and fine-tune their effect and therefore concentrate on making a material perfect.

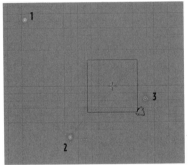

The desktop with the three lamps.

The provided scene, rendered with no materials.

If you've worked through the modeling and lighting chapters, you should be able to easily make a nice approximation of this setup. For later in the tutorial, you will also need a simple model of the power supply and cables. If you are just working on materials and don't feel like modeling anything right now, you can find the file, called "materials_tutorial.blend", with the models and lights preset in the "examples" folder on the included CD.

An Approach to Materials

Adding a New Material

In order to begin, you need to create a new material for the plane surface. Select the plane that is your desktop with RMB.

The Links and Pipeline tab, before clicking Add New.

Under the Links and Pipeline tab in the Material buttons is the Add New button. Select this so that a new material will be created for your desktop object.

As you can see, Blender creates a default gray material for your object. It's from this default that you will make modifications to turn the material into more of a wooden, desktop-like surface. Don't worry about all those controls. At this stage only a few of them are necessary to produce your wooden desktop.

The default Material.

An Approach to Materials

Material Base Color

One of the easiest things to do is to set up the base color of the material.

Just below the preview tab you should see a Material tab with settings for the color. LMB inside the gray color area just to the left of the Col button, popping up the color picker.

Here you can drag across the color panels to select any color you like. Try it. LMB a color then confirm it by pressing the Enter key.

The material will now have a diffuse color based on your choice. You are also able to manipulate the R, G, and B sliders directly in the material tab or to enter values with the keyboard to accurately obtain the color you require.

That is what I want you to do now. LMB on the R value (Red) so that the number there becomes highlighted for direct numeric input.

Blender's color picker palette.

- Enter 1.0 for R(ed) and press TAB to move down to the G(reen) entry.
- Enter 0.837 and press TAB to move down to B(lue) entry.
- Enter 0.438 and press the Enter key.

I chose that color after very careful observation of the desk in the original photograph (obviously, the real desk is not black and white like the photo). When trying to determine the base color to use for a material, you must try to imagine what the real material would look like if illuminated evenly with a balanced white light.

Diffuse and Specular colors are set on the Material tab.

Even though you've defined the basic color of the material, you haven't told Blender anything about how this material reacts to light. Is it shiny, like wet rock, or does it have a soft, extremely diffuse appearance, like pool table felt?

Blender implements both Diffuse and Specular shader models under the Shaders tab of the Material buttons.

The Shaders tab.

The Lambert model is one of several available for Diffuse shading and the CookTorr is one of a series of Specular models. Later you will learn about the others but for now we are going to stick with the defaults. In fact, the default specular model settings of Spec 0.50 and Hard of 50 are fine for your desk surface.

Diffuse and Specular shaders are chosen on the Shaders tab.

Variation Across the Material Surface

Almost no surface has a totally uniform color, shininess, or flatness. In fact, variation across a material surface is the single most important thing that will transform a dull and obviously computer-generated material into an authentic surface representation, or at least a more interesting one. Observation of the desk surface reveals that apart from the wood grain there are some subtle and random variations in color across the surface. You therefore need a similar random texture to give color variation to your shading model. In order to simulate these variations it's necessary to add textures to your material.

Material Base Color

Textures

Blender offers the ability to apply up to 10 texture layers within a standard Blender material. Each texture layer offers a huge range of possibilities to help modify your material. For this reason, things can appear a little daunting when beginning to work with textures. We will be covering the details of textures in the discussion section. So for now, just follow along with the suggestions and see what happens.

- Switch the buttons view window to Textures (F6 or LMB the textures icon).
- LMB on the Add New button.

The Textures tab, before adding any textures.

The same tab after clicking "Add New"

A new texture is created in the first slot with a default name. Currently there is no texture type assigned so the preview is blank.

- Click the Texture Type button, where it says None, to display a list of available textures, and from the list, select "Clouds".

The Preview tab gives an indication of what the texture looks like. This one, as its name suggests, looks sort of cloud-like.

- Change the Noise Size to 0.158 and the Noise Depth to 3.
- Switch back to Material buttons (F5 or LMB the materials icon).

The Texture tab and Preview tabs with a preview of the Cloud texture type.

Textures provide variation to a material.

As soon as a material has a texture attached, a lot of new options appear. We will be dealing with most of these later, but for now you only need to worry about three things:

- How will the texture be projected ("mapped" is the proper CG term) onto the surface?
- What will be the size and orientation of that projection?
- And how will the texture interact with the underlying material?

Mapping

The default mapping is called "Flat", and fortunately, you have a nice flat surface to which we would like you to apply the texture. Obviously, there are other ways to map textures onto models, several of which will be covered in the discussion section. One, UV, is so useful, it has its own chapter (Chapter 10).

The tab that has these settings is called Map Input. If you don't see this tab in your Material buttons window, either MMB-drag the window or use the scroll wheel inside of it to show the additional tabs at the bottom of the view.

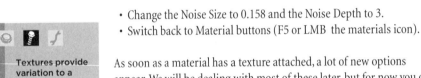

Ensure that the Flat and X, Y and Z buttons are turned on as in the illustration. These are the defaults for new textures though, so you shouldn't have to change them.

Textures

Size and Orientation

Although you have already set a Noise Size in the Texture buttons you are able to have greater control over the texture's size and orientation in the Map Input tab. Alter the sizeY to 10.00. This will squash the Y axis mapping of the texture (front to back) which makes it look more like a variation caused by the direction of the wood grain.

If you were to render now the material would look very strange (try F12 and see!)

Currently Blender doesn't know what you want the texture to do, so it's applying it as a default Magenta color.

Texture Interaction with the Material (Map To)

The Map To tab in the Material buttons also has a host of options that we will cover later. For now, it's a color variation that you're interested in, so the Col (Color) button and the Mix color are the important options. Set the Map To tab to match the highlighted portions of the illustration.

The Map To panel.

If you render this time you will see that the desk material looks much better (F12).

Bumps

It's very common for a surface to have bumps, either due to its natural makeup or as the result of damage and erosion. Adding these details can raise a material's believability. As you're shooting for believability, not an exact copy of reality, such details don't have to be exact photographic duplicates of what you can see. For instance the wood grain on the desktop would be very difficult to copy exactly. However, it should be possible to come up with similar patterns and colors so that it looks like the simulated desk was produced from the same materials as the original. Let's have a go at creating the wood grain.

If you look closely at a real wood surface like that of the desk, you will see that it has both depth and color. In this case, it appears that a covering of varnish or stain has been added, which pooled slightly in the grain dents, causing them to darken a bit. In fact, the grain is quite pronounced and much darker than the wood surface. Once again, careful observation is the key. It is often not good enough to work from what you imagine as "wood" — unless you are a practiced artistic observer, your memory will have already done a good bit of shorthand and simplification to it. Find a real piece of wood (or a detailed picture) and study it.

Don't worry. You won't have to do this for every material for the rest of your life. Once you get the hang of artistic observation and visualization, you'll often be able to do "good enough" materials just by detailed visualization.

Textures Are Your Friends

Since you have 10 Texture slots available within any single material, you have plenty of space to add wood grain to your material.

It's possible to add a new texture right from within the Material buttons.

• Find the Texture panel in the Material buttons.
• LMB on the empty texture slot below the one you have already created.
• LMB on the Add New button to create a new texture in that slot.

You will notice that the name of the texture appears to be identical to the last one, called "Tex". However, the actual texture name is Tex.001. You could change it here by LMB on the name and entering one of your choice. It's easier to do that however, in the Texture buttons.

Creating a new texture directly within the Material buttons.

• Press F6 (Texture buttons)

The Texture buttons also have a Texture tab where you can Add New textures.

New textures can be added from either the Material or Texture buttons.

You can change the name of any texture that's selected by clicking the name and entering one of your choice. Here I have changed the name of both textures as a reminder of their function.

If you can't think of a name (or if you are completely lazy!), you can use the little motorcar icon. This will generate an automatic name based on the type of texture.

The textures have been renamed so they are easier to keep organized.

Back to your wood surface. Careful examination shows that the grain is made from 2 elements. There are some broad elongated concentric rings that are slightly darker than the overall surface. Within those, there is some thin and dark wood grain that has a pronounced indentation in the wood. You will

It's always a good idea to give meaningful names to Blender objects, and Materials and Textures are no exception. You can easily lose track of what you are doing without the discipline of a good naming scheme. Although names are restricted to 19 characters, it should be more than enough to keep things straight.

start with the broader concentric rings.

I have chosen Wood texture and RingNoise with a Noise Size of 0.250 and a Turbulence of 16.10.

Go back to the Material buttons (F5) so that you can decide how it will be mapped to the material.

More Mapping

This texture will only be mapped to the Nor value.

The "Nor" button refers to "surface normals". The Normal of a surface is simply the direction that the surface is facing at any given point. Using a texture to change the surface normal alters the way that the shader calculates light and shading for that particular point. Changing the direction the surface faces at different places simulates bumps. They are not "real" bumps, i.e. bumps made out of triangle meshes, but when done properly they can give a fairly realistic interpretation of bumps and indentations across a surface. They will react to light shining on them and will appear as though they are self-shadowing. This is commonly referred to as "bump mapping".

Stencil

You can see that the "Stencil" option has been set. This uses the texture as a mask that will hide some portions of the textures below it in the Texture layers. The reason it is being used here is because you want some small tight grain to only show on some parts of the material, leaving some of the original surface showing through. The "Neg" (Negative) switch simply reverses the incoming texture information, in effect reversing which portions of the following textures are hidden or shown by the Stencil.

Size

Note that we have also changed the size of the texture in the Map Input tab to:

- $sizeX = 0.300$
- $sizeY = 3.00$
- $sizeZ = 2.00$

Those sizes were arrived at by trial and error, but guided by observation of the reference.

Previewing

It's possible to preview a material without resorting to a full render. The Material buttons have a very capable tab that actually uses Blender's renderer to generate its previews. Although small, you get an impression of how the material might look when applied to a variety of surfaces.

Don't forget: you can always use the Shift-P 3D window preview (See Chapter 2) to see how your Material and Texture settings look, and it's much quicker than doing a full render!

The Materials preview panel, showing the different ways to preview materials.

Multiple Effects from a Single Texture

So far you have used single effects for each texture (Col, Nor). It's possible, however, to apply a texture to more than one effect. On your next texture, which will represent the thin wood veins, you will do just that.

- With the desktop object selected, switch to the Texture buttons (F6).
- Add a new texture with the following settings:

This is another cloud texture with settings of Hard noise, NoiseSize set to 0.162, and NoiseDepth set at 4.

New settings for a Cloud texture.

Stencil

Mapping

Under the Map To tab both Col and Nor are set. As you are applying a color, a dark brown has been set with:

- R(ed) = 0.301
- G(reen) = 0.217
- B(lue) = 0.000

You will also notice that the Nor value is set to 8.00. This is quite a high Nor value, although not the maximum. The texturing effect that you are after has very pronounced sharp edges in the reference, so you have to turn the value up.

A full render at this point is a good idea (F12). In this render, you can really see how the previous texture that was set to Stencil is only letting this new effect show through in certain areas.

Not bad, but the original desktop surface is more random. In fact there is probably a simple explanation, and therefore a simple solution to how that random-ness occurs.

You will remember that the initial texture that you applied to the material was there to add the color variation that you could see on the wood's surface. As a

A full render of the desktop with materials and textures

tree develops, different seasons and weather vary the growth rate considerably. This can lead to denser areas within the wood which affect the way the grain evolves. So, not only is there variation within the material, but there is a variation in the way that it varies. Since you know that the cloud texture when applied as a color looked fairly authentic, why don't you use that texture to warp the two grain textures just as it might have done in reality?

Fortunately, Textures have a Warp feature for textures in slots below them, so let's go back to that texture and set a warp value so that it will vary the wood grain for you.

- From the Material buttons select the top texture slot — the one named "2nd-diffuse" in the illustrations.
- In the Map To tab LMB the Warp button to turn it on.
- Set the amount of warp to 0.30. Although this may appear small, the range is only 0 to 1, so a little variation can go a long way.

Adding Warp to the first texture channel.

Before you re-render to see the results, try this trick: get to the Render window, which should have a nice render of the desktop before you added the Warp control. While the Render window is in front, press the J-key. The render disappears. Now, re-render (F12). When the render is finished, press the J-key again. The old render shows back up. Press J-key yet again. The new render appears.

Pressing the J-key in the Render window allows you to save the original render in a separate "buffer", so that when your new one is complete, you can toggle between them to quickly compare their differences. Using this technique, it is easy to see how much more believable the material has just become.

A new render with warp in effect.

Reflections

Up until this point, you have used the Specular shader to provide a shiny highlight on the desktop. However, shiny materials also reflect the world around them. A mirror, for instance, will reflect almost all of the world around it. Polished or glazed surfaces will also reflect their surroundings to some extent.

Blender, like many powerful 3D applications, has an excellent "raytrace" render engine. It works by tracing a virtual ray of light from the camera back to a light source, calculating any reflection, refraction, or absorption that occurs between the two. This type of rendering gives the most realistic simulation of a scene. However, because it has to trace back to every light source, the render calculations take much longer than the standard Blender rendering method (for the curious, it's called "scanline").

In the early days of 3D design, before raytracing renderers, the only way of simulating reflection was by using complex image maps or by careful use of lighting to represent reflected light from surfaces. Blender itself has an older method of mimicking reflection called Env (Environment) mapping. However, on modern hardware, Blender's raytrace renderer is now relatively efficient. As a result, it is much easier to achieve a reflection using Raytrace, so that is the method you will use here.

Indiscriminate use of raytracing for reflections and transparency can still drastically raise your render times. For rendering still images, this is not usually a big deal. For animation work, where you might be rendering thousands of frames, those extra minutes can add up. If you will be using reflection in your animation work, you are urged to investigate the Env Map method.

Reflective Materials Need Something to Reflect

Currently your scene has nothing to reflect, as only the desktop has been modeled. However, you don't need to model an entire office around your desktop. You can simulate the reflected color from the office walls by changing the world color to approximate the real environment.

- Select the World button (F8) and change the Horizon color.

- Set the HoR to 0.540, HoG to 0.427, and HoB to 0.275
- Press ENTER to confirm those settings.

The World panel from the World buttons.

Adding the Power Supply for Some Close-Up Reflection

Apart from the walls and the world around the desktop, there is a power supply on the desk as well. If you look closely at the reference photo at what appears to be shadow below the supply and its cable, you will see that it is in fact a reflection on the desk surface and not really a shadow.

If you are building your own power supply and cables for modeling practice, now would be a good time to do so. If, however, you are using the included sample .blend file, then Shift-LMB on the Layer 2 button on the 3D header to show the pre-made models.

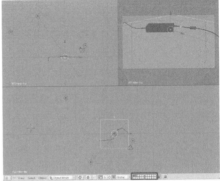

The objects on Layer 2 are now showing.

Set Raytrace Reflections for the Material

• Select the desktop object and move to the Material buttons (F5), selecting the Mirror Transp panel.

This tab may appear complex, dealing with things like Fresnel, Falloff, and IOR, but for uses where you only need simple reflection, there are only 2 settings and one button that need concern you.

Mirror Transp tab with raytrace reflection settings highlighted

Ray Mir is the amount of raytraced reflections and varies between 0 and 1, with 0 reflecting 0% of light from the surroundings and 1 reflecting 100% of it.

• Set it to 0.49

Depth refers the depths of calculation that Blender makes to trace the ray. For example, a ray that must bounce off two different mirrors before hitting its light source would require two levels of calculations. The default is 2 but its range is from 0 (no raytrace reflections) to 10 (significantly longer but more accurate raytracing renders).

• Make sure it is set to 2.
• To enable the Ray Mirror material effect, turn on the Ray Mirror button.

Render the scene so far.

Raytraced reflections are enabled on the Mirror Transp tab.

A render with Ray reflection enabled. Note the subtle reflection, distorted by the bump mapping on the desks surface.

If you don't see any reflection in your render, use F10 to enter the scene buttons and make sure that the Ray button is turned On for the renderer.

Enabling the Ray option in the Scene buttons.

The whole surface is looking much more realistic. However, real materials and surfaces will have subtle details on them that will tell the eye whether or not what it sees is "real", or at least believable.

Adding a History to a Material (Getting Dirty)

Close examination of a real desk surface shows polish and dust accumulation, as well as a few knocks and marks here and there. If you can add these subtle hints to the material's history, you can produce a much more believable material simulation.

A Material's History Can Be Broken Down Into 3 Possible Areas

Dirt

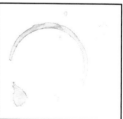

Adding dirt and irregular flaws will enhance a material's believability.

All real materials get dirty, either from accumulated dust or from interaction with liquids or staining substances.

- Dust will collect in crevices.
- Dirt will transfer from mucky hands or dirty objects onto a surface over time.

Damage

Given time, any surface will sustain damage either through interaction with the atmosphere (erosion/corrosion), or by being knocked or marked directly.

Deliberate Alteration

In this modern age, it seems that we can't leave a natural surface alone. Labels either stuck on or sometimes embossed into a surface are commonplace.

Although the real desk surface in the reference is fairly clean, there is nothing to stop you from adding a little dirt and damage. I sometimes enjoy a cup of coffee at my desk. While I typically use a coaster to protect the desk's surface, let's pretend that I have in the past placed an overfilled coffee cup on the desk's surface. The stain of a coffee cup is a unique shape and you therefore can't use a procedural texture to imitate it. However, such a stain is very easy to produce and get into Blender.

A digital photo of coffee stained paper.

Adding a History to a Material (Getting Dirty)

The image above was created by placing a coffee cup on paper, allowing it to dry, and then placing the paper in a scanner. I touched up the picture in a paint program to give more contrast. You could also take a digital photo of the paper, or, if your 2D digital painting skills are developed enough, just paint the stain pattern directly in the image editor of your choice. For your convenience, the image file for this stain has been included on the CD.

Image Textures

As with any decent 3D suite, you need a way of applying photographs, or graphic images created in a paint package, to a material simulation. Blender is no exception and has some wonderful tools that make the job easy.

There are 2 strategies for applying an image to a texture.

> • Standard image mapping — where a picture is projected onto a surface from a single direction, and;
> • UV mapping — where a mesh is unwrapped to a flat surface upon which the image is placed. This method allows precise control of how the image lays across the mesh model.

UV mapping is the preferred method of mapping for professional work, and you can learn about Blender's incredibly simple and powerful UV mapper (see Chapter 10). For this example, though, we will stick with the basics.

Mapping an Image to a Surface

Standard image mapping can use one of four methods to project an image onto a surface.

> • Flat — Projects the image along the Z axis of the object. The easiest way to think of this is like a texture up or down onto a ground plane.
> • Cube — Here the flat image is projected along each axis. Therefore a cube would receive the same image on each of its six sides.
> • Tube — As its name suggests, the image is projected around the Z axis of the object from a central point. In other words the projector pans around the tube.
> • Sphere — Here the image is projected from a central point in all directions.

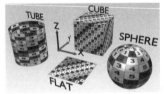

Blender's different image mapping methods.

There will inevitably be some distortion if the object is not a perfect plane, cube, tube or sphere. Fortunately, we only need to map a simple image to a plane. You can therefore use Flat mapping without having to worry about distortion. However, you also need to position and scale the coffee cup mark so that it appears to occur "naturally". Let's start by adding a new texture to your desktop material.

> • With the desktop object selected press F6 to change to the Texture buttons.
> • Select the next free available texture slot and select the Add New button.
> • From the available Texture Type rollout select Image.

The final Image that will be used for the texture.

This is the image you will use for the coffee stain.

It was created, as explained earlier, by scanning a real coffee stain on paper and adjusting the contrast in a paint program. It was also converted to grayscale and inverted. You will use the Map To panel to add color later.

• From the Image tab select Load Image and locate the coffee-stain1.jpg file.

I will explain the settings in a moment, but for now those shown are the defaults.

Return to the Material buttons (F5) so that you can see how the image will be mapped to the desk surface.

Orienting and Scaling an Image Texture to a Surface

These are just the defaults, apart from setting the mixing mode to Add. In a moment I will explain the mixing modes in detail, but for now the reason I have set it to Add is so that it will be clearly seen on the desk surface.

• Press F12 to render the scene.

As you can see, the coffee stain has lightened the desk surface. It is far too big, though, unless you are someone with a serious caffeine addiction. The image has been mapped to fill the whole texture space of the mesh plane. For our purposes we need to change the size, or scale, of the image and position it on the desktop in an appropriate place. You can change the scale and position of an image texture by altering the sizeX, Y, Z and ofsX, Y, Z ("ofs" stands for "offset") in the Map Input tab of the Material buttons.

There are several ways in which you can position and scale an image texture to a surface. You will learn other methods later, but the one I show here will help further explain the Map Input controls and their uses.

Map Input

Currently the image is mapped to fill the entire space of the mesh. This type of mapping is called Orco(ORiginal COordinates) in Blender and is the default. As you can see from the Map Input settings there are quite a few others available. Although you'll need to consult the Blender documentation for a full explanation of all the settings, here are some of the more useful attributes of the map input types:

- Glob(al): As its name suggests, the material will be scaled and oriented to the global co-ordinates. This would mean that if the object moved in an animation the material would remain in place, giving the illusion that the object was moving "through" the material.
- Object: With this type you can attach the material coordinates to another object such as an Empty. The other object must be named and, of course, exist. This is incredibly useful, as you can animate that other object to move, scale, and rotate, which causes the material to do so as well.

Orienting and Scaling an Image Texture to a Surface

- Orco: The default mapping method; uses the object's texture coordinates. If the object moves, the material will move with it. In most circumstances this default works just fine. It is possible to translate the Orco coordinates in scale and position.
- Win(dow): The texture is mapped as though being projected from the camera. Therefore if the camera moves so does the texture.

There are other exotic mapping methods which, although useful, are not usually necessary for the majority of texture needs.

Back to the Coffee Stain Texture

After playing around and using the preview render window, these are the settings that I found work best for positioning the coffee stain:

Size

- Set sizeX, sizeY, and sizeZ to 6.20

The final Map Input settings for the coffee texture.

Position (offset)

- Set ofsX to -2.300, ofxY to 1.200, ofsZ to 0.000

If you find it odd that the sizeX, Y and Z buttons make textures appear smaller as their values increase, think of them as "how many times will the texture fit into the area" values. Therefore, a number like 6.2 for the size values indicates that the actual texture image grows small enough that 6.2 of them could fit within the texture coordinates.

One last thing to do. Back in the Texture buttons (F6), change the repetition/stretch settings from "Repeat" to "Clip." Otherwise, you'll find that the coffee stain will repeat itself across the surface. If you render the scene now, you see a rather disappointing coffee stain that barely shows up, only appearing in the wood grain. Why is that?

When you started creating the textures for your desktop you set some Warp and Stencil effects on previous texture layers. These affect all textures below them. Although the Warp effect can be turned off on a subsequent texture layer, Stencil cannot. This means to get an undistorted coffee stain, it really should have been the first texture.

Reordering Textures

You may have wondered what those up and down arrows were in the Texture panel of the Material buttons. These give you access to a temporary storage area called the buffer. You are able to copy a selected texture to this buffer then paste it into another texture slot. All material settings, like Map Input and Map To, are copied with the texture.

The copy and paste buttons for texture channels.

To move a texture down one slot, you must first select it, choose the "Copy" button, select the channel below it, and choose "Paste". Start by moving the coffee texture down several slots, then proceed up through the stack, moving each entry down one level.

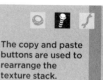

The Texture stack after shifting and duplicating.

Finish by making a copy of the coffee texture and pasting it into the topmost Texture slot. You should end up with this:

You will notice that the Texture stack shows that there are now two copies of the coffee stain texture in this material. Don't worry about that, as you can use the other copy for a nice special effect in a bit. However, LMB the checkmark by the second coffee stain texture to temporaly turn it off while you set the Map To settings for the first.

The copy and paste buttons are used to rearrange the texture stack.

Setting the Map to Options for the First Coffee Stain Texture

With the first texture slot selected in the Material buttons, select the Map To panel so that you can set the way this texture will be combined with the material color. The Mix blend mode will mix both the black background of the image as well as the stain mark itself. You need to get rid of the black background. Once again Blender has the ability to do this.

- Switch to the Texture buttons (F6) and in the Image tab select CalcAlpha and UseAlpha. This will make the black area of the image transparent.

Alpha (opacity), in materials, is quite complex, and even experienced users find themselves trial-and-error toggling alpha related buttons from time to time to get things just right. If things don't work exactly as you expect at first, don't lose hope!

- Switch back to the Material buttons. I am sure you don't need to be reminded of how to do that. (HINT: F5. No more hints.)
- F12 to re-render.

Quite a subtle effect has now been produced. The stain has slightly bleached the surface, and because the coffee contained far too much sugar, the specular and reflective difference between the normal table and the stain can be seen.

You can now use the second copy of the coffee stain texture. The image texture itself is shared between the two slots, but each instance here can have its own unique Map To settings.

- Set Col and Nor on to give you both color and a bump map effect.
- Change the blend mode to Subtract to give a darker color to the stain.
- Change the Col slider to around 0.50, so the new color isn't overpowering.
- And set the Nor value 2.00 to increase the bump size.

A full render at this point will show that some of the wood grain has become darker, as though coffee has spilled and dried in the crevices. However, it's a bit random. Why might that be?

The Map To settings for the second coffee stain channel.

Order of Textures and Their Effects on Each Other

Previously you set both a Stencil texture to mask some areas of following textures, and a Warp.

Once a Stencil is set, it applies to all following textures. A Warp, however, can be switched off further down the stack.

- Select the texture slot immediately before the last coffee stain texture.
- Set Warp to "on" but make sure the fac(tor) amount is set to 0.00.

These settings tell Blender that all following textures should have no Warp.

The final render.

The desktop is now a reasonable simulation of the reference, with a few artistic interpretations and additions, such as the coffee stain, on its surface.

Through thinking about and carefully observing materials in the real world, you have a reasonable chance of using Blender's tool to make a believable approximation of those materials. Combined with decent modeling and good lighting, working in this fashion can lead to significantly more believability in your renders.

Blender Materials - Discussion

This is a practical primer on Blender's material and texturing system. Its goal is not to comprehensively explain every option available to the user — the 2.3 guide and online references will be good for that — but to provide a basic understanding so you can better grasp the tutorial in this book, as well as online resources, and start branching out into your own work.

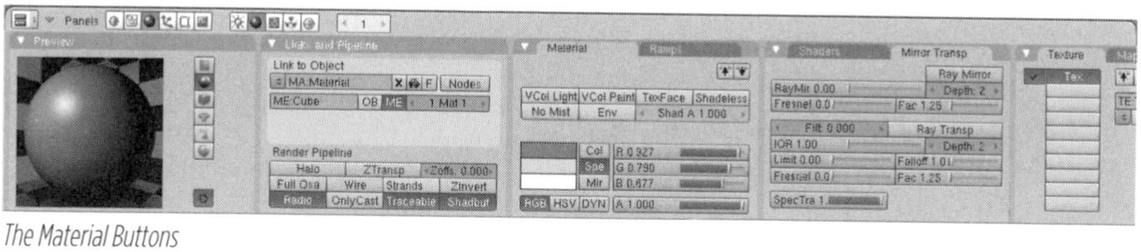

The Material Buttons

Managing Materials

Materials are created and linked to objects in the Links and Pipeline tab of the Material Buttons (F5). The Material buttons will display the material for the active object in the 3D view. If there is no material already linked to the active object, the Links and Pipeline tab will display a button with the label "Add New". To its left is the activator for a drop down menu. At this point, you can choose to either add a new material (Add New), or use the drop down to pick from the list of existing materials. When you've added a new material (or chosen an existing one from the menu), the Add New button changes into a text box that displays the material's name. It is a good idea to use the text box to change the name to something that will help you remember what it is for, should you revisit your project six months from now.

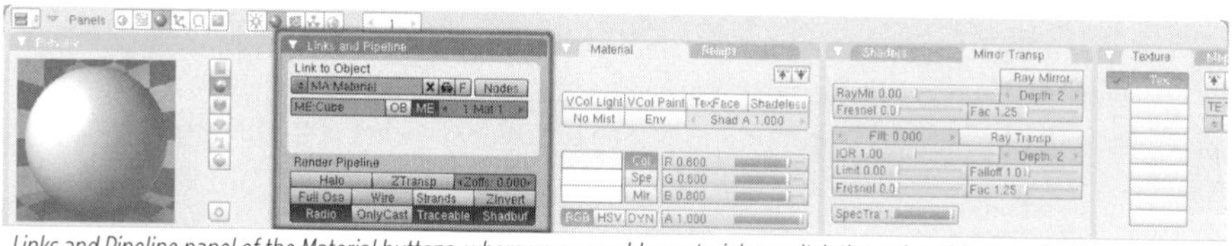

Links and Pipeline panel of the Material buttons, where you can add a material or switch the active object's material.

Blender does not come with a set of pre-built materials, but several community projects have filled that gap — a quick Internet search will reveal a number of freely available Blender material libraries.

Once a material is linked to an object, it is quite simple to change or remove that link. Changing which material is linked to an object is just a matter of choosing a different material from the drop down menu. To completely remove the link between a material and an object, click the "X" button to the right of the material's name.

Material Preview

To the left of the Links and Pipeline tab (or above it, if you are working in a vertical buttons window) is the Preview tab. The previews shown here are actual renders generated on-the-fly by Blender's internal rendering engine, so they are highly accurate. The vertical row of buttons to the right of the preview indicates which shape

Managing Materials

Material previews are generated by the internal renderer and are very accurate.

will be used by the renderer to make the preview, from the standard cube and sphere to hair strands and the ever-popular monkey to represent more complex objects. For an even higher quality preview, you can enable the "O" button below the shape choices to use anti-aliasing in the previews.

Material Preview

Components of a Material

Blender materials each have four main components: base color, shaders, reflection/transparency and textures.

1. Base color

Color and Specularity buttons, and RGB sliders.

These controls set the basic color of the material. "Col" sets the overall color, while "Spe" and "Mir" set the base colors for Specular highlights and Reflections. You can use the familiar RGB sliders, choose to use Hue/Saturation/Value sliders with the HSV button, or LMB on the color swatches at the left to pop up the graphical color picker.

2. Shaders

The Shaders panel. The Diffuse and Specular shader selectors are here.

Blender's renderer has several options available for how exactly to shade the 3D geometry you've created. The top set of controls is for Diffuse shading, which is the way that the renderer calculates the general shading of the object. Here's a short breakdown of most of what is available, and for what each might be best suited.

Lambert: Blender's default shading option. This is a good shading model for plastics and other glossy, fairly smooth substances.

Minnaert: This shader allows you to affect the way that light plays on the portions of your geometry that face the camera directly, as well as the portions that are perpendicular to it. Varying the Dark slider and watching the Preview panel will quickly give you a feel for how it reacts. This shader is useful for cloths, especially deep ones like velvet, and can also be used (with Dark set carefully to lower values) for giving an ever present backlight effect to objects.

Oren-Nayer: A great general shading model for matte surfaces. Unless you are working with one of the special cases mentioned in the other shader descriptions (cloth, plastic, etc.), try this. Although it doesn't actually generate any texturing based on the "Roughness" value, it does simulate the more diffuse scattering that such a surface would produce. As such, it works well as a basis for human skin materials.

Toon: Toon shading breaks the shading into three flat regions — shadow, mid-tone and highlight, and allows you to control the sharpness of the boundaries between them. Used correctly in combination with the Toon specular shader and the edge rendering option, this can produce an effect much like the standard three-part shading of the majority of today's hand-drawn animation.

Although each Diffuse shader has slightly different controls, they all have a Ref (Reflectance) value. This represents the amount of light that reflects from the surface and reaches the camera. A Ref value of 0.8 means that 80% of the light that reaches the surface from the scene's lamps is used for shading purposes. It is up to you to determine how reactive your material will be to light, but for most cases 0.8 is a good starting point.

The lower set of controls is for materials that have specular highlights. Specular highlighting is a way of faking the reflectance of a light source itself on a surface. Don't go overboard with specular highlighting — just because it's there doesn't mean you have to use it. Many times real world materials that you are trying to simulate will appear more believable if you set the Spec value to 0 or very near it. In general, the Spec value indicates the intensity of the highlight (using the Spe color from the Material tab — remember that metallic objects should have highlights colored near to their base color), while the Hard value controls the size of the highlight ("Harder" substances like glass or diamond exhibit tiny, tight highlights, while softer substances like cloth would have a larger highlight area).

The Blinn specular shader pairs well with the Oren-Nayer diffuse shader for most matte and naturally occurring surfaces. Phong works well for glossy plastics. Phong and CookTorr seem to produce good results for shiny metallics, as long as the Spe color is adjusted properly.

3. Reflection and Transparency

We just did reflectance in the Shaders tab, didn't we? Although named in a similar fashion, this is different, and refers to actual visible reflections, like those most commonly seen on a mirror.

The Mirror Transp tab, where reflection, transparency and refraction settings are made.

Components of a Material

The simplest way to create reflective surfaces in Blender is to enable the "Ray Mirror" option in the Mirror Transp tab. Adjust the RayMir slider between 0 (no reflection) and 1 (all incoming light is reflected, like a mirror). This method of creating reflections uses Blender's raytracer, which is a way of following light rays from the camera back to their source. It creates great effects, but can be costly in terms of render time. In order for "Ray Mirror" to work, you must make sure that the "Ray" option is turned on in the Scene buttons (F10). If you want your reflective objects to have an overall color cast (like the tinted reflection in red and green Christmas balls), you will need to set the "Mir" (Mirror) color in the Material tab.

The other method of creating reflections is called Environment Mapping. It is not as accurate as raytraced reflections, but has some advantages. You can find information about Environment Mapping in the next section on Texturing.

The Ray option on the Render panel of the Scene buttons.

Alpha and Opacity

The CG term for how much light passes through a surface is Alpha. Many people make the mistake of initially conceptualizing Alpha as "transparency." The reason this is a problem is that the Alpha scale runs from 0, which represents completely transparent, to 1, completely opaque. So, when someone thinks about "increasing the amount of transparency", they think they should make the Alpha value higher, when that is the exact opposite of what they should do. It's better to think of Alpha as Opacity from the beginning, so the scale will always be intuitive. Higher Alpha = higher opacity, while lower Alpha = lower opacity.

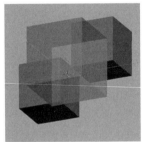

However you choose to think of it, the Alpha value slider is on the main Material tab with the RGB color sliders. Changes to the Alpha slider, labeled "A", will be reflected immediately in the Material preview. If you want to have the alpha visualized in the 3D view, you must then select the object you wish to see (3D View Alpha is done on an object-by-object basis), switch to the Object buttons (F7), then enable the "Transp" button on the Draw tab.

The effects of enabling "Transp" in the 3D view

The Draw tab on the Object buttons.

As there are two ways to accomplish reflection, likewise there are two ways for Blender to render Alpha. If you don't need to simulate refraction (the way that light bends when it passes through materials of differing density, i.e. the lens effect), the best way to do it is to use something called zTransparency.

The Links and Pipeline tab where zTransp is located.

To use this very basic method, enable the "ZTransp" button on the Links and Pipeline tab of the Material Buttons. Unless your visual demands are exacting (close ups of faces wearing glasses, beauty shots of pouring water, etc.), ZTransp should serve most of your Alpha needs quite efficiently.

If you need that last bit of refractive realism, though, you will need to use raytraced transparency. To use this method, make sure that zTransp is disabled in the Material tab, then enable "RayTransp" in the MirrorTransp tab. The IOR slider just below the RayTransp button controls the Index of Refraction. You can find the Indices of Refraction for commonly occurring materials like glass, water and different types of gems and stone quite easily on the Internet. Just be aware that, as with Ray Mirror, using RayTransp can drastically slow your render times if used indiscriminately. Always try zTransp first to see if it will be good enough for your purposes.

Two objects rendered, the one of the left with ZTransp, the one on the right with Ray Transp.

Before we move onto the fourth component of materials, Textures, you may have noticed that we have ignored almost half of the controls on the tabs so far. There are a lot of special-purpose items there that don't fit the scope of a "basics" text, but we'll highlight a few of them, just in case you were looking for a way to achieve a specific effect.

Wire: toggle button on Links and Pipeline tab. Renders only the edges of the model, creating a nice wireframe effect in renders.

OnlyCast: toggle button on Links and Pipeline tab. Causes faces linked to this material to not appear during a render (making the object invisible), but to still cast shadows. This is a handy trick for compositors and special effects, when a real-world object must cast a shadow within your 3D creation.

Tralu: slider on Shaders tab. Translucency. Renders the faces of an object with light and shadows as they strike the face from behind. While this will not produce the popular Subsurface Scattering effect seen when you hold your fingers up to a bright light source, it can be used to enhance the believability of thin organic materials.

Emit: slider on Shaders tab. This slider determines how much of an object is "self-lit". This will neither cast light on objects, nor produce a glowing halo, but models that emit light in the real world (like a light bulb) should have this value turned up to prevent them from being excessively shaded by surrounding light sources.

Fresnel: two sliders on Mirror Transp tab, one each for Mirror and Transparency. The fresnel slider can be used to enhance the realism of raytracing for certain materials. The fresnel value controls how much of the raytracing effect is limited to portions of the object facing perpendicular to the camera. Changes to these values display in the material preview, so you can get a good idea of how they work just by playing around in the Material Buttons.

4. Textures

Up to this point, the material settings have allowed only a single color for each type of shading (diffuse and specular). Almost nothing in the real world is completely uniform in color, and so we turn to Textures to create the variations in color and other characteristics that occur across an object's surface.

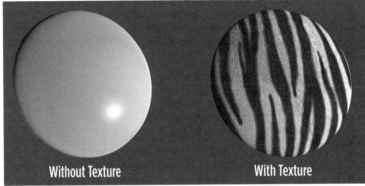

A shape rendered with and without a zebra skin texture.

Textures are organized and layered in the Texture tab of the Material Buttons. Each of the buttons in the stack represents a different channel for textures, so you can layer up to ten textures in a single material.

The Texture tab, with a stack of empty texture channels.

Each texture in Blender has three components: its actual content (e.g. computer-generated noise, digital photo of a brick wall, etc.), how that content wraps around the geometry of the object, and settings for which material properties (color, specularity, etc.) it affects.

Texture Management

Texture management is much the same as material management. To create a new texture, you select one of the empty channels from the texture stack, then press the Add New button that appears to the right of it. Different textures can be linked to the material by selecting a channel and choosing an existing texture's name from the drop down menu. A texture can be unlinked from a material by selecting its channel and clicking the Clear button.

Please note the check mark to the left of the default texture channel in the illustration. Sometimes, you may want to prevent a particular texture channel from being rendered or previewed, perhaps to isolate and tweak the look of a different channel. Turning the check mark "off" by clicking it will cause the renderer to ignore that texture channel.

Texture Content

Textures come from two places: external images and Blender's internal texture generator.

For external images, Blender will let you use many formats, including Targa and PNG which allow Alpha channels, and many video formats, depending on your system type (Mac, Windows or Linux).

Although it's easier to get believable results with image textures, creating them can be time consuming. To help with all the times you don't want to use an external image, Blender has a powerful texture generation system.

When a new texture is created or selected in the Textures tab of the Material buttons, you can access its texturing properties through the Texture buttons (F6). Although it is simple to switch between the Material and Texture buttons (F5 to F6) in a single window, it is often useful to split the buttons window, setting one window to Materials and the other to Textures.

A custom Blender screen with Material and Texture buttons existing simultaneously.

Create a new texture (or select an existing one) in the texture stack, then go to the Texture buttons (F6).

The Texture Type dropdown menu control contains all of the different kinds of textures, including external images, that are available in Blender. Here is a brief rundown of some of the more useful texture types and some suggested uses.

The Texture Type dropdown menu.

The majority of the textures are created by noise functions, which produce a random but patterned variation throughout 3D space. Each of these noise-based textures has their own set of controls, but most share some similar basics. The controls labeled NoiseSize, NoiseDepth and Soft/Hard are common throughout. NoiseSize refers to the "zoom" level at which the texture is used. Adjusting the NoiseSize slider and observing the Texture preview will quickly show you how this functions.

Texture Content

The Soft/Hard settings control whether the noise moves softly from light to dark, or whether there is a sharper transition

The other common control, NoiseDepth, is a little less obvious. NoiseDepth concerns how detailed the texture will be. If it will only be seen from far away, NoiseDepth can stay at 1, as it will only go "one level deep" when doing texture calculation. Higher values will add more detail to the texture, which is perfect for close-ups, but at the cost of rendering time. The default value of 2 seems to be a good general starting point, but people wanting to completely optimize their render times should consider the level of texturing detail they will need.

Also, each of the noise-based textures can use one of several different methods for calculating noise. The illustration shows you the default previews of each noise type for a quick reference.

On to the texture types:

Clouds: an excellent general purpose noise generator. Great for making texture layers for clouds (of course), overall dirt and stains, and color variations over natural surfaces.

Marble: this texture type is good for any surface or material whose variation runs along parallel veins.

Wood: a noise texture that is useful when you need noise patterns to appear in bands or rings, as you would for cross sections of wood (surprise!), or concentric rings in a disturbed liquid surface.

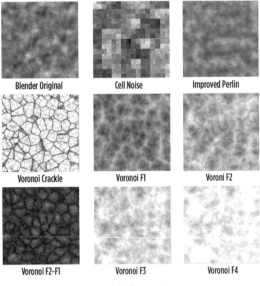

There are many noise types available for texturing.

Stucci: think Stucco. Apparently no one, not even Blender's shepherd Ton Roosendal, knows the origin of the term. This is the texture type to use for creating small divots or peaks in surfaces similar to the rough patterning found on finished stucco and gypsum walls. Almost all non-metallic and non-glossy manufactured items (desktops, kids toys, interior car molding, your computer monitor) can be simulated with a stucci texture.

Distorted Noise, Voronoi, Musgrave: these are more direct implementations of the different noise models, where the mathematically or experimentally inclined can tweak obscure settings until four o'clock in the morning.

Noise: this texture just creates dithered noise, which does not animate well. Use this only for truly noisy things like static snow on an un-tuned television. Do not use this to add fine detail to surfaces — it will result in an ugly "crawling" pattern during animation. Instead, use the stucci texture for that sort of thing.

Those are the noise-based texture types. Targeted experimentation and the Texture preview tab will be your best friends when using these tools. On to some of the non-noise based tools:

Blend: the blend texture (called "gradient" in some other applications) creates smooth value transitions across the texture space. You have your choice of blend types: Lin, Quad and Ease are all slightly different left-right blends, Flip XY creates a top-to-bottom blend, Diag runs from corner to corner, Sphere and Halo make blends from a center point outward, and Radial spins the blend around a central point like a clock arm or radar sweep.

Magic: if you choose the Magic texture, then start spinning through different depth value, you see a series of seemingly unrelated color shifts. When layered together, these different color patterns make excellent overlays for iridescent materials like oil slicks, insect bodies and different metals.

EnvMap

The last type of Blender-generated texture is the EnvMap, which was mentioned in the section on material reflections. An EnvMap (Environment Map) is a special kind of image map that Blender generates on-the-fly to simulate reflections. When an EnvMap is called for, Blender makes six mini-renders of the scene from the standpoint of the object, stitches them together, then uses them to fake a reflection from the object's location. It works very well, and can save valuable time when working on an animation project.

If your object needs to have a reflective surface, and those reflections will not change over the course of an animation, you can set the EnvMap to Static, which will do the mini-render once, and use it as an image map for the rest of the anima- tion. You can even use the save/load

The EnvMap tab, for controlling Environment Maps.

buttons to save EnvMaps to disk, allowing you to render them only once and reuse them later without further calculation time. One other advantage of using an EnvMap is that you can set the CubeRes (the resolution of each rendered mini-tile) fairly low, then turn up the Filter value, which will create a blurry reflection that is not achievable with raytraced reflections.

To use an EnvMap, you need to give the "Ob:" text box the name of the object that is the center of the reflection. Enabling the Anim button in this panel will re-render the EnvMap on every frame of your animation.

Image Textures

As mentioned earlier, images created either by digital photogra- phy, scanning or a 2D image editing program (like the GIMP or Photoshop) can be used as a texture in Blender. To do this, set the Texture Type dropdown menu to Image.

The Map Image tab is laden with buttons, not all of which you need in order to get basic functionality. To load an external

The Map Image and Image panels.

image, click the Load button on the Image panel beside it, then select an image from the file browser window. If you have images loaded for several different textures, you can change them by using the dropdown arrow button to the right of the image name. As with Materials management, clicking the X to the right of the name unlinks the image file from the texture.

In general, you will not need to mess with the other settings in this tab. If your image has built-in alpha (like some Targa and .png's do), you will need to enable the UseAlpha button to make use of it. The row of buttons across the middle of the tab, Extend/Clip/ClipCube/Repeat/Checker, deal with how the image repeats within the texture. The two most common settings are Clip and Repeat. Clip puts only a single instance of the image in the middle of the texture space with transparency all around it, which makes it ideal for texturing labels and decals. Repeat (the default) pops up two new buttons, X and Y spinners that show how many times the image is repeated along each axis. These repeats are shown in the Texture preview, so it is easy to adjust it properly.

Texture Mapping

Once you have textures, either generated by Blender or brought in as images, Blender has to know how to apply those textures to the 3D geometry of your object. This process if called Texture Mapping and is controlled in the Map Input tab of the Material buttons.

The four sections of the Map Input tab.

Coordinate systems buttons: this set of controls tells Blender what coordinate system to use for mapping. This question is one of "where do I want my mapping to start from?" and the answer is dependent on what you want the texture to do. Here are the most frequently used choices:

Orco: This stands for ORiginal COordinates, and is the most useful coordinate system. The texture follows the object as it translates and rotates through 3D space. Using this setting will make it appear that the texture is a part of the object itself.

Glob: Global Coordinates. The texture uses the coordinate system of the entire Blender 3D space. As the object moves or rotates in space, the texture stays in place, so it appears that the object is moving "through" the texture.

Win: Window Coordinates. This is another system where the 3D space is not attached to the object. With Win coordinates, the texture appears to be projected from the viewpoint of the camera. In this case, objects will appear to move "through" the texture if they move across the viewport of the camera, but the texture will also appear to move if the camera changes its position or view of the object.

Refl: Reflection Coordinates. Use the Refl setting in conjunction with the EnvMap texture type to produce properly mapped fake reflections.

UV: This is a user controlled, very precise method of texture mapping. If you are interested in this (and you should be), you will find an entire chapter (10) devoted to Blender's UV Mapping tools in this book.

2D Projection buttons: these four buttons determine how 2D textures such as Images will be projected onto 3D geometry. But what about the other textures, like clouds, wood, etc.? Those Blender-generated textures are already considered "3D". An irregular rock shape textured with Clouds and the Orco button is textured as though it was a solid object. If you cut the model in half (and put faces on the cut portion), it would appear as though the Cloud texture continued inside the object.

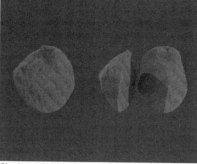

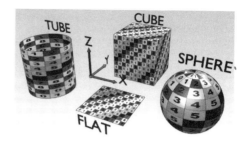

Blender-generated textures are three dimensional.

Very simply, you should select the projection type that most closely suits the object you are texturing. If you cannot get satisfactory results from these buttons, then you most likely need to use the more complex but excellent UV mapping method that Blender offers.

Axis remapping: The mysterious voodoo of the axis remapping tools will have to wait for a more advanced text. If you like, you can click around with these buttons, but you're better off getting the basics down first.

The ofsX/ofsY/ofsZ controls stand for Offset X, Y and Z. These spinners can be used to finely adjust the positioning of the texture on the object along the specified axis. If you are using an image texture with the Clip setting, which will only place one copy of the image on the material, you can use these controls to position it on your object's surface.

Likewise the sizeX/sizeY/sizeZ controls can alter the scaling of the texture along the relevant axis. However, it's important to note that raising the size value above 1 *decreases* the size of the texturing element, while values descending from 1 to 0 will *increase* its apparent size. To keep this from confusing you ("Raising the size decreases the… size?"), think of it as "How many times will my texture fit on the object along that axis?"

What the Texture Actually Does

The final component of texturing is deciding what properties of the material a particular texture channel will affect. Many properties from other tabs in the Material Buttons are able to be affected by textures: basic color, mirror color, specularity, reflectance, alpha and translucency to name a few. These texturing options are in the Map To tab.

The simplest way to use a texture is with the Col (Color) channel in the Map To tab.

The Map To tab.

What the Texture Actually Does

There are lots of options in the upper set of buttons, and these determine which properties of the material the texture will affect. Mousing over the buttons will bring up a tool tip that describes what each button does. The most commonly used ones are Col, Nor, Spec and Alpha, which we'll look at now.

Col: Color. When this button is enabled, the texture works in conjunction with three other controls on this panel: the mixing dropdown (which shows Mix as a default), the Col slider just below it, and the color picker immediately to its left. As this is just the basics, leave the Mix dropdown alone (if you are familiar with mixing modes like Add, Multiply, Screen, etc. from other applications, you'll find all of your favorites there.) The Col slider sets the strength of the texture's affect on the base color of the material on a simple scale — 1 is 100% strength, 0 is 0%. The color picker sets the color that will be used for blending.

Nor: Normal. Using textures to vary the normal of a material simulates bumps and detail across the surface. Use this button with the Nor slider to set how deeply the bumps appear. This is commonly referred to as "bump mapping".

Spec: Specularity. A piece of metal that has dirt and corrosion on its surface will be rather shiny in clean places, but dull in the dirty spots. Using a texture to affect specularity allows you to simulate this effect. The Var slider determines how much of the texture is used for specularity, from 0 to 100%. It's important to note that properties like specularity (and emit, translucency, alpha, etc.) still use the settings from their main sliders in the Material Buttons as their baseline. This means that if you leave the Spec slider on the Shaders tab at 1, you most likely would not see any effect from the texture. Think of it this way: the Spec slider in the Shaders tab sets the lowest amount of specularity for the material, while the Var slider sets the maximum amount of specularity that will be created by the texture. So, the way to show the greatest range in values of specularity would be to set the Shaders tab Spec slider to 0, while setting the Map To tab Var slider to 1.

Alpha: Opacity. The alpha setting works exactly the same way as the Specularity one. Just a reminder, though, to think of alpha as opacity, not transparency, so everything works intuitively. The greatest range of Alpha variation will be achieved by setting the Material tab "A" slider to 0 and the Texture tab Var slider to 1. Make sure to click ZTransp in the Links and Pipeline tab to get an accurate material preview and correct rendering with Alpha.

Many of these buttons are not normal toggles, but three-stage toggles. For example, clicking the Nor button once turns it on, while clicking it again leaves it on and turns the label yellow. Clicking once more turns it off. That third state with the yellow label is a "reverse" setting. It uses the texture, but backwards. Under the Nor setting, what would have bumped out now bumps in, while what would have bumped in now bumps out. Likewise, the Neg (Negative) button can be used to invert a texture, and due to complex technical reasons this will not always produce the same result as the third toggle state of one of the property buttons.
You are not constrained to using a single property on each channel of the texture stack. Careful selection and adjustment of the property buttons (say, Col, Nor, Spec and Alpha) along with their respective sliders (Col, Nor and Var) can produce complex effects within a single channel. So, with ten channels to work with in the texture stack, you can produce some incredibly complex materials.

We've reviewed the four main components of Blender materials (base colors, shaders, reflection/transparency and textures), and explained the most common options relating to them. There is a wealth of additional features and options within Blender's material and texture system that we did not cover, but the basics

What the Texture Actually Does

presented here will give you a good starting point to begin exploring on your own. The Blender 2.3 guide and official online documentation contain explanations for every button and switch in the Blender interface and would be a good companion for users wishing to go beyond these basics.

CHAPTER 10

UV Mapping

UV and Painting: Hands On
by Modron

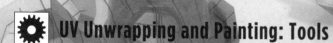

UV Unwrapping and Painting: Tools

Modron

Greetings. Though I don't care to reveal too many details about myself publicly, here is a provocatively mysterious description:

I was born in, and have lived in Washington State for most of my life, and have traveled somewhat around the United States, and Europe. I have always studied various forms of art, including musical composition and performance, but only recently began using the computer as a tool to make art.

I downloaded Blender, originally intending to use it to set up perspective for a drawn animation, and I have not put it down since.

Thanks go out to the rare collection of individuals known as the Blender community, whose generosity and enthusiasm are unparalleled on the web. I salute the Blender community, for it is great.

UV Unwrapping and Painting: Hands On

The process of UV Mapping a mesh is very much like taking a physical paper model of an object, cutting it in various places, and flattening it onto a table. Once that is done, photographs can be fastened to it, or it can be painted directly. Then, the flattened paper is reassembled into its original 3D configuration. In UV Mapping in Blender, mesh models are cut and unwrapped into a flat UV Editor window where textures and images are applied. Of course, because this is 3D graphics, you can do other cool things once you have this basic procedure down, such as painting directly on your model in the 3D view and baking lighting and texturing information for later use.

Although there are several methods for unwrapping mesh objects, Blender's automated unwrapper does such an excellent, easy job that it's the one we'll cover.

In this tutorial, you'll unwrap an organic shape using Blender's live unwrapping feature, and do some texture painting in the UV window.

Unwrapping an Organic Shape

Before you begin, either run Blender or, if it's already running, start a new session with Ctrl-X. When the default screen appears, use the MMB to split the 3D view into two separate windows (see Chapter 2 if you need a reminder of how to do this). Then, change the right hand 3D view into a UV/Image Editor window using the Window Type icon menu on the far left of the header.

You could unwrap the default cube, but that would be boring. RMB select it, and get rid of it (X-key). You need something worthwhile to unwrap, so go into a front view (Numpad-1) and add Suzanne to your scene by choosing Add->Mesh->Monkey from the spacebar toolbox. (Suzanne is the pet name of Blender's default Monkey primitive.) If you know how from the Mesh Modeling chapter, you can Set Smooth on Suzanne and add a Subsurf modifier (Shift-O) so she looks a little nicer.

Defining Seams, or How the Mesh Will Be Cut

The default screen, with the 3D view split and set to a UV/Image Editor window.

The Suzanne mesh is added in Edit mode, which is what you want. If the mesh you are working on is not in Edit mode, use the Tab-key to get there. Imagine for a moment that Suzanne is made out of a skin of rubber, or fabric, and the idea will be to make cuts in a way that the surface could be laid out flat, with minimal stretching or bunching.

The main consideration is to place the seams in areas that will create "islands" of faces where continuous detail will be needed. If there is going to be a highly visible area with lots of detail or a smooth gradient, you do not want to put a seam there. Seams should be placed in unobtrusive areas, as though you were a plastic surgeon trying to hide your cuts.

To make a seam, select an edge and press Ctrl-E. From the Edge Specials menu that pops up, choose "Mark Seam." Any edges marked as seams will display with twice the thickness of a normal mesh edge, and will be a dark orange in color. Seams that are mistakenly marked can be cleared with the "Clear Seam" option in the Ctrl-E menu.

In the illustrations below, you can see where we have chosen to set seams on the Suzanne model. Really though, you can make your seams wherever you like. We encourage you to experiment with different seam placements later to get a feel for how unwrapping works. For now, though, try to at least approximate the configuration in the illustrations, so that the rest of the tutorial follows what you are doing. One thing to keep in mind while making selections for seams is that Edge Select mode and Alt-RMB Edge Loop select can be very useful.

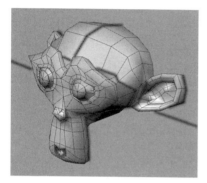

Getting the Faces Into the UV Editor

Let's ask Blender to unwrap and flatten Suzanne based on the seams you've marked, then transfer that configuration to the UV Editor.

Press the Tab-key to put Suzanne into Object mode. Now, you'll learn a new mode specifically for dealing with faces and UV unwrapping. Press the F-key, and see that you've entered a new mode called UV Face Select mode.

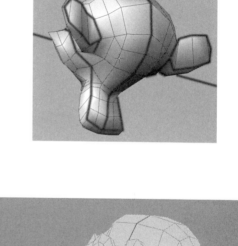

Press the A-key to deselect all your faces (deselected faces are white) and press it again to reselect them all (selected faces are

Face mode can be identified on the modes menu on the 3D header, and by the broken lines designating selected faces.

pink). This double A-key technique is a good habit to get into to make sure that all faces are included in the unwrap. If your Suzanne turned pink on the first tap of the A-key, that's okay — it just means that it began with no faces selected. When in Face mode, the Tab-key still works to enter and exit Edit mode. Any face selections made in Edit mode will be carried back into Face mode when you return.

Getting the Faces Into the UV Editor

With all faces selected in Face mode, press the U-key (for Unwrap). A menu pops up with a number of options. Choose "Unwrap." In the UV Editor window, the sliced and unwrapped version of Suzanne appears.

Many of the commands and tools that work with mesh editing also work when dealing with the flattened mesh in the UV Editor window. One of the more useful commands is Ctrl-L, which selects an entire continuous section of faces from a single selected node.

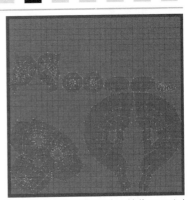

Your unwrap will be different than this if you created different seams than the previous samples. Note how the front of the face, which will be an area of continuous detail, has been kept as a single piece.

For technical reasons, the "vertices" you see in the UV Editor aren't exactly vertices as they are in the mesh. In the UV Editor, they are referred to as "nodes."

RMB select a node in the UV Editor, then press Ctrl-L. That will select the entire UV "island" that the node belongs to.

You can move, rotate and scale UV nodes and islands using the G, S and R-keys as in other editing situations. The mouse gestures work here, too.

Arranging the Islands

As you'll be painting a texture, it would be nice to have the islands oriented in a way to make it simpler. The arrangement of the islands in the previous illustration would require you to paint textures at odd angles. It would help to rearrange them.

There are a couple of things to note in this illustration. First, see how the front face island has been scaled up a little bit. It will be the visual focus of the monkey model and should be given more area in the unwrap so it can have more detailed texturing. Second, the two eye islands have been placed on top of each other. You'll see why later. And finally, notice how the nose has been separated from the rest of the front face mesh. In some cases, it might be okay to leave them apart, but since you'll be painting the entire front of the face as one piece, you should reconnect them.

The nose island

The UV islands rearranged and rotated to assist with texture painting.

The nose island is shown in the illustration, but you should look at how to identify parts of an unwrap in case it's not so clear. In the 3D view, RMB select one of the faces on the nose. In the UV Editor, you'll see that all the

Arranging the Islands

UV nodes disappear except the one you have just selected. Now, keeping your eye on the UV Editor, but keeping the mouse over the 3D view, press the A-key twice. All faces are again selected, and all the nodes reappear in the UV Editor. You will be able to see which portion of the UV nodes contained the one you had selected.

Select the nose island (hover the mouse over the nose island and press the L-key) and use the G-key to move it into the middle of the hole on the front of the face. If you need to, use the S-key to scale the nose island until it is slightly smaller than the hole.

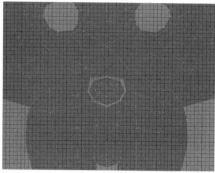

The nose island in place inside the nose hole on the main face's island.

Select all the nodes around the outer edge of the nose island and press the P-key. The selected nodes turn red. This means they are "Pinned." Pinned nodes form the basis of the "Live Unwrap Transform" feature, which we will look at next.

In the "UVs" menu on the header, select "Live Unwrap Transform."

Now RMB select the pinned nodes one by one and drag them roughly to where they will attach to the face.

Notice that the unpinned nodes on the nose island follow along and optimize themselves in real time to keep the rest of the faces in proportion to the ones being fixed. Your goal is to stitch these two islands back together, so you would like to get the nose nodes fairly close to their corresponding face nodes. You don't need to be exact, though, because Blender has some handy tools to help with the job.

To use the stitching tool, you need to select all of the nodes that will be stitched: the outer nodes of the nose island and the inner ring of nodes on the nose hole on the face island. Since these nodes actually share vertices in the 3D mesh, there is a different selection mode that will help you to access corresponding nodes, no matter where they are in the unwrap. On the Select menu in the header, choose "Stick UVs to Mesh Vertex," or use the Ctrl-C hotkey.

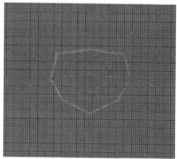

This is all the closer you need to get.

Now, when you RMB select the nodes on the nose island, the corresponding node on the face island is also selected for you. Using Shift-RMB select, build a selection of the outer ring of the nose island.

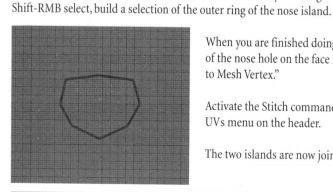

When you are finished doing that, you should see that the inner ring of the nose hole on the face island is also selected, due to "Stick UVs to Mesh Vertex."

Activate the Stitch command by pressing the V-key. It's also in the UVs menu on the header.

The two islands are now joined.

To show the use of the "Live Unwrap" tool a little better, let's do one more thing to the unwrap before you begin painting.

Select all UV nodes in the UV Editor by pressing the A-key. When everything is selected, clear the pinning you made before with Alt-P. All of the pinned red nodes should return to normal. Now, from the Select menu, choose "Stick Local UVs to Mesh," which is the opposite of the setting you used before. For the next part, you only want the nodes that you directly select to be active, not any extra nodes that might be connected to this one in the 3D mesh.

With that done, RMB select the uppermost node of the face island, then Shift-RMB select the lowest. Also, Shift-RMB select one node on either side of the mouth. Use the P-key to Pin these four nodes.

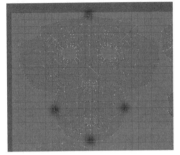

Make sure that "Live Unwrap Transform" is selected in the UVs menu.

RMB select the node at the top of the face island, and using the G-key, start to move it around. The UV faces change shape and location to try to keep everything in proportion, but the other three pinned nodes stay exactly where they were put. They do not move. Pinning tells the UV unwrapping procedure to use those nodes and their locations as its new baseline for calculating the unwrap. As you move any pinned node by hand, the unwrap is recalculated for the new positioning of all pinned nodes and displayed.

And so, if you knew that you would be painting significantly more detail in the forehead area, you could drag the top pinned node slowly upward, expanding the area covered by the upper part of the face island, while having everything automatically adjust to stay proportional. Likewise, you could select the pinned nodes on either side of the mouth and S-key scale them, expanding the space given to the mouth faces, while the unwrapper used the other two pinned nodes as pivot points for determining the rest of the unwrap.

When you're satisfied with the unwrap, turn off "Live Unwrap Transform" in the UVs menu. Select all the nodes in the UV Editor and use Alt-P to unpin them.

Painting a Texture in the UV Editor

You're going to be working with the texture painting tools next. Although you may be happy with the unwrap of Suzanne you have achieved in the first part of this tutorial, you are encouraged to make use of the file "UVUnwrap.blend" in the "examples" folder of the provided CD for the next section, as it has some textures and images that will be needed already included. If you're the kind of person who likes to make everything from scratch, though, please feel free!

You'll use the pre-created images later. Make sure that Suzanne is the active selection in the 3D view and create a brand new, blank image in the UV Editor by choosing "New" from the "Image" menu on the header. When you make a new image, a popup appears, asking for an image name and a size. We've called our image "monkey paint" and changed the size to 512x512 pixels.

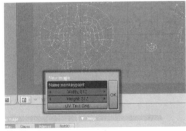

The New Image pop-up panel.

Over in the 3D view, use the Draw type menu on the header to change to Textured mode, one you haven't used before.

Suzanne turns black in the 3D view, but that's okay because the new image you created is filled with black.

To enable texture painting in the UV Editor, either click the Pencil icon on the header or choose "Texture Painting" from the Image menu. Then, press the C-key to bring up the painting tools palette.

Selecting a Draw type from the header.

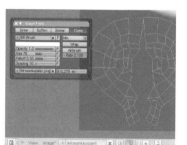

In the palette, click the "Clone" button, and choose the "monkeyskin" texture from the browse button at the bottom of the palette. You'll see the ghosted image of the "monkeyskin" file superimposed on your original image.

Using RMB drag, position the skin texture behind the face island.

Now, use the LMB to paint the area of Suzanne's face in the UV Editor. As you paint, you will see the areas you've LMB dragged become lighter and show a more distinct version of the "monkeyskin" image. What the clone brush does is to duplicate whatever is in the texturing image into the image that is loaded in the UV Editor. To see the effects of your painting

The UV Editor in texture paint mode, with the painting tools palette.

without the texturing image showing in the background, you can either click the "X" beside the texturing image's name on the palette to unlink it, or turn the "B" (Blend) slider down to 0. The B slider controls the opacity of the texturing image in the display.

In any case, keep using the LMB to paint the "monkeyskin" texture onto the canvas, for the face and ear islands. You may need to move the texturing image around with the RMB in order to clone it onto all the different parts. As you paint, watch the texture show up in the 3D textured view.

If you find that the UV Editor window doesn't give you quite enough room to work, try using the Ctrl-Down/Up Arrow key to have the UV Editor temporarily take over the entire workspace. When you need to see other windows, just use Ctrl-Down/Up Arrow to set things back to normal.

When you're done, you should have something like this:

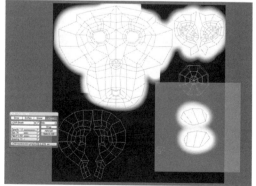

The monkey skin cloned into place on all of Suzanne's skin areas.

Switch the texturing image to "monkeyhair" and clone it into the remaining areas. To get a softer edge to the areas where the hair texture transitions to the already-painted skin texture, adjust the Falloff slider on the Image Paint palette downward. A brush Falloff setting of 0 makes a diffuse, smooth brush, while a setting of 1 gives it a very hard edge.

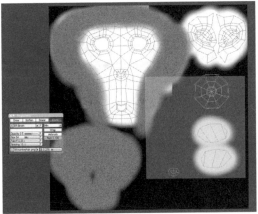

Both the skin and hair texture images cloned into place.

Let's use the non-texturing paint tools to finish up.

Click the Draw button on the Paint Image palette, then set the other controls to match the illustration:

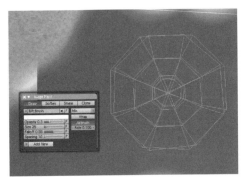
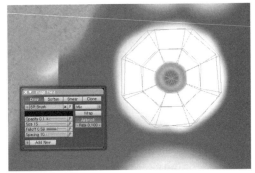

The Paint Image palette set to paint the eyes.   *The eyes, painted.*

From the color picker swatch in the palette, choose a fairly white color. Using LMB, paint the eyes white. With the color picker, choose several colors, first a dark blue, then a light blue, then black, and paint the pupils and irises of the eyes.

One great thing you'll notice in the 3D view is that both eyes are now painted! This is because the UV faces for those eyes are taking up the same space in the UV Editor, and receive the same texturing.

Painting a Texture in the UV Editor

Set Falloff to 0, Opacity to 0.1, Size to 20 and choose a medium brown color. Use this brush to paint a bit of shading around the eyes, nose and ears.

Back in the 3D view, use the MMB to rotate your view of the model and see how the painting has been applied based on the UV unwrap.

Painting In the 3D View

It's possible to use the painting tools directly in the 3D view, and have the painting apply to the image loaded in the UV Editor.

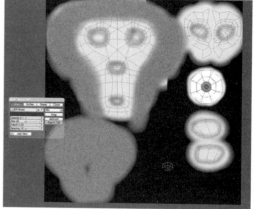

Shading has been painted in certain areas.

In the 3D view, switch the object's mode from UV Face Select to Texture Paint. If the Edit buttons aren't showing in the buttons window, bring them up with F9. Find the Paint panel.

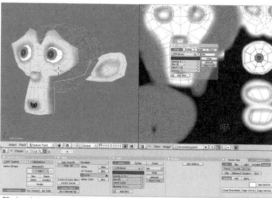

3D view in texture paint mode, and edit buttons with Paint panel.

Using the color picker swatch on the Edit buttons Paint panel, select a deep red color. Click and drag with the LMB on Suzanne's mouth in the 3D view. As you paint in the 3D view, the painting shows up on the flattened version in the UV Editor.

Saving the Image Texture

In the UV Editor, choose "Save As" from the Image menu. This will bring up the file browser window so that you can type a name for the image you've just painted and save it. If you had quit Blender before doing this, all the work you had put into painting that image would have been lost!

It's now okay to leave Texture Paint mode in both the 3D view (by changing back to Object mode on the header menu) and in the UV Editor (by un-checking "Texture Paint" in the Image menu or clicking the Pencil icon on the header).

Painting In the 3D View

Adding the Image to a Material Using the UV Unwrap

You can see Chapter 9 for a full explanation of Materials and Texturing, but we'll give some additional information here so you can quickly use your UV Unwrap and painted texture.

With Suzanne selected, bring up the Material buttons (F5). Add a new material in the Links and Pipeline panel with the Add New button, then switch to the Texture buttons (F6). Click Add New in the texture buttons, and set the new Texture Type to Image. As the image is already in Blender, you don't need to go looking for it on disk. Select the "monkeypaint" image from the Image panel's dropdown menu.

Back in the Material buttons, find the Map Input tab, and change the coordinate type from "Orco" to "UV." This tells the renderer to use the UV unwrap for the texture coordinates.

At this point, the default camera and lamp should be enough for you to make your first render of an unwrapped, texture-painted mesh.

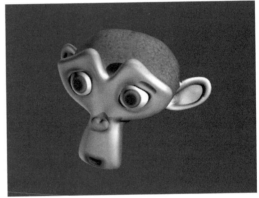

Press F12 to render.

Well, there she is. My, but you look lovely this evening Suzanne!

UV Unwrapping and Painting: Tools

Blender gives you an excellent and easy-to-use toolset for slicing and flattening mesh models in order to make the application of 2D textures more detailed and efficient. Don't be confused: "UV" unwrapping has nothing at all to do with "ultraviolet," the common expansion of the "UV" acronym. It has to do instead with assigning a set of 2D coordinates to all vertices.

Don't they already have 3D coordinates? Yes. As you know, each vertex of a mesh already has an X, Y, and Z coordinate. But if you make a copy of the mesh, slice it and flatten it out, each vertex will also have another set of coordinates, ones more appropriate to a flat workspace. Normally, you'd label the axes of a 2D space X and Y, but those are already taken. So, it's U and V. Where's W? Don't ask.

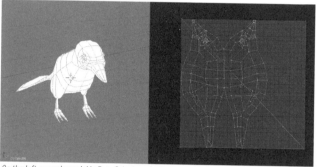

On the left, a mesh model in Face Select mode. On the right, that model unwrapped in the UV Editor.

If you've never dealt with UV unwrapping and mapping before, we strongly urge you to work through the tutorial section first in this chapter. Blender's UV Unwrapper is a highly interactive feature, and one that can be best grasped by actually using it.

Unwrapping

The Modes menu, with Face Select mode highlighted.

The unwrapping process itself is found in Face Select mode, accessible on the 3D header's modes menu.

Most times, you will be unwrapping an entire mesh at once. In this case, simply using the A-key to make sure that all faces are selected will be good enough.

The U-key brings up the Unwrap menu in the 3D view. It only works in Face Select mode.

There are a number of UV calculation methods, but only a few will be immediately useful.

Unwrapping

The simplest ones to conceptualize are "Project from View" and the closely related "Project from View (Bounds)." These options take the mesh exactly as seen in the current 3D view, and squash it right into the UV Editor. (Technically, it's the "UV/Image Editor," but since we're only working with UVs right now, we'll call it the UV Editor for short.)

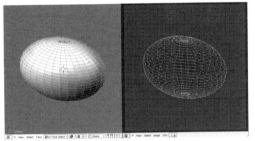

3d view of sphere, flattened with project from view (bounds).

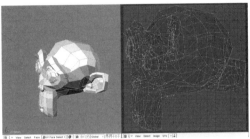

3d view of Suzanne, flattened with project from view (bounds).

Project from View can be good when you need to create a quick texture that corresponds closely to the profile shape of the mesh.

The only difference between the two is that "Project from View" creates UVs at roughly the size that the mesh appeared in the 3D view, while "Project from View (Bounds)" fills the entire UV space with the projection.

A fish texture, done with Project from View.

Some of the other options are also good for making quick unwraps on objects that will appear as background items, or only for a short time. These are the Cylinder, Cube and Sphere options. Each is good for unwrapping (surprise!) objects that closely match those primitives in shape. There will be sections that don't map quite correctly or show distortion. If you're not sure if the job they do will be good enough, give it a shot. You never now until you try.

> Meshes are unwrapped by entering Face Select mode and using the Unwrap command from the U-key menu.

Other options aside, though, the most useful unwrapping method is simply called "Unwrap." It uses a procedure called "Angle Based Flattening" in conjunction with seams marked in Edit mode to give excellent results with very little effort.

Seams

In order for it to work properly, you must first tell the Angle Based Flattening unwrap tool where to make cuts on the mesh. This is accomplished by adding seams to your model.

In Edit mode on a mesh model, seams are added by selecting edges, pressing Ctrl-E and choosing "Mark Seam" from the Edge Specials menu that pops up. Marked seams appear as heavy orange edges. A seam can be unmarked by selecting that edge, pressing Ctrl-E and choosing "Clear Seam."

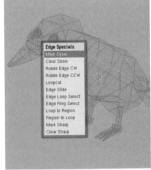

The Ctrl-E Edge Specials menu for marking seams.

Although any selection method will work, it is often helpful when making seams to work in Edge Select mode and to use Alt-RMB to select entire edge loops at once.

Seam placement is crucial. The best way to think about it is to visualize actually cutting slits into your model so that, if it were made of paper, it would be able to lie flat on a desk.

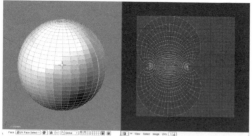

A sphere with a single, poorly chosen seam produces a bad unwrap.

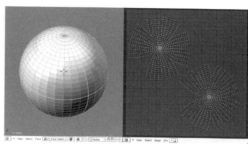

A sphere with better seams makes a more useful unwrap.

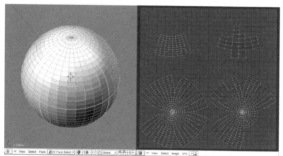

Notice the island created by seams in the 3D view and in the UV Editor.

Seams can also be placed so that entire portions of the model are separated from the others. These separate pieces of the model are called "islands.".

Once you have seams marked, you can return to Face Select mode and choose "Unwrap" from the U-key menu.

Seams are set in Edit mode with Ctrl-E: Mark Seam, and removed with Clear Seam.

Selecting Nodes in the UV Editor

If the configuration achieved by the Unwrap command is not exactly what you need, it is possible to adjust it. When dealing with node selection (nodes are the name for vertices in the UV Editor), the following rules and options apply:

RMB, B-key border select and double-B-key circle select all function as they do in mesh Edit mode.

Pressing the C-key allows you to select entire faces in the UV Editor with a RMB click. When in this "Active Face Select" mode, which is also available from the Select menu on the header, a small purple square is displayed in the lower left corner of the UV Editor.

Like working with distinct groups of vertices in mesh Edit mode, hovering the mouse over an island of nodes and pressing the L-key will select the entire island.

There is another set of selection modes here that may be a little hard to understand at first, both found in the Select menu: "Stick UVs to Mesh Vertex" and "Stick Local UVs to Mesh Vertex."

The "Local" option is the default. The tricky thing to realize in the UV Editor is that a single vertex from the 3D mesh can have as many instances in the UV Editor as it has faces. This illustration demonstrates:

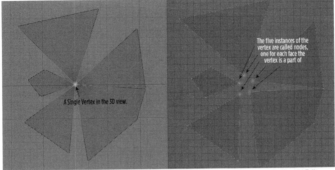

A single vertex in the 3D view, spanning five faces, each with a separate instance in the UV Editor.

When in "Local" mode, RMB selecting one of these nodes will select all instances of the 3D mesh vertex that share that particular point in UV space. It won't feel any different than selecting and transforming vertices and edges in mesh Edit mode.

The difference comes when switching to "Stick UVs to Mesh Vertex" (non-"local") mode. When this option is chosen, a little box icon with two yellow vertices appears in the lower left corner of the UV Editor. Selection now works like this: RMB selecting any node will also select all other nodes that share the 3D mesh vertex, regardless of their location in the UV space.

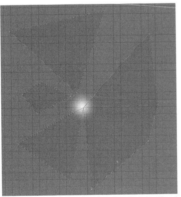

Selecting a node in local mode only selects itself and other nodes it's touching.

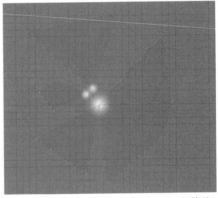

Selecting in non-local mode selects all nodes connected in the 3D view.

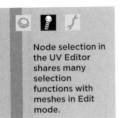

Node selection in the UV Editor shares many selection functions with meshes in Edit mode.

This is particularly useful when your mesh is divided into many islands and you need to find which parts of one island correspond to which parts of another.

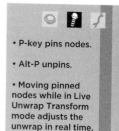

Fixing the Unwrap

Although the default unwrap is usually pretty good, you will probably need to optimize it for texture painting. Areas that will be a focus of rendering and detail need to be carefully painted, and an even, proportional unwrap can only help.

Pinning and Live Unwrap Transform

Areas of an unwrap that you are happy with can be frozen by "pinning." Pressing the P-key pins selected nodes. Fixing portions of an unwrap that you are unhappy with is as simple as pinning a few key nodes within the bad area and moving them into a better configuration. Then, after also pinning the good areas, Blender can re-unwrap the mesh, hopefully giving better results. It uses all the pinned nodes as a starting point for its next attempt.

Asking for another unwrap can be done from the 3D view with the U-key menu as before, or directly from within the UV Editor with Ctrl-E.

One great thing Blender can do to make this process much more intuitive is called "Live Unwrap Transform," and can be accessed only through the UVs menu on the UV Editor's header.

Once Live Unwrap Transform is enabled, there is no need to re-unwrap your meshes after pinning and adjusting. The unwrap adjusts itself in real time as you pull and push pinned nodes, giving you great visual feedback that helps to quickly optimize the unwrap.

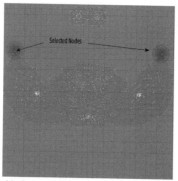

A bad unwrap, with several nodes pinned, and one selected.

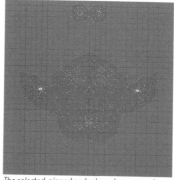

The selected, pinned nodes have been moved, causing the rest of the unwrap to adjust itself.

When you have the unwrap the way you want it, be sure to turn off Live Unwrap in the UVs menu so you don't accidentally move a pinned node and ruin your work.

• P-key pins nodes.

• Alt-P unpins.

• Moving pinned nodes while in Live Unwrap Transform mode adjusts the unwrap in real time.

Paint Tools

Blender's painting tools can be used to paint onto existing images or to create new ones, and can be used either in the UV/Image Editor or directly within the 3D view. To be able to texture paint a model in the 3D view, you need to have assigned UV coordinates to the mesh's faces by unwrapping.

Texture Painting mode is accessed through the Image menu on the UV Editor header, or by changing the object mode on the 3D header to "Texture Paint".

The Image menu in the UV/Image Editor.

Texture Paint mode, with the Image Paint panel.

Whether you are painting in the 3D view or in the UV/Image Editor, you must have an image selected in the UV/Image Editor (just called the Image Editor from now on, as we're done with the UV functionality). If you have an image loaded for some other reason (a texture, a background, etc.), you can select it on the Imageblock selector dropdown on the Image Editor header.

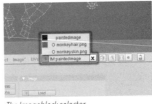

The Imageblock selector.

If you would like to create a completely new image, choose "New" from the Image menu, then set a resolution in the dialogue that pops up. A new, black image is created and loaded into the Image Editor.

You can paint directly on images by setting the Image Editor or object to Texture Paint mode.

Pressing the C-key in Texture Painting mode in the Image Editor brings up the Image Paint palette. A nearly identical panel, called Paint, is available in the Edit buttons (F9) for use in the 3D view.

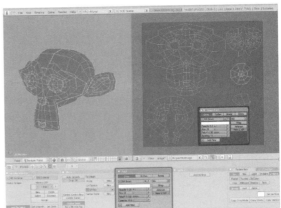

The Image Paint and Paint panels.

Paint Tools

Painting is accomplished by LMB dragging across either the image itself or the model in the 3D view. The general brush controls are:

Color: Chosen by LMB clicking on the color swatch. This is the main color that is used for painting.

Opacity: How strongly the painting blends with the current image. An Opacity value of 1.0 causes the painted color to completely cover the existing image. 0.50 would cause the color to be applied at only 50%.

Size: Adjusts the size of the paint brush.

Falloff: The hardness of the brush. Setting Falloff to 1.0 creates a hard-edged brush. Reducing it to 0.0 creates a brush with a very soft edge.

Spacing: How frequently the brush "stamps" its color as you drag. Painting in Blender isn't truly continuous as it is if you were to drag a brush loaded with oil paints in the real world. The Image Editor simulates continuous painting by stamping the color every few pixels, in the shape of the brush. The Spacing value is a percentage of the Size value and determines how far apart these stamps occur. If Size is set to 45 and Spacing is set to 10, the brush will paint a new blob of color every 4.5 pixels (10% of 45).

If you happen to have a pen and art tablet for your computer, you'll find that it works very well with texture painting. Clicking the little "P" icon beside any of these settings will allow them to be controlled by your pen's pressure.

Airbrush: Enabling this option causes paint to continue to flow for as long as you have the LMB pressed, even if the brush is stationary. Normally, painting only occurs as the brush moves.

In addition to painting with a color, it is also possible to paint with a Blender texture, giving even more detail to your painted image. Any texture that has been created in the Texture buttons (F6) can be selected in the dropdown at the bottom of the Image Paint palette. That texture is then used along with the palette color when painting.

See Chapter 9 for information on using the Texture buttons. Textured brushes can be created in the Texture buttons by selecting the Brush button in the Preview panel.

Draw Modes

The top of the Image Paint and Paint palettes control the brush mode.

Draw: This is the normal painting brush that you have been using.

Soften: This brush blurs the image as you use it.

Smear: Dragging with this brush pulls and smears the image.

Clone: The clone brush lets you paint portions of other images into the one you are working on. The clone brush is not available when painting in the 3D view.

When the clone brush is selected, the texture dropdown at the bottom of the Image Paint palette is replaced by an image selector dropdown. You can select any other image that has already been loaded into Blender. When you do, that image shows up in the background at 50% opacity. Painting with the clone brush copies the portion of the image under the brush into the active image. The background image may be moved around with the RMB in order to align portions of it with different sections of your main image.

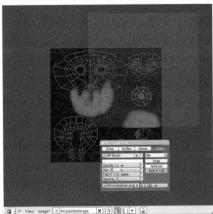

A clone image used in the background.

Image File Management

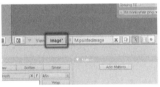

Unsaved image indicator

It is important to remember to save any images you create or alter in the Image Editor. If you don't, any changes you've made will be lost when you quit Blender. To save your changes to an image, or to save a new image for the first time, select "Save" from the Image menu in the Image Editor. Blender will let you know that an image has unsaved changes by placing an asterisk (*) beside the Image menu.

One Last Bit of Fun

For a final cool trick, try clicking the Lock icon on the Image Editor header. If your object is visible in the 3D view while painting in the Image Editor, the Lock will show you the painting in the 3D view in real time. To be able to see it, either enable Texture Paint mode in the 3D view or set the object's Draw mode to Textured.

CHAPTER 11

Lighting and Rendering

 Lighting: Hands On

 **Lighting Discussion**
by Mathias Pedersen

Mathias Pedersen – (The M.h.p.e.)

Mathias Pedersen is a young, aspiring artist, currently 16 years old and living in Denmark. At the age of only 10 years, he began seriously working on his art. Only a couple of years later, 3D came along as well, and he has been using Blender for 2 years. Lately, he's been getting on early start on his professional career by doing working as a freelance artist. Although he enjoys the technical aspects of 3D, they are not his driving force. In his art, Mathias prefers to have something of importance to tell. He hopes to make 3D his future profession, using it to convey stories and messages, possibly in movies.

Lighting: Hands On

While lighting is extremely important to the quality of a final render, and good setups can run the gamut from basic to complex, Blender's lighting tools themselves are simple to use.

Open the scene called "Lighting Tutorial.blend" that is found in the "lighting" folder of the included CD.

The "lighting tutorial.blend" file when first opened.

If you were to render this scene right now (F12), you would get nothing but a completely blank image. Although the models and textures are complete, nothing will render without lamps.

Use the toolbox (Spacebar) to add a standard Lamp to the scene.

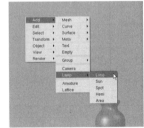

Like any other Blender object, new lamps are created at the current location of the 3D cursor. They can be moved (G-key) or rotated (R-key), with the transform manipulators and mouse gestures working as well. Scaling should be avoided. In fact, scaling Lamps in Blender can create serious problems with your scenes. Distance, energy and shadow settings can be sensitive to the scene's overall scale, and using the Scale tools can lead to unexpected results. The transformation manipulators and mouse gestures will also work with lamps.

The toolbox adding a lamp.

With the new Lamp selected, find the Lamps subcontext of the Shading context, commonly referred to as the Lamp buttons. In the example file, the buttons window is already set to the Lamp buttons.

The lamp buttons.

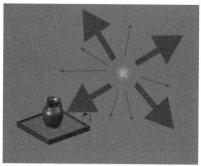

The arrows show how light shines in all directions from the standard lamp.

The type of lamp you have added to your scene is often referred to as a "point lamp," although that term is not used in the Blender interface. A point lamp casts light equally in all directions, using the lamp's location as the light source.

Try a render (F12) to see what the scene looks like with a single point lamp at default settings.

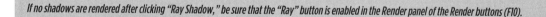

You can also use the Shift-P preview panel that was demonstrated in Chapter 2 to get a faster idea of how your lamps affect the scene.

Rendering without shadows makes the vase seem to float.

One thing you'll notice about the render is that while the objects are illuminated on the side facing the lamp and dark on the side facing away, there are no cast shadows. You would think that light sources should always cast shadows like they do in the real world. Shadows, however, require extra calculations at render time, which can slow things down. In addition, some scenes may have complex lighting setups using dozens of lamps, not all of which need to show shadows for the scene to be believable. For these reasons, shadows in most CG programs, Blender included, can be enabled or disabled.

Let's turn on shadowing for your point lamp. In the Shadow and Spot panel, press the "Ray Shadow" button. Now re-render. That's all there is to using a point lamp.

If no shadows are rendered after clicking "Ray Shadow," be sure that the "Ray" button is enabled in the Render panel of the Render buttons (F10).

The vase now looks like it makes contact with the tiles.

From a top view (Numpad-7), press Shift-D to duplicate the point lamp and move it to the other side of the scene.

If you have added the wrong kind of lamp to your scene and would like a different kind, you don't need to delete it and create a new one. The Lamps panel in the Lamp buttons lets you switch the actively selected lamp into a different type. Change the duplicated lamp into a Sun lamp by pressing the "Sun" button on the Preview panel.

A Sun lamp has the same set of options as a standard Lamp in the Lamp buttons, but works a little differently in the 3D view and has a very different effect on a render. Recall that the standard Lamp broadcasts light in all directions from its location. A sun lamp does not shine light from a single location, regardless of where the lamp is located in the scene. It creates uniform lighting coming from a single direction.

All light from a sun lamp flows in the same direction.

The direction is controlled by the rotation of the lamp in the 3D view, visualized by the dashed line attached to it. All of the light generated by a Sun lamp will shine parallel to this line. To see the difference between the parallel shading and shadows of a Sun lamp and a standard Lamp, move the lamp fairly close to the vase and rotate the lamp to face it.

Render the scene. With the Render view still up, press the J-key. This will move the render to an alternate render buffer, so you can easily compare it to the next step.

Back in the 3D view, change the Sun lamp into a standard lamp and render again.

When the render is finished, press the J-key several times to toggle between the two versions of the render. It's quite obvious when doing this how the light sources differ greatly in their effect, even though their controls are mostly the same.

The sun lamp render is on the left. Even though the lamp is nearly touching the vase, notice the parallel shadows it casts.

Now that we've introduced you to the absolute basics of lamps (creation, positioning and shadow activation), you'll create two different lamp setups, one each on a different layer, to learn the rest of the lamp controls.

Lamp Basics

Three Point Lighting

The discussion section of this chapter talks about some of the weaknesses of this very traditional method, common in studio lighting, but using it will give you a good chance to learn some additional techniques.

Three point lighting makes use of… three lamps! Surprise. One lamp provides a direct light to show the details of the subject. Another lamp shines from a different direction and fills in the areas that are cast into shadow by the first lamp. A third lamp shines from behind and above, throwing a bright rim of light around the back and top edges of the subject.

You'll start by creating the first light, called the "key" light. Select and delete (X-key) the two lamps that are already in your scene.

Add a new Spot lamp at about the location shown in the illustration. We've split our 3D view into two separate

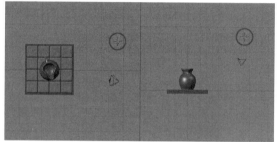

The 3D cursor positioned before the creation the Spot lamp.

views so you can better see the placement of the lamps.

Using either the hotkeys, the manipulators or mouse gestures, rotate the spot lamp until its central targeting line

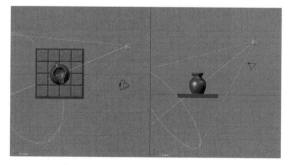

passes through the vase.

Spot lamps have more controls than the other types of lamps you've seen so far. Almost all of those settings are related to shadows, and we'll examine them in a moment. For now, duplicate the Spot lamp twice with Shift-D and position and rotate the two new lamps as shown in the next illustration.

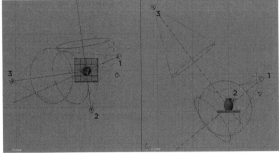

See if you can get close to this lamp configuration.

Three point lighting with three identical lamps.

A render with this setup produces bland results.

What you need is to adjust the intensities of the lamps to give the image better contrast. Select Spot number 1, the key light, and adjust the value of the Energy slider on the Lamp panel to around 2. Also, change the R and G values in the RGB sliders to 0.6. As you can see in the color swatch below the sliders and in the Preview panel, this will change the key lamp to a light blue.

Spot number 2 is called the "Fill" lamp, because it fills in the areas that are not illuminated by the key lamp. It should be a more subtle light, so turn its energy down to 0.60, and reduce its Blue slider to 0.5.

Finally, select Spot 3, the "Back" light, so called because of it's placement behind the subject. It will give the vase a bright rim around its upper edges. Leave the color alone (R, G and B all stay at 1.0), but change its Energy slider to 5.0.

A much more interesting render.

There are a couple of ugly things about this render that need to be fixed. First, the specular highlighting from both the fill and back lamps looks bad on the wooden frame of the base, as well as on the highlight on the left side of the vase. You don't want to lose the highlights from the key lamp, though, so you can't just turn off specularity in the vase's material. Blender allows you to enable and disable both specular and diffuse shading on a lamp-by-lamp basis.

Select the fill lamp (number 2), and click the "No Specular" button on the Lamps panel. Do the same for the back lamp (number 3). You can re-render to see the effects.

Another problem is the shadow being generated by the back lamp. If you examine it closely in your render window, you can see that it becomes pixelated (boxy) around the edges. In our first experiments, we enabled the "Ray Shadow" button on the standard and Sun lamps. That type of shadow generation always results in sharp, accurate shadows with no user configuration. Those shadows come at the cost of speed. In contrast, the default shadowing method for Spot lamps is called "buffered shadows."

Each time an image is rendered using a lamp that has a buffered shadow, a special mini-render is done of the scene from the point of view of the spot lamp. An image is created of how far the objects in the scene are from the lamp. This kind of image is called a "shadow map." When the final render is done, that shadow map is used to decide if there is anything between the part of the object being rendered and the lamp, creating shadows.

If you're thinking ahead, you may already realize why the shadow being generated by the back lamp looks pixelated. It's because the shadow map, being an image, doesn't have enough resolution (enough pixels) to cover the area of the scene it is being asked to cover.

You can control the size of the shadow map with the "ShadowBufferSize" spinner in the Shadow and Spot panel. Select the back lamp and set its ShadowBufferSize to 2000. Re-render to see the shadow from the back lamp with a much nicer edge this time.

Some problems have been cleaned up, but light is bleeding through the vase.

There is one other huge problem with the shadow from that back lamp, one you may not have even noticed: there seems to be light leaking through the vase!

Where is that coming from? Without being too technical, we'll just say that at some point during the creation of the shadow map, the wall of the vase was too thin to be detected. The result is an inaccurate map and a bad render. To fix problems like this, turn the Bias setting on the Shadow and Spot panel to 0.3. Re-render, and the problem has gone away.

Much better.

You might be thinking at this point that tweaking buffered shadows is a pretty big pain and wondering why you shouldn't just use ray shadows all the time. The first reason is speed, and the second is flexibility. If you like, note your render time for using buffered shadows on the Render window. Then, switch each of the lamps to use ray shadows, re-render and see the time difference. On the test computer for this simple scene, the difference is that buffered shadows are almost 20% faster than ray shadows.

The back light's shadow, softened.

The second advantage, and probably the most important, is flexibility. Buffered shadows allow you to easily create blurred shadows, which can give an image a softer, more realistic look. To show this effect, set the Soft value of the back lamp to 10 and re-render. To increase the quality of the softening calculations, you can raise the Sample value.

When working with buffered shadows, there are several things to watch out for:

• Pixelated (blocky) shadows can be fixed by raising the ShadowBufferSize.

• Light leaks in a shadow, as well as a shadow not quite meeting the bottom of the shadow-casting object, can be fixed by reducing the Bias value.

• Buffered shadows can be blurred by raising the Soft value.

There are two more things you can do to increase the quality of your buffered shadow. The first is to adjust the Spot lamp's cone that appears in the 3D view. The cone that emanates from the lamp shows the area of light that is projected. Nothing outside of this cone receives any light from the lamp. Your goal as a lighting technician in Blender is to get that cone to be as small as possible, while still encompassing the objects in your scene.

Adjust the area the spotlight covers by reducing the SpotSi (Spot Size) slider on the Shadow and Spot panel. In the case of the example, we were able to reduce it to 15.00. Note in the illustration how much smaller the cone is than before.

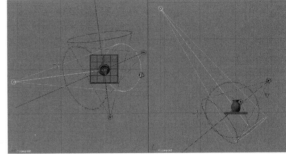

The second adjustment that can assist with spot quality deals with something called clipping. Clipping is just another way to limit what the shadow buffer creation process sees. The defaults that you can see at the bottom of the Shadow and Spot panel are 0.50 for ClipSta

Try to achieve the tightest light cone that will cover your objects

(Clip Start) and 40.00 for ClipEnd. This means that Blender will create a shadow map for objects that are between 0.50 and 40.00 units from the lamp. Nothing outside of that range will be able to cast a shadow. Like the size of the Spot lamp's cone, you want to keep this range as small as possible while still encompassing all of the objects that need to be included.

The newest version of Blender allows you to set the clipping values automatically. To do so, click the "Automobile" button (Get it? Auto?) to the left of each Clip spinner on the panel.

In a rudimentary scene like this example, none of these optimizations make much of a difference to rendering speed or quality. It is when scenes grow in complexity, to hundreds of thousands of faces, and are rendered thousands of times for an animation that these controls really begin to prove their worth.

One final word about buffered shadows. If all of these settings seem overwhelming, but you want the speed of buffered shadows, you are in luck. In addition to the default method of buffered shadow creation (called "Classic-Halfway" for technical reasons), there is another method called "Irregular."

Select the key lamp (number 1) and change the drop down menu below the "Buf Shadow" button to "Irregular." The ShadowBufferSize and several other controls disappear. Irregular shadow buffers give very nice edges without the downsides of raytracing. Adjust the Bias on this lamp to 0.300 and turn on Auto clipping for both ClipSta and ClipEnd.

That's a decent lighting setup for your scene. We'd like you to make one more, but you've spent so much time on this one that it seems wrong to completely discard it. Rather, we'd just like to get it out of the way. Select all three lamps, then press the M-key, which, if you remember from the Object chapter, will bring up the Layers palette.

Final render with three point lighting setup.

Adjusting Settings

Use the mouse, or press the 2-key, to put the lamps on Layer 2. Unless they are on a visible layer, lamps will not add light to a scene. Therefore, using layers to hold different sets of lamps is a great way to manage different lighting setups.

With those lamps sent to Layer 2, let's create a new lamp directly above the scene. This time, select the "Hemi" style of lamp from the toolbox. If you create the lamp in a top view, it will be facing directly downward. If it isn't, use Alt-R to remove any rotations.

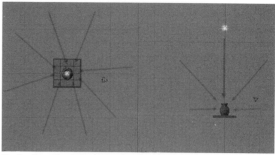

The Hemi lamp illuminates from an imaginary hemisphere.

The purpose of a Hemi lamp is to light every object in the scene as though it were in the middle of a giant, glowing hemisphere. Hemi lamps are like Sun lamps in that their location doesn't matter — only their orientation. Hemi lamps do not cast shadows.

Here is a render of the scene with the Hemi lamp's default settings.

Obviously, Hemi lamps aren't really suitable by themselves. They are good, however, for adding a little bit of light to a scene whose shadowed areas appear too dark, or to give an overall color cast.

Since you'll be using it as a sort of background illumination, let's reduce its Energy slider to around 0.4, and turn off specularity by pressing the "No Specular" button.

The scene lit with a single Hemi lamp.

Now, you'll add the last kind of lamp: an Area lamp. Create one with the toolbox, and position it as shown in the illustration.

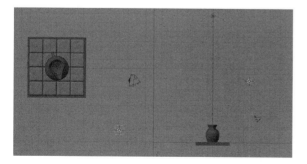

Area lamps are directional, so you will need to point it at the vase. The fastest way to do this is to first select the Lamp, then Shift-RMB select the vase and press Ctrl-T. Choose "TrackTo Constraint" from the menu that pops up. Ctrl-T tells the selected object to point toward the Active object, regardless of where it is. A lamp that is tracked this way will automatically follow an animated object.

With the Area lamp as the Active object again, enable "Ray Shadow" in its Shadow and Spot panel. Turn "Samples" up to 4. Set Energy to 0.25.

When you render, you should see something like this:

Notice the softening shadows? Although it uses raytracing to calculate the shadows, they aren't sharp. Why not? An Area lamp simulates what would happen if you had a grid of ray-traced Sun lamps. The Sample spinner tells the Lamp how many raytraced lamps to include in its calculations. In this case, the value you assigned, 4, told it to make a grid that was 4 lamps by 4 lamps, giving a total of sixteen lamps.

Here, you can see a real Sun lamp arrayed on a 4x4 grid. The resulting render looks much the same as the one from the Area lamp.

Area lamps can give a realistic effect with respect to shading and shadowing, but it comes at a cost. Because their shadows are raytraced, rendering can be slow. As the Samples value increases, quality goes up, but speed suffers.

Another issue with Area lamps is that distance from the subject can be important. They are tuned for optimal lighting conditions at the distance noted in their Dist control on the Lamp panel. This value is shown by the central targeting line extending from the lamp in the

The render from a grid of Sun lamps is similar to that of the Area lamp

3D view. Moving a lamp much closer or further from the subject than its distance value suggests can result in drastically increased and reduced energy levels, respectively.

Before we move on to the final method of lighting a scene, we'll look at one more technique. Although you'll do this to the Area lamp, it will work for any of Blender's lamp types.

The Lamp Texture and Input panel.

On the Texture and Input panel in the Lamp buttons, use the menu selector below the Add New button to find the texture called "Branches." Then click on the "View" button below the texture selector to change the way the texture maps with the light. Lamps can have standard Blender textures attached to them. Those textures change the color of the light. One of the best uses for this is to fake the way that light filters through a tree's branches and leaves.

Of course, you could also model an actual tree with leaves, and have the lamp shine through it, casting real shadows. But most times, going to such trouble will not be worth the difference in the resulting renders.

Render again, and see how the Branches texture affects the light.

The Branches texture was already created for you, but you can use any of the texturing tools reviewed in the Materials and Texturing chapter to create textures for your lamps. They can be layered, just like Materials, and their scales and offsets adjusted and animated separately. For example, if you wanted to make a fairly convincing animation of a branch shadow pattern moving in the wind, you could create three different branch textures, stack them, and animate them each to move in a slightly different way. While that probably wouldn't hold up if it were the featured element of a scene, it would certainly suffice for background work.

The branch pattern of the image texture is cast from the lamp.

At this point, you can push the Clear button to remove the texture from the lamp.

In addition to lamps, there is one more method of adding light to a scene. It produces excellent results, but can be slow. Do you see a trend here?

Ambient Occlusion

Select and delete the Hemi lamp you created earlier. Select the Area lamp and send it to Layer 3 to get it out of the way for a moment.

Find the World buttons (F8), which are another subcontext of the Shading buttons, like Lamps. Click on the "Amb Occ" tab to bring it to the front. Ambient Occlusion refers to a technique that raytracing renderers can use that causes faces that are both near and pointing toward other faces to appear darker, and faces that are far, or pointing away from, other faces to appear lighter. To see the effect in practice, click on the "Ambient Occlusion" button in the Amb Occ tab, then render.

The render is grainy, but notice how the tiles under the vase have a subtle shading to them, which makes it look like the vase is casting a slight shadow. Also, the lower portion of the vase is darker than the top, as its lower faces are pointing toward the tiles, while the faces on the upper part are facing the "sky." And all of this with no lamps! This method of lighting a scene can be excellent when you want believability with very little configuration and have rendering time to burn.

Default Ambient Occlusion settings.

Raising the Samples value for Ambient Occlusion smoothes out the graininess, but, of course, takes longer. It's quite common to work on a scene that will include Ambient Occlusion with a very low sample value, like 2, to enhance speed while you tweak the rest of the scene. After that, you can turn it up to 10 or so for your final render and get yourself a cup of coffee.

A render lit only with Ambient Occlusion.

Ambient Occlusion

To demonstrate how believability in an image can be significantly enhanced by using Ambient Occlusion (usually referred to as "AO"), let's bring back our Area lamp. Enable Layer 3 (Shift-LMB on the Layer 3 button on the 3D header, or Shift-3). Since the AO is already adding a significant amount of light to the scene, turn the Area lamp's Energy slider even further down to 0.1. Render.

The result is a softly lit scene with a high degree of believability. If you would like to really remove the grain in the render, change the AO samples to 10 and check the new result. AO samples can be set as high as 16, but excellent results are usually achievable without going that far.

The final render.

Conclusion

Lighting is an art form in itself. Large CG companies have artists on staff who do nothing but lighting. It is a complex topic - one that can make or break a scene. While we've shown you the mechanics of using Blender's lighting tools in this tutorial, we encourage you to work through the discussion section of this chapter, and to seek out other resources to enhance your artistic abilities.

Lighting: Discussion

While good lighting has some technical aspects to it, it is largely artistic, based on observation and interpretation. Looking at the way light behaves in real life is the only sure way to achieve convincing results in 3D. Find all the references you can. Don't rely on your memory for the little details — there will always be something that you failed to notice.

Light in 3D is comparable to the light you experience in the real world. Light illuminates objects so that you can see them. In the real world, light sources cast rays of light into space that are eventually reflected back to your eyes, enabling you to see the world. In Blender, each surface that is seen by the camera receives a certain amount of light from each of the Lamps in the scene, allowing the camera to render those surfaces.

Why is Lighting Important?

Obviously, if there is no light in your scene, you'll get a completely black render. Of course, even bad lighting can fix that. Second, and more importantly, lighting can help to bring out details in your scenes. And third, lighting sets the overall tone and mood for a scene. Great lighting can evoke drama and emotion in an otherwise static scene, while poor lighting can ruin the most carefully designed meshes and materials.

Lighting can either help you convey your message, or not.

Basic Tools

Blender comes with a set of basic lighting features that you need to be familiar with before you can focus on their more artistic aspects.

Lamps are added like other Blender objects, through the toolbox.

All the lamp types share a basic set of controls on the Lamp panel.

Adding a lamp from the toolbox.

Crop of Lamp buttons, with Lamp controls highlighted

Energy: The Energy slider determines the actual brightness of the lamp.

RGB: The RGB sliders set the color of the light that comes from the lamp. The color swatch below the sliders can also be LMB clicked to bring up the color picker.

Layer: This button restricts light from the lamp so it only affects objects on the same layer. If you wanted to make one object in a night scene appear much brighter than others, it could be placed on a separate layer and lit with layer-restricted lamps.

Why is Lighting Important?

273

Negative: Sometimes you need to actually subtract light from an area. Using the Negative setting inverts the effects of the lamp, taking light away.

No Diffuse/Specular: Prevents either the Diffuse or Specular render calculations from recognizing the lamp. Non-key lights can have their Specular components turned off to avoid visual confusion in a scene.

Lamp Types

Blender is equipped with 5 lamp types — lamp, sun, spot, hemi and area — each with unique purposes and uses. Once a lamp has been added to a scene, its type can be changed using the buttons on the Preview panel.

Lamp

The Lamp type is Blender's basic light. It works very much like a real light bulb, shining in all directions. The Lamp has a few options, and most repeat themselves in the other lamp types. The standard lamp can cast shadows using raytracing, a very accurate technique that produces sharp-edged shadows.

Sun

The sun type is a "directional" light. This means that all shading from this lamp appears to come from parallel light rays, as though they were emitted from an infinitely distant, infinitely large object. Although the real sun is neither of those things, its size and distance relative to the Earth make it appear to be so for all practical purposes. Sun Lamps can only cast shadows using raytracing.

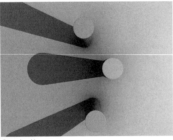

Standard Lamp

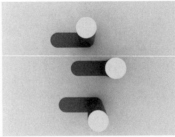

Sun Lamp

The difference between the shadows of an ordinary lamp (left) and a Sun Lamp (right). Notice how the Sun Lamp casts parallel shadows.

Spot

The Spot Lamp is very much like a real world spot light. It illuminates objects within a controllable cone-shaped area. It also has the benefit of a different method of shadow calculation: buffered shadows. This is handy if you want to have softer shadows than those produced by the common raytracing method, but don't have time to wait for the soft raytraced shadows of Area Lamps.

Hemi

The Hemi Lamp is a little different than the other light types, as it doesn't have any form of shadow calculation. It functions as a big, illuminating half-sphere surrounding the scene. Hemi Lamps are useful for giving a scene an overall color tone.

Lamp Types

Area

Area Lamps are the most realistic lights in Blender, but have the drawback of involving more in-depth calculations during shadowing, leading to longer render times.

When you need soft and realistic shadows, the Area Lamp is the one to use. In the real world, no shadows are completely sharp, even in direct sunlight. They get softer the farther away they get from the shadow-casting object.

Standard Lamp

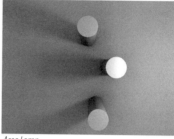

Area Lamp

The difference between the shadows of an ordinary Lamp (left) and an Area Lamp (right). The shadows of the area lamp blend out the farther away they fall, exactly the way they do in real life.

Shadows are enabled and controlled in the Shadow and Spot panel.

Ray Shadow: Using shadows based on raytracing is pretty much "fire and forget." Press the "Ray Shadow" button, and make sure that the "Ray" option is enabled on the Render panel of the Scene buttons (F10). Ray-based shadows are perfectly crisp and are slower to render than the other shadow method.

In addition to the standard lamp controls, both Spot and Area Lamps have additional capabilities and settings.

Controls That Only Apply to Spot Lamps

Buf.Shadow: A non-raytracing method of generating shadows. Buffered shadowing creates a special type of image from the point of view of the lamp, then maps it onto the objects in the scene to simulate shadows. Many of the controls on this panel are used to fine-tune shadow map creation. The most important are:

The Buffered Shadow options for Spot Lamps.

ShadowBufferSize: The resolution of the shadow buffer "image." The higher the resolution, the more detailed the shadow can be. If you see pixelization around the edges of your buffered shadows, try raising this value, 1,000 at a time, until you get acceptable results.

Bias: Corrects for problems around edges of objects and with objects that might be too thin to be seen by the shadow mapping calculations. Reduce the Bias value if light seems to be leaking through your object, or if the shadow doesn't come the whole way to the base of your object.

Controls That Only Apply to Spot Lamps

Soft: One of the great advantages of buffered shadows is that they can be blurred using this setting. Soft shadows can add realism to a scene. If you are planning to raise the Soft value to blur shadows, you will have to also raise the Samples value to prevent ugly artifacts.

Buffered Shadow dropdown menu: Choose from "Irregular," which doesn't allow blurring, or "Classic-Halfway," the default method. Ignore "Classic" — it's only there to support older files.

SpotSi: Spot Size. This control sets the angle that the Spot Lamp covers. Although it can be set as high as 180 degrees, shadow mapping at very high values will be mostly useless. The Spot Size is visualized by the cone attached the Spot Lamp in the 3D view. For best results with buffered shadows, try to keep the Spot Size as small as possible while still covering all the objects it needs to light.

SpotBl: Spot Blur. This value determines how hard or soft the edge of the Spot Lamp's circle of light will be. A value of 0.0 gives a very sharp edge, like a spotlight on a stage. Setting it to 1.0 results in a gradual reduction in light from the very center of the lamp, with no visible edge.

ClipSta, ClipEnd: Objects can only be seen by the shadow creation process if they fall within a certain distance from the Lamp. The ClipSta (Start) and ClipEnd (End) values define this distance. They are visualized by the central line extending away from the Spot Lamp. Although you can set these manually, you can also click the "Automobile" button beside each control to have Blender determine the optimal values for objects within the light cone.

Controls That Only Apply to Area Lamps

The Area Lamp options.

As mentioned above, Area Lamps are capable of producing soft shadows with raytracing. There are two settings that control this.

The Size spinner on the Lamp panel controls the actual apparent size of the light source. It is visualized by the square panel in the 3D view. The larger the light source, the more quickly the shadow will diffuse as it moves away from its casting object. This can also be changed to Rectangle, allowing you to adjust the vertical and horizontal sizes of the Area Lamp independently.

Once you press the Ray Shadow button, several new controls appear.

Samples: This controls the quality of the blur effect. Very low values will produce obvious artifacts that look like several hard-edged shadows overlaid and slightly offest. Higher values (up to 16) produce progressively smoother shadows, but can drastically slow render times.

Dither: The dither button applies a little bit of noise to the sampling, resulting in smoother shadows.

Remember when working with Area Lamps that they are tuned to have their Energy setting work optimally at the Dist (Distance) setting, shown by the line extending away from the lamp in the 3D view. Objects significantly nearer the lamp than this distance will receive much more energy.

Ambient Occlusion (A.O.)

Ambient occlusion approximates the lighting conditions of an overcast day, where light comes equally from all directions. This gives very soft shadows and darkens corners and places where objects are close to one another. Used alone, it does look very much like an overcast day, resulting in a flat, boring render. But used as a supplement to standard lights, it adds a great touch of extra realism.

Without AO, very careful and complex lighting is needed to give the right shading and shadowing to objects that touch each other. It can be difficult to get correct, and even a couple of little mistakes can ruin the believability of your scene. The inclusion of AO can go a long way toward fixing this.

The Ambient Occlusion panel is found in the World buttons (F8). One control to check out on the AO panel is the "Plain/Sky Color/Sky Texture" series of buttons. These let the AO calculations use the color of your world background (which can even be an image) to determine the color of light coming from that part of the sky, and can add even greater realism and interest to a scene. Another good way of giving ambient occlusion more color is to use it along with low intensity colored Hemi Lamps.

A render lit only by Ambient Occlusion.

Light in Animation

Lights can be animated just like any other object in Blender. In addition to animating the location and rotation of lamps like standard objects, though, a lamp's color and energy can be animated, as well as Spot Size for Spot Lamps and Size for Area Lamps. Key frames are created for lamp settings by pressing the I-key with the mouse over the Lamp buttons and choosing the appropriate key type from the menu that pops up. Ipos for lamp settings can be adjusted exactly like Ipo curves for standard objects, as shown in Chapter 3.

Lighting Techniques and Methods

Three point lighting

Three point lighting uses three light sources to light a scene (hence the name). The first and most important light is the key light. The key light can be positioned anywhere in a scene and sets the general mood. It is followed by the fill light, which does very much what its name says: fills out the areas not touched by the key light. The last light, the back light, is placed behind the subject, often a bit to either the right or left, and gives a nice highlight around its edges. The highlight visually separates the subject from the background. As it is a widely used technique, there is plenty of detailed information on three point lighting available on the Internet and in other resources.

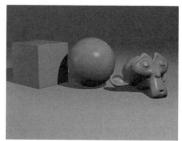

Rendered with a three point lighting setup.

Three point lighting in the GUI.

The Law or Merely a Suggestion?

It has become a common notion that the three-point setup is "the way to go" when lighting in 3D. It really works better as a guideline, though, than as an ironclad rule. Following it to the letter won't automatically make for good lighting in your scene. Unfortunately (or fortunately depending on how you look at things), lighting is about thinking for yourself. There are not any final rules or complete recipes, just guidelines, tips and techniques.

Is Three-point Lighting Even Good at All?

While it's hard to doubt that it has some useful elements, its status as a superior way of lighting is probably unjustified. It tends to look unnatural, which can make it hard for spectators to connect with a scene. Also, it has come to be associated in viewers minds with studio interviews, making its appearance elsewhere feel odd.

What follows is a general approach for lighting that might possibly lead you to a three-point setup if the situation demands it, but will most likely produce a much more organic solution for your scene.

Generic Lighting

"Generic Lighting," to coin a term, relies on common sense, reality and some basic theories of light.

You are not constrained to three light sources here. You can have as many, or few, as needed. If the lower right corner of your image is not bright enough, you add a light or two there. In real life, complex rigs might be necessary to achieve such a little enhancement, but in 3D, there is no cost to adding a little lamp in a corner.

Think Realistically

If you're creating an image that is supposed to take place around midday, think realistically. For instance, setting the Sun Lamp too low in the sky wouldn't be realistic. Neither would it be if you had two Sun Lamps lighting things from opposite directions. Don't laugh — we've all seen rendered images from artists that just look horrible, and it's often because of nonsensical setups like that. As humans we're used to seeing things in real life, and keeping within the boundaries of what we're used to actually seeing will make your lighting look better. If you have two Sun Lamps in an image, it just won't feel right. Keeping it down to one Sun Lamp in a scene, and making all other lights more diffuse and soft will look much better. Keep it looking real. It doesn't have to be exact, which is called photorealism. But it should be believable.

Light Tracing and Bouncing

In real life, light bounces off surfaces. Take a typical room as an example. Light comes in the window and hits the floor, but doesn't stop there. It bounces off the floor, illuminating the walls and ceiling. In Blender's renderer, when a lamp illuminates a surface, the light dies there. It does not go on to reflect to other objects. So, in 3D, you would have to fake this bouncing effect by putting a lamp where the light hits the floor, at a lower intensity, so it can cast more "reflected" light around the room. This method can be expanded as far as you like, and light can be traced multiple times. With this technique, though, less is often more, and only one or two bounces will be needed to give your scene believability.

A lamp has been added to the floor to simulate the way the reflected sunshine lights the room.

Single-point Lighting

"Single-point lighting" is a good term for setting up a single light source, then letting ambient occlusion take care of illuminating the rest of the scene. It causes longer render times due to AO's relative lack of speed, but can get good results with very little work. Some people find this rather easy method to be "cheating." Of course, another way to approach that is to say "If it looks good, it worked!" While this method gives passable results, getting the last bit of believability out of your scene will take a little more work.

Circle Light

Using a circle light is a way of faking ambient occlusion. It doesn't give quite as nice a result as AO, but can still be useful to some extent. To do this, place a number of lamps in a circle in the scene, a little above everything that needs to be lit, and render.

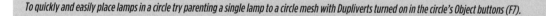

To quickly and easily place lamps in a circle try parenting a single lamp to a circle mesh with Dupliverts turned on in the circle's Object buttons (F7).

Rendered with a circle of lights, set to Ray Shadow.

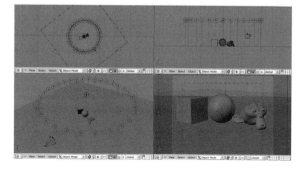

If you find the hard-edged raytraced shadows in the illustration disturbing, try using soft buffer shadows instead. With a little work put into making the spots focus on the scene, this can turn out even better as a fast, faked Ambient Occlusion.

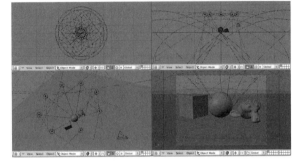

Circle lighting with buffered shadows.

Focused Lights

Focused lights are lamps that focus on a single object, or just a few objects, in a scene. A good example of focused lights is seen when lighting character shots, with spots placed just to illuminate the eyes. Under certain conditions, the eyes could be cast into shadow, making a character lack life. In the real world, this would be difficult to fix, but in 3D, you can put two focused lights on the eyes with just enough Energy to bring them out, then make them the children of the head so they follow its every movement.

Focused lights can be applied to any scene where an area needs a bit more light. It is a good idea to go easy on the intensity though, as overuse can look unnatural. One technique that helps to blend it smoothly with the rest of the lighting is to use Spot Lamps with buffered shadows and to raise the SpotBl (Spot Blur) value to soften the edges in the lit area.

How Light Affects a Scene

Lighting setups create a certain mood, one which is usually linked to a symbolic interpretation. Knowing your way around the basics of this can help your lighting to better express the feel of your scene.

Color

Lamps can be colored — and should be! If you only use white lights, your scene can quickly lose its soul and appeal. Although we think of most lights we see in the real world as "white," that is really just our brains correcting for the color casts of the light sources. Sunlight is slightly yellow, even at midday. Fluorescent lights can have a variety of casts, from pink to blue. Normal incandescent lights usually have a warm, yellow glow. While you don't want to go overboard, giving subtle color to your lights can add a great deal to your scene.

The color of the lighting in your scene should be influenced by general color theory and symbolism. Here are a few of the most common colors and a little about how they work in relation with lighting.

White

Pure light is white. It lights your scene in a plain way, not expressing much: just illuminating. In some cases, to give a sterile or medical feel, white light can be preferable. In others, it looks boring. White lighting is common in studio photography, like product photos, where the aim is to give a pure feel.

Red

Red is intense and aggressive. It can be a symbol of things like love, warmth, anger and also danger. Strong red light demands attention, while a slight red cast to a scene's illumination can add subtle warmth.

Blue

Traditional color symbolism suggests that blue stands for trust, faithfulness and security. However, when dealing with lighting, blue tends to give a cold feeling to an image. Keep in mind, though, that blue is a less aggressive color than red, and can feel quite natural in many settings due to the fact that the illumination from an empty sky is blue, and is often found in nature to one degree or another.

Green

Green can mean anything from nature and health to jealousy or wealth. In lighting, though, green gives an ugly, creepy cast, especially to interior settings. In exterior settings, subtle green lighting seems to be a more natural phenomenon, as reflected light from grass and other kinds of vegetation has a green cast.

Intensity

Light intensity, called Energy in Blender, is another fun property to play with. Low intensity lighting will obviously give a darker, more mysterious feel. When several low intensity lamps are used at once, though, it can give a soft, luxurious feel that enhances beauty. High intensity lamps give a high contrast result that's visually more edgy and can feel tense.

Location

The location of a light can have a tremendous effect on how a scene is interpreted. The basic positions and their characteristics are listed below.

Front light

Lighting a subject directly from the front removes quite a bit of depth from the resulting image. To accomplish a front lighting effect without losing your depth, have a light on each side of the camera, about 45 degrees upward, pointing down at the subject. This setup gives a wider front light that seems less intense and can preserve the depth of the subject.

A bust lit from the front.

How Light Affects a Scene

Back light

Back lighting

Back light is wonderful for accentuating edges, and emphasizing the depth of an image. Back light often gives a thin edge of light around objects, called rim lighting, although it's hard to see it if the light is positioned directly behind the subject. Giving a foreground object a rim light will make it stand out from the background, accentuating the division in depth.

Side light

Side light is great for emphasizing the shape and texture of an object. It clarifies an object's form, bringing out roughness and bumps. A blend between front and side light is common, as it communicates shape and form, while softening the flaws that direct side lighting can reveal.

The bust lit from the side.

A brick wall lit from the side. Notice how apparent bumps and shape become.

Top light

Direct top light alone can make for a very sad and almost spooky feeling. Although we're used to seeing subjects lit from above (sunlight and most indoor lighting), there are usually other light sources filling in the shadows. Therefore, to achieve this effect, fill lights, if used, must be dramatically reduced in intensity.

Bottom light

Bottom light is the light we're least accustomed to seeing. It has an intense impact when used, making objects look completely different and often sinister.

The bust lit from the top.

The bust lit from beneath.

How Light Affects a Scene

Shadows

Shadow control is half of good lighting.

No shadows

If none of your lamps have shadows turned on, it will look like your objects are floating, as in the illustration below. To achieve any kind of believability, you need some kind of shadowing. However, you don't necessarily want every lamp in your scene to cast shadows, for both technical and artistic reasons.

A render with no shadows at all.

Hard vs. Soft Shadows

Turn on Ray Shadows for a standard Blender lamp, and you'll get hard edged shadows. Very seldom are true, sharp shadows seen in reality. In the physical world, the smaller the light source, the harder the shadow, and vice versa. Of course, that means that the 100% hard shadows generated by Ray Shadow don't really exist in the real world, simply because they would require an infinitely small light source.

There are countless examples of images that have been ruined by hard shadows from several light sources, crossing each other and confusing the eye. If the artists had paid as much attention to shadowing as they had to the rest of their scene, this would not have happened.

A guideline to remember: every shadow is soft, even the ones that you remember as hard. We are not really used to seeing completely sharp shadows, so our eye finds it distracting in rendered scenes. It is especially noticeable in close-ups, where shadows are always soft to some degree.

To illustrate the difference between hard and soft shadows in real life, look at these two almost identical photos:

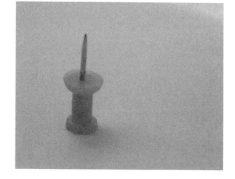

The shading defines the object more clearly, but the hard shadow actually becomes part of the composition of the photograph.

The object is less defined, as the light has been spread out by the more diffuse source. There are, however, no hard shadows to distract the eye, and it makes the photo softer and the subject more dominant.

In photography, you generally try to avoid hard shadows. In some cases, hard edged shadows can serve to make the right mood: one of tension or roughness. Hard shadows also bring out a surface's texturing and bumps, which is why they are not used when attempting to give a sense of beauty or diffusion to a scene.

As already mentioned, hard shadows can be a tremendous distraction when they litter a scene, crossing each other in inopportune places. Let's look at an example.

Spots with hard edged ray traced shadows.

Spots with soft buffer shadows.

Notice the difference between the images above. With soft shadows, the scene becomes much clearer, as we don't have the hard shadow edges competing with the composition of the rest of the scene.

There are a couple of ways to create soft shadows in Blender. The first option is the more physically correct, using time consuming area lamps. They give you a fairly realistic simulation of shadows as they spread and wash out. This is often preferable for close-ups where details like these can make a significant difference.

The second option is to use Spot Lamps with soft buffer shadows. You don't get quite the same crisp and realistic effect as with area lights, but this is not always enough of a drawback to matter. Combining soft Spots and Area Lamps is often a preferable solution.

Hard sunlight.

Soft diffuse light.

Shadows

Lighting Examples

No two images require the same lighting setup, but knowing where to start can sure help. Below are some of the most common types of lighting situations you'll encounter. These are also included on the CD for you to explore in detail.

Please don't stick to these examples as though they are law. They are only places to begin, not out-of-the-box lighting solutions. Remember, no two scenes will work out optimally with the same light setup.

Outside

Exterior settings require you to stick as closely to reality as possible to be credible to the viewer. Experimentation with alternative lighting in these settings shouldn't come at the cost of believability.

Clear day

Imagine a clear blue sky with a glaring sun. To obtain lighting like this, you must first understand what illuminates objects in a real world situation, then try to mimic that in Blender. First, you have slightly yellowish sunlight. In Blender, this can be done with, you guessed it, the Sun Lamp. Place it above your scene, pointing downwards at the desired angle (consider whether you want a morning, midday or afternoon feel).

Clear day render

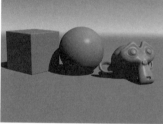
Sunlight alone

Sky illumination alone

Apart from the sun, you have the blue sky surrounding the scene, illuminating everything with a soft blue cast and turning every bit of shadow blue. This is called sky illumination.

To properly obtain that effect in Blender, you need to apply some AO to the scene, and add a sky blue hemi light for the correct color in the shadows. There are alternatives to AO, like setting up a couple of blue lights around the object, but they struggle to give the nice all-round soft shadows that AO delivers. The circle light method described earlier can perhaps give a good enough effect, and is worth a try.

Sun light on right side of a tower gives direct illumination, while sky illumination lights the rest.

Cloudy day

A day with clouds drifting around, blocking the sun every so often. The setup for this is much like the clear day setup. The only differences are that the sunlight is lower in intensity, depending on how much cloud cover there is at the time of the render, and the sky illumination color is toned more toward gray. The energy of the Sun Lamp can be slowly animated to produce the feeling of the sun moving into areas of greater and lesser cloud coverage.

Cloudy day render

Overcast day

We've all experienced one of those days with completely dull, overcast weather. In those cases, there isn't any direct sun light at all, and the only natural light source left is the gray glow coming from clouds. Ambient Occlusion with little to no key light source, or circle lighting, will achieve this effect.

On overcast days, shadows are diffuse.

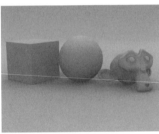

Overcast day render

Sunset/Sunrise

Staging a scene at sunset or sunrise can add a lot of mood. Set a sun lamp at a very low angle and give it an orange/red color. Make the sky illumination color (from Hemi Lamps and AO using Sky Color) a mix between blue and red.

A wide range of colors can actually be applied to a situation like this. From yellows to oranges, onto reds and sometimes even pinks. Shadow colors from the Hemi Lamps can be dark blues and purples. It's a very beautiful time of the day that seems to be completely new and different each time you see it, so there is more than enough variation to play around with.

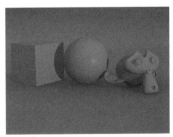

Sunset/sunrise render

Lighting Examples

Clear night

This render represents a night with no clouds, and the moon shining brightly. Moon light can be cast by a Sun Lamp with a white or slightly blue color. Apart from that, low energy blue/gray sky illumination is needed as well. When lighting a night scene, though, focus on keeping everything visible. Instead of turning down lamp energy so low that you cannot see your subjects, tint the light blue and use detailed rim lighting to show forms.

Clear night render

Overcast night

Like a clear night, except you remove the moon and make the sky illumination even grayer. This setup is the hardest to get to work, as it doesn't look very natural if it's bright enough to be able to see anything clearly. In reality, these lighting conditions (overcast night) mean that there is almost no discernible light to begin with, so no matter what you do, it won't look natural.

Overcast night render

Interiors

In interior settings you encounter a new type of light: artificial. Light bulbs can be divided into two types: incandescent and fluorescent. Although the difference in the light they cast has become increasingly small in the last few years due to new technologies, most people can still tell them apart at a glance.

Incandescent lights

Incandescent light is the kind generated by typical filament bulbs or halogen lamps. Depending on the bulb, it can have anywhere from a warm yellow/orange to white (typically for newer types). This form of light is widely used in homes.

In 3D you set up lights where you would place them in real life: on walls and ceilings. A little AO with an orange cast to it (maybe done with Hemi Lamps), can be used to fake the way that light bounces around in the room.

A render with incandescent lights.

Light sources in homes are mostly incandescent.

Lighting Examples

Fluorescent lights

Fluorescent lights are common in public places, like offices, and sometimes in private households. Older fluorescent lights have a strong green cast to them (especially on photos where the photographer used the wrong filter), but newer ones can appear completely white as well. Some fluorescent lights are even warm in color like incandescent lights, so there's a pretty broad range of colors to choose from.

A render with fluorescent lights hints.

Fluorescent tubes are often used in industrial and utility settings.

Windows

A window is another light source to keep in mind when working with interior settings. It lights differently depending on the weather and time of the day.

On a clear day, you would have a Sun Lamp shining through the windows, with some blue sky illumination, very much like the exterior setup explained earlier. In some cases, though, sky illumination isn't needed and can be excluded from the light setup without much loss of believability. One can use pretty much the same method described for outside settings to obtain a cloudy day, overcast day, night, etc.

For the more overcast weather, or to suggest the windows on the shady side of a house, an alternative, and more realistic, method is to use Area Lamps.

A render of light from windows, on a clear day.

Area lamps outside the windows give a different effect.

Sunlight through windows.

Sunlight through windows with blinds. Notice the beautiful reflected light.

Placing an Area Lamp just outside each window gives wonderfully diffuse lighting.

Special Cases

From time to time you encounter situations that just don't fit in with the standards you're used to observing.

Space

In space, things are a bit simpler than here on Earth. There is no big blue sky casting illumination from all directions. A single sun lamp, in most cases, is all you need. Illumination from the surrounding universe of stars is there, but it's negligible and not worth setting up in most cases. Notice how most entertainment productions that include space scenes use nebulae and other large scale structures to give color and light to scenes that would lack it in reality.

A render of a planet.

Studio lighting

The key word when it comes to studio lighting is control. The lights can be set up to exactly suit the photographer's needs. Studio lighting is an enormous subject that could have a chapter, a book, or an entire book series of its own. If you're really interested in replicating studio lighting in 3D, there are many books and resources already available. What follows is just one of many ways to achieve a studio lighting effect.

The studio setups most commonly encountered by the average person are product shots. Big, soft lights, often with diffuser panels, are used to light subjects evenly while eliminating distracting shadows. In 3D, this means that you must use Area Lamps or Spot Lamps with soft buffered shadows. This type of setup usually has lights arrayed around a subject for uniform illumination at a high level of intensity, "burning" any details completely out of the background.

A render simulating studio lighting for a product shot.

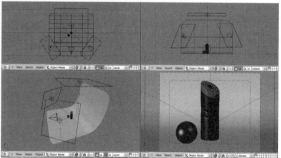

The shot set up in Blender.

Camera flash

We all know the kind of amateur photos where the light from the camera's flash is way too prominent, almost destroying the image. However, if you want to make a 3D image appear like it was indeed snapped with an amateur camera, adding a bright lamp just above the camera can easily give an extra level of realism. Nothing is perfect in reality, neither cameras nor cameramen. Sometimes duplicating bad real-world practices in 3D can enhance believability.

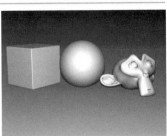

Camera flash render

Conclusion

Hopefully this chapter has given you a good start on the way to lighting your scenes effectively. Don't forget that without proper lighting your weeks of hard work on that model and materials will be so much less than it could.

Let there be light!

Particles: Hands On

Strands by Tommy Helgevold

Particle Toolset Discussion

Tommy Helgevold – (Hamsterking)

Tommy Helgevold is a former student of the animation workshop in Denmark where he studied to become a character designer / Animator. He has used Blender to produce countless visualizations like packaging design, product mascots for children, and industrial products visualization.

He is currently working as a 3D Graphics Designer at Stieler & Co in Denmark, a company that produces and invents merchandise gimmicks from scratch and is now using Blender 3D to create visualizations for customers like Carlsberg, Tuborg, Dong Energy and many more.

His personal webspace can be found at: www.hamsterking.com

Particles: Hands On

Blender's particle system allows you to create a variety of effects, including smoke and fire, sparks, dirt and "magical" lights. Unlike other Blender objects, particles are generated on-the-fly, and have no real dimensions. They are like groups (or clouds or blobs) of points in space, which can be set to glow, appear as textured cloudy areas, or even appear as duplicates of normally shaded objects. Many of the differences between these effects are based on the kinds of materials applied to the particles.

Particles are used to simulate the sand grains.

On the included disk, you will find a number of .blend files with example particle systems for fire, smoke, dust and other effects, from which you can obtain and reuse the settings and materials for your own purposes.

In this tutorial, you will create a basic particle system that resembles sand. You will learn how to give particles a starting velocity, how to fake the effects of gravity, and how to make them react to their environment.

You'll need a playground for your particles:

The scene consists of an icosphere, 2 planes, and a cube with the top removed, oriented as seen in the illustration. You can find a file, called "particles.blend," with these objects already created in the "examples" folder of the included disk. If you would rather just create your own, follow the illustration and annotations below.

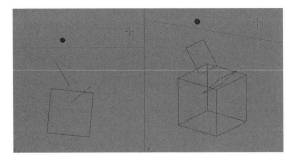

Particle systems and forces are sensitive to scale. For the tutorials in this chapter to work properly with the provided settings, you should try to recreate the exact conditions present in the illustration.

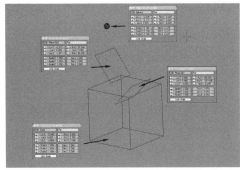

The object settings needed to recreate this scene.

Creating the Particle System

RMB select the sphere, then display the Object buttons (F7, if you're using the hotkeys). With the Object buttons up, switch to the "Physics Buttons" subcontext. The Physics Buttons contain panels for working with particles, forces, and Blender's soft body and fluid simulations.

Creating the Particle System

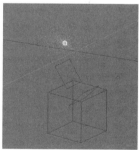

The Physics buttons.

On the "Particles" panel, click the "New" button to indicate that the sphere you have selected should be used as the "emitter" for a particle system. The emitter is the object that will "shoot out" the particles. When you create a particle system, the base emitter object will not show up on your final renders, although it will still appear in the 3D view to help you keep track of what's going on.

When you click "New," an entire panel of controls shows up, most of which you don't have to worry about for now.

The Particles panel.

The most important settings in this panel are found under the "Emit:" heading. Here, you will find the total number of particles to create, on what frames the emitter should start and stop creating particles, and how long each particle will live before it disappears. Obviously, the more particles Blender has to calculate, the slower it will respond. It does very well, however, with even tens of thousands of particles on most up-to-date hardware, so don't be overly stingy with your particle amounts.

For this tutorial, set things up like this:
- Amount: 20000 — make a total of 20,000 particles;
- Sta: 1.0 — have the emitter start to create new particles on frame 1;
- End: 150.0 — have the emitter stop creating new particles on frame 150;
- Life: 75.0 — each particle that is created will live for 75 frames, then disappear;
- Disp: 25 — The "Disp" control tells Blender what percentage of the total particles to calculate and display in the 3D view. So, the "25" value means that you will see only 25% of all 20,000 particles in your 3D preview.

Put the mouse cursor over the 3D view and press Alt-A to preview the particle animation. It seems like nothing happens, but if you watch carefully, you will see that little white particles are appearing on the surface of the sphere. In order to get them to do something, you'll have to give them a velocity.

The Particle Motion panel.

Switch to the "Particle Motion" panel.

This panel tells particles how to move. Set the "Normal:" and "Random:" spinners both to "0.030" and press Alt-A to see the results.

Particles flying off in the direction of the surface Normals.

This time, the particles fly off the sphere, which is what you wanted. The reason you entered a value into the "Normal" control was that you wanted each particle to shoot off along the "normal" of the emitter object. The short description is simply that giving a velocity in the "Normal" control will cause particles to emit away from the surface of the object. A better description of normals is available in Chapter 4.

Creating the Particle System

Particle Patterns

You may have noticed in the animated playback that the particles seem to be flying off the sphere in a certain pattern. This is because Blender emits the particles from the object based on the order of faces and vertices within the object. When a primitive object like a sphere is created, the faces are ordered very neatly.

In order to truly randomize the way that particles emit from a mesh, you must enter Edit Mode on the mesh (Tab-key), select all vertices (A-key), and then click the "Hash" button on the Mesh Tools panel of the Editing buttons (F9). The Hash function scrambles the order of vertices, meaning that particles will now seem to emit in a much more random fashion.

What you would really like, though, is for your particles to fall down through the other obstacles in the scene. This is where the "Force" controls come in.

The upper bank of X/Y/Z force controls exerts a constant force on particles along the global axis of your choice. So, to make your particles "fall" as though they are affected by gravity, you need to assign a velocity along the global Z (vertical) axis. Set the "Z" force control to "-0.50," and preview with Alt-A.

If you find that your computer shows the animation slowly or sloppily, reduce the "Disp" on the Particles panel in order to show fewer particles. If things are running fine, and you have a fast enough machine, try setting the "Disp" value to 100, to show 100% of the particles.

Barriers and Deflection

RMB to select the rotated plane immediately below the emitter, then click the "Deflection" button on the "Fields and Deflection" panel to the left of the particle panels.

The Fields and Deflection panel.

In this tutorial, you're only concerned about the upper section, labeled "Particles." By turning on Deflection, you tell the particle system to treat the object as a barrier.

Pressing Alt-A now shows this, which is clearly wrong:

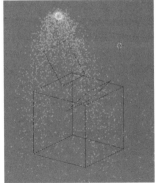

These particles are going crazy!

The problem is that by default, particle paths are calculated at a fairly low resolution. You can adjust this with the "Keys" control of the particle motion panel.

Barriers and Deflection

RMB to reselect the particle-emitting sphere, then set Keys to "50." What this value actually means is that along the total life of the particle (75 frames in your example), it will have its location calculated 50 different times. Before you changed the value, it had been set to 8, which meant that Blender was only calculating the particle position about once every ten frames. Obviously, 50 will be much more accurate.

Particles properly deflecting from the top plane.

Alt-A again, and this time you will see that the particles bounce off the plane.

Let's do one more thing with the deflection settings of the plane. RMB select the plane, then change the Deflection "Damping" setting to "0.8." Damping takes motion energy away from particles, slowing them down when they collide with the deflection object.

Pressing Alt-A doesn't seem to show any difference. Annoying. Certain changes to the scene will not be detected or automatically taken into account by particle systems. When this happens, you have to tell the particles to recalculate manually. Fortunately, this is easy to do.

To force a particle system to recalculate, RMB select the particle emitter, then click the "RecalcAll" button in the main Particles panel.

Alt-A now shows the particles sliding off the end of the plane, as opposed to rebounding like they did before you changed the "Damping" value.

There's one more thing to learn about Deflection. The deflection calculations are sensitive to which way mesh faces are pointing. Select one of the deflection planes and use the Tab key to go into Edit mode. In the "Mesh Tools 1" panel of the Editing buttons, enable the "Draw Normals" button and set the NSize value immediately above it to 1.0. You will see a light blue line extending upward and away from the plane. This line indicates the Normal, or facing direction, of the plane's quad face.

The deflection tools consider the Normal direction to be the "hard" side of the plane. If you were to rotate the plane 180 degrees and recalculate the particle system, you would see the particles no longer bouncing and sliding off the plane, but passing through it and slightly changing direction afterward. Be sure to keep surface Normals in mind if your objects are not deflecting correctly.

The particles sliding off the damped plane.

One at a time, select both the other plane and the open-topped cube, enable Deflection for them, and set their damping values to "0.8." When you're done doing that, don't forget to reselect the emitting sphere and manually recalculate the particle system.

Preview the particle animation with Alt-A, and you will see your particles fall from the ball, deflect off each plane, then end up in the bottom of the cube.

Particles seem to be escaping from the bottom of the cube, and occasionally a particle may pass through one of the planes. The particle physics system is not a full, actual physics simulation and will be subject to little annoyances like this.

Applying Other Environmental Forces

Create an Empty and position it between the sphere and the first deflection plane. Use Alt-R to clear any rotations that might be on the Empty. With the new Empty selected, choose "Vortex" from the "Fields" drop down menu in the Fields and Deflection panel.

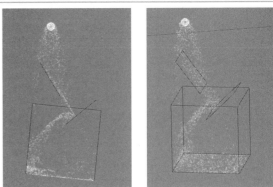

The particle system cruising along.

The Fields drop down with Vortex selected.

Set the "Strength" field to "50," and play the animation. If you are in a front or side view, the effect might not be obvious, so use the MMB to rotate the 3D view a bit. Now, you can see that the particles, as they fall, are swirling in a cyclonic fashion. You can also see that the empty now has ghosted "vortex" lines.

Now that you've seen what Vortex can do, reduce its strength to 15 or so. That will cause the particles to follow the vortex force a bit, but to still stay pretty much within the confines of the rest of the scene.

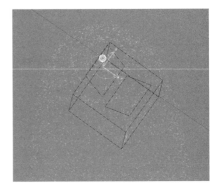

You can save this file for later reference if you like. After that, start a new Blender session with Ctrl-X for the next part of the tutorial.

Strand Particles

Blender's particle generator is not only capable of making standard particles as seen in the previous section, but also creates "Strands" that can be used to simulate hair, fur or even feathers.

Let's start by adding a sphere from the Spacebar toolbox: Add -> Mesh -> UVsphere. You can accept the default creation values of 32. Put the sphere into Object mode with the Tab key.

The default particles panel.

In the buttons window, press F7 to bring up the Object buttons. Press F7 once more to cycle forward to the Physics buttons. Press the New button on the Particles tab, and you will again see the controls as they appear in the following illustration:

Since you're about to create hair Strands, you need to make the particles static. Static particles are Blender's way of showing all of particles positions along its life at one time. The net effect is that a static particle looks like a long chain of particles that fill the path that a standard version of the particle would have followed. Press the "Static" button. To draw the Strands properly, you need to activate the "Vect" option. If you want the emitter mesh to show along with the particle Strands, press the "Mesh" button in the Display section.

So where are the Strands? Like the previous example, strand particles need a velocity to be more than just points. Go to the Particle Motion tab and set Normal to 0.010. Your sphere and Strands should look something like the illustration, which is shown in solid view (Z-key).

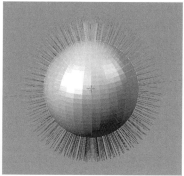 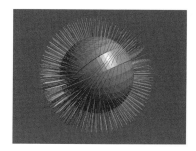

An OpenGL and Rendered view of Strands.

They look quite boring don't they? That's because they're just a bunch of Strands sticking out of a round ball. Let's make them look better! Right now, the rendered Strands stop abruptly and are the same size along their entire length. Real hair and fur tapers away to almost nothing, giving them their soft, whispy appearance. Let's take a look at how you use textures and material to get the same effect with Strands.

The Strand Shader

If you haven't already done Chapter 9: Materials and Texturing, the next part may go a bit too quickly for you. Although many parts of this book are independent, Strand rendering is quite dependent on proper materials and texturing. You are encouraged to work through Chapter 9 for a better understanding of this.

Material buttons Map Input and Map To panels.

Blender has a special shader for dealing with Strands. You'll use the Blend texture type along with the Strand shader to make rendered Strands appear to thin out toward their tips.

The illustration above shows several panels of the Material buttons (F5). You will need to add a new material, and then add a texture to that material. Set the panels as shown. The "Strand" button on the Map Input panel activates Strand mapping and the Alpha button on Map To activates the opacity channel. Also, turn off the Col button (Color) in the Map To panel.

Let's work on the "fading texture." You're going to set the texture in the first texture slot to a Blend. Check out the next illustration:

The Texture buttons Texture and Blend panels.

The Strand Shader

We have torn off the Colors panel from behind the Textures tab where it began and adjusted the panel layout for clarity in the illustrations. Refer to Chapter 2 if you need help with this.

Let's adjust the color and opacity of the Blend texture. On the Colors panel, press the Colorband button to show the Colorband controls. Set the "A" slider to 1.0 and pick a pure white from the color swatch right above it. Then, change the spinner that reads "Cur: 0" to 1. The Alpha and RGB sliders will change. Set A to 0.0 and pick a pure black from the color swatch. When you've done it correctly, it should look like this:

You've now finished the Blend texture that will create the fade effect on the Strands.

The Texture buttons Colors and Preview panels.

Let's give your Strands a color by going to the Material buttons and selecting a color from the Col button's color picker on the Material panel. Also, to let the Alpha from the Blend texture take effect, turn the "A" (Alpha) slider on this same panel down to 0.0. In the Links and Pipeline panel, be sure to turn on ZTransp to allow the renderer to use transparency.

To get a good preview of the effect all of this will have on your Strands, you can switch to the "Hair Strands" preview type in the Preview panel, and enable anti-aliasing by clicking the "O" button at the bottom.

Preview, Material and Links and Pipeline panels.

If you did everything as described above and press F12 to render, your render should look something like this:

It's a little hard to see in the book, but on your screen the difference between the old render and the new render will be obvious. You now have much softer hair Strands.

There is one more thing you can do to give an even more tapered feel to the Strands before you start to add a lot more particles. Blender renders Strands with a width of one pixel, no matter how near or far they are from the camera. If you click on the "Strands" button in the Links and Pipeline panel, you can adjust the beginning and ending size of the Strands that the renderer uses. They can start out or end thicker or thinner, and you can even tell them whether to make the transition from thick to thin.

A render of the textured strands. You may have to adjust your camera angle and lamp position if you want to duplicate this exactly.

In this example, we've set the Start size of the Strand to 12.0 and changed the Shape to -0.900 so it's really "spiky."

The Strand palette.

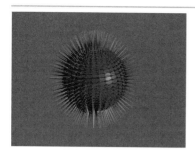

If you render now, it looks like the image on the left:

Now that you've done all the footwork, you're ready to have a *lot* of fun with hair and fur. Let's go back to the particle settings and create a lot more fur.

In the Physics buttons (F7), turn the Emit amount up to 20,000. If you don't have a faster computer, you can change the Disp value to 20. All 20,000 particles will still show up at render time, but it will let you work much more quickly in the 3D view.

Now that you have a lot more particle Strands, let's hit them with some gravity. Without being relativistic, gravity is just a downward force, so you change the Z value in the Force section of the Particle Motion tab to about -0.06. To make your fur a bit frizzy and random looking, set the Random value in the Velocity section to 0.015. To create an even better looking distribution of the particles, enable the Rand and Even buttons in the From section of the Particles tab.

If the fur Strands move in a direction other than downward when adjusting the Z force value, it could be that the emitter was created with a rotation. To remove this and see the Strands bend down with gravity, make sure the emitter is the active object and press Alt-R to remove any rotations.

The Particles and Particle Motion tabs.

If you render this, it will look something like the next illustration. The lighting setup that was used to render the images for this book is simply the default lamp switched to a spot lamp and tracked (Ctrl-T) to the particles. The spot uses a Classic-Halfway buffered shadow.

Curve Guides

What if you want to do something a little better than just some fur hanging off of a ball? All that you have to do in order to nicely shape the hairs in your new hairball is to add a Curve object and set it to be a "curve guide."

Curve Guides are extremely sensitive to their initial conditions, different settings and the actual shape of the curve. Do not worry if you don't exactly duplicate the images in this section. What's important to take away from this is how to create a Curve Guide and have it influence Strand particles.

Add a Curve object to the Scene by using the spacebar toolbox and choosing Add->Curve->Bezier Curve, then pressing the Tab key to leave Edit mode. With the Curve selected, go to the Object buttons (F7) and take a look at the Fields dropdown menu in the Fields and Deflection panel:

The Force Fields menu.

When you designate the Curve object as a Curve Guide, you see it instantly affect your particle furball. Each strand now mimics the shape and orientation of the Curve Guide. If you'd like, you can enter Edit mode on the Curve with the Tab key, then use the standard selection and transformation tools (RMB, G/S/R-keys) to change its shape, while watching the Strands update in real-time to follow the changes.

Don't worry if your first attempt looks nothing like this. Curve guides can take a while to get the hang of.

A curve guide, modified to nicely shape the hair.

It cannot be stressed how important lights and shadows are to achieving good quality hair. Buffered shadows with large (greater than 2,000) buffer sizes usually produce prettier results than Ray shadows. Good materials also help: turning Specularity values up to 1.0 and using high Hardness (150-200) will give great renders.

Nice hair, huh? Here are the Material and Particle settings for it:

The Material and Particle buttons for the last render.

Let's take a look at what we've done to get that nice hair. We scaled the emitter object down a bit so it was less prominent in the scene. Then, the Normal (speed) value in the Particle Motion panel was increased to 0.04. Also, the Random value was upped to 0.4. Of course, the Curve Guide was altered too. You'll be surprised how flexible Curve Guides can be.

Want to get even more advanced? Read on...

You can use multiple Curves to guide your hair. Select the current Curve and use Shift-D to make a duplicate. Tilt them each at a slightly different angle as shown here:

Two Curve Guides, offset.

This section is very dependent on how you shaped the Curve Guide in the previous example. Don't take the values given here too seriously, as they may not be appropriate for your particular model. The goal is to see how multiple guides can affect different sections of Strand particles, not to reproduce the final render exactly.

Now check out the Fields and Deflection panel for each Curve Guide, and press the "Additive" button. This button creates an approximation field on your Curve Guides, so that when you blend two or more together it will affect parts of your Strands depending on the settings in the MinDist and Fall-off spinners. Set a small MinDist value (try 1.5) for each Curve, and set the Fall-off to around 3.25. These values will depend on your Curves, the number of segments and emitter size, etc. In other words, they will vary with your own creations, so you may have to change something to get it to work.

The real trick, though, is that once you have made those settings, you must move each curve guide until the solid circle around its head is intersecting part of the emitter mesh. Particles that come from the portion of the mesh that falls within that circle will follow that particular Curve Guide.

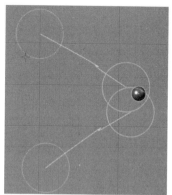

If you've done everything correctly, you should be able to control your hair well enough to split it into sections like this:

You can even vary the length of each Curve so it will affect the length of the Strands near that particular Curve.

The Curve Guides converging on the emitter mesh.

There is almost no end to how much you can do with particles in Blender. You can twist them around, knit them, swirl them, toss them and yes, do almost anything you want with them. Your characters will never go bald again!

Particle Toolset Discussion

Particle systems are different from other Blender objects in a number of ways. First, instead of being made of faces, edges and vertices, they are composed of a large number of points (up to 100,000). Second, the locations of these points are calculated by Blender and are based on velocity and force values, instead of being modeled by the user into exact shapes.

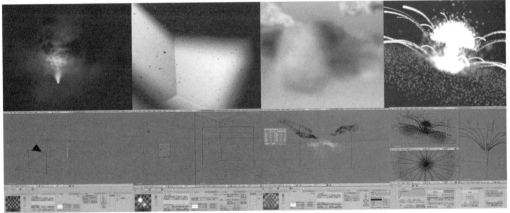

Various particle systems, both rendered and in the GUI. Smoke and detonation particle setups by Liubomir Kovatchev and Jason Saville.

Particle systems can be used for a variety of effects, but are most commonly found when making "aerial" effects like smoke, fire, clouds, dust motes floating in sunlight, magical sparkles swarming around an actor...you get the idea.

Emitters

Particle systems need a place to start. That place is an "emitter."

In Blender, an emitter can be any mesh object you choose. The shape of the mesh will form the starting point for the particles.

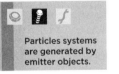

Particles systems are generated by emitter objects.

A particle system is created by RMB selecting a mesh object, and clicking the "New" button in the Particles panel of the Object buttons (F7), found in the Physics buttons subcontext.

The Particles panel. In the default configuration, the Particle Motion panel is nested as a tab behind the main Particles panel, but we've pulled it out to show you everything at once.

Before you examine the particle tools, a couple of points about particle systems in general are in order:

- There are two kinds of particle systems, Static and Dynamic, each of which has its own tutorial.

Static particles are used for systems of Strands like hair, fur and grass. Dynamic particles are used for the previously mentioned fire, smoke and dust effects.

- Unless you take special steps, the emitter mesh itself will not show up in a render.

The most basic settings for particles are found in the "Emit" section of the panel.

Amount: This is the total amount of particles in the system. How many you use will vary in relation to exactly what you are trying to do. Keep in mind that more particles will take more calculation time, and, depending on the speed of your computer, may slow things down significantly.

Sta: This stands for start, and refers to the frame number on which the emitter will begin to create particles.

End: The last frame on which the emitter will create particles.

An emitter will create particles at a constant rate between the Start and End frames. So, with only these three controls, you can cause some serious differences in the way particle systems can act. 10,000 particles being created between frames 1 and 1,000 will make 10 particles per frame, a fairly low rate. On the other hand, 10,000 particles with a Start of 1 and an End of 2 will cause a burst of all 10,000 particles within 1 frame. Think of a fireworks explosion.

Life: How long each particle will live. Particles hang around in the scene for only as long as this parameter will let them. After they die, new particles will be emitted to take their place, up until the End frame is reached.

A low Life value (a couple of frames) will have particles blipping into and out of existence rapidly, like short-lived sparks thrown from a welding torch. Life settings that are longer than the amount of time the particles are actually being emitted will cause a build-up effect, with all emitted particles hanging around in the scene long after the End frame.

Disp: Percentage of particles to display. This is indispensable when you are working with particle systems that have enough particles to slow down your Blender experience. The value here is a simple percentage: 10 shows only 10% of the total particles, 50 shows 50%, etc. The really nice thing is that it is not just a display speedup. Until render time, Blender does all of its particle calculations on this reduced amount, giving good speed boosts for any particle-related activities. When you render your scene, though, the full particle amount is used.

You can also control which parts of the mesh emitter the particles come from, in the appropriately named "From:" section of the panel.

By default, both the "Verts" and "Faces" buttons are On, meaning that particles can be emitted from either vertices or faces. For certain effects, you could restrict it to one or the other by setting either to Off. For example, if you wanted to create an effect where particles emitted in a burst from several points on a grid, you would turn off the Face option.

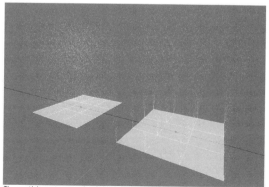

The particle system on the right shows particles emitting from faces and vertices. The one on the left only emits from the vertices.

Emitter Settings

Rand: Creates a truly Random distribution. The normal distribution of particles looks pretty random to the untrained eye, but from a mathematical perspective it isn't. Without getting all math-geeky, really random things tend to cluster and clump. Their elements are not as orderly as the standard particle layout. When looking at the illustration, you can see patterns in the standard emit, but none in the Random emit.

The particle system on the left has the normal particle distribution. The one on the right is using the Rand option.

Even: Attempts to distribute particles evenly over the surface of the mesh emitter. Usually, Blender assigns particles on a per-face basis, meaning that in a 20,000 particle system, each face of a 100 face mesh gets to emit 200 particles. That sounds fine until you realize that some areas of the emitter mesh might have more densely packed, smaller faces. Particles will be denser in those areas.

Using the Even option attempts to alleviate this by assigning each face a number of particles in proportion to its part of the area of the mesh. You need to be careful when using this option with things that could change the shape of the mesh though: shape keys, character animation through armatures, lattices, etc. These tools can change the relative sizes of faces in your mesh, causing particles to seem to jump around as they are reapportioned for different face areas.

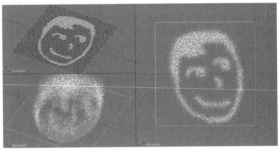

A mesh with a vertex group of a face saved. The particles are set to emit from the "face" vertex group.

Vgroup: Vertex Group. Vertex groups are covered in Chapter 4. You can enter the name of an already-created vertex group here to cause only that portion of the mesh to act as an emitter.

Materials: What do the particles look like?

Particles use a material option that is not covered in the Materials and Texturing chapter. We'll go over it here. To get the most out of this, you should probably have read Chapter 9 so you understand the basics of creating and working with materials and textures.

By default, particles are rendered with the Halo material. Halos are rendered at a different stage than normal geometry, and are strictly 2D effects placed into the final render.

Note: Halos do not react to raytracing, so they will not show up in Ray reflections or Ray transparency. Also, as they are a 2D post-render effect, Halos cannot cast shadows.

The following illustration shows what halos can look like:

Emitter Settings

A particle system, showing two different Halo settings.

A material's halo options can be accessed by enabling the "Halo" button on the material's Links and Pipeline panel.

Tuning Halos to get them to do what you want is not an exact science. A lot of trial and error will be involved, so try not to become frustrated.

The Halo options for materials.

HaloSize: This controls the overall size of the Halo. When working with Halos, this is the first setting to start playing with.

Hard: This control varies Halos from rendering as tiny dots with a small lightness surrounding them (127) to diffuse circular blobs with no discernible center (1). Particles that should look like "magic" would have high Hard values, where smokes and other less defined effects would require near-zero values.

Add: Determines the level to which Halo effects reinforce themselves. Normally, several halos stacked in front of each other would only render the values for the nearest halo. With Add turned up to 1.0, stacked Halos reinforce each other, accumulating their brightness. Particle systems that are meant to simulate fire should have high Add values.

In addition to the "glowing ball" look, Halos can be given other properties, too.

The particle systems in the illustration show the effects of the Ring, Lines and Star buttons on the Shaders tab. The buttons can be combined, as seen in the system on the lower right. The numbers of Lines and Rings are controlled by the corresponding spinners on the same panel. Line and Ring color can be adjusted individually through the color pickers on the Material panel, where the Spec and Mirror colors normally reside.

Ring, Lines, Star, and all three together as Halos.

Shading

By enabling the "Shaded" button on the Shaders panel, you can make Halos react to light.

Any particle effect that would be shaded in real life, like smoke or clouds, should use this setting. "Magic" effects, or anything that appears to glow, like fire, should avoid the Shaded option.

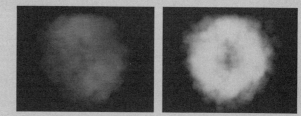

The same particle system, rendered as both Shaded Halos and non-Shaded.

Alpha

In most cases, good particle effects will require reducing Alpha and enabling ZTransp. For example, when making a cloud effect, you could simply make a low number of particles (100 or so) and give them a large HaloSize and high Alpha value (0.9). This would produce a cloud, but it would have very low detail. A better way to go about it would be to increase the number of particles (say, to 5,000), drop the HaloSize and drop Alpha to around 0.1. This would produce a cloud of the same overall density, as the drop in Alpha would offset the larger number of particles, but with much better detail and more of a sense of volume.

Halo Settings

Display

The set of buttons that is labeled "Display" contains controls that determine how particles appear both in the 3D view and at render time.

Material: the Material spinner selects which material index of the emitter you want the particles to use. In Blender, meshes can have several materials attached to them. You will need to refer to the emitter's Material buttons panels to see which number corresponds to the material you would like to use. If you are not enabling the Show Mesh option, though, there will almost certainly only be a single material linked to your emitter.

The Material panel, showing material index numbers.

Mesh, Unborn, Died: These buttons control whether or not the mesh, unborn, or dead particles show up in the final render. If you want particles to show up before they are emitted (unborn) or after they have reached the limit of their Life setting (died), you can do so with these buttons. For example, you may want your particles to represent "fairy lights" or some such thing, which begin their life speckling the outside of a tree. As the animation progresses, they fly off and about. In this situation, you would enable the "Unborn" option so that particles that have yet to leave the tree are still visible.

Under normal circumstances a particle's mesh emitter will not show up in a render. The Mesh button makes it visible.

Vect: Causes particles to render as lines instead of points, with the line facing along the direction the particle is moving. The "Size" spinner beside this button controls the render size of the vectors, not their lengths.

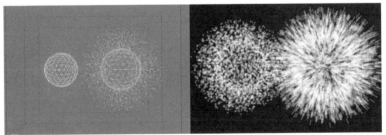

Difference between standard particles, and vector particles.

Children

If you want your particles to generate new particles when they die, you use the Children tools.

In the interface presented here, the Generation: 0 in the spinner is the first, main emission of particles. To make particles create children when they die, adjust the "Prob:" spinner, which refers to the probability that a particle will emit a child when its life ends. At the default setting, 0, no particles will emit children. If you

Particles with children.

choose 1.0, this corresponds to a 100% chance that a particle's death will result in a child, meaning that all particles will spawn children when they die.

To add additional generations of particles, use the Generation spinner to move into generations 1, 2 and 3 and adjust their probabilities to something other than 0.

Currently, child particles use the same motion settings as their parents, so children are limited to doing simple fireworks effect.

Particle Motion

Once you have decided how many particles to emit, how long they live, and how they will be visualized, you have to define how they will move.

Motion is controlled on the Particle Motion panel that shares tabs with the main Particles panel.

The Particle Motion tab.

Velocity Controls

Normal: This spinner gives particles a velocity based on the surface or vertex normal of the emitter at the point where the particle is created. The non-technical explanation is that this will cause particles to shoot straight out from the surface emitter. This control can give very fast motion, so you might want to begin by clicking on the spinner's right arrow section which will advance the value by small increments.

Object: When emitted, particles have the same direction and velocity as their emitting object at that point in the timeline. If your object is not animated and moving, this setting will have no effect. However, if your emitter object is moving and spinning in 3D space, you get nice animated particles. With values approaching 1, all of the emitter's motion is used, and the particles will appear to fly off of it as though under the object's momentum. Lower values, for example 0.2, will have the particles string out behind the emitter, but with a small amount of following motion, like a smoke trail.

Random: This control adds a bit of random motion on top of that generated by the other controls. Usually, very low values (0.001-0.025) will add believability to certain effects. However, this control can easily override and essentially destroy other carefully refined control values, especially if it is cranked the whole way up to 1.0. Try it and see.

Damping: Damping is a sort of friction control. 0.0 damping means that particles will continue at their initial velocity until the end of their lives: they will not slow down. Turn damping up to 1, however, and the particles will quickly slow to a stop, almost immediately after they are emitted.

Force controls

The force controls are simple. There are three spinners, one each for the X, Y and Z axes. The spinners can range from -1.0 to +1.0, and apply a constant force along the indicated axis.

As an example, let's pretend that you would like your particles to appear to be affected by gravity. The Z axis represents up and down, so to fake the effects of gravity, you could try a value of -0.5 in the Z force spinner. This applies a constant downward (negative Z) force on all particles. -0.5 may or may not be the right value to enter, but simply playing the animation in the 3D view will give you good feedback on whether it looks correct or not.

On the opposite end, you could add a small positive value to the Z spinner in order to simulate the way that smoke climbs into the air after it is emitted.

Texture Motion and Other Controls

There are a number of other controls for particle motion, many of them concerned with textures and groups. Using 3D textures to control and alter the motion of particles can be tricky, and is a topic that, if covered thoroughly, would double the size of this chapter. That being the case, it will not be covered in this book.

Force Fields

Particle motion can also be affected by Force Field objects. These are usually Empty objects that have been activated in the "Fields and Deflection" panel of the Physics buttons.

The Fields and Deflection panel, once a field type has been chosen

There are several kinds of force fields that can affect particles. To create one, add an object to your scene (an Empty is good for this), then select one of the field types from the Fields dropdown menu on the Fields and Deflection panel.

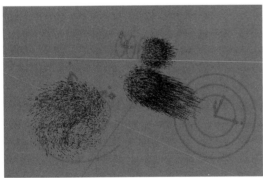

Wind, Sphere and Vortex fields.

The different types of fields shown in the illustration are:

Wind: A wind field pushes all particles in a uniform direction. The strength and direction of the wind are visualized by the row of circles trailing away from the field object.

Sphere: Sphere fields act like magnets. Positive strength values attract particles toward the center of the field object, while negative values repel them.

Vortex: A vortex field causes particles within its area of influence to move in a spiral.

The field types have a common set of controls:

Strength: Determines how pronounced the particular effect is.

Texture Motion and Other Controls

Falloff: How quickly the effect dissipates as you get further from the field object. A value of 0.0 means that there is no falloff and the field affects all particles regardless of distance. The best way to determine a good falloff value, if you need one at all, is to experiment in the 3D view as feedback from moving field objects occurs in real-time.

The MaxDist feature, if enabled by clicking the "Use MaxDist" button, sets an absolute cutoff beyond which the field will have no effect. This Maximum Distance of effect is shown by a dashed circle around the field object.

Particles as Object Duplicators

In addition to showing up as points and vectors, particles can also be used to make duplicates of other objects. This technique can be a good way to distribute custom grass blades, small pebbles and other objects.

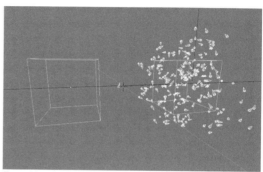

To use this feature, make the object you wish to duplicate the child of the particle emitter (Ctrl-P). Then, with the emitter as the active object, enable the "DupliVerts" button on the "Anim settings" of the Object buttons. If you want the duplicated objects to follow the rotation of the particles, enable the Vect option on the Particles panel of the Physics buttons.

The particle system on the right is set to duplicate the small object in the center.

Strands for Hair and Fur

There is a completely different way of using particles than the ones you have seen so far. Blender is capable of dealing with particles as "Strands," which can be used to simulate hair, fur and grass, among other things.

To use particles as Strands, enable both the "Static" and "Vect" buttons in the Particles panel. When you do that, the way particles are displayed changes completely.

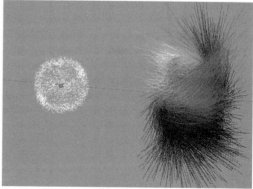

Strand particles operate under the same set of rules, and with the same set of controls, as standard particles, with only a couple of exceptions. The main difference is that Strand particles, often called static particles, have no "start" and "end" values — they are always there — and the "Life" value takes on a different meaning.

A normal particle system on the left, with a Strand system on the right. Both of these systems have identical motion and emit settings.

Strand particles are really a drawing of the path that a normal particle would have followed, but frozen in time. Just like a particle with a long Life value would travel farther than one with a short Life value, Strands with long Life values are correspondingly long.

Also in the Particles panel, the Sta and End spinners are replaced by a "Steps" spinner.

The Steps control tells Blender how much detail to put into the Strand. If you think of a Strand as the drawing of the path a normal particle would follow over its lifetime, Steps controls how closely the Strand follows that path. A step value of 5, the default, draws the Strand using every 5th frame that the normal particle would have followed, in essence "connecting the dots" between those locations. It's easy to see this effect with very high Step values.

Strand particles with a life of 50 and Steps set to 25. See how each Strand is made of two straight lines. Particle "dots" have been connected for frames 1, 25 and 50.

The same particle system with Steps set to 1. The curves are now very smooth, as the "dots" are connected on every frame.

With Strand systems, the RLife spinner on the Particle Motion tab becomes particularly useful. RLife adds a random factor to particle life, and in this case to Strand length. Very few strand applications (hair, fur, grass) benefit from having strands of uniform length. Raising this setting can help to alleviate that.

If you are going to use the Strand particles on an animated emitter — by that we mean an emitter mesh that will be deformed in some way — you will need to enable the "Animated" option on the Particles tab.

The real power of Strands, though, comes from rendering and material options that aren't available with any other kind of object. Strands render with a special shading model called Tangent Shading that attempts to create shading and highlights as they would appear in real hair situations.

On the Links and Pipeline panel in the Material buttons, you will find a popup button labeled "Strand" hidden amongst several toggle buttons. Pressing the Strand button brings up a configuration palette.

The Strand configuration popup in the Material buttons

Strands render differently than other types of objects. By default, each strand renders as a single pixel in width, regardless of how close or far it is from the camera. This single pixel size can be changed on the Strands configuration panel. The Start and End sliders control the pixel size of the Strand where it begins and ends, and the Shape slider controls how quickly it blends between those values.

Strand Materials

Before you finish this chapter, we'll show you the controls for creating a material and texture that will map along the length of a Strand, allowing you to create a variety of hair, fur and other looks. This is not a full description of the material tools, though. If you haven't already worked through Chapter 9, you should probably do so before tackling this.

A default Blend texture added to a Strand system's material.

The Blend texture type, chosen from the Texture Type dropdown in the Texture buttons is where the magic happens. Once "Blend" has been chosen, the "Colorband" button on the "Color" panel needs to be activated.

In these illustrations, we have collapsed some panels and pulled some tabs off into their own panels so you can see everything at once.

The default colorband.

The Colorband tool consists of different markers along a band of color, each holding values for color and Alpha. When Colorband is enabled, the panel looks like this:

The markers are selected with the LMB, at which point you can alter their values with the RGB and Alpha controls below. Markers can also be LMB dragged to change their position along the blend, or even to rearrange their order. As you move them, the blend updates in real-time.

If you need more than just the two default markers at either end, new ones can be added by Ctrl-LMB clicking at the location in the blend where you would like a new marker.

The next illustration shows a good Colorband for light hair:

Notice the last view of the panel with the fourth marker highlighted. Its Alpha value is 0.0, indicating that the Colorband is completely transparent there. Alpha is shown in the Colorband preview by a checkered background showing through.

Strand Materials

The reason this makes a good hair texture is that light hair is often darker at the root (marker 1), and lighter and more transparent at the tip (marker 4).

Back in the Material buttons, there are only a few things to do in order to make this work.

Material panel settings

The coordinate system in Map Input should be set to Strand. This will use each Strand's individual texture coordinates, mapping the Colorband from the Texture buttons along the length of the Strand.

The texture should be set to affect both Col (Color) and Alpha in the Map To buttons.

Finally, in order to take advantage of the Alpha from the texture, the "A" (Alpha) slider on the Material panel should be turned down to 0.0, and the ZTransp button on the Links and Pipeline panel should be enabled.

For a preview of the Strand material, you can click the "Hair Strands" preview type button in the Preview panel. Turning on preview anti-aliasing with the "O" button can really help with the Strand preview.

This image is a render of some Strands with a material similar to the one shown here. As you can see, the Strands are darker near the root, and become lighter and apparently thinner near the tip. The thinning is the effect of the texture's Alpha, and not due to reducing the End size in the Strands popup palette.

Coming Soon!

There are some great new particle features coming in the next release of Blender that you can read about in Chapter 15.

Strand Materials

CHAPTER 13

Rendering and Compositing

 Composite and Rendering: Hands On
by Colin Litster

 Composite and Rendering: Discussion
by Colin Litster

 Rendering Settings: Discussion

Composite and Rendering: Hands On

Why Composite?

You have reached the point where you have created a good mesh and designed a great material to shade it. You have applied lights to illuminate your scene for maximum effect. Surely, you only need to press the render button to be finished!

Although your render might seem to be done, in a real production environment you would almost certainly have to color correct or composite the render with a pre-created background, or possibly even put it together with several different renders, building a final image in layers. While it is possible to add all the potential elements of a completely finished scene into a single render, it is an inefficient and time consuming approach to a production. The process of combining different elements into a single image is called "compositing."

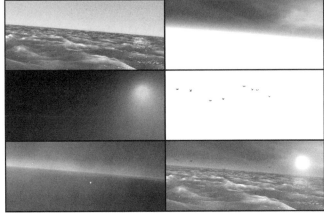

A stormy ocean scene composited from several images.

Blender has a Compositor and post-production facility built in. It can be used to finely control the look of the finished render while drastically reducing render times in animations. More importantly, it gives you complete control over the end result.

The only difference between the images is that the one on the left is a raw render, while the one on the right has gone through the compositor.

The Production Pipeline

You probably have heard this phrase in relation to the motion picture or graphic still production industry. It refers to the workflow that begins with the organization of 3D objects, materials, textures, scenes and animation, proceeds through the rendering of these elements, and ends up by combining all of these assets into finished images.

Blender gives artists the ability to do all of these things in one package, while allowing the integration of content from other sources and giving the opportunity to produce images and files that are useful in the scheme of a larger pipeline.

While a complete understanding of the Blender render pipeline can help you make even more efficient use of the Compositor, you can start to use this versatile tool with only a little knowledge. In this chapter, we will introduce compositing techniques to produce effects that would not be possible otherwise. With only a few tools, you can subtly or even radically improve your renders.

Rather than bog you down with too much detail at this early stage, we'll have you do a simple composite effect to learn some core facts about the system. Later, you'll do a more complex exercise that teaches more about individual node types, as well as some common techniques like bloom, color correction and vector-based motion blur. These later exercises will also show how the composite system can save you considerable time in the render process.

A Beginning Compositor Exercise

Let's use the Compositor to apply a sort of background shadow to a simple mesh model.

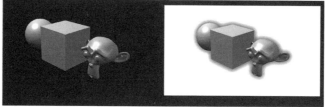

A raw render beside the composited version.

Run Blender and start a new scene (Ctrl-X). You should have a default cube in the center of your view. If you want to match our example exactly, you can use the spacebar Toolbox to add a sphere and monkey. As the compositor needs a render to work with, render the scene now by pressing F12.

A Screen Layout for Compositing

Although Blender comes with a default screen for many tasks, it does not come with one that is optimized for compositing.

The screen layout used in this chapter is as follows:

If you're comfortable with the interface modification tools from Chapter 2, you should be able to recreate this layout from the illustration. Also, this setup can be found as the "composite_screen.blend" file from the "examples" folder on the accompanying CD.

A good compositing layout.

The default render setup has the Compositor turned off. You need to tell the renderer to send its output to the Compositor, and also to create a window in which to set up your composite effect.

In the Anim panel of the Render buttons (F10), enable the "Do Composite" button. From now on, any render will send its result to the compositor in order to achieve a final image.

If you are not using the compositing screen shown earlier, you will need to change one of your windows into a Node Editor. Select "Node Editor" from the Window Type popup on the left side of the main 3D view's header.

In the Node Editor's header, click on the face icon to tell the window to work with composite nodes (it can also create node-based materials), and on the "Use Nodes" button, which tells the scene to calculate the current node configuration. When node trees become very complex, it can sometimes take several seconds to calculate when you make a change. If you plan to make several minor adjustments and don't feel like waiting each time, turning off the "Use Nodes" button temporarily disables recalculation.

Select the "Node Editor" Window Type.

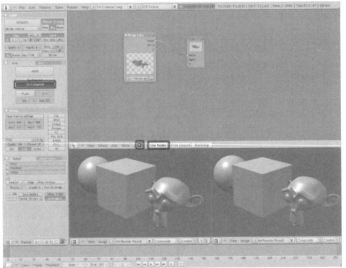

Both the Composite and Use Nodes buttons must be enabled.

A default node system will be created for you, consisting of an input node called "Render Layer" and an Output Node called "Composite."

Nodes

The process of compositing usually involves taking an input (like a render), applying filters or other modifications, and specifying an output, which is often a render result. This type of process can be illustrated very well by a diagram in which each process, like input, filters and output, is represented by a panel and is connected to other panels by lines that indicate their relationships. These panels are the nodes.

Use the mouse's scroll wheel to zoom in on the Node Editor window.

A node consists of:

- input and/or output connectors;
- a title bar

with:

- a down arrow to collapse the entire node;
- the node's title;
- a plus sign toggle that will hide unused input/output connectors to clean up the display;
- a "double bar" button that hides and shows the node's controls;
- and a round preview toggle that hides or shows the node's preview.

The default nodes.

A line that represents the connection between the nodes is shown in the above illustration. Lines that join nodes are called "connectors." This connector is flexible, and will grow, shrink and change shape to maintain the connection regardless of where the individual nodes are moved.

Basic Node Tasks

You already know the standard Blender methods of adding, moving and deleting objects. Blender uses many of the same interface conventions for mesh and object manipulation as for node editing, and gives you a few extra shortcuts.

Arranging Nodes

Nodes may be selected with the standard RMB click, either on the node's title bar, or on any non-control space within the node. As there is no 3D cursor in the Node Editor, a LMB click will also work as a selection tool.

Nodes can be moved with the Grab (G-key) tool, or simply LMB clicked and dragged.

Move the Composite node to the far right of the view to make some extra room between the nodes. You will notice that when you select a node, its title is highlighted and the part of the connector nearest the selected node turns white.

With the Composite node still selected, press the X-key to delete it. If you ever delete a node by mistake, remember that you can Undo (Ctrl-Z).

Adding a Node

New nodes are added in the same fashion as objects in the 3D view: the spacebar toolbox. Bring up the toolbox with the spacebar, and choose Add->Output->Composite. A new composite node appears. If it isn't already there, move it to the right side of the view.

Making Connections

The labeled dots on the sides of the node panels are sockets. Sockets that appear on the right side of a panel are outputs. They have some kind of information to offer: usually an image or a value. Sockets on the left side of a panel are inputs. They accept information sent by output sockets. To join an output from one node to the input of another, LMB click and drag on the output socket toward the desired input socket on another node. When you are near enough to an input socket, the connector will snap to it.

LMB drag from the "Image" output socket on the "RenderLayer" node to the "Image" input socket on the "Composite" node. When you successfully connect them, the Composite node will show a small version of the render in its preview window. If nothing is showing in the nodes at this point, you probably forgot to render the scene originally. If that's the case, do it now (F12).

Deleting a Connection

There are a couple of ways to remove connections between nodes. The first is by LMB clicking on the input socket with a connector attached, dragging it away from the node, and releasing the LMB. Another way that is useful for removing a number of connections at once is to LMB drag over them in the workspace of the Node Editor. When you release the LMB, any connectors that fell within the described area are removed..

Don't confuse the LMB-drag motion for deleting Compositor connections with the typical LMB-drag selection method of other programs. If you tried to select multiple nodes by LMB-dragging, you'll find your connections gone. Of course, if this happens, an Undo (Ctrl-Z) will fix it.

Experiment by deleting the connector now. When it's gone, also select and delete (X-key) the Composite node. There's one more node creation and connection trick to learn.

Automatic Node Connection

Make sure that the RenderLayer node is selected (LMB or RMB), and use the spacebar toolbox, Add->Output->Composite again. This time, when the new node appears, it is already connected to the RenderLayer node. If you create a new node while an existing one is selected, Blender will attempt to make a connection between the two nodes, and makes a guess as to the best way to connect them. This can make the creation of entire node networks go very quickly.

Resizing a node

You may have noticed that the new Composite node is a little smaller than the one from the default setup. You can shrink or grow a node panel by LMB or RMB dragging on its bottom right corner. Using this technique, make the Composite node match the size of the Render Layers node.

A Simple Shadow Outline

It's time to implement a simple node network to produce an effect that would be difficult to do if you only had access to 3D objects and a plain renderer. In this example, you will remove the render's background and substitute an "outer glow" shadow effect.

Remove the link between the RenderLayer node's output and the Composite node's input by LMB dragging across the connector. Make a new connection by LMB dragging between the Alpha output of the Render Layer node and the Image input of the Composite node.

Render the scene with F12.

RenderLayer's Alpha socket connected to Composite's Image socket.

Why did it show this result? The Alpha output socket on the RenderLayer node contains the Alpha channel of the raw render. An Alpha channel is a grayscale image that shows the opacity of different parts of the render: white for opaque, black for completely transparent and everything in between. By connecting the Alpha output to the Composite node's Image input, you told the Compositor to use the Alpha channel as the final Image.

Alpha channels (sometimes called Alpha masks, or just masks) are useful for separating and overlaying renders in the Compositor.

Now, you'll use that white, opaque area to create a shadow behind your objects. At the moment, though, it's the wrong color. Also, as it's exactly the same size as the objects themselves, it would be hidden. In order to turn this mask into a shadow that can be seen, it will be necessary to:

    1. enlarge it slightly;
    2. blur it;
    3. invert its values (white for black and vice versa);
    4. put the original render layer over the shadow; and
    5. add some color.

If you haven't been doing so already, now would be a good time to save your work.

Enlarging a Mask

If you have used a paint package before, you may have heard of a dilate/erode or shrink/grow filter. In short, its task is to either add or remove pixels around a selection. The Composite nodes have such a filter, which is found, not surprisingly, in the Add->Filters section of the spacebar toolbox.

Press the spacebar to Add a node and select Filters->Dilate/Erode.

Connect the RenderLayer Alpha output socket to the Mask input of the Dilate/Erode node, and connect the Mask output of the Dilate/Erode node to the Composite node's Image input. Set the "Distance" value on the Dilate/Erode node to 10.

The Dilate/Erode node in place.

One thing you'll notice as you do this is that you do not have to re-render to see the new results. That's because the render itself has already been done. You're just pushing things around with the compositor.

You should see that the alpha mask has grown somewhat from the first render. This is the effect of the Dilate/Erode filter node. If its Distance value had been negative, the alpha mask would have shrunk. The Composite node in the editor also shows a small preview of the effect. While these small previews are okay for a quick idea of what might happen, it would be better to have a larger preview without sending the node's output to the Composite result node, which should really be reserved for your final composite.

Making Previews Better

The Add menu on the Node Editor header also contains all of these same commands.

Blender has a much better way to preview different stages of the compositing process.

Use the spacebar tool to Add an Output->Viewer node to your network.

Sometimes, depending on the zoom level and size of the window, Blender creates new nodes off-screen. When this happens, it is quite easy to bring them into the view, as newly created nodes are always selected. So,

Enlarging a Mask

pressing the G-key will allow you to move the node into view. Alternately, you could use the scroll wheel to zoom, and MMB drag in the window to pan until all nodes are showing. Even easier, you could use the Home-key, which, as in other window types, will auto-zoom and pan the view to show all objects.

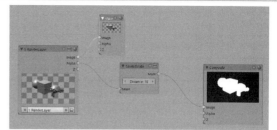

A good place for the viewer node.

There are a couple of things to notice here. If you created the Viewer node with the RenderLayer node selected, it will have been automatically connected to the Image output socket. If not, you will need to connect the RenderLayer's Image socket to the one on the Viewer node. Secondly, if nothing shows up in the Viewer node's preview upon connection, you may need to re-render (F12).

A tidy Viewer node.

Although the Viewer has an image displayed, it is still rather small. Grab the bottom right corner of the Viewer node and drag outward to enlarge it. Make it as large as it will go. Since you don't need the Alpha or Z input sockets for this exercise, click the "+" sign on the Viewer's header to hide them.

Let's create another Viewer node to show the Alpha channel before it runs through the Dilate/Erode filter. You could create another viewer with the toolbox, and then resize and tweak it to make it look like the one you already have, but why not duplicate the existing Viewer and move it? Duplicate in the Node Editor is the same as in other window types: Shift-D.

Make sure the Viewer node is selected and press Shift-D. An exact copy is produced and placed into Grab mode. Move it below the Dilate/Erode node.

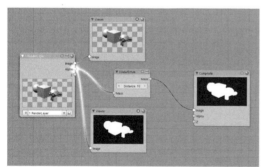

Note how multiple connectors branch out from RenderLayer's Alpha socket.

Drag a new connection from the RenderLayer Alpha output to this new Viewer's Image input.

It is possible to have multiple connectors originate from a single output socket. We won't go into that in detail yet, but it's good to know that it can be done.

While useful, these viewer nodes don't seem to give any kind of better preview than the little images in the other nodes. Wouldn't it be great if you could make these as large and detailed as a standard render window?

Setting a window to the UV/Image Editor type.

If you're using the composite layout file from the CD, you already have two UV/Image Editor windows available. If not, split one of the windows in your workspace (MMB on a window border, see Chapter 2), and change it to a UV/Image Editor window.

In the header of the new UV/ Image Editor window, select "Viewer Node" from the popup menu.

From now on, this window will display a full resolution image of the currently active viewer node. You can zoom the view using your mouse scroll wheel and pan by MMB dragging.

Up until now, all renders have brought up a separate Render window. It is possible to direct render output to appear as a Render Result in the UV/Image Editor window as well. This can be set on the Output tab in the Render buttons (F10).

With this setup, composite structures become much easier to create. Although you cannot even see your 3D scene directly from a screen like this, remember that compositing is a post-production process. Modeling, materials, and animation will almost certainly be completed before you start to create a compositing work flow.

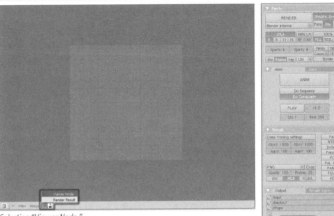

Selecting "Viewer Node."

Selecting "Image Editor" for the default Render Display

Blurring the Mask

Back in the main example, you need to blur the alpha mask image to produce the nice feathered look you would like the shadow to have. There are several nodes, all in the Add->Filter section, that produce blurs:

- Vector Blur: A very fast method of creating motion blur for animations.
- Defocus: Simulates various camera blurs for Depth of Field and other effects.
- Blur: Simple image blurs, using several different methods.

As you're not using motion or trying to simulate camera effects, the basic Blur will suffice. Add a Blur node with Add->Filter->Blur.

Connect the Dilate/Erode node's Mask output to the Image input of the new Blur node. Then, connect the Blur node's Image output socket to the Image input on the Composite node.

When you attach a new connector to an input node that already has a connection, Blender may attempt to rearrange some connections for you. Often, this can be useful, but sometimes (e.g. when you have an Alpha socket connected directly to an Image socket) it can make the wrong choice. If this happens, you can always delete any incorrect links by LMB dragging over the bad connectors.

The node network with Blur added.

From the filter type selector on the Blur node, choose Gauss, which is a good general purpose blur. Set the X and Y values to 30. Ignore the Size value — it only sets the Blur size as a percentage of the X and Y values and should stay at 1.00.

Setting up the Blur node.

If you have set your views up as suggested, you may have noticed that the UV/Image Editor window that is set to "Render Result" will have updated to show the blur without you having to re-render.

To make this blurred image into a shadow, you will need to reverse it, exchanging black for white and vice versa.

Inverting the Image to Produce a Shadow

The Composite nodes often provide several ways to achieve a particular effect. There are a number of ways to invert an image, and in this example we'll show you a method that will also allow you to add some color.

The updated composite Render Results appear automatically.

Zoom out with the scroll wheel if you have to, and move the Composite node to the right to make room for more nodes.

RGB Curves

Add an RGB Curves node with Add->Color->RGB Curves.

The RGB Curves node.

Place it between the Blur and Composite nodes, connecting Blur's Image output to RGB Curves Image input. Then, connect RGB Curve's Image output to Composite's Image input. You should be getting the hang of building connections like this by now.

The RGB Curves node can be quite tricky, but it is one of the most powerful and generally useful nodes available. It provides fine control over the contrast and color of an incoming image.

In its default state, the node shows a straight line running diagonally from bottom left to top right. This represents a mapping of the value from the input socket to what the node sends to the output socket. The horizontal axis represents the input color with black at the left, moving through 50% gray in the center, and with white at the extreme right. The vertical axis represents the output values, with black at the bottom, 50% gray halfway, and white at the top. The curve represents how the input will be changed to produce

Inverting the Image to Produce a Shadow

the output. The default diagonal line in the node is the "curve" mentioned in the node's title. Although it doesn't look like a curve at the moment, it is.

If you were to alter the curve, the relationship between input and output color would also change, depending on how you shape it. You can use this curve to remap the colors of your image so that an input of black becomes white, and white becomes black.

Move the mouse to the bottom left-hand point of the curve and LMB drag it up as far as it will go along the vertical axis, while keeping it flush with the left side of the work area. By doing that, you have told the node to take any input of 0% (black, along the horizontal axis) and change it to an output of 100% (white, along the vertical axis).

Now, LMB drag the point on the curve in the upper right of the work area the whole way down, until it looks like the image on the right.

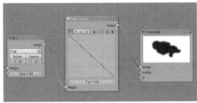

Remember that if you make a mistake, you can quickly remove it with Undo (Ctrl-Z).

The default RGB curve reversed.

The second move tells the node to change any inputs of 100% (white, along the horizontal axis) into outputs of 0% (black, along the vertical axis). The line that runs between the two points gives a blend between those two transformations.

The UV/Image editor render result window should update to show the inverted image, which now looks a lot more like the shadow you are shooting for.

We will come back to the RGB Curves node later to add some color variation. Now, though, let's place this shadow behind the original objects.

You will need to take the original render layer, with its original alpha, and place it over the node-generated shadow image. To do this, you will use the AlphaOver node.

The effects of the inverted RGB curve, shown in the Render Result.

Placing the RenderLayer Image Over the Shadow

Add an AlphaOver node with Add->Color->AlphaOver. You're getting a small cluster of nodes now, and it might be useful to either zoom out or to start rearranging things. Put the AlphaOver node between the RGB Curves and Composite nodes.

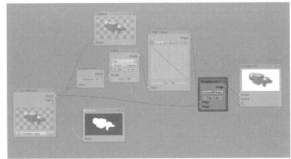

The node network with AlphaOver connected.

Notice how the AlphaOver node has two Image input sockets? That's because it takes two images and combines them into a single output. Connect the Image output of the RGB Curves node to the top Image input on AlphaOver. Connect the original Image output on the RenderLayers node to the bottom Image input on AlphaOver. Finally, connect the Image output from the AlphaOver node to the Image input of the Composite node.

The UV/Image editor Render Result should update to show the objects over the top of the shadow.

Compositing Issues

Before we move on to the final section of this exercise, let's take a closer look at the render and composite you just achieved.

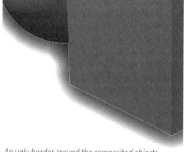

The render result shows a slight blue edge around the objects. This is not really a problem with the node network, but with the original render settings. The odds are that until now, you've been rendering everything with the default, Sky background.

The renderer set to Premul.

In the Render buttons, the Render panel has a set of radio buttons: Sky, Premul, and Key.

An ugly border around the composited objects

Since you're compositing now, you won't be using the Sky for a backdrop. Switch the renderer from Sky to Premul. Without being too technical, Premul, which stands for "Premultiplied," combines a render with its Alpha channel before handing it off to the compositor, creating very nice edges.

The "render this node" button.

At this point, you could hit F12 to re-render the whole node network, or you can LMB click on the little Render icon next to the RenderLayers popup selector, to trigger a render of only that node.

The composite, now with Premul in use.

Order of Processing

Several compositing nodes have multiple inputs, just like the AlphaOver node. It's important to know the order of processing so you can achieve consistent results.

In the example, you wanted the original RenderLayers image to be on top of your shadow image. The stacking order in Blender is upside down from what you might expect. That means that the lowest image input in fact layers over the image input above it. There's no good way to learn that other than simply getting it wrong a few times and seeing the result.

Just remember that multiple node inputs treat the lowest socket as the most important.

Compositing Issues

Adding Colors

A black and white shadow may be exactly what you were after, but the RGB Curves node offers much more to help liven up an image. As the illustrations in the book are grayscale, you'll have to look to your own display to see the results of this section.

Let's start with the shadow and add a little color.
In the RGB Curves node are four buttons marked C, R, G, and B. When pressed, the R, G, and B buttons allow access to the adjustment curve for only that component of the image (Red, Green and Blue), leaving the others as they are. The C option (Combined), which is what you used in the above example, changes all three channels at once. This means that you can alter individual colors in an image as well as the combined values.

You already have the Combined curve set to invert the image. LMB on the "R" to work with the Red channel only, and LMB again somewhere near the center of the curve. This creates a new point on the line.

Drag that point upward until it is about halfway up the next grid division as shown in this illustration:

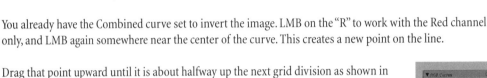

Switch to the "B" (Blue) button and LMB click to create a new point on its curve. Move it close to the position shown on the right side of the illustration.

Because the Combined curve has already inverted the image, the effects of moving the individual Red and Blue curves are the opposite of its normal behavior. However, adjusting the color with these curves is fairly intuitive, and you are welcome to experiment a little, moving any of the curves to see its effect on the shadow color. Before you continue, though, try to get back to something that resembles the curves from the above illustration.

This image shows two curves superimposed.

The render result window should now show a nice inky-blue shadow. As a last exercise, let's try to add a yellow tint to both the background and the shadow. You could do this by continuing to fine tune the RGB Curves. Instead, though, you'll use a new node type that will give you more control.

Make room for a new node in your network by moving the AlphaOver and Composite nodes to the right.

Remove the connection between the RGB Curves and AlphaOver nodes. With the RGB Curves node selected, add a Mix node with Add->Color->Mix. Its Image input socket should be automatically connected to the output of the RGB Curves node.

The Mix node added to the network and connected.

Connect the Image output of the Mix node to the upper input of the AlphaOver node.

Mixing Images

The Mix node has two Image input sockets. If only one of those sockets has an incoming connection, the other defaults to a color swatch, which can be set by LMB clicking on it and using the standard Blender color picker that pops up. This lets you mix an area of uniform color into an image.

As mentioned earlier, the bottom socket on the Mix node's inputs will represent the highest image in the composite, so LMB drag the connector downward from the upper socket to the lower one.

LMB in the color swatch beside the upper Image socket and set the RGB values in the color picker to something like this:

Set the color to R 0.98, G 0.92, B 0.79.

Set the Mix mode dropdown menu to Multiply, and Fac (Mix Factor) to 0.65. This factor indicates that the dominant image (the lowest in the stack) will be blended at 65% opacity.

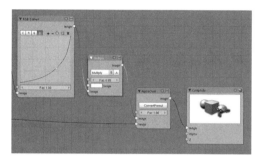

You may have noticed that there is a vast array of mix modes when you selected "Multiply" from the dropdown list. In the current release, there are sixteen different mixing modes. Although these ways of blending images will be familiar to you if you have used 2D painting packages, it's easy to try them out within the Node Editor and see how they affect the final composite for yourself.

Without any more experimentation, though, you are left with the image on the right.

The node network to generate that from a simple grayscale render of three objects is found below it.

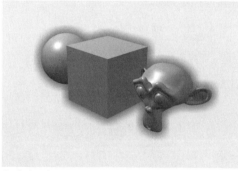

Our final render.

Conclusion

In this basic tutorial, you have learned that Composite node networks, though complex when finished, are fairly simple to build. All the core operations of creating, moving, deleting and connecting nodes have been covered, as well as a good work flow for approaching a compositing problem. Next, we'll look at several common post-processing tasks and how to accomplish them with the Composite nodes. As you will see, the nearly instant response to changed node settings will speed up your creative process and help to make you much more productive as a 3D artist.

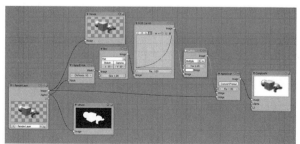

The final Composite node network.

Compositing and Rendering: Discussion

Discussion Exercise: A Steam Gauge

Although other chapters have contained a more academic discussion section, the compositor lends itself to an extended example. Its usefulness comes not from individual settings, but from combining components and practical understanding. If you are interested in a blow-by-blow rundown of Render settings, they can be found in a third section to this chapter: Render Settings: Discussion.

This section, however, will show you how to approach the compositing process, as well as several common compositing setups.

To do this, you'll become the compositing and rendering department of a virtual movie studio, tasked with finishing a shot from the highly anticipated feature film, "Blender Hothouse." The modeling, texturing and lighting have all been completed by other departments. Your job will be to devise the look and feel of the scene by compositing its various elements into a completed 10 second animation without altering the models, lighting or materials.

A steam gauge from the "movie" Blender Hothouse

From the screenplay:

An oily brass steam gauge within a dark steam room. The dial initially increases from zero to a quarter of its travel as though steam pressure is rising. The dial hovers at this position, gradually becoming more agitated, as though the pressure is about to blow. The dial then rapidly turns to maximum and shakes: pressure is at its highest level and explosion is imminent...

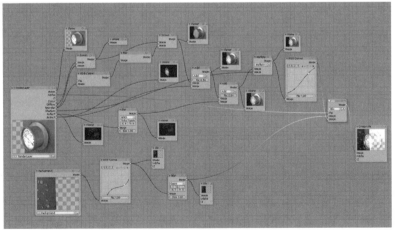

The node network for this composite.

The Composite Node network for this exercise appears to be staggeringly complex. However, it can be broken down into four distinct portions, each one covered here in depth. There are a number of files that will help with this chapter, all found in the "examples" folder on the included CD. The first exercise will require you to create the node network from scratch, but later ones will use pre-made files for you to examine and play with.

Let's start with the file as delivered to you from the production department. Load "CompositeStage1.blend" and perform a test render (F12). If you find that the render takes longer than a couple of minutes, you may want to consider working with the renderer set to 50% size in the Render buttons.

If you examine the scene, you will see that some of the materials use raytracing. A simple textured plane outside of the camera's view provides something for the dial's face to reflect.

The file as provided.

Creating the Source Renders, Scenes and Components to Composite

Change the wide window at the top of the screen from a 3D view to a Node Editor. Switch to Composite Nodes with the face icon on the header, and make sure the Use Nodes button is enabled.

The window on the left side of the screen shows the Render buttons. Both windows at the bottom have been set to UV/Image Editors for showing Preview and Composite result nodes. You'll be focusing on the main gauge for the majority of this discussion, so disable Layers 2 and 11 to hide the background and wall elements.

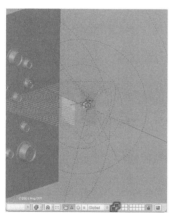

Shift-LMB click on these two layer buttons.

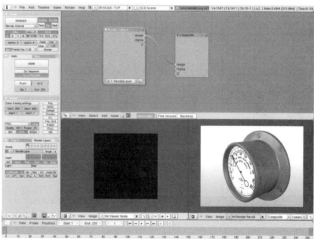

A good setup to begin compositing.

When turning on Use Nodes for the first time, the default is to have a Render Layers node connected directly to a Composite node. However, you are not limited to a single render input. It is possible to set up different Render Layers, each with their own node input, pulling elements from various modeling layers and scenes which can then be dealt with separately in the Compositor.

The Render Layers tab.

These controls are found in the Render Layers tab of the Render buttons, nested into the same panel as the Output tab.

Render Layers

From this tab it is possible to control exactly what will be rendered, as well as what will be passed to the compositor for processing. In short, a Render Layer is a selection of scene layers that will be rendered in a single pass: a set of Layers that will be rendered together. Each Render Layer can have its own Input node, allowing you to perform different composite operations on different sets of objects from your scene, as you'll see later.

Let's look at the controls on the Render Layers tab:

Scene

Scene layer buttons

This refers to the set of layer buttons at the top of the panel. These controls are a duplicate of the layer buttons found on the 3D view headers, and are included here as a convenience. As you will be indicating which layers should be included with which render input in this same tab, it is nice to be able to check the contents of layers without leaving the panel.

Below this is the name and selector for the active Render Layer. Like other name popups, new Render Layers may be created by selecting Add New and may be removed by clicking the "X" to the right of the control.

Layer

Layer Layer buttons

Further down is the Layer control, which again shows the familiar layer selector. Unlike the one above, which controls what displays in the 3D view, this selector is the one that determines which scene layers will be included in this Render Layer. When a Render Layer is created, it defaults to including all scene layers.

Why would you need separate access to so many scenes and layers? You could, for example, divide a scene between background and foreground objects, sending the background objects to the compositor in a different Render Layer for blurring. It's also possible to have part of your project in a completely different Scene, allowing you to composite objects with completely different render settings.

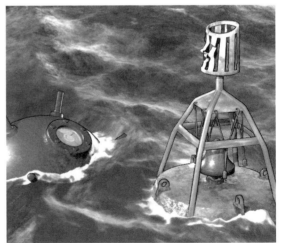

A render composited from two scenes. The ocean scene used standard render settings, while the mine and buoy scene used the Edge settings.

Render Process

Render process buttons

Below the Render Layer selector are toggles for which portions of the renderer to use. Blender treats different types of objects in different ways, and each of these can be enabled or disabled here. For example, if you were to turn off the Solid button, no objects with solid faces would be rendered, leaving only the background.

The other buttons can be used to disable rendering of Halos, Edges, Transparent (zTra) objects and the Sky background or BackBuffer image, on a Render Layer by Render Layer basis.

Just below the render process buttons are two text fields: Light and Mat. If the name of an object group is entered in the Light field, the Render Layer will use lamps from that group, ignoring any other lamps in the scene. A material name entered into the Mat field will cause all objects in the Render Layer to be rendered as though they were temporarily linked to that material. These fields are useful for doing test renders and special effects. For example, you might need to substitute a simplified lighting rig and material to test object placement without actually replacing lamps and materials throughout your entire scene.

Render Passes

Render passes buttons

At the bottom of the Render Layers tab are the controls for render passes. As Blender renders an image, it performs a number of calculations that are combined to deliver the final color of the rendered pixel. Render Passes allow you access to each stage of these calculations individually from within the Compositor. For instance, you could separate the Diffuse, Specular, and shadow calculations, and recombine them in the compositor. By adjusting the way they mix, you could make the shadow darker or blur and lighten the specular highlights. Using a work flow like this gives you the freedom to drastically improve and alter the look of the final output without re-rendering, potentially saving enormous amounts of time.

On new Render Layers, only two render passes are enabled:

- Combined, which delivers the final RGB and alpha results; and

- Z, the depth information of objects from the camera's viewpoint. Each pixel in a render has a Z value, which refers to the distance between the camera and the face that was rendered. If you look in the Node Editor, you will see that the Render Layers node has three outputs: RGB, Alpha and Z. These outputs correspond directly to the Render Pass settings.

Enabling any of the other pass buttons adds additional outputs to the associated Render Layer node.

The other twelve passes are:

Vec: Provides vector motion data for the rendered geometry. Mostly useful for calculating fast, vector-based motion blur.

Nor: Provides the Normal information from objects in the render layer. If looking at the output of this pass in a Viewer node, the strange colors are the visual encoding of the Normal.

Render Process

UV: The UV information from objects that have UV mapping. This pass makes it possible to replace the colors on objects that use UV mapped textures, without re-rendering or changing the materials directly.

IndexOb: You can assign any object an index value in the Object buttons and use this to create selection masks.

Col: Provides an un-shaded color pass, as though everything had been rendered with a Shadeless material.

Diff: The diffuse shading of objects, including colors, but without shadows or specular highlighting.

Spec: Specular shading.

Shad: A pass representing shadowing information. This pass is Multiplied with others to get a final image, so non-shadowed areas appear in white, with shadowed areas being progressively darker.

AO: The result of Ambient Occlusion, without any materials applied.

Refl: The reflection pass, if Ray is enabled on the Render panel and an object has a reflective material.

Refr: Refraction, if Ray is enabled on the Render panel and an object uses ray refraction.

Rad: A radiosity pass. Radiosity is another method of lighting that is not covered in this book.

If you would like to see the actual outputs from any of these passes, it's as simple as connecting their output sockets to a viewer node and re-rendering. Of course, if you already rendered after the different passes were enabled, no re-render would be needed.

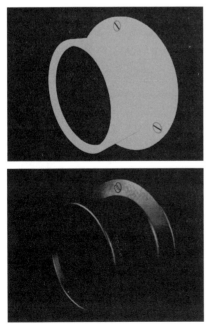
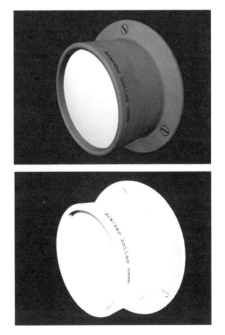

The Col, Diff, Spec and Shad passes.

Recombining Passes

For the first part of this exercise you will recombine the Diffuse and Specular passes to make the brass of the gauge's body a little brighter and shinier.

You can either follow the simple instructions to set this up yourself, or if you prefer, load up the completed stage for examination. The file "CompositeStage2.blend" can be found in the "examples" folder.

If you want the practice of building your own, here's what to do:

Enabling the Diff and Spec passes

In the Render Layers tab of the Render buttons, enable the Diff and Spec passes.

Add a color Mix node (Add->Color->Mix), connecting the Render Layer node's Diff output socket to Mix's upper image input and the Spec output to the bottom image input.

Create a View node with Add->Output->Viewer, and connect the output socket of the Mix node to the Viewer node. If something was already connected to the Viewer node, that connection will automatically be replaced by the new one you make.

The nodes systems doesn't like loops or ambiguity, and will frequently delete connections when you replace them with others, or warn you of problems should they occur.

The Mix Node

The Mix node is one of the most frequently used and important nodes in the compositing system. It defines how color passes or images from two separate inputs will be blended into a single output.

A list of available mixing methods can be viewed by clicking the popup selector.

In this case, choose Screen.

Screen brightens an entire image, based on the image being mixed into it. Light areas brighten more, with white turning the other image white. Dark areas brighten less, with black leaving the image unaffected.

The specular pass in the example is mostly black with some lighter areas, so it won't brighten the other image much. We would like you to enhance the specularity, though, so you need a way to increase the brightness of the Spec pass. It could be run through an RGB Curves node and adjusted, but there is an easier way.

The available mixing methods.

The Specular pass.

The Fac (Factor) spinner on the Mix node controls the strength of the bottom image in the mix. Values of 0 through 1 represent 0 to 100%. The mix factor can go as high as 5, though, meaning that you can mix the Spec pass at 500% of its actual intensity.

Set the Fac spinner on the Mix node to 4.77.

As you adjust the mixing Factor, the Viewer node updates without having to re-render.

The brass gauge now looks a lot shinier, but could still be better. To do that, you'll apply a common post-process effect: bloom.

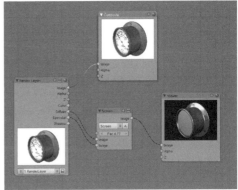

The current node network.

Increased specularity following the Screen Mix node.

Bloom/Glow

Real highlights, such as a specular reflection, tend to behave differently than mathematically calculated highlights in a 3D package. Light intensity in the real world can cover a huge range that our eyes find difficult to view. As a result, very strong highlights can cause our eyes to actually overload in certain places, perceiving this dramatic contrast between light and dark as a kind of glow. Adding this subtle effect can make a render look more authentic and is a simple way of adding believability without the extra processing requirements of more complex raytracing algorithms.

Load the file "CompositeStage3.blend" from the "examples" folder. The nodes will appear empty until you render (F12). Also, it's okay that the dial appears blank right now. The dial is seen through a refractive object and won't show until you make use of the Refract pass later.

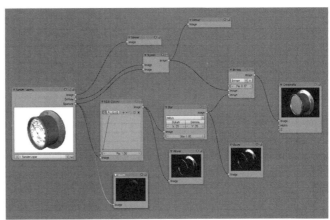

The Bloom Node network. Viewer nodes have been attached so you can easily examine the various stages.

Bloom/Glow

As you can see from the node tree, we have collapsed some of the nodes from the previous section using the controls described earlier. That should make it easier to focus your attention on the bloom effect. Once you are happy with a section of a complex composite node tree, it is a good idea to collapse it like this to keep clutter to a minimum.

Source of the Bloom

Although there are several ways to produce a bloom effect, the simple approach we've taken is to use the Specular pass again, brightening it and applying some blur before mixing it back into the existing image.

Using RGB Curves to Brighten an Image

The network uses an RGB Curves node, taking its input from the same specular pass you used before. In the basic back-shadowing tutorial, you used the RGB Curves node to invert and colorize an image. Here it is used to brighten the Spec pass by drawing the top right point of the Combined curve over three quarters of the way to the left.

Here's a neat trick: enable the "Backdrop" button on the Node Editor's header. Now, clicking on a Viewer node shows that preview right in the background of the Node Editor. This is particularly useful if you are working with your nodes in a Maximized window (Ctrl-Up Arrow/Down Arrow), or if there is no room in your screen layout for a UV/Image Editor window. The backdrop preview may be moved around with Shift-MMB.

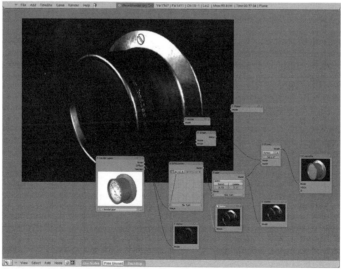

Backdrop enabled on the header. This preview shows the result of the RGB Curves node on the Spec pass.

Blurring an Image

After the RGB Curves node, you have a Blur node, which can be found under Add->Filter->Blur.

Although there are seven different blurring styles to choose from, two of the most commonly used are Gauss and Mitch.

The Blur node with settings for the bloom effect.

Gauss

Gaussian is a good, general purpose blur. It provides an even effect across the image.

Mitch

Mitchell-Netravali blur gives a more accurate effect for bright objects. It does not reduce highlights by evenly spreading them like Gaussian blur. Because of that, this type of blur is excellent for working with highlights, as you are here.

Of course, other blur methods like CatRom will produce similar effects, so the choice is yours. With the speed of the Compositor, it's easy to switch between different blur methods to see which works best in your final production.

Blur Settings

In the previous illustration, the Blur node's X and Y values are set to 35. Above the X and Y settings are two buttons that, although not used here, are worth explaining.

Bokeh

This is a more complex blur setting that attempts to simulate optical blurring, the kind that would happen with an out-of-focus camera, as opposed to the simple mathematical blurring of other methods. This setting will slow renders and composite updates considerably, but when attempting to fake a camera blur effect, it is much more realistic.

Gamma

Using the Mix node in Screen mode again.

This setting will give bright parts of the blur precedence over darker portions, instead of averaging them. This will usually lead to a brighter blur.

Mixing the Bloom Effect

You need to mix this brightened and blurred image with the results of the diffuse and specular combination from earlier. Notice how the title of the Mix node has changed to "Screen," making it easier to tell the mix type at a glance, even on a collapsed node.

A new Mix node, in Screen mode.

We have used a Screen Mix node (Add->Color->Mix), as once again you have to blend an image that needs to brighten another. In this case, the Factor has been adjusted to 0.37, but try taking it as high as 0.80 to see if you like it better.

Reflection/Refraction Adjustment

So far, you have improved the look of the metal and added a nice bloom to the highlights. You're still missing the reflection and refraction, though.

Load "CompositeStage4.blend" from the disk and render to fill all the buffers and passes.

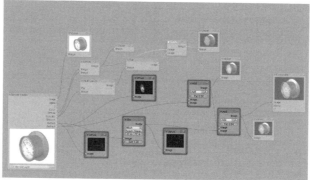

The additional nodes for reflection and refraction.

You have both a reflection and refraction pass available because the brass material uses raytraced reflections and the glass dial uses raytraced refraction. To see what these passes produce, follow the connectors to their associated viewer nodes and select each in turn.

Neither is much to look at in this state, but there is a lot of information hidden in these apparently dark passes.

The reflection pass.

The refraction pass.

You need to properly mix these passes with the output from your previous compositing result. To do this, you'll need to use another Mix node.

The Add Mix node's lower Image socket receives its input from the Refract socket the whole way back on the Render Layers node. This makes it the "primary" image — the one being layered over your previous Diffuse/Spec/Bloom network result.

The Mix node in Add mode.

Setting the Factor to 0.50 means that the Refraction pass is only used at half-strength, de-saturating the dial. This is actually ideal, because if mixed at full strength (1.0), the reflection pass would not be visible. Try setting the Add Mix Factor to 1.0 and see what it does to the final composited image. Once you've done that, change it back to 0.5. This is a great example of how using the Compositor can improve an image without re-rendering.

Modifying a Pass Before Recombining

One of the down sides of using raytraced reflections is that they are razor-sharp. In the real world, unless a reflection comes from a polished mirror, it will have some degree of blur. If you were not using the Compositor, the only way to accomplish blur in a reflection would be to use high Filter settings with Env Maps (see Chapter 9). By now, though, you should be able to see a simple solution to this problem.

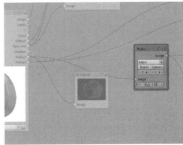

Examine the Blur node that is connected to the Reflect output of the Render Layers node. It uses the Mitch blurring method and only a small value, 4, for X and Y.

The Blur node set to affect the Reflection pass.

The blurred Reflection pass is then composited with the Diffuse/Specular/Bloom/Refraction result with a Mix node in Add mode, set to 0.84.

Varying this factor will increase or decrease the amount of reflection and apparent oily film on the brass. Experimentation is the key, and you are encouraged to modify any of these factors to see how it affects the composite.

The render with reflection and refraction passes added.

Adding the Shadow Pass and Color Correcting the Image

A Mix Multiply node to blend the shadow pass into the rest of the image.

Load the file "CompositeStage5.blend" and render to fill the passes.

The final pass to recombine is the shadows.

Mixing the shadow pass is relatively straight forward. It uses a Mix node set to Multiply, with a Factor of 1.0. The lower input socket runs the whole way back to the Shadow output of the Render Layers node. The upper input socket connects to the previous Add Mix node that is producing the final composite.

Multiply mode is the opposite of Screen. When multiplied, black turns the underlying image black, while white leaves it untouched. As you can see in the next illustration, areas not in shadow on the shadow pass are white, so they will not affect the final image when blended in Multiply mode.

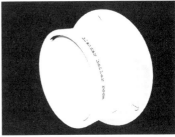

The shadow pass.

Screen and Multiply offer superb after-render control of both shadowing and highlights. If you like, increase or decrease the Mix Factor to change the way the shadow blends into the final image.

Color Correction

As it is, the final composite looks a bit milky. Let's raise its contrast with an RGB Curves node.

The Contrast S Curve.

Although the RGB Curves node was used in the basic tutorial to completely change the color of the drop shadow, it can be used for more subtle effects too. One of those is enhancing contrast. In fact, this technique is so common and useful that it has its own name in the world of image processing: the "S Curve."

A detail of the final rendered, sweetened image.

As you can see, it's a subtle alteration to the default diagonal line, but when applied to an image it can significantly enhance its appeal. It works by darkening the already dark areas (pulling down the bottom left of the curve) and brightening already light areas (pushing up the upper right of the curve), while leaving the middle areas alone.

Even though you have split apart the different passes, tweaked them and put them back together into a much better image, there is more you can do. Currently, the gauge just floats on a black background, rather than existing as part of a steam room.

Adding a Background with Render Layers

Load the file "CompositeStage6.blend" and render to fill the passes. You will notice that the two layers with additional objects, Layers 2 and 11, have been re-enabled.

With the other layers showing, the gauge now rests against a simple plane, textured with an altered copy of the brass material,

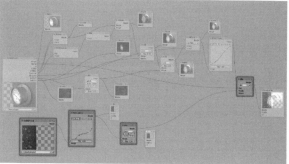

The node network to composite the layers with different settings.

and given a custom paint job to show oil staining with the Image painting tools. Also, a bunch of duplicates of the gauge appear in the background, attached to a wall. The main gauge's wall is on Layer 11. The gauges and wall in the distance are all set to Layer 2.

The node setup in this file uses two separate Render Layers: one for the foreground gauge you have been dealing with up until now and its wall, and a separate one for the distant background elements. Having the background appear on a separate Render Layer will let you perform a completely different set of composite effects to those objects.

Render Layer settings for the foreground.

Render Layer settings for the background.

Notice that the bottom set of Layer buttons for the "1 Render Layer" layer only includes objects from scene Layers 1 and 11. The Layer buttons for the "Background" layer include objects from scene Layer 2.

Looking at the node network, a new Render Layer node has been created with Add->Input->Render Layers, and set to use the "Background" render layer at the bottom of the panel. As you will only be darkening and blurring this layer, you can stick with the default "Combined" pass.

Immediately after the "Background" Render Layer, we have added an RGB Curves node to darken and reduce the contrast of the render. Contrast can be reduced by performing the opposite of the "S Curve" — darkening the light areas and brightening the shadows.

The "Background" Render Layer node.

Before putting both layers together, though, you can use an old trick to help bring out the foreground objects.

Quick and Dirty Depth of Field

A simple blur applied to the background makes it look as though the camera lens is focused on the gauge.

A Gaussian blur has been applied with X and Y settings of 5. We have used the Gamma button to emphasize the bright parts of the image, ensuring that the out-of-focus dials remain visible. Also, as we're pretending that the background is blurred due to camera focus, it might be worth it to use the Bokeh option.

The Blur node for the background.

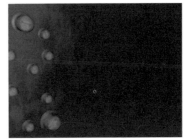

The blurred, darkened background layer.

The combination of the steam gauge with the background can be accomplished, once again, with the Mix node. This time, however, you will use the default Mix mode. How can you get the node to not blend the entire area of the images together, though? As you've already learned, adjusting the Factor affects how much of the image from the lower input socket is composited over the other. In addition to just being a number, though, the Factor setting can also use an image as its input.

By connecting the Alpha pass from the original Render Layers node, portions of the image that were completely opaque (the gauge itself) receive a Factor setting of 1.0, while the non-rendered areas receive a Factor of 0.0.

The result is that the Alpha pass is used as a mask for the Mix node.

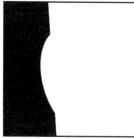

Mixing the background with the
rendered element.

The Alpha Channel from Render Layer 1.

The rendered, composited image with background.

Before you finish, you'll look at one more excellent use of the Compositor, one that's suited to animation but that can also enhance single-frame renders.

Vector-Based Motion Blur

Load the file "CompositeStage7.blend" and render to fill the passes.

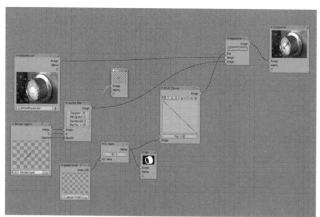

The node network for compositing the spinning pointer

With this file, you will produce the animation. However, as the only thing that moves is the pointer on the gauge's face, it would be a waste of time to render the entire image once for each frame. The animation for this piece is 250 frames long, and each frame takes, on the computer used for this discussion, almost a minute to render. That is almost four hours of render time. If you use a single minute-long render to produce a background, then render only the pointer as it spins, you can reduce the per-frame render time to around two seconds, saving nearly three hours and fifty minutes of render time!

In this new file, you will see that only three objects exist: the pointer and the main body and face of the gauge. You will only use the render of the pointer when you make the final composite, but the shape of the gauge itself will be useful too.

When producing an effect like this, you will need to have already rendered the rest of the image, without the animated portions, to use as a background. We have already done that in the example file, bringing the image into the Compositor with an Image node found in Add->Input->Image.

Also, the only 3D objects left in the file are the pointer itself, the main gauge body and face, and the lamps. If you had wanted, you could have simply moved the extra objects to a disabled layer.

Blender has two methods of producing motion Blur. The older method, available with the "MBLUR" toggle in the Render buttons, relied on rendering an entire scene several times on fractional frame numbers, then combining the results. Of course, this came at the cost of having to render your whole scene up to sixteen times per frame. Vector-based Motion Blur, on the other hand, uses the Compositor to examine how the objects in a scene are moving, then builds a new image with moving objects smeared along their trajectories and blended into the scene.

The Vector Blur node.

Vector Blur is found under Add->Filter->Vector Blur. To make it work, you will need to have some sort of image to blur (either a Combined pass or a composited image), and the Z and Vec passes enabled in the Render Layers tab of the Render buttons. In this example, all three input sockets connect directly to their output counterparts on the "1 Render Layer" node.

Obviously, objects will need to be in motion on the rendered frame for Vector Blur to have any effect.

The pointer blurred on Frame 189, before compositing.

Key mode on the Render tab.

As you need a good Alpha channel with which to composite, remember to switch the Renderer from Sky to Key mode on the Render tab.

Completing the Shot

To finish this example, the dial needs to be mixed back over the background image.

When compositing an image with built-in Alpha (a render of a lone object like the pointer), the AlphaOver node does the job. AlphaOver is found in Add->Color->Alpha Over. It follows the same socket stacking rules as the other nodes, with the base image in the upper socket and the image with Alpha in the lower socket.

The Alpha Over node.

In the example, the saved image of the gauge is used as a backdrop in the top Image input, while the vector-blurred pointer with built-in Alpha fills the bottom Image input. You can see from the final composite, though, that something is wrong.

One last trick, then, to properly mask the pointer. This is why you still have the gauge body and face hanging around.

Composite with the pointer sticking out.

In this file, both the gauge body and face have been placed on Layer 2, and a separate Render Layer created for them called "Gauge Body." With the body itself selected, it has been assigned an Object Index by using the "PassIndex" spinner on the Objects and Links panel of the Object buttons (F7).

In the Render Layer settings for the "Gauge Body" layer, you can see that all passes have been disabled with the exception of the IndexOb pass. You don't need to care about colors, materials or shading here: you want a pass that will generate a mask of this object to use on the pointer. The PassIndex value of all objects defaults to 0 unless changed by you. By assigning a PassIndex of 1 to the gauge body in the Object buttons, you will be able to single it out in the Compositor.

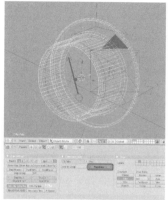

The PassIndex of the body set to 1.

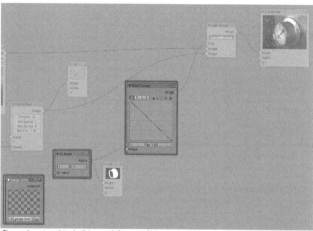

The node network to build a mask from an Object Index pass.

The IndexOb pass from the Gauge Body Render Layer (note how with no Combined pass sent, there is no image at all in the preview) is connected to an ID Mask node, from Add->Converter->ID Mask.

The ID value in the ID Mask node is set to 1, to correspond with the value you set on the 3D object. After that, an RGB Curves node is used to invert the resulting mask. That image fills in the Factor input socket on the AlphaOver node, correctly masking the spinning pointer and completing your shot.

Getting the Shot Out of Your Department

So, you've finally finished the job. The managers who have been planning the production had allocated five hours to your department on this shot for rendering and sweetening. Because you're a pro with the Compositor, you were able to set up the nodes in only a half hour (perfectly reasonable once you're experienced), and rendered the finished animation frames before the rest of the first hour was up.

Have a sandwich. Grab some coffee. You've earned it.

Well, the Compositor's earned it, but you can take the credit.

The final shot, correctly composited with the animated blurred spinner.

Render Settings: Discussion

There are only a few useful settings for the renderer that are not related to compositing.

The Render Buttons.

The Render buttons are accessible from any buttons window, and can be found by clicking on the Scene context and Render sub-context on the header, or by pressing F10.

When rendering, there are several things you need to specify: the render size, where and in what format to save the finished product, and the quality options you would like the renderer to use.

Render Size

The finished size of the render is chosen in the Format panel, with the SizeX and SizeY controls. The column of buttons to the right contains preset values for different rendering tasks.

Setting render size and preset buttons on the Format panel.

Output Format

Rendered images are not automatically saved. You must press F3 to save them, or select "Save Image…" from the File menu. When Blender saves the image, it uses the format specified on the Formats panel.

The default image format is Jpeg, but, as Jpeg compression can leave ugly artifacts, you should probably change it to PNG, and set the Quality spinner to 100. With this menu, you can also choose from the animation formats appropriate to your computer (Quicktime, AVI codec), which will bring up your operating system's animation saving dialogue.

If you want to save an image's Alpha channel along with the rest of the render, you need to select the "RGBA" button at the bottom of the panel, as well as an image format that supports Alpha channels (Targa, PNG, OpenEXR and MultiLayer).

The different image formats available for saving

If you are rendering an animation and have chosen a still image format (PNG, Targa, Jpeg, etc.) instead of an animation format (.avi, Quicktime), Blender will save a series of numbered image files, one for each rendered frame. It is then up to you to put the images together into a playable animation, using either Blender or some other program.

Animated image sequences are saved automatically to the folder specified in the top file selector of the Output tab.

Animation file path selector on the Output tab

Oversampling

The render is basically a system that looks at the 3D scene for every pixel of the final image and asks "What color should this be?" In the simplest case, it just takes the object nearest to the camera on that pixel, figures out the location on the object that the pixel covers, and calculates the final color based on lamps, shadowing and the object's material. What should it do, though, if one of the pixels in the final image happens to show the edge of an object? Should the renderer use the color and shading for the closest object, or the one showing from behind it?

Jagged edges anywhere one object ends and another begins.

This is the problem that anti-aliasing tackles. If the renderer only chose the foremost object, final renders would look like this:

However, the renderer could actually pretend that that single pixel is made up of, say, four smaller pixels. Then, it could calculate a color for each of those, giving a more accurate picture of what's really going on at that object's edge. After those four values are calculated, the results could be averaged, giving the final color for the image's pixel. This process is called oversampling, which is one method of anti-aliasing. For images to look natural, it must be enabled.

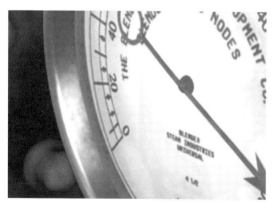

The same scene, with anti-aliasing.

Anti-aliasing is enabled with the "OSA" button, which stands for "oversampling." Different levels of OSA can be set: 5, 8, 11 and 16. Lower levels give a less nice, though often acceptable, result. The higher levels will take longer to render, but give smoother edges. Always start at the bottom and only raise the level if the edges of your objects still show the kind of "stair stepping" visible in the first sample image.

The Oversampling buttons

Rendering Controls

The large Render button on the Render panel triggers a render. That's kind of obvious, but it must be said. A render may also be triggered from any window type or screen within Blender by pressing F12.
If you will be rendering an animation, the large Animation button on the Anim panel does the trick. Blender will render all the frames in the range between (and including) the Sta (Start) and End values at the bottom of the panel.

Oversampling

At any time during either a single frame or animation render, the rendering process may be stopped by pressing the Esc-key.

Technical Details

The Render and Animation render buttons

If you have a computer with a dual core processor (or more), you can have the renderer take advantage of it. The "Threads" spinner on the Output tab tells Blender how many different render processes to run at once. Dual core processors will be able to efficiently run two threads at once, while quads or two duals could run four at once.

If your computer has an Intel Core Duo or Athlon X2 processor, you can set Threads to 2. If you have a different multi-processing architecture than those two, you probably don't need us to tell you what you have.

Speeding Up Test Renders

You don't always want to wait for a full quality render. Sometimes, it's good enough just to see how a moved lamp or tweaked material looks in place with the rest of your scene.

The Threads spinner set to 2 for use with a Mac Dual G5 computer.

If you don't want to use the Shift-P Preview Render panel in one of the 3D views, your only option is to actually trigger a full render. There are several ways to speed it up, if you are willing to compromise certain aspects of the result.

- Disable OSA: Turning off OSA will give a drastic speedup, as each pixel in the image will only go through a single round of calculations.

- Disable Shadow: Disabling the Shadow button on the Render panel tells the renderer to entirely skip shadow generation and mapping. If there are several lamps that cast shadows, this will give the render a nice speed boost. This button disables both buffered and raytraced shadows (see Chapter 11).

- Disable Ray: Disabling the Ray button on the Render panel skips all raytracing calculations, including ray shadows, transparency and reflection. For test renders that don't directly involve raytraced objects or effects, turn it off. In fact, unless you really need it, Ray should be disabled as a general principle.

- The percentage buttons: If you don't need to see your render at full resolution, you can use these buttons to tell the renderer to work at a percentage of the set output resolution. For example, setting this to 50% would generate a 400 x 300 pixel image if the output size on the Format panel was 800 x 600. Remember that a reduction to 50% in dimension means that the renderer only has 1/4 of the full number of pixels to calculate, which could give you a great speed increase.

A test render ready to go at 50% size, with no shadows, raytracing or oversampling.

One final way to speed up test renders is to render only part of your image instead of the entire scene. Pressing Shift-B in a camera view brings up the same sort of marquee selection mode as using the B-key for border selection. LMB drag a box around the portion of the view you would like to have rendered. When you release the LMB, a dashed red box describes the area.

When you activate a render, only the outlined area is rendered.

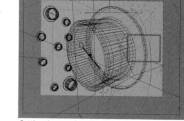

Setting the area for a Border render.

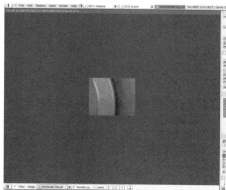

The selected area is rendered.

This border render mode will persist until turned off by disabling the "Border" button on the Render panel.

The "Border" render button.

CHAPTER 14

Preferences and Options

Customizing Blender

Preferences and Options: Customizing Blender

In Chapter 2: The Blender Interface, you learned how to configure screens, windows and panels to suit your workflow, and how to save that configuration as your default (Ctrl-U). Blender offers even more customization than that, in a "hidden" preferences screen.

Open Blender and take a look at the header at the very top of the screen.

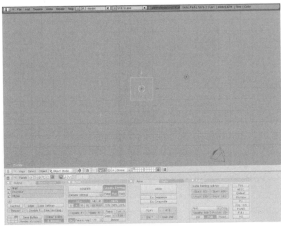

The main header.

This header is just like any other in Blender, and if you carefully examine the screen layout, you will realize that the 3D Window below it already has a header. So, which view is this one the header for? Place the mouse over the line between this top header and the top of the 3D view. The cursor changes to the double-headed arrow symbol, indicating that you can LMB drag to change view sizes. LMB on the line and drag downward. You've just expanded and shown the User Preferences window.

The "super-secret" user preferences panel, exposed.

Let's go through the different sections of the User Preferences, highlighting some of the more useful options. Feel free to experiment with the options that aren't covered here — the tooltips you see when hovering the mouse over a control can give you some more information about available settings —and don't worry about messing things up. As long as you don't use Ctrl-U, the changes you make will not be saved as your default.

View & Controls

If you really cannot stand the way that Blender uses the RMB for selection, you can change it here. The "Select With" option allows you to swap the left and right mouse button functionality. Just remember that if you set Select to use the LMB, all tutorials and instructions will be backwards from now. If you think that getting used to new selection methods is tough, try doing a tutorial with inverted instructions!

The "Select With" preference for switching the left and right mouse buttons.

The "View rotation" control can be useful when you will be focusing your work on a single object for a while. Setting this to use "Turntable" and "Around Active" will cause MMB view rotation to keep the Active Object as the center of view rotation, allowing you to easily change the viewing angle of the object in question without having to worry about losing it in the 3D View.

"Around Active" is great when working for long periods on a single object.

Other helpful options are:

The "View Name" button in the Display controls on the far left. View Name displays the name of the current view (Front, Top, Camera, Side, etc.) in the upper left corner of all 3D windows, helping you to maintain your orientation at a glance.

"Emulate 3 Button Mouse." If you are working with a mouse that has no middle button, or on a laptop with a touchpad or ministick, enabling this option will allow you to simulate a MMB click by holding down the Alt key while use the LMB. So, the Shift-MMB combination that pans the view would be accessible by using Alt-Shift-LMB instead. Zooming is Ctrl-Alt-LMB. View rotation becomes Alt-LMB.

Edit Methods

The "Auto keyframe" controls are a handy tool for animators. You will recall from the animation chapters that keyframes are set by using the I-key, followed by a LMB click on the appropriate key types. Turning on the "Action and Object" button in this control set will cause Blender to automatically insert keys at the current frame whenever an object or bone is transformed.

View & Controls

The "Available" button will modify this behavior slightly, only setting keys for Ipo channels that have already been keyed. This means that if you have manually set keyframes for an object's location, then both move and rotate it, only keys for the translation will be automatically set, while the rotation will not receive a key.

Auto keyframe controls can speed up your animation workflow.

Undo

If you are dealing with enormous scenes that contain large amounts of high-polygon meshes or animation data, Blender's Undo system might cause your computer to drastically slow down due to memory requirements. If you find this happening on a particular scene, you can alleviate the problem by reducing the Undo "Steps" that Blender keeps around, or take the even more drastic measure of turning off "Global Undo" altogether. Of course, this means you're working without the safety net of Undo. Just remember to save backup copies of your previous work!

Language & Font

By default, only a single un-activated button appears in this section of the preferences. Turning on "International Fonts" will cause an immediate change to the whole Blender interface. The font changes and becomes nicely anti-aliased. This alternate method of viewing the interface can slow Blender down a bit, but if you like the look, it may be worth it for you. Once International Fonts have been enabled, you can change the main font and font size for the interface and even select from (at this point) eighteen different translations. Please note that not all translations are complete.

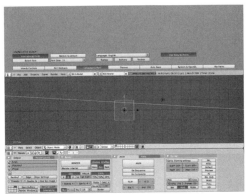

Blender can change its display to anti-aliased fonts.

Themes

Themes affect the way that Blender draws the interface elements themselves. The simplest way to see this is to change from "Default" to "Rounded" in the dropdown menu.

After you change from the Default theme, all of the theme configuration tools are exposed. If you want to spend the time, you can use these controls to customize the drawing of every widget in the interface. You can even save a Theme you've created through the File menu. Choose "Export" near the bottom of the File menu and select "Save current theme..." to bring up a

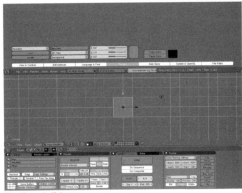

The "Rounded" theme.

window that will save your current theme into your Scripts directory. The created .py file can be shared with other Blender users so that they too can experience the genius of your theming skills.

Of course, you can also obtain themes from other users as well (do a web search on "Blender Themes"). To activate a theme that you've downloaded, place it in your scripts folder, then run Blender. Change one of your windows into a Scripts window (the one with the snake icon), then find the Themes entry within the Scripts menu on the header.

Selecting a named theme here will add it to the selectable themes menu in the User Preferences window.

"Save current theme..." in the File->Export menu.

Selecting a created Theme from the Scripts menu.

If you like the theme, remember to use Ctrl-U to save it into your default configuration. Otherwise, you will have to re-import it every time you run Blender.

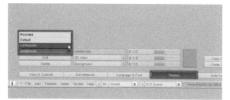

Once you click the Theme's script, it is added to the Themes selector in the preferences window.

Auto Save

While you work, Blender saves temporary files for you behind the scenes. This can be great, especially if your system (or Blender) crashes, leaving you with unsaved work. Go to this preferences screen and press the "Open Recent" button, which will load the most recently saved temporary file,

Auto Save settings.

hopefully resurrecting at least some of your work. If you are a paranoid person with an unstable system, you may want to set "Minutes" as low as "1," so a backup file is saved once every minute.

System & OpenGL

The three Solid OpenGL light controls affect the way that Blender draws the Solid style in the 3D Window. In fact, these are the virtual "lights" that Blender uses to shade the Solid drawing style. The "Light" buttons enable and disable the three lamps, while the color swatches set diffuse and specular colors by LMB clicking on them. LMB dragging on the spheres moves the light source.

The Solid OpenGL lights controls.

The other useful control in this panel is "Emulate Numpad." When using Blender on a laptop or with any keyboard that lacks a separate number pad, this button will cause the standard numeral keys that are normally used for layer assignment to be used as their Numpad equivalents instead. For example, the 1-key that would normally trigger Layer 1 would be used to set Front View, which is usually Numpad-1. Enabling this option loses the layer hotkeys, but if you don't have access to the number pad for view switching, it's definitely worth it.

File Paths

Unless you find that you are constantly browsing to a certain directory to find your renders and texture images, this set of controls won't be of much use to you at first. They mainly set the default locations where Blender will either look for or place something. If you want to change the default Render or Texture paths to a different folder, just click on the folder icon to the right of the control. This pops up a file browser from which you can select your new default folder.

The one setting you should definitely take a look at in this section, though, is the "Temp" path. Many of Blender's background functions like animation rendering, auto save, and crash recovery require that this path be set to a real, existing folder on your hard drive. Some systems already have the default directory ("/tmp/") in place, and some do not.

Perhaps the simplest way to test whether or not your system is configured correctly without doing anything technical is to click the "Open Recent" button in the Auto Save set of preferences. If it gives an error stating that the file was unable to be opened, then the Temp directory is not configured. In that case, you have two options:

1. Go to your home directory (c:\ in Windows; ~/ on Linux and OS X) and create a new folder called "tmp."

2. Click the folder button on the right of the Temp control and use the file browser that pops up to locate a directory somewhere on your hard drive where Blender can store temporary files.
Now that we've gone through the different sections of the preferences, you can hover the mouse back over the dividing line between the preferences window and the 3D view. LMB click and drag it back up.

Lest you think that the Preferences view is some kind of "special" window, take a look at the Window type menu:

That's right. In addition to hanging out at the top of the Blender work space this entire time, the User Preferences have been available from each and every window you've worked with so far. Any window in Blender can be set to any window type, including the User Preferences.

Now that you know where they are, though, you are sworn to secrecy.

Files Path preferences.

CHAPTER 15

Blender Bonuses

 **Blender Bonuses**

Blender Bonuses

Blender's functionality goes way beyond what has been shown in this book. You've no doubt seen a lot of buttons that were never touched in the tutorials, and settings that were not explained in the discussions. In addition, there are entire sections of Blender that we haven't even mentioned. Just to give you a sense of what to tackle after you've mastered the basics, here is a brief look at some of those items.

Rigid Body Dynamics: Bullet

A rigid body dynamics simulation environment lets you create setups of solid objects and have the system treat them as though they were real objects, conforming to the laws of physics. Rigid body dynamics can simulate something as simple as a brick wall breaking to pieces, or something more elaborate like a complicated Rube Goldberg device. Blender has built in support for rigid body dynamics simulation using the Bullet Physics SDK (Software Development Kit).

This is mainly used to support a Game Engine. Through the use of built in programming tools and internal logic and control systems, you can create a fully-functional game directly within Blender. A "game" could be a complex racing simulation like "Club SILO" from Luma studio (http://luma.co.za), or a ball that you push around a maze. Within any game, though, the Bullet physics engine is at work behind the scenes, making things happen in an efficient, realistic manner.

Even if you don't want to create games, though, Bullet is useful to the animator and still artist. Many times, you need an added touch of realism, mostly where gravity and collision are concerned, and it can be tough to keyframe such things believably. In Blender, you can use the rigid body dynamics of Bullet to do the heavy lifting.

Record Game Physics to Ipo

Blender can record Bullet rigid body simulations into an object's animation curves. On the main header is a "Game" menu, under which you will find the option "Record Game Physics to IPO." By enabling this setting, the game engine will bake the locations and rotations of any dynamic physics objects into animation Ipos that can be played back later as a standard animation.

A Basic Rigid Body Sample

On the included disk in the "examples" folder is a file called PhysicsAnimationBakingDemo.blend. Open this file, position the mouse inside the 3D view and press the P-key to start the Game Engine. After a while, press the Esc-key to stop the simulation, and the newly generated Ipo curves should be visible inside the Ipo view.

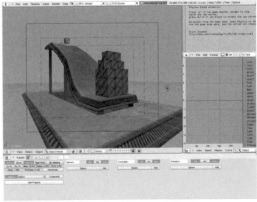

The Physics Baking Demo

Rigid Body Dynamics: Bullet

Rigid Body Settings

Objects are identified for use by the physics engine as Static objects by enabling their Actor button in the Logic buttons. Static objects are useful to represent environments in a simulation: the ground, buildings and other non-movable objects. If objects need to be moved by the physics engine, the Dynamic and Rigid Body buttons must also be enabled.

The Logic buttons.

Collisions

Any objects that have their Actor button enabled are detectable for collisions. Objects that collide with other objects will react as they would in the real world, knocking each other around based on their mass settings and momentum. Blender 2.43 added support for compound collision shapes for rigid body objects that are part of a parent-child hierarchy. You can enable compound objects by choosing the new Compound button for the parent objects:

Compound collision objects.

Compound collision objects let you build complicated structures, with each part having its own type of collision boundaries.

Rigid Body Constraints

Some objects may be dynamic rigid bodies, but their movements should be limited. For example, a door can normally only rotate around its hinges. This hinge would be a constraint. To simulate a chain of connected objects, you can limit the motion of each part in the chain so that the objects stay within a certain distance of one another. These types of constraint relationships are built with the Rigid Body constraint type, in the Object buttons.

Rigid Body Constraints

Rigid Body Settings

More About Rigid Body Physics and Bullet

You are invited to visit http://www.bulletphysics.com for some cool demos, and lots more information.

COLLADA Physics Support

Several other 3D tools and game engines support COLLADA, an open interchange format for interactive 3D. One of the unique features of COLLADA is it's capability to represent rigid body information. Blender 2.42 and later supports COLLADA Physics import and export. This means that the rigid body information that has been set up can be exported and imported through COLLADA 1.4. This can be useful when authoring rigid body data for external game engines like Ogre 3D and C4.

Soft Body Dynamics

Blender has another physics simulator, one for working with soft bodies. Think of gelatin wiggling on a moving plate, a banner flapping in the wind, or the bounce of body fat as a character jumps across a landscape.

A mesh object is set to use Soft Body dynamics by enabling the Soft Body button on the Soft Body panel of the Physics buttons, where the Particle controls are found.

The Soft Body controls

If you load the file "softbellyhank.blend" from the "examples" folder on the included disk, you will find that Hank from the character animation and rigging chapters has put on a few pounds. Soft body dynamics have been applied to his enlarged stomach so that it rebounds as he walks.

Soft bodies work with the concepts of "goals" and "springs." In short, the goal is the original, modeled shape of the mesh, and the Goal controls on the panel tell the simulator how rigorously the mesh should attempt to meet that goal shape. The Edge controls at the bottom of the panel control "stretchiness," or how and how much the edges of the mesh can act as springs and stretch as they go about their soft body business.

Soft belly Hank

In the case of Soft Belly Hank, only the stomach is affected by the soft body system. This is because soft bodies can be restricted based on a vertex group. By creating a vertex group with a low weight on the stomach and a high weight on the rest of the mesh, the soft body system can be told to use those vertex group weights for goals.

Soft bodies can also be used to simulate cloth, although at this time a full cloth simulation for something like an animated character's clothes isn't practical.

In addition to the basic soft body simulations, the system can take colliding objects into account, as well as check for self-collision within a soft body object to keep it from intersecting itself. Standard and self-collision detection add another level of realism to the soft body simulator.

Fluid Simulation

In addition to rigid and soft body physics, Blender has an integrated fluid simulator. Based on the Lattice-Boltzmann Method, the fluid system produces excellent results that are limited only by the computational strength (RAM and CPU) of your particular machine.

A fluid simulation requires several components: a domain (the area within which the simulation takes place), a fluid (a mesh that defines the starting shape and location of the fluid) and obstacle objects. You can also include objects that will add fluid to the simulation over time (inflows) or remove it (outflows). These are all defined by adding separate objects to your scene, then enabling each for fluids on the Fluid Simulation panel of the Physics buttons. From there, you use the buttons to define which role the object will play in the simulation.

The Fluid Simulation assignment buttons.

After all of the objects are defined, the simulation is run by pressing the Bake button. Using high resolutions can take enormous amounts of time and memory, but most modern systems should be able to handle small-scale needs like water pouring into a glass, etc., without much trouble.

The final product of the fluid simulation is an animated mesh object that can use any standard Blender material, with careful settings to mimic water or other fluids producing excellent visual results.

Some examples of Blender's fluid simulator, courtesy of Mike Pan.

Creating your own fluid simulation is simple.

Start a new scene, select the default cube and Enable it as a Domain in the Fluid Simulation buttons.

Click Enable, then Domain.

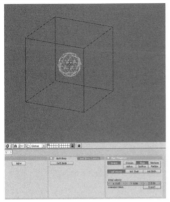

The icosphere inside the cube, enabled as a Fluid.

Add an Icosphere, positioning it within the cube and scaling it down to fit completely inside. Then, Enable the sphere as the Fluid.

One thing to be aware of before you actually do any simulation is that the Domain object, in addition to defining the area in which the simulation takes place, becomes the actual animated fluid. Don't be surprised when you see your nice fluid sim, but your Domain object is gone. The Domain object *is* the fluid sim.

In a timeline (or Render buttons) window, set the animation End frame to 75 or so. Reselect the cube and click "Bake" on the Fluid Simulation panel. Wait a couple of minutes. The progress bar on the main header will show how far the simulation has progressed. It will also show itself working in the 3D view. When it's done, just press Alt-A in the 3D view to see the simulation. For a better look with higher resolution data, you can change the dropdown menu that reads "Preview" to "Final."

If your fluid simulation is taking too long to calculate, you can press the Esc-key to cancel.

Python Scripting

Blender includes a programming language called Python. By writing or loading Python programs within Blender's text editor, you can extend Blender's functionality in almost any way you can imagine.

A simple script to select an object's parent looks like the image on the right.

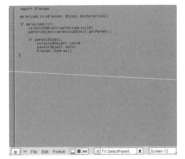

Of course, you don't have to be a programmer to take advantage of the creativity of others. Tucked away inside several of Blender's menus are Python scripts, ready to use. In fact, you may have already used them without knowing it. Here are some of the places you can find them:

The second from the left image shows one of the UV Mapping pop-up menus, where the last item "Unwrap (smart projections)" is a Python script. In the other menus, you can see the little Python snake icon beside the entries. Each and every one of those is a Python script that is loaded and placed in the menus when Blender runs.

A script called "MakeMonster" linked to a selected object, and set to update every time the frame number changes

In addition to being integrated into the menu system, Python scripts can be executed in a number of different ways. If they are loaded as a text file like the first example, placing the mouse over the text window and pressing Alt-P will run the script. Scripts in the text editor can also be linked to scenes, materials and objects in the 3D view. Such linked scripts can be set to run whenever the screen redraws, whenever the frame number changes, or at render time. This kind of link gives scripts the ability to control and alter objects in real-time as you work, over the course of an animation, or just during the render.

Some of the more complex Python scripts can do things like create an entire system for exporting to and driving Renderman compliant renderers, or simulate crowd motion with full character animation.

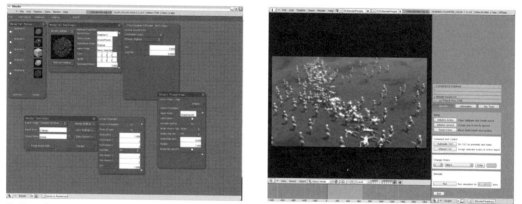

The Neqsus Renderman exporter (courtesy of Bobby Parker), and BlenderPeople crowd simulation.

Although a Blender installation comes with a Python interpreter built in, if you have the full Python programming language installed on your system already, Blender's Python environment will happily use your installation, including any special modules or packages you have installed. This means that your capabilities with Python scripting in Blender are almost limitless. Future development plans for Python within Blender include the ability for Python scripts to create and control their own UI panels directly within the main Blender interface.

Coming Soon!

With an active and creative development team, there are even better things on the horizon.

Coming Soon!

Currently in the Works:

- The ability to remap hotkeys and control events, meaning that users can truly customize their own experience. Keyboard maps that simulate other 3D applications to ease transitioning users will no doubt become popular.

- A completely new particle system with excellent support for hair and fur that includes intuitive, interactive controls for combing, growing and cutting hair, as well as a host of new methods of particle visualization and control.

- The next Google Summer of Code will no doubt include several great Blender projects. In the past, the GSoC has brought us the modifier stack enhancements, multiresolution sculpting, FFMPEG, the IK rewrite and improvements, and the fluid simulator.

Symbols

3D Cursor **45, 66**
3D Space **47, 65**

A

Action Editor 133, 148
  Commands and Functions 148
  Managing Actions 150
Actions
  Editing Keyframes 201
  Shape Keys 200, 208
Active Object 53
Add New 36
Animation 25, 44, 74
  Automatic Keyframing 351
  Constraints 61
  Insert Key 52
  Key View 56
  Keys 52, 75
  Lamps 277
  Playback 53
Armatures 154
  Bone Layers 160, 180, 182
  Bone Naming 157, 158, 179
  Bone Roll 162, 180
  Bones 177
  Constraints 182
  Constructing 155
  Deform Options 181
  Display Modes 180
  Edit Mode 155
  Extruding Bones 156, 178
  Extrusion, Symmetrical 178
  Full Body IK 168
  Hinge 181
  Hybrid IK 168
  IK Chain Length 167
  IK Constraint 163
  LockTrack Constraint 164
  Modes 177
  Parent/Child 160, 179
  Skinning *See* Skinning
  Transformation Locking 166
  Workflow 176
  Working with Bones 178

  X-Axis Mirror 157
  X-Ray 156, 131, 180
Axis System 65

B

Bullet 356
Buttons Window 35
  Add New 36
  Contexts 35
  Drop Down Menu 36
  Panel 36
  Spinner 37
  Subcontexts 35
  Tab 36
  Text Block 36
  Toggle button 36
  X (unlink) 36

C

Changing Interface 39
Character Animation 25, 146
  Action Editor 130, *See* Action
    Editor
  Armature 26
  AutoIK 132, 148
  Automatic Keyframing 131
  Blending Actions 142
  Converting Actions to Strips 141
  Creating an Action 131
  Creating Poses 146
  Flipping Poses 138
  Inverse Kinematics 147
  Keyframing 146, 147
  Manipulators 132, 147
  Non-linear Animation *See* NLA
    Editor
  Offset Bone 143
  Posing 131, 132
  Repeat 141
  Screens 130
  Walkcycle 135
Color Correction *See* Compositing
Compositing 314
  Alpha Blending 342
  Bloom/Glow 334

Application Glossary

Although most 3D applications share functionality, the terms used to refer to different tools and procedures can vary from program to program. Here you will find several items and procedures in Blender that use names that may not be familiar to you. We've listed them by their more generic names and added a short description and a page number in this book where you can learn more about it.

Also, Blender has an extensive set of importers and exporters to help it fit right into your existing work flow (.3ds, .obj, .lwo, COLLADA, DirectX). Just look at the Import and Export items in the main File menu to see the entire list.

Animation Blocks/Curve Blocks/Tracks: A set of curves for an object or skeleton bones that are grouped together and visualized as a single piece of animation. *Blender term "Action" 201*

Curves/Animation Curves: The visualization of the interpolation between key frames. Often shown as Bezier curves, but can usually be interpolated in ways as well. *Blender term "Ipo Curves" 58, 76*

Depth Mapped Shadows/Shadow Maps: Using a pre-calculated depth map to render shadows, as opposed to ray tracing. *Blender term: "Buffered Shadows" 268, 275*

Deformers: Functions attached to objects that accomplish live effects, such as smoothing, subdivision surfacing, array duplication, Booleans and displacement. *Blender term "Mesh Modifiers" 84*

Directional/Direct Light: This lamp type casts parallel light rays. *Blender term: "Sun Lamp" 264, 274*

Graph/Curve Editor: An editing screen that allows you to directly manipulate the animation curves and keys of an object. *Blender term: "Ipo Editor" 58*

Hair and Fur: *Blender term: "Strand Particles" 296, 309*

Maps: Some 3D packages refer modules and images that vary colors and settings across materials as "Maps." *Blender term: "Textures" 234*

Non-linear Animation/Trax Editor/Motion Mixer: An editing screen that allows you to blend different sets of animation data, as well as to see, adjust and freely rearrange blocks of animation data. *Blender term "NLA Editor" 140*

Null Objects: Used as reference points, placeholders and assistants when building complex animations, these objects do not show up in renders and usually have limited object attributes. *Blender term "Empty" 52*

Omni/Point Light: This lamp type casts light in all directions at once.
Blender term: "Lamp" 274

Paint Deform: This is a method of "painting" on a mesh to push and pull faces and vertices along their normals. Several packages have full-blown sculpt modeling interfaces, and this functionality falls under that heading. *Blender term: "Sculpting" 113*

Scripting/Plug-ins: The use of an embedded scripting language and pre-written plug-ins to expand the functionality of the program. *Blender uses Python as its embedded scripting language. 360*

Shape Animation/Morph Targets/Mesh Targets: The process of causing a mesh to reshape itself into a different form by modeling the different shapes and interpolating between them. *Blender term: "Shape Keys" 194, 203*

Skeletons: A construction of bones used for character animation. *Blender term "Armature" 154*

Sky Light/Hemisphere Lamp: This usually refers to the effect seen with lighting that mimics a cloudy day, i.e. no directional light, but general illumination and shading where objects are nearer to each to other. *Blender term: "Ambient Occlusion" 271, 277*

Soft Selection/Selection Falloff: The ability to transform selected portions of a mesh and have the transformation also affect non-selected vertices (or edges and faces) to create a smoother transformation. *Blender term: "Proportional Editing" 89*

UVW/Unwrapping: The process of assigning texturing coordinates to faces of a model. *Blender term: "UV Unwrapping" 244, 253*

Widget: Graphic elements that can be grabbed by the mouse and manipulated on-screen to transform (translate, rotate, scale) objects. *Blender term: "Transformation Manipulator" 49*

Support Blender Open Projects: http://peach.blender.org

RUBY BY EXAMPLE
Concepts and Code

by KEVIN C. BAIRD

There may be no better way to learn how to program than by dissecting real, representative examples written in your language of choice. *Ruby by Example* analyzes a series of Ruby scripts, examining how the code works, explaining the concepts it illustrates, and showing how to modify it to suit your needs. Baird's examples demonstrate key features of the language (such as inheritance, encapsulation, higher-order functions, and recursion), while simultaneously solving difficult problems (such as validating XML, creating a bilingual program, and creating command-line interfaces). Each chapter builds upon the previous, and each key concept is highlighted in the margin to make it easier for you to navigate the book.

JUNE 2007, 312 PP., $29.95 ($37.95 CDN)
ISBN 978-1-59327-148-0

THE BOOK OF JAVASCRIPT, 2ND EDITION
A Practical Guide to Interactive Web Pages

by THAU!

The Book of JavaScript, 2nd Edition teaches readers how to add interactivity, animation, and other tricks to their websites with JavaScript. Rather than provide a series of cut-and-paste scripts, thau! takes the reader through real-world JavaScript code examples with an emphasis on understanding. Each chapter focuses on a few important JavaScript features, shows how professional websites incorporate them, and shows readers how they might add those features to their own websites. This thoroughly updated and completely reworked second edition includes coverage of Ajax, revised appendices, and new examples throughout.

DECEMBER 2006, 528 PP., $39.95 ($49.95 CDN)
ISBN 978-1-59327-106-0

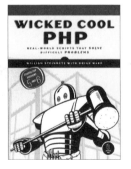

WICKED COOL PHP
Real-World Scripts That Solve Difficult Problems

by WILLIAM STEINMETZ *with* BRIAN WARD

Rather than focus on the basics of the language, *Wicked Cool PHP* provides (and explains) PHP scripts that can be implemented immediately to simplify webmasters' lives. These include unique scripts for processing credit cards, checking for valid email addresses, templating, overriding PHP's default settings, and serving dynamic images and text. Readers will also find extensive sections on working with forms, words, and files; ways to harden PHP by closing common security holes; and instructions for keeping data and transactions secure. By exploring working code, readers learn how to customize their webserver's behavior, prevent spammers from adding annoying comments, scrape information from other websites, and much more.

FEBRUARY 2008, 216 PP., $29.95 ($32.95 CDN)
ISBN 978-1-59327-173-2

THE ARTIST'S GUIDE TO GIMP EFFECTS
Creative Techniques for Photographers, Artists, and Designers

by MICHAEL J. HAMMEL

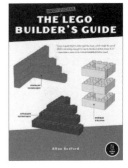

The GIMP, an image editor whose power and ease-of-use rivals that of
Adobe Photoshop, is one of the world's most popular free software projects.
The Artist's Guide to GIMP Effects shows you how to harness the GIMP's powerful
features to produce professional-looking advertisements, impressive photographic effects, as well as logos and text effects. The book's extensively
illustrated step-by-step tutorials are perfect for hands-on learning and
experimentation.

AUGUST 2007, 360 PP., $44.95 ($53.95 CDN)
ISBN 978-1-59327-121-3

THE UNOFFICIAL LEGO BUILDER'S GUIDE
by ALLAN BEDFORD

The Unofficial LEGO Builder's Guide combines techniques, principles, and
reference information for building with LEGO bricks that go far beyond
LEGO's official product instructions. Readers discover how to build everything from sturdy walls to a basic sphere, as well as projects including a mini
space shuttle and a train station. The book also delves into advanced concepts
such as scale and design. Includes essential terminology and the Brickopedia,
a comprehensive guide to the different types of LEGO pieces.

SEPTEMBER 2005, 344 PP., $24.95 ($33.95 CDN)
ISBN 978-1-59327-054-4

PHONE:
800.420.7240 OR
415.863.9900
MONDAY THROUGH FRIDAY,
9 A.M. TO 5 P.M. (PST)

FAX:
415.863.9950
24 HOURS A DAY,
7 DAYS A WEEK

EMAIL:
SALES@NOSTARCH.COM

WEB:
WWW.NOSTARCH.COM

MAIL:
NO STARCH PRESS
555 DE HARO ST, SUITE 250
SAN FRANCISCO, CA 94107
USA